Social Welfare in Canada

Andrew Armitage

Fourth Edition

OXFORD
UNIVERSITY PRESS

OXFORD
UNIVERSITY PRESS

70 Wynford Drive, Don Mills, Ontario M3C 1J9
www.oup.com/ca

Oxford University Press is a department of the University of Oxford.
It furthers the University's objective of excellence in research, scholarship,
and education by publishing worldwide in

Oxford New York

Auckland Cape Town Dar es Salaam Hong Kong Karachi
Kuala Lumpur Madrid Melbourne Mexico City Nairobi
New Delhi Shanghai Taipei Toronto
With offices in
Argentina Austria Brazil Chile Czech Republic France Greece
Guatemala Hungary Italy Japan Poland Portugal Singapore
South Korea Switzerland Thailand Turkey Ukraine Vietnam

Oxford is a trade mark of Oxford University Press
in the UK and in certain other countries

Published in Canada
by Oxford University Press

National Library of Canada Cataloguing in Publication

Armitage, Andrew
Social welfare in Canada / Andrew Armitage. – 4th ed.

Previous eds. published under title: Social welfare in Canada.
Includes bibliographical references and index.
ISBN-10: 0-19-541783-6
ISBN-13: 978- 0-19-541783-8

1. Public welfare – Canada   2. Canada – Social policy.   I. Title.
HV105.A7 2003   361.971   C2002-905260-2

Cover Image: Jen Petreshock/Getty Images
Cover Design: Brett J. Miller

3 4 - 07
This book is printed on permanent (acid-free) paper ∞.
Printed in Canada

Contents

Tables

To my wife, Molly
To our sons, Mark, Paul, and Timothy
To our daughters-in-law, Karen and Mary Jane
To our grandchildren, Nicholas, Spencer, Eric, and Emma
In trust that we may all live our lives in a peaceful and just society.

Andrew Armitage
July 2002

Preface

Social Welfare in Canada is written primarily for students preparing for careers in social work and the human services. For all those in such careers the institutions of social welfare provide the context of their work. As a result, an understanding of the issues dealt with in this book is essential to informed and professional practice in the social services and constitutes a required part of the curriculum of all accredited Schools of Social Work.

The book you are reading is a summary of ideals, ideas, and conclusions developed during a career working in the social services, administering them, and teaching about them. My first experience as a social worker involved administering financial aid and providing child protection services in Prince George and Fort St John, BC, for the BC Department of Social Welfare in 1962. My first experience as a teacher was teaching community organization and development as a social work field instructor in Vancouver in 1967. From these beginnings in the 1960s I have been fortunate in having had a dual career. As a social worker and government bureaucrat I became a policy analyst, researcher, ministry executive, and Superintendent of Child Welfare. In the university I became a Professor and had the opportunity to undertake research and write about the social services.

This book is written from a social justice perspective. The objective is to provide the reader with an understanding of the principles of social justice and an analysis of the social services that encourage, indeed insist upon, determining right from wrong. In other words, some policies, programs, and services meet the objectives of social justice better than others. To make such judgements one needs information, values, and critical analysis. This book provides an overview of Canadian social welfare services,

who they serve, and how they are organized. The social work values presented here offer a way of judging the effectiveness of these provisions in achieving the objectives of social justice for Canadians. The critical analysis is the responsibility of the student of social work.

Social justice is a controversial and political subject. There are disagreements about what constitutes social justice, how important it is to pursue social justice, and how best to pursue social justice. Thus, this textbook invites both controversy and discussion. As the author, my commitment is to state clearly the values I hold and to apply them as consistently and fairly as I can to the analysis of Canadian social welfare. As the reader I do not expect that you will always agree with me; indeed, I would be disappointed if you did. I expect only that you will think about the issues raised by the book and come to your own view in an informed way. The principal values that are foundational to this book are:

1. All people are to be valued equally.
2. All people are to be respected in their beliefs and culture.
3. All people are capable of making their own decisions and have potential for growth and change.
4. Obstacles to achieving growth and change are primarily social constructions, not individual pathologies.
5. Social constructions are political and can be changed.
6. Over the last 100 years we have learned that some social objectives can be achieved while others appear to be beyond our ability. Sometimes our efforts to achieve what seemed like worthwhile goals caused more harm than good.

7. Canada cannot separate itself from the surrounding world and needs to pursue social justice in a global and international context.

The book is divided into five sections. The first section (Chapter 1) provides a general overview of Canadian social welfare, the values that inspired its development, and the people it serves. The second section (Chapters 2 and 3) examines more closely the social welfare objective of achieving some degree of fairness in the distribution of income and the reduction of poverty in Canada. The third section (Chapters 4 and 5) examines the role of social welfare in building communities that have tolerant, fair, and just social relationships. The fourth section (Chapters 6 and 7) explores the political and ideological context of Canadian social welfare. These chapters aim to show the student how and why change has occurred. The last section (Chapter 8) looks to the future of social welfare in Canada.

Each chapter opens with a list of student learning objectives and ends with a series of discussion questions designed to encourage the application of the ideas in the chapter and to promote critical thinking. Also, at the end of each chapter is a list of additional readings chosen to expand on ideas and perspectives referred to in the text.

Acknowledgements

The opportunity to prepare this fourth edition of *Social Welfare in Canada* was provided by the University of Victoria through an administrative leave. Members of the School of Social Work have had a major influence on my understanding of social justice and social welfare since I joined them in 1987. In particular I want to acknowledge the influence of Leslie Brown, Gord Bruyere, Marilyn Callahan, Mehmoona Moosa Mitha, Michael Prince, Brian Wharf, and Barbara Whittington. I am indebted to Gayle Ployer for having clipped and kept many of the newspaper articles that are included in this edition.

The first two editions of *Social Welfare in Canada* (1975 and 1988) were published by McClelland & Stewart; the second two editions (1995 and 2003) have been published by Oxford University Press. To my publishers, thank you for the encouragement and advice you have provided and for the assistance of Richard Tallman, in this and earlier editions, in making my prose more readable.

PART I

Overview

CHAPTER 1

Social Welfare: Ideals and Context

This chapter introduces the concept of social welfare and looks at the major issues that have shaped the development of social welfare policy and services in Canada. In terms of conducting a social welfare policy analysis, the main subject headings of this chapter constitute a check list of items that must be considered.

Learning Objectives

1. To establish a working definition of 'social welfare'.
2. To distinguish the influence of six major viewpoints (ideologies) in the analysis of social welfare policy.
3. To understand seven central concepts in 'liberal' Canadian values that have had a strong influence on the development of social welfare policy.
4. To recognize the role of seven structural forces on the development of social welfare policy.
5. To understand how ideology, values, and structural forces interact with each other in shaping social welfare policy.

Social Welfare

What is social welfare? Today, in common parlance, 'social welfare' is defined by the social services and in particular by the services directed towards income security and personal and family life. The services themselves are examined later in this book, but before commencing this detailed examination of Canadian welfare services, it is important to look at the concept of social welfare and the context in which it has been developed.

The *concept* of social welfare has a much broader objective than the individual social services that are its most visible manifestation. This objective is to so design social welfare measures that they form a major component of the organized pursuit of social justice. This broad definition of social welfare, and in particular its application in Canada, is at the heart of this book.

This view of social welfare, based in the pursuit of social justice, is often referred to as the 'liberal' view. This is not a reference to the Liberal Party or to any particular government. Instead, the term 'liberal' is used to distinguish a school of philosophical thought and understanding. As such, the 'liberal' view is one of the six major viewpoints that have influenced popular and academic understandings of social welfare, the others being the conservative, socialist, feminist, anti-racist, and Aboriginal points of view.

The conservative point of view is illustrated by a recent social policy publication from the C.D. Howe Institute:

Canada's social programs need repair. They are too elaborate. They are too expensive. And they may not be good for the people they are supposed to help. They may not have caused Canada's current huge debt problem, but they are too large a component of public expenditure not to be part of the solution.[1]

The label 'conservative' includes what is sometimes referred to as 'neo-conservatism' and sometimes as 'neo-liberalism'. The 'neo' prefix indicates the assertion of the anti-welfare, pro-economic values that were asserted during the 1980s and 1990s by both the Mulroney Progressive Conservative government and the Liberal Chrétien/Martin government.

The socialist viewpoint is illustrated by Bob Mullaly's *Structural Social Work*:

> It [the social welfare state] can be used as a stepping stone towards a socialist society. Because social welfare programs and services represent a break with the free-market doctrine of distribution, social democrats think that the advantages of such a system would be seen by the general public as preferable to that of the free market, thus aiding in the transformation from a capitalist to a socialist society.[2]

The feminist perspective is not based in an ideology per se but in a separate experience of social welfare. Patricia Evans and Gerda Wekerle, in *Women and the Canadian Welfare State*, write that:

> The welfare state has always been a site of struggle and contestation for Canadian women. Today it frequently appears that women are fighting a rearguard action as hard-won gains are dismantled by economic restructuring and public sector cutbacks. In this climate, in which women often seem to bear a disproportionate share of the costs, it is easy to lose sight of how women have been and continue to be active in constituting and redefining the welfare state.[3]

The impact of feminism extends beyond a vigorous critique of social welfare. Feminism has also been the source from which new policies, programs, and services have been developed.

This influence includes major contributions in such areas as child and elder care, employment equity, sexual assault and family violence, and abortion and birth control services.[4]

An anti-racist critique of social policy has also been developed on the basis of a distinct experience of social welfare. In the experience of First Nations, blacks, South Asians, and other visible minorities, the policies and provisions of the welfare state have features that make them part of the institutional racism of Canadian society. Racism in this sense does not mean personal racial slurs and discrimination; instead, as Naidoo and Edwards define the term, 'Racism results from the transformation of race prejudice, ethnocentrism, or both through the exercise of power against a racial group defined as inferior by individuals and institutions with the intentional or unintentional support of the entire culture.'[5]

The Aboriginal critique of social policy shares with that of the anti-racist school a concern with racism in all its forms. However, the Aboriginal critique of social policy has many distinctive elements of its own based on the historic experience of Aboriginal peoples, both in Canada and internationally. These include the impact of colonialism, the continued connection to the land, and the continued experience of poverty and other forms of deprivation. Chief Strater Crowfoot writes:

> We need a paradigm shift in our thinking from the cynical, defensive, dependant, entitlement mindset that has been inculcated in us under the colonial Indian Act regime, and towards a more trusting, assertively proactive, persevering, visionary, affirming, meritocratic and inclusive orientation. We must summon the courage to take calculated risks in adapting to a changing environment, for our survival depends on that adaptability, just like it did in our ancestor's time.[6]

Because of the importance of the Aboriginal experience to social welfare the Aboriginal writers and critics deserve independent recognition.

The liberal point of view has a central place in this text because the other five points of view are agreed that liberalism is (or was) the driving force behind the institution of social welfare. It has also been the impetus for the aspirations and commitment of the majority of professionals in social welfare institutions. The other points of view are having a major impact on social welfare in Canada and on the development of critical thinking about social welfare. Each has also brought about significant changes in the original liberal conception of social welfare. However, the liberal view continues to best represent the aspirations for the social welfare in Canada as a whole. It represents historic mainstream thinking that the other approaches take for granted in developing their distinctive critiques. The contribution to understanding and policy formulation of each viewpoint is found throughout this text. In particular, Chapter 7 provides a more thorough treatment of the ideas, research, and knowledge base that inform each.

The Liberal Values

The liberal point of view, as applied to social welfare, ascribes particular importance to the following shared values: (1) concern for the individual; (2) faith in humanity; (3) equity; (4) equality; (5) community; (6) diversity; and (7) democracy.

1. *Concern for the individual.* All liberal conceptions of society place high value on the individual. The literature of social welfare illustrates this concern. In their interpretation of the role of social welfare in industrial society, Wilensky and Lebeaux[7] find a distinguishing characteristic in its 'direct concern with human consumption needs'. By this is meant that if government activities are placed on a continuum from activities directed to maintenance of the social system as a whole, such as national defence, monetary policy, and the administration of justice, to

activities focused on providing benefit to individuals, for example, schools, recreational facilities, and health services, then social welfare must be classified among those activities organized primarily with respect to the needs of the individual.

In social work, the concern with the individual finds expression in the commitment of professional codes of ethics to the principles of client-centredness, confidentiality, self-determination, and advocacy. At the international level the United Nations Universal Declaration of Human Rights expresses the concern thus:

> Article 22. Everyone, as a member of society, has the right to social security, and is entitled to realization through national effort and international co-operation, and in accordance with the organization and resources of each State, of the economic, social and cultural rights indispensable for his dignity and the free development of his personality.[8]

In Canada the Canadian Charter of Rights and Freedoms provides a central anchor for this value.

2. *Faith in humanity.* Concern for the individual is matched by a high degree of faith in the individual. This finds expression in social welfare programs and social work activities directed towards change in both institutions and individuals. In the former case, the basic thesis is that people are restricted and prevented from the fulfillment of their potential by ignorance and by ill-designed and inhumane social institutions. If these factors are changed, then people will achieve not only greater happiness and greater realization of potential but will be able to contribute to and receive more from their peers. When change in individuals is considered, the same basic thrust emerges. People can be helped to liberate themselves from their self-constructed prisons of ignorance, fear, and anger and thereby obtain greater personal fulfillment. The 1971 Senate Committee on Poverty expressed the value thus:

A recent development in Canadian social philosophy is the emergence of the more positive human resource development approach. This philosophy recognizes the inherent value of the literate, educated and trained population. . . . Development of human resources to their greatest potential is regarded as a desirable objective in itself.[9]

The value is expressed, too, in the rejection of the basically suspicious thrust of economic theory. The rejection of the idea that productivity depends on economic rewards and penalties is captured in the following quotation:

> that man is by nature greedy, lazy, etc.; that money incentives are required to make him work; and that it is perhaps an unfortunate necessity for industry to have a pool of unemployed and therefore miserable people from which to draw the energy (manpower) to work the machines, or to do the 'dirty work' of a society. . . . the 'market mentality' [is not only] seen as corrosive of human dignity and identity, it is increasingly seen as inefficient, even in its own terms, for society as a whole.[10]

Here, a high degree of faith is held in the positive aspects of our humanity. Failure to obtain these high aspirations is usually interpreted as a failure in institutions, socialization patterns, or opportunities. Such failures can be prevented or corrected. Failure to obtain the best is regarded as an unfortunate and correctable aberration.

These ideas are also connected to the concept of 'anti-oppressive' social policies and social work practice and to the concept of 'structural' social work, both of which make the assumption that oppression and injustice occur because of choices that have been made, deliberately or inadvertently, in the way that society has organized its affairs. If these mistaken choices in the way society has organized its affairs were corrected, human nature would be more tolerant, generous, not racist, not homophobic, etc.[11]

3. *Equity.* The commitment to equity indicates a willingness to listen to, search for, and reduce, if not eliminate, those features of the social condition that create relative differences of power and privilege, and hence of advantage and disadvantage. Examples of such differences include the relationships between children and adults, the relationships between men and women, the relationship between those who are able-bodied and those who have different physical or mental capacities, the differences that visibly or culturally distinguish people from one another, and the relationship between people of differing sexual orientation.

The liberal Oxford philosopher John Rawls has suggested two principles of social justice that are sufficiently broad to provide a beginning point for discussion of equity in this wide range of social relationships:

> First: each person is to have an equal right to the most extensive basic liberty compatible with a similar liberty for others. Second: social and economic inequalities are to be arranged so that they are both (a) reasonably expected to be to everyone's advantage, and (b) attached to positions and offices open to all.[12]

Applying these principles to the relationship between a child and his or her parents permits some inequality of status and freedom between parent and child, but only to the extent that such inequality can be reasonably expected to be to everyone's advantage. Thus a parent has no right to mistreat, exploit, or neglect a child while still holding to the right to parent. A moral basis thus exists for a social welfare function that aims to protect the welfare of children. An analysis of how children are treated in our society, including how they are treated by social welfare, is an important corollary.

Applying these principles to the differences between men and women requires that men and women be treated equally in employment, marriage, divorce, inheritance, ownership, and civic life while permitting women to advance differing claims based on their exclusive role in child-bearing. It also requires that social policy be subject to a feminist analysis that examines how the welfare state deals with women.

Applying these principles to race and ethnic relationships would exclude any consideration of differences based on appearance while permitting an ethnic group to articulate its right to resist cultural practices that act to its disadvantage. The 'Report Card on Racism' described in Box 1.1 indicates the concerns that lie at the heart of a commitment to equity.

It should not be supposed that the principle of equity is easily applied. For example, between parents and children the words 'reasonably expected to be to everyone's advantage' require interpretation, and frequently interpretations differ among parent, child, and social welfare authorities. A teenager who needs an abortion or who lives with a lesbian companion may hold that her liberty in no way infringes on the liberty of others, but not all would agree. Some parents and social groups would consider that they, or the state, have a right to intervene. In recent years there have been differences of view on these matters within Canadian society, and much wider differences of view exist between societies.

4. *Equality*. A strong egalitarian thrust is a central feature of social welfare values and is a particular expression of the general concern with equity. The value finds expression in two related concerns: a general concern with the extent of inequalities and a particular concern with poverty. The concern with the extent of inequalities directs attention to the relative standards of living of different groups of persons. The concern with poverty directs attention to the minimum standards of living that are to be tolerated in the society, regardless of the individual poor person's financial contribution to the society. In both cases, there is a clear rejection of the idea that the income distribution resulting from inheritance, property, productivity, bargaining, and the like should be allowed to stand.

Beginning with Rawls's principles of justice, the social policy analyst W.G. Runciman approaches the subject of inequalities with an initial assumption that economic equality between persons should be the beginning point for any discussion of difference.

> Starting, therefore, from the assumption that all social inequalities require to be justified it can, as a minimum, be shown that rational persons in a state of nature would agree on three broad criteria, or principles, in the light of which, subsequent inequalities of reward could be claimed to be just.[13]

These three principles are need, merit, and contribution to the common good. Of the three, *need* is regarded as the most basic. A person who is sick needs additional resources to obtain the most basic type of equality with others in the society. *Merit* is accepted as a criterion only to the extent that it equates with the willingness of individuals to do things that are difficult to do, involving demonstrable hardship and sacrifice to the doer. *Contribution to the common good* is accepted because everyone stands to benefit. It follows that the extent of financial advantage should be proportionate to the extent of the general benefit obtained for all. Thus the ideal world would be characterized by those differences in wealth and income that all had agreed are justified, rather than by wealth and income being privately determined. In particular, in Runciman's approach to inequality and equity, there would be sensitivity first to the situation of those who are least well off.

5. *Community*. The values of community are attentive to the need of individuals for a social context for their lives. Community values take the form of assertions that people should have the opportunity to fulfill themselves through their relationships with others. Ideally, people should live in a community from which they draw satisfying social relationships, which provides adequate developmental opportunities for their children, and in which participation, in

Box 1.1 Unequal Access: A Report Card on Racism

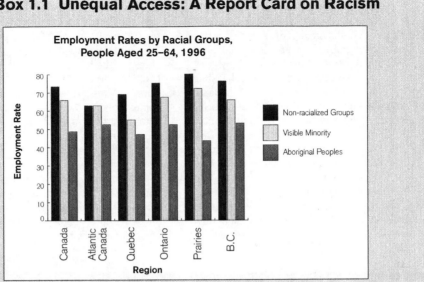

Employment Rates by Racial Groups, People Aged 25–64, 1996

Legend:
- Non-racialized Groups
- Visible Minority
- Aboriginal Peoples

On January 9th, the Canadian Race Relations Foundation will release *Unequal Access: A Canadian Profile of Racial Differences in Education, Employment, and Income*, a 'report card' on racism in Canada. The report, written by Jean Lock Kunz, Anne Milan, and Sylvain Schetagne of the CCSD [Canadian Council on Social Development], shows that good jobs and promotions elude many visible minority and Aboriginal men and women in Canada. The report uses the most recent statistics available, primarily data from the 1996 census and from focus group discussions held with visible minority and Aboriginal men and women in five cities across Canada. Here are some of the highlights of the research.

Aboriginals still have low educational attainment

The high school non-completion rate is highest among Aboriginal youth, compared to rates among visible minority youth and young people who are neither visible minority nor Aboriginal (non-racialized youth). Aboriginal youth also lagged far behind in their rates of university completion.
- Even with post-secondary education, job opportunities may still be out of reach for Aboriginal peoples. As one Aboriginal participant comments: 'When I send out my résumé and I'm totally qualified for the position, they'll look at the courses I've taken (First Nations resources). Maybe that's why I don't get the job.'

Immigrants have difficulties with credential recognition

Despite their higher educational attainment compared to non-racialized groups, visible minorities trail behind in terms of their employment and income.
- For recent immigrants, the challenge is to have their credentials recognized. One focus group participant said, 'I have a university degree from Algeria, where there is no CEGEP. When I came to Canada, they subtracted three years from my educational attainment in order to compensate. This makes no sense.'
- Foreign-born visible minorities experience greater discrepancies between their education levels and their occupations, compared to other groups. Less than half of foreign-born visible minorities who have a university education work in jobs with a high skill level.

Good jobs are elusive to minorities

- In times of economic prosperity, it is not as difficult to find a job, but for men and women who are members of minority groups, it is still difficult to find jobs that match their qualifications. There was consensus among focus group participants that some groups of people in Canada have more difficulty than others in finding employment. These include Aboriginals, members of visible minority groups, recent immigrants to Canada, young people, and seniors. Employment rates for these groups are lower in all regions of Canada.

- Visible minority men and women still face 'polite' racism when job hunting. One focus group participant said: 'I've called about jobs and had people say "come down for an interview," yet when I get there, I get the feeling they are surprised to see that I'm black because I sound like the average guy on the telephone. They've said, "Oh, the job has just been filled,"

or during the interview they'll say that I'm overqualified or ask me questions like "Are you sure you want to work at this type of job?"'

- Even when members of minority groups gain access to the labour market, they still have difficulties advancing in their position. As illustrated by one focus group participant: 'I had applied for a promotion, but I didn't get the job. A guy that I had trained (who is white) got the promotion instead.'
- Compared to non-racialized groups, members of visible minority groups and Aboriginal people with a university education are less likely to hold managerial or professional jobs. For those who do obtain managerial jobs, more than half are self-employed, compared to only one-third among non-racialized groups.

Source: Canadian Council on Social Development, *Perception* 23, 3 (Dec. 1999): 10–11.

deciding how the collective welfare is to be obtained, is open to all.

The concept of community includes the geographic local community but also includes communities based on any common tie, such as age, interest, employment, leisure, or ethnic origin. Community is seen as providing the primary means of social control and socialization and the first level of collective support to the family. The community is also the site of such organized measures of support as family life education, daycare, homemaker services, and mental health services.

In addition, the community has increasingly been seen as a source of employment and economic development through such activities as community development, community economic development, and community social services. All of these activities have a goal of improved relationships among people, less alienation, less class separation, and less racial or ethnic conflict.

6. *Diversity.* Earlier statements[14] of the goals of social justice failed to recognize that differences arise not only between individuals but

also between religions, cultures, and social groups. Rawls refers to these differences of world view as 'reasonable comprehensive doctrines':

Thus, it is not in general unreasonable to affirm any one of a number of reasonable comprehensive doctrines. We recognize that our own doctrine has, and can have, for people generally, no special claim on them beyond our own view of its merits. Others who affirm doctrines different from ours are, we grant, reasonable also, and certainly not unreasonable.[15]

In the discussion of equity and equality we noted that the application of these principles differs with individual situations. Recognizing diversity as a value requires that respect be shown as well to differences of peoples' collective historical and cultural experience. In relation to social policy this means that:

Liberals can and should accept a wide range of group differentiated rights for national minorities and ethnic groups, without sacrificing their core commitments to individual freedom and social equality.[16]

An example is provided by the relationship between First Nations and general Canadian society. Let us grant that the inequality between persons of Native origin and others is an injustice. Until the 1970s it was generally assumed that the way to correct this injustice was to adopt policies that promoted the assimilation or integration of First Nations into the general society. However, this view was rejected by First Nations and the view now is that they should have the opportunity to form their own societies and govern their own affairs. There are many questions about how such a separation can be made and sustained, but the need to recognize a separate Aboriginal presence is now entrenched in the Canadian Constitution and is central to the development and administration of social policy by and for Aboriginal Canadians.

Opening the discussion of social welfare to issues of diversity has led to major changes in the scope of that discussion and requires us to see social welfare as it was developed as a historical expression of Western culture rather than as a universally applicable institution. Major differences reflecting the values and culture of each society also exist between countries that have developed social welfare systems.

7. *Faith in democracy.* The example of the change in First Nations policy illustrates another important feature of the values of social justice, which is that their application is fallible and subject to change. Kymlicka, in his discussion of liberalism and individual freedom, notes that:

> [The] assumption that our beliefs about the good life are fallible and revisable is widely endorsed in the liberal tradition from John Stuart Mill to the most prominent contemporary American liberals. . . . As Rawls puts it, individuals 'do not view themselves as inevitably tied to the pursuit of the particular

conception of the good and its final ends which they espouse at any given time'. Instead they are 'capable of revising and changing this conception'. They can 'stand back' from their current ends to 'survey and assess' their worthiness.[17]

In practical terms, the revision of public policy lies within the boundaries of the political process. Hence, the importance of the attachment to, and confidence in, democracy. 'Democracy', meaning rule by the people, is an extension of faith in humanity, from the individual to the collective. In ideal terms, democracy is the participation of all affected parties in processes of decision-making to an extent proportionate to how much they are affected by the results. Decisions are expected to be based on rational argument, respect for difference, and negotiated compromise rather than imposed through the assertion of differences of power.

Realistically, it must be conceded that such is not the real state of Canadian political affairs or of any other political jurisdiction, and there is a search for more participatory and consensual ways to make public choices. However, until better ways can be devised a basic commitment remains to the typical form of democracy found in liberal societies generally and in Canada in particular (a universal adult electorate, a choice of political parties, periodic elections). The accepted instruments of change are thus persuasion, argument, protest, publicity, organization, interest group politics, and alliances. On the other hand, subversion, intimidation, violence, and personal attack, not to mention terrorism and warfare, are the antithesis of the objectives of social welfare.[18]

The Context of Social Welfare

Social welfare, as we know it, is the product of a particular time and culture. The fact that it has been established within the last 100 years and is a creation of Western developed societies provides it with a familiarity that would be lacking if it had occurred in another time and place. This familiarity can distract us from understanding the context in which social welfare both was developed and now exists. The importance of seeing social welfare in context cannot be overemphasized, for the principal reason that social welfare is changing is that the context in which it arose has changed. Some of these changes are affecting all Western developed societies, while some are distinct to Canada.

1. *The global economy, the information age, warfare, and terrorism.* The global economy is not a new phenomenon. There was international trade in rare objects from the earliest time, and by the nineteenth century a global economy of sorts was founded on colonialism and on European military and technological supremacy. During the twentieth century America and developed post-colonial societies, including Canada, Australia, and South Africa, became full members of this colonially based international economy. It was a global order characterized by great inequalities and it was managed to the benefit of the Western developed societies as a matter of military, financial, and economic policy. During this period the institutions of social welfare were developed.

The current global economy has undergone major changes from this earlier pattern. One change was marked by the OPEC oil cartel in the 1970s. The cartel showed that a determined group of non-Western countries could take control of a critical commodity and manipulate its price and supply to their benefit. A more profound change, however, was the development of a much more complex manufacturing and trading world in which major growth in the proportion of production took place outside the Western developed market economies, first in Japan and in Southeast Asia and increasingly in India, Latin America, North Africa, and the Middle East. Until the 1990s, the centrally planned and managed economies of Eastern Europe, Russia, and China offered an alternative Communist economic model. However, the collapse of this alternative system symbolized by the destruction Berlin Wall heralded their participation, too, in a global economy that remains dominated by the Western developed societies in which it originated.

Concurrent with the development of the global economy has been the development of transnational corporations (TNCs) and financial systems that lie outside the control of any national government and are only loosely regulated through international conventions and agreements. Thus, the manufactured goods we buy in our stores come from all parts of the world and are frequently made through production processes that occur in more than one country and often on more than one continent.

The development of the latest form of the global economy and its associated financial systems has been made possible by a new technology—the computerized information systems on which we now depend. The speed with which information can now be processed and communicated anywhere in the world has produced fundamental changes in the way the world does business, organizes its affairs, and understands itself. Furthermore, we are still in the early stages of this revolution in our collective affairs. We do not know where it will take us, but the changes that have already occurred are such that we know the world of the twenty-first century will be as different from our own as the world of the nineteenth century was from ours.

Warfare also had a major influence on the development of social welfare. World War I led to the development of social welfare for veterans and seniors; World War II led to the framing of the concept of the 'welfare state'. The Cold War challenged Western societies to provide a sufficient measure of internal equality to offset the attraction of the Communist model. The great Swedish welfare state economist and architect Gunnar Myrdal saw the connection when he wrote in 1958 that 'We will never be able to come to grips with the international problems of today and tomorrow if we do not squarely face the fact that the democratic Welfare State in the rich countries of the Western world is protectionistic and nationalistic.'[19]

In the present period a single military power, the United States of America, plays a dominant role in providing the military framework for the global economy. Its hegemony is challenged less by other nations than by international terrorism, as the events of 11 September 2001 and their aftermath showed all too clearly. It is possible that social welfare has a role to play in alleviating the social conditions that support the development of international terrorism, but this would require the development of international social welfare institutions on a scale not yet begun.

2. *Capitalism.* The capitalist free-market economy provides the economic context of social welfare. The economic historian Robert Heilbronner points out that there have been only three mechanisms for the exchange of goods and labour between people and societies in the history of mankind. The first is tradition: the sharing of goods and labour on the basis of cultural expectations as occurred (and continues to occur) in First Nations communities (e.g., through ceremonies like the potlatch). The second is command: the authoritative distribution of goods and labour as occurred in the building of the pyramids and in the command economies of Eastern Europe prior to the 1990s and as occurs today in the government sector of our economy. The third form of distribution is through the market economy in which goods and labour are exchanged at a price. The capitalist form of the market economy has developed since the eighteenth century as a mechanism that encourages the private ownership of the means of production and distribution and hence the accumulation of wealth by individuals and corporations.

The capitalist form of the market economy has many problems. It is exploitive, unstable, and environmentally insensitive, creates extremes of wealth and poverty, and is devoid of any moral character. However, it has provided a mechanism for a dynamic series of social and economic revolutions that have transformed all capitalist societies, whether they wanted such transformation or not.

> The first of these was the industrial revolution of the late eighteenth and nineteenth centuries that brought with it the cotton mill and the steam engine along with mass child labour; a second revolution brought with it the railway, the steamship and along with them a new form of economic instability—business cycles; a third brought electrification . . .; a fourth introduced the automobile . . .; a fifth has electronified everything. . . . Over the entire period of humanity children had lived lives that were essentially the same as their parents. . . . From the mid-nineteenth century on that sense of continuity was ever more noticeably displaced by a sense of change.[20]

With each revolution has come, too, an increase in individualism, freedom, income, health, and longevity of life for the wealthy, for the middle classes, and for most but not all members of developed Western societies. The affluence and advantage enjoyed by participants in capitalist market economies have exercised an attraction wherever they have become known. Where they have had the choice people have, more often than not, chosen the market economy over having their affairs organized by either tradition or command. Once such a choice has been made it has never been permanently reversed. Furthermore, the alternative developed under socialist auspices in Eastern Europe and the Soviet Union has disintegrated and been replaced by new capitalist systems. For the foreseeable future there is no alternative to capitalism in sight.

In this capitalist economic order individuals are expected to provide for themselves. The pages of Canadian government statements of social policy are filled with obeisance to the goals of economic growth and with exhortations as to the values of economic self-reliance and independence. Further, these values have been increasingly emphasized as insecurity about the future of Western society has grown. The society's rhetoric entrusts its future to the private initiative of individuals rather than to institutions—whether unions, governments, or corporations. Social welfare provision is closely related to this capitalist view of economic freedom and responsibility.

As a result, many of our social welfare policies can be viewed as the secondary consequence of this series of social and economic revolutions and as a reaction to the amoral character of capitalism. Based on a varied mixture of concerns—the unfairness of the capitalist economic order, human sympathy for the unfortunate, recognition of the claims advanced by those who have been disadvantaged by change, and fear that organized opposition might disrupt the market economy—social welfare measures have been developed. The large field of income security policies can be viewed as a response to the problems of social dislocation caused by unplanned changes in demand for different types of labour and the consequent impossibility of private citizens providing for themselves in all circumstances. The large field of personal and community social services can be viewed as a response to the dislocation of community and family life caused by urbanization.

In the early years of capitalist economic growth there was little or no attempt to mitigate the social effects of continuous change. The social costs of social change were allowed to lie where they fell. Latterly, there has been more understanding that economic change creates both winners and losers, and that losers should receive some compensation or adjustment assistance from the state. Thus, a case was made that the James Bay Cree should be compensated for lost lands due to hydro development, that a workman dispossessed of usable skills by technological change should be compensated by the society, and that an elderly renter, whose neighbourhood is to be destroyed for new

construction, should be rehoused. We have also come some way towards recognizing that there should be a settlement for losses and damages that occurred in the past. Examples here include First Nations who were dispossessed of their land without compensation and victims of poor industrial working conditions. Finally, the claims of farmers and fishermen to compensation have been partly recognized where they have lost their livelihood due to change in either international prices or environmental conditions.

Some parts of our social welfare policies can be seen as necessary activities to the market economy but are undertaken outside it. Examples include universal education, public health systems, transportation and energy infrastructure, and the criminal justice system. Moreover, the need for social welfare is also a product of the positive achievements of capitalist society: people live longer and hence need more care. They live more by their brains and hence need more sophisticated education and training.

With each change in the market economy has come a change in the social environment, in the demand for labour, in the types of education that are relevant, and in the disparities of wealth and income that are generated. Each of these changes has made some features of our social welfare systems less relevant than they were while creating new issues that need a response. One indicator of these changes is the proportion of the Canadian workforce in various types of employment. Table 1.1 provides an overview of these changes. The change in the proportion of the working population in the blue-collar (manufacturing), primary (resource extraction), and transportation sectors is particularly significant, as these groups represented the majority source of employment when the social welfare systems were developed. Our unemployment insurance provisions were designed in the 1940s for an economy dominated by male workers in blue-collar and primary industries who were assumed to be the principal source of family income. It is not surprising that they did not anticipate the 1990s distribution of employment and gender roles.

James Ife makes the case that capitalism and globalization have now led to a new juncture in which inequalities will increase as more and more people are considered to be 'irrelevant' to the global economy.[21] Included in their number are all of those of greatest concern for social welfare—the poor and the unemployed. However, Ife does not encourage pessimism, noting that:

> Globalization, then, is a complex and contested field. It is clear that we live in a globalized world, but far from clear what form that globalization will take. It is currently dominated by economic forces and imperatives, but the same criticism can be made of this (as was made of earlier forms of capitalism) . . . , namely that the market alone is not always the best mechanism for the equitable meeting of human needs. Social conditions have to be taken into account as well as economic concerns, and social policy must be considered along with economic policy if some form of global civil society is to be developed and maintained.[22]

3. *The nation-state and international relationships.* The national state remains the fundamental political unit of society, but its power to control its affairs has been reduced by the advent of the new form of the global economy. The transnational corporations have proved to be difficult to regulate, control, or tax. Each country wants and needs the employment that the TNCs generate, but since the TNCs can choose where they operate the individual countries are placed in a situation of competing with one another to offer the most favourable (that is, profitable for the TNCs) operating conditions. Taxation of TNCs has also been difficult, partly because when production and trade processes are distributed globally it is difficult to establish where profit has been generated. In addition, countries with high rates of corporate tax risk driving away new TNC investment.

Social welfare remains an internal jurisdiction of each country. State actions may range from inactivity through support to such institutions as churches, philanthropic groups, and the family, to the active creation and administration of state-provided services. Indeed, one of the strengths of social welfare is that each country has been able to devise the system that expresses its own need and social character.[23] This same strength, however, can lead to each country being involved in a competition aimed at minimizing the costs of welfare in order to provide a more profitable and attractive environment for international investment. The European Community has recognized this

Table 1.1   Distribution of the Labour Force, 15 years and Over, by Occupation Division, 1941–1991 (numerical distribution by 000s)

Occupation Sector	1941		1961		1981		1991	
	No.	%	No.	%	No.	%	No.	%
All	4,183	100	6,458	100	12,267	100	14,220	100
Blue-collar	1,058	25	2,446	38	3,465	28	3,017	21
Primary	1,134	27	830	13	929	8	867	6
Transport	266	6	496	7	939	7	1,060	7
White-collar and Service	1,496	36	3,246	50	6,864	56	9,829	69

SOURCE: *Census of Canada*, various years.

danger and agreed on a series of conventions governing the regulation of industry, working conditions, and social benefits. Although European proponents of the welfare state see many limitations to what has been accomplished,[24] the European model provides more support for the welfare systems of each member state than is available in North America.

In North America, Canada is partnered with the United States and Mexico in the North American Free Trade Agreement (NAFTA). As neither of the other partners has had as strong a social welfare system as has Canada, there is no support through NAFTA for Canadian welfare provisions. This is not to say that Canada cannot have its own social welfare system, but it has to be designed, financed, and managed in a manner that supports, or at least does not harm, Canada's external economic competitiveness.

In some circumstances nations have had to ask for international assistance to develop or support their internal economies. Where this has happened, as was the case in New Zealand in 1988, international bodies have played a more active role in requiring changes in social welfare as a condition of assistance. For New Zealand, this included adopting policies of financial restraint that influenced social welfare expenditures through such effects as creating unemployment and limiting the government revenues available to finance programs. In the early 1990s, Canada was close to being in this situation and as a result made deficit reduction a major policy goal, cutting some long-standing social programs and limiting others. This raises the question of the extent to which social welfare is under the control of national governments and the extent to which Canada can now have policies of its own. It has become increasingly clear that national governments require the support of international social policy agreements that limit corporate power. For this reason, activist supporters of social welfare have been among those critical of the World Trade Organization's failure to recognize sufficiently the connection between international trade policies and social policies (see Box 1.2).

4. *Ethnonationalism and cultural pluralism.* The post-war social welfare service state was founded in the aftermath of the Holocaust at a time when racism was seen as an extremely dangerous force in social policy, and it was believed that one way to counteract this dangerous force was to develop social welfare on the principle that common social services would be available to all citizens, regardless of culture or ethnic origin. However, this principle was based on another assumption—that 'modern' Western institutions would be or could be made appropriate for all peoples and, sooner or later, would gradually displace traditional ones such as the tribe, local community, and extended family. The approach to social policy favoured treating people as individuals with human rights rather than as ethnic groups with collective rights.

In the 1990s it became apparent that the issues of ethnicity, culture, and race had not been dealt with to people's satisfaction and that a policy paradigm that disregarded cultural differences constituted a form of institutional racism. Instead, there has been a reawakened understanding that the nation-state has to accommodate a variety of claims to different types of collective identity within its boundaries. The name given to one of the claims of these newly recognized identities is *ethnonationalism*, which occurs where there is more than one nation within a state, occupying lands of their own and sharing a distinct historical and cultural tradition. Levin defines both the objectives and the dilemma of ethnonationalism:

> The demand of a state for every people is the strong sense of ethnonationalism, the extreme political expression of cultural identity. Reconciling the strong version of this ideal with the institutional realities of a state for every people is, however, a practical impossibility. That there are far fewer states than ethnic groups makes the depth of the attachment to the ideal and the sense of deprivation in its frustration all the

more poignant. The politics of ethnonationalism worldwide draws its importance not from this disproportion of numbers, but from the fact that more than half the governments of these independent states must deal with political claims made on an ethnic basis where there are few if any workable solutions. . . .

Acceptance of the right to self determination—the weak sense of ethnonationalism—also presents problems, since it leaves unattended the question of what forms of institutional autonomy can meet the aspirations of 'people' for autonomy. . . . New political forms which offer autonomy without sovereignty are difficult to imagine. Furthermore, any new solution bears the burden of achieving acceptance without a history to give it legitimacy.[25]

Canada faces two major ethnonational forces, the recurrent issue of establishing Quebec as a separate state (the first sense of ethnonationalism) and the issue of Aboriginal government (the second sense of ethnonationalism).[26]

In addition, Canada, along with all other developed states, has become, through immigration, a polyethnic multicultural state in

---

Box 1.2 The Road to a Better World

The failure of the World Trade Organization to agree on the agenda of a new trade liberalization round was predictable. Beyond the complex negotiations and the street protests, the failure is rooted in a profound imbalance in our efforts to benefit from and cope with globalization. This imbalance is plain: World governments are investing enormous efforts in regulating and liberalizing the world economy, but they neglect the multilateral institutions dedicated to social and environmental issues.

There is no mistaking the high price paid for last month's failure in Seattle. There will be lengthy delays in progress on key trade issues: the curbings of agricultural subsidies, the removal of trade barriers in information technology, agreeing on the tax treatment of electronic commerce, moving forward on trade and environment, and opening the rich markets of OECD countries to exporters from the developing world. Such delays are particularly damaging to Canada, which, with 40 per cent of its production exported, always benefits from the stability and predictability that comes with an enhanced legal framework for international trade.

The WTO failed in 1999 like the Multilateral Agreement of Investment did in 1998 because its agenda was outmoded, out of sync with the times. Pure liberal economics are not the entrenched foundation of social organization they were 100 years ago. It is no coincidence that the scrappy protests in Seattle looked more like the anarchist anti-capitalist demonstrations at the turn of the century than the student marches of the sixties: The target of the protesters looked dangerously like a corporatist manifesto from 1900. The isolation of negotiators lent an undeserved credibility to those who would fight such a manifesto through street violence.

Most opponents of the WTO are neither against globalization—though they may like the slogans—nor against the opening of borders. What they demand is that the international regime follows the same key principle that underpins domestic governance in the 20th century: a relative balance between the market, social justice and environmental protection. These opponents can be rallied behind a strengthening of the international trade regime by deploying as much vigour in co-operating and negotiating on non-economic issues as is shown in trade rounds. This is the way to push trade liberalization forward and reap its undeniable benefits.

But too many proponents of free trade simply defend it as being modern and forward looking, as compared to the 'antiquated' positions of their nationalist, social democratic and environmentalist opponents. They forget too easily that there is nothing particularly modern, forward or progressive in promoting laissez-faire economics at the expense of other values.

SOURCE: Pierre-Marc Johnson and André Beaulieu, 'The road to a better world', *Globe and Mail*, 30 Dec. 1999.

which Aboriginal peoples and peoples of French, British, other European, Asian, and African origins live together using common social institutions. The changes taking place in this mix of peoples of different origins are substantial. For most of the twentieth century those of French and British origins dominated all others by a wide margin. This is no longer the case. Table 1.2 shows the historic pattern and the recent change.

Until the 1970s the assumption of Canadian social policy was that immigrants (and Aboriginal peoples) would assimilate to either the English or French majorities. This is clearly no longer the case. For most of the twentieth century, too, 'Other' in the census reports represented people of principally European origin. This is rapidly changing. At the time of the 1981 census, 70 per cent of the 'Other' were of European origin, but by 1991 only 56 per cent of these were European. The rapid growth in the numbers of people declaring non-European origin is also apparent when the 1986, 1991, and 1996 censuses are compared (see Table 1.3). Some of this increase is the result of immigration, but some is the result of a greater willingness to declare a non-European origin.

It is now apparent that the origins of the peoples in Canada are complex and that the old British/French paradigm and even the later British/French/Other European paradigm no longer represent the basis on which social policy can be developed. The challenge is to build, or rebuild, social institutions that serve all peoples with equity. Genuinely common institutions have to be developed. Assimilation was too simplistic and spoke only of a one-way street towards integration. Instead, we are finding that Canadian social policy and its administration have to change to provide for a society of many peoples.[27]

5. *Feminism.* European culture was (and is) not only racist but also patriarchal. Women were denied the vote until long after voting had been extended to all men. A woman's property rights were limited and on marriage were lost to the man. Women were subject to discrimination in employment both by being denied access to some types of employment and by being paid less in all employment. Roles performed by women, particularly caring roles, were taken for granted and not valued at all. As late as the 1950–60 period the common wisdom was that 'a woman's place is in the home', where she would care for the children, prepare the meals, keep a clean and tidy house, and remain faithful to her husband. The man, on the other hand, was expected to be a 'breadwinner', bringing home a wage from which he would give his wife what was needed for the household; he would

Table 1.2 Population of Canada by British, French, and Other Origin, 1901–1991 (000s)

Ethnic Origin	1901 No.	%	1921 No.	%	1941 No.	%	1961 No.	%	1971 No.	%	1981 No.	%	1991 No.	%
British	3,063	57.0	4,869	55.4	5,716	49.7	7,997	43.8	9,624	44.6	9,674	40.2	7,595	28.1
French	1,649	30.7	2,453	27.9	3,483	30.3	5,540	30.4	6,180	28.6	6,439	26.7	6,146	22.7
Other	659	12.2	1,466	16.7	2,308	20.0	4,792	25.8	5,764	26.7	6,370	26.4	7,429	27.5
Total	5,371		8,788		11,507		18,238		21,568		24,084		26,994	

NOTE: Until the 1981 census respondents could only report one ethnic origin determined by their paternal ancestry. In the 1996 census respondents were offered a wider range of reporting categories for the ethnic origin question and comparability to earlier data ceased to be possible.

SOURCE: *Census of Canada*, various years.

be part of the children's lives but on a more limited basis, with work taking precedence; he was also free to use the balance of his income for his interests and there was to some degree a 'double standard' of fidelity.

These cultural assumptions were the understanding of men's and women's roles that were held by men. Dissenting women's voices were not heeded, or were treated as marginal or extreme points of view. As a result, social welfare was based on patriarchal assumptions and upheld male privilege. These assumptions are now regarded as wrong by most women and some men, but the institutions established on these assumptions, and on the male privilege that they created, continue to exist. Changing the institutions to provide for equity between men and women has been proceeding for the last two decades. The process is by no means complete and the privilege that resulted (and results) from their unreformed character remains. There also have been reactions to uphold male privilege by resisting, or reversing, those modest actions that have been taken, for example, to provide greater equity in the workplace.

In addition, feminism as a reforming and reframing influence on social welfare poses a deeper challenge than correcting androcentrism. This challenge is to look at what the pursuit of social welfare means based on the life experience of women, as is seen, for example, in the Baines, Evans, and Neysmith text, *Women's Caring: Feminist Perspectives on Social Welfare* (1991, 1998).

6. *The extent and scale of social spending.* All developed countries devote a substantial portion of national revenues to social welfare measures. However, major variations exist in the percentage of various countries' economies devoted to social spending (see Table 1.4).

Social spending includes public expenditures on pensions, unemployment insurance, health care, and families (including family allowances), as well as active labour market measures such as retraining and assisted job placement. Some of the variation between countries can be partly accounted for by differences in the number of beneficiaries and the age structure of the population. Other differences, however, are the result of deliberate public policy choices. Table 1.5 shows some of the major differences that exist. For example, variations in pension expenditures are largely the result of demographic differences, while the differences in non-health service costs are largely the result of public policy decisions in areas like daycare and active labour market programming.

One major change that is readily apparent from Table 1.5 is that Canada sharply reduced

Table 1.3 Peoples of Non-European Ethnic Origin, Canada, 1986, 1991, and 1996 (000s)

Ethnic Origin	1986	1991	1996
Aboriginal peoples	373	470	1,100
Arab/West Asian	75	144	244
South Asian	260	420	671
Chinese	360	585	860
Filipino	93	157	234
Korean	26	44	69
Other East and Southeast Asian	73	114	240
African, Caribbean, Black	223	323	574
Latin American	32	85	177

SOURCE: *Census of Canada*, 1986, 1991, 1996.

its social expenditures between 1992 and 1997 while most European countries increased theirs. Although Linda McQuaig[28] and other social welfare writers argued that Canada's social spending was not out of line with that of other OECD countries or out of control and could indeed be increased on a European pattern, Canada moved in the opposite direction to decrease social expenditure and to make its overall expenditure profile similar to that of the United States. There were several reasons for the change. Since the 1970s Canada has incurred an unbroken succession of annual public expenditure deficits. Each year more has been spent than has been raised by taxation, and each year the difference has been financed by borrowing (Table 1.6).

In the period up to 1983 Canada's public debt was similar to that of other OECD countries, at around 50 per cent of gross domestic

Table 1.4 Social Spending among G-7 Countries as a Percentage of Gross Domestic Product, 1960, 1980, 1990, and 1997

	1960	*1980*	*1990*	*1997*
France	13.4	24.7	26.7	29.6
Italy	16.5	21.2	26.3	26.9
Germany	20.5	24.6	22.0	26.6
United Kingdom	13.9	18.0	16.9	21.6
Canada	12.1	17.5	20.2	16.9
United States	10.9	13.1	12.4	16.0
Japan	8.0	14.3	14.4	14.4

SOURCE: OECD, *OECD Economic Survey 1993–4, Canada,* (Paris 1994); OECD, *Society at a Glance: OECD Social Indicators* (Paris, 2001), 73.

Table 1.5 Social Spending in G-7 Countries by Broad Social Policy Areas, 1997

	Cash Benefits		Services		
Country	*Income Support to Working Age Population*	*Pensions*	*Health*	*Social Services for elderly, disabled, families and 'active' labour market programs*	*Total*
France	12.4	6.6	7.5	3.1	29.6
Italy	3.5	16.0	5.9	1.5	26.9
Germany	4.7	11.0	8.1	2.8	26.6
United Kingdom	6.5	7.1	5.8	2.2	21.6
Canada	5.1	5.0	6.4	0.4	16.9
United States	2.2	6.8	6.5	0.5	16.0
Japan	1.4	6.6	5.8	0.6	14.4

SOURCE: OECD, *Society at a Glance: OECD Social Indicators,* 73.

product (GDP), but by the 1990s it had risen substantially higher, to around 90 per cent.[29] This was requiring Canada to spend an increasing proportion of public expenditure each year to pay debt service costs. By 1992 the level of debt service costs had reached 9.4 per cent of GDP (21 per cent of all government revenues), exerting an enormous pressure on all other public expenditures. Consequently, Canada came under considerable international pressure to reduce its government deficits to a much lower proportion of GDP. In 1988 Canada had also entered the Free Trade Agreement (FTA) with the United States, and with the FTA came accumulating pressure from the business community to make Canadian revenue and tax policies more similar to those in the United States. In the later 1990s the Liberal Chrétien/Martin

government, and 'conservative' provincial governments, addressed the 'problem' of deficits and began to deal with the 'problem' of tax differences from the United States. The result was that by 2000 there was a government surplus, some tax cuts had been effected, and social program expenditures had sharply decreased. The decreases in social expenditures, however, did not hit everyone equally. Pensions and health expenditures were largely exempt, leaving the burden of reduced programming to fall on families and children and on the working poor. In the year 2003 it is very difficult to see how these changes will be reversed. The late 1990s appear to have been a threshold period for social expenditure in Canada, marking the point when Canada gave up the idea of pursuing an independent social policy, let alone one modelled on

Table 1.6 Canada: Trends in Federal and Provincial Revenues and Expenditures as Percentage of GDP, 1961–2000

	1961	1975	1981	1985	1992	2000
Revenues	29.7	37.4	39.8	40.0	44.8	44.6
Expenditures	30.5	39.9	41.3	46.8	51.4	42.8
Surplus or (Deficit)	(1.8)	(2.8)	(1.5)	(6.8)	(6.7)	1.8
Program Spending	27.5	36.1	35.0	38.4	42.0	36.0
Debt Service	3.0	3.8	6.3	8.4	9.4	6.8

SOURCE: John Richards, *The Case for Change* (Ottawa: Renouf, 1994), 41; John Richards, *Now That the Coat Fits the Cloth: Spending Wisely in a Trimmed Down Age* (Toronto: C.D. Howe Institute, 2000), figures estimated from graphs.

Table 1.7 Population Projections by Age Groups

	Population by age (000s)			Percentage by age		
Year	0–17	18–64	65+	0–17	18–64	65+
1991	6,616	16,986	3,155	25	63	12
1996	6,525	17,701	3,579	23	63	13
2001	6,172	18,445	3,934	21	65	14
2006	5,653	19,115	4,279	19	66	15
2011	5,072	19,466	4,800	17	66	16

SOURCE: Statistics Canada, *Projections for Canada and the Provinces, 1989–2011,* Catalogue no. 91–520 (Ottawa: Supply and Services, 1990).

Box 1.3 Health Care Is No. 1 Concern

Canadians are becoming more and more alarmed about the state of the health-care system, a new poll shows. The Angus Reid poll shows that 55 per cent believe political leaders should make the health system their top priority. That is a jump of 17 percentage points since December, a clear sign that concern about health care is rising.

Health now dwarfs other issues on the national agenda. Education comes a distance second, with 23 per cent calling it the top priority. Education was followed by taxes (19 per cent), unemployment (15), poverty (15), government spending (12) and national unity (11).

'It's something we've been tracking for two years and concern about health care has been climbing steadily,' said Darrell Bricker, a spokesman for the Angus Reid Group, which conducted the poll for The Globe and Mail and CTV. 'It's emergency care, it's nurses, it's waiting lists—there's a whole variety of things people are worried about.'

The poll comes amid a clamour about the state of the country's much-admired, publicly funded health-care system. Reports about overcrowded emergency rooms, waiting lists for surgery and patients flooding to the United States for better treatment have filled the media.

Canada's premiers told Prime Minister Jean Chrétien last week that Ottawa must inject as much as $6.3-billion into the system or watch it collapse. Only last year, Ottawa pledged to spend $11.5 billion more for health care over the next 5 years. But that was not enough to calm public fears.

Another Angus Reid poll, published last week, said eight in 10 Canadians believe the health-care system is in crisis. Only one in four gives high rating to the health-care system and the quality of its medical services. The latest poll was conducted for The Globe and Mail and CTV between Jan. 27 and Feb. 2.

It shows that concern about health care is strongest in Quebec, where 67 per cent called it the most important issue. Among age groups, those over 55 were most concerned about health care. Sixty per cent of them called it the top priority. Those 24 to 54 were almost as concerned, at 58 per cent.

The poll showed concern about national unity has fallen sharply since December, when the federal government's so-called clarity bill on the rules for a possible Quebec referendum was dominating the headlines.

Apart from the rising concern about health care, the poll showed that the Liberal government still enjoys strong public support.

The Liberals had the backing of 46 per cent of decided voters, more than three times the level of the second-favourite party, the Progressive Conservatives, who had 15 per cent. Reform tied for third with the NDP at 12 per cent.

The Liberals strong showing came despite an uproar over the mismanagement of $1-billion in grants by the Human Resources Department.

The poll was taken just before an Ottawa convention that gave birth to the Canadian Reform Conservative Alliance, a grouping of reformers and other right-of-centre politicians who are teaming up to beat the Liberals at the next election.

The poll was based on the responses of 1,500 randomly selected Canadians. It has a margin of error of plus or minus 2.5 percentage points, 19 times out of 20.

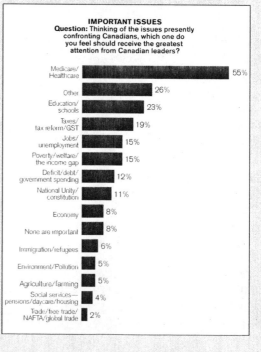

IMPORTANT ISSUES
Question: Thinking of the issues presently confronting Canadians, which one do you feel should receive the greatest attention from Canadian leaders?

Issue	Percentage
Medicare/Healthcare	55%
Other	26%
Education/schools	23%
Taxes/tax reform/GST	19%
Jobs/unemployment	15%
Poverty/welfare/the income gap	15%
Deficit/debt/government spending	12%
National Unity/constitution	11%
Economy	8%
None are important	8%
Immigration/refugees	6%
Environment/Pollution	5%
Agriculture/farming	5%
Social services—pensions/daycare/housing	4%
Trade/free trade/NAFTA/global trade	2%

SOURCE: Marcus Gee, 'Health care is No. 1 concern: poll', *Globe and Mail*, 7 Feb. 2000.

European precedents. Instead, a North American model, dominated by the revenue and expenditure pattern of the United States, has been adopted.

7. *The aging Canadian population and competing priorities.* Social welfare was developed at a time when the baby boomers—those born from the late 1940s to about 1960—were children. They are now in the middle of their working lives, with those born earliest in the post-war years now well into their fifties. They will soon be leaving the labour force, pushed out by globalization and the information age, into a 'retirement' that is a euphemism for unemployment.[30] Table 1.7 shows the rapid aging of the Canadian population.

There will be many more retired people in the years ahead and most will not have been able to organize their lives and personal affairs so as to retire in comfort at age 55. Instead, they will depend on the provisions of the public-sector social welfare system. They are also strong supporters of the Canadian health system, knowing well that they will need it. In public opinion surveys health care is the number-one concern (see Box 1.3). This concern far outranks concern with poverty or social services, making it unlikely that poverty or social services will be priority items for governments.

Values and Social Context

When the liberal values of social welfare are related to the social context there are many obvious sources of conflict. Concern for the individual is in conflict with global economic processes and values that see all transactions in purely financial terms.[31] The value of equality conflicts with the propensity of capitalist societies to create and maintain inequality through such mechanisms as inheritance, private ownership, and the resolution of scarcity through competitive bidding. The desire to maintain viable communities conflicts with the processes of change that disrupt them in the course of technological and environmental change, industrial development

(or decline), and urbanization. The values of equity and diversity are in conflict with established positions of privilege and power and with the rights of private ownership, which always favour the status quo.

One view of the relationship between social welfare values and economic processes is that there has been a progressive shift in the relationship with the passage of time and the development of social welfare institutions. Eric Trist, writing in 1967, held this view:

> The relationship of welfare and development takes three principal forms: when development is a function of welfare; when welfare is a function of development; when welfare and development are interdependent functions.[32]

The first of these represents the circumstances of pre-industrial society, in which welfare is conserved by such traditional structures as the family, stable social classes, religion, and community. The study of First Nations and other Aboriginal peoples shows what such a society was like. The 'development' brought by contact with capitalist society was an overwhelming threat to welfare. When the European colonizers and their market economy gained ascendancy, Aboriginal peoples suffered a loss of cultural and social institutions, and at the same time they lost much of the ability to manage their own affairs or provide for the welfare of each other.

The second form, where economic growth (development) takes precedence over welfare, typifies capitalist society. Economic growth is the major focus of attention, and welfare (i.e., social welfare) is identified with those special situations that require attention because of unmet human needs. These 'special situations' lead first to what Wilensky and Lebeaux define as a 'residual' conception of social welfare that 'holds that social welfare institutions should come into play only when the normal structures of supply, the family and the market, break down.'[33] As society's understanding of the endemic nature of its needs has grown, it is held, so have the depth and continuity of commitment to social welfare measures. Wilensky and Lebeaux use the term 'institutional' to refer to this second concept of social welfare:

> [This institutionalism] implies no stigma, no emergency, no abnormalcy. Social welfare becomes accepted as a proper, legitimate function of modern industrial society in helping individuals achieve self-fulfilment. The complexity of modern life is recognized. The inability of the individual to provide fully for himself, or to meet all his needs in family and work settings is considered a 'normal' condition; and the helping agencies achieve 'regular' institutional status.[34]

In the writings of Alfred Kahn these ideas are identified with the 'social planning phase of the welfare state',[35] and in the works of Romanyshyn such ideas are linked with the concept of 'social development':

> Social welfare as social development recognizes the dynamic quality of urban industrial society and the consequent need to adapt to change and to new aspirations for human fulfilment. It goes beyond the welfare state to a continuing renewal of its institutions to promote the fullest development of man.[36]

These ideas begin to approach a third concept of the relationship of welfare to development, where both are planned for together in a manner that is environmentally sustainable. The National Welfare Grants division of Health and Welfare Canada sponsored a series of projects in the early 1990s to explore these ideas more thoroughly. One product of this work was the publication by the Roeher Institute of the booklet *Social Well-being*, in which the concept of well-being is introduced in the following manner:

> One weakness of the post-war framework for well-being was the incapacity of social,

economic and political institutions to fully grasp the interdependence among people, their communities, their society and the environment. The promotion of individual well-being came to be seen as achievable independent of investments in the social and economic development of communities and independent of the establishment of social entitlements. Social investments and entitlements have been withdrawn in the name of economic restructuring and budgetary deficit, without due recognition of the impact on individual well-being. In the name of societal well-being global economic integration has been pursued, but in a manner that has resulted in the loss of economic and social security for households and communities. . . . *A new framework for well-being must take into account the interdependence of various levels within society.*[37]

This concept of the relationship between social welfare values and economic processes represents a plea for a balanced integration of one with the other.

A second, conservative, view of the integration required between social welfare values and economic processes is provided by Courchene and Lipsey:

> In their view [that of Courchene and Lipsey], the social contract must change to complement the nature of the economy on which it rests. In other words, the welfare state should complement the underlying economy, and should not—and probably cannot—be used in the long run merely to offset the fundamental changes happening there. Key symptoms of this inability to reconcile changed economy with an entrenched social contract are growing transfer dependency, persistent and unsustainable public sector budget deficits, growing mismatches between economic opportunities and available skills and growing inequality in the distribution of income.[38]

In this view the institutionalized social welfare

measures that Canada has established have only served to delay processes of inevitable social change. The costs of this delay are now mounting and have reached the point where they can no longer be paid. Social welfare has to be changed, not only in scale but in form, and, by this view, must be integrated with (i.e., dominated by) economic policy. The liberal values that social welfare represents can only be preserved (and then in a reduced form) by making them subordinate to financial imperatives. This requires major changes in social welfare programs.

A third view of the relationship is provided by socialist writers of the political economy school of analysis. Writers from this perspective support resistance to any reduction in the scope or form of social welfare but are increasingly pessimistic as to whether such resistance will achieve anything useful. Their analysis of social welfare in capitalist society is that it arose out of:

> the attempt by government to contain intractable conflict arising from the contradictory interests of the subordinate and ruling classes, and to implement redistributive or 'averaging' mechanisms as a response to resistance by working classes to intolerable conditions surrounding the reproduction of their labour. Such reforms are a compromise response to the outcomes of the contradiction between labour and capital in a system with no inherent mechanism for addressing such conflicts.[39]

Today, with the new global economy and the weakening of the nation-state, the capitalist economic system appears to be an overwhelming and uncontrollable force for the deepening of social inequalities and the establishment of hegemonic power.

However, one should be careful not to overstate this case. Mishra (1999) provides three strong reasons why the arguments for globalization and the dismantlement of the welfare state are not as strong as they at first appear to be:

1. *Overgeneralization.* The European countries are coping successfully with globalization while preserving much higher levels of social expenditure than are the English-speaking ones. Furthermore, the 1990s was a period of prosperity for the developed economies in which their internal economies grew. Thus the argument that globalization leads to an inevitable decline in resources for social expenditures is not supported.
2. *Downplaying democracy.* Politicians do pay attention to opinion polls and public protests and to election results. While it is true that limits to social expenditure are set, broadly, in a comparative and global context, internally each country responds in its own way in the context of its own democratic politics.
3. *The contradictions of global capitalism.* Capitalism triumphant has been a recipe for social instability wherever and whenever it has been practised. It undermines the capacity not only of the state but also of the family, voluntary organizations, and corporations to provide for welfare. An unfettered free-market system leads to the development of forms of resistance, sabotage, and terror with which it cannot cope and for which it needs the powers of the state.[40]

The problem for Canada is that Canada's economy and social policy choices have become constrained by the close trading relationship to the United States. This relationship, rather than the overall scope for choice in social policy, has come to dominate Canadian social policy. This influence favoured the dominance of a classical (pull-yourself-up-by-your-own-bootstraps) liberalism, which focused on the individual and his/her freedom to make choices and to get rich or remain poor. The practical consequence of this predominance was that social welfare institutions were forced to conform to a more restricted role in which the pursuit of some functions, particularly the goal of equality, was weakened. However, the cuts in the social safety net during the 1990s were also complex, with some equity categories faring much better than others. Sharp benefit reductions affected the unemployed and poverty and homelessness grew considerably. Benefits for seniors, on the other hand, were much less affected, and health-care expenditures continued to grow. At the same time there were some changes in welfare provision for women, children, Aboriginal peoples, and persons with disabilities that increased horizontal equity for these groups, albeit in the midst of greater overall vertical inequalities. The impact of these changes on individual families and persons was complex, as many were in the situation of having some benefits increased at the same time as others were cut.

Additional Readings

Strater Crowfoot, 'Leadership in First Nations Communities: A Chief's Perspective on the Colonial Millstone', in R. Ponting, ed., *First Nations in Canada: Perspectives on Opportunity, Empowerment and Self-Determination*. Toronto: McGraw-Hill, 1997, 299–325. Chief Crowfoot presents an articulate statement of the challenges that Aboriginal leaders face in establishing social justice for their communities.

James Ife, 'Localized Needs in a Globalized Economy', *Canadian Social Work*, Special Issue on 'Social Work and Globalization' 2, 1 (Summer 2000): 50–64. Ife discusses how to work for social justice and social welfare at the local level.

Stephen McBride and John Shields, *Dismantling a Nation: The Transition to Corporate Rule in Canada*. Halifax: Fernwood, 1997. Chapter 4, 'Dismantling the Post-War Social Order', is a step-by-step account of the turning point in Canadian social welfare policy, from independence to a more North American (US) model.

James Midgeley, 'Globalization, Capitalism and Social Welfare', *Canadian Social Work*, Special Issue on 'Social Work and Globalization' 2, 1 (Summer 2000): 13–28. Midgeley's article provides good background material on the relationship between globalization and social welfare.

Study Questions

1. Find a newspaper article that deals with some aspect of social welfare policy or social services. What ideologies are reflected in the opinions reported in the article and which is dominant in the article as a whole?

2. Sooner or later all of us have a personal experience with the social services, either as a consumer or as a service provider. Think about one such episode in which you participated (or observed closely what happened to a family member or close friend). What 'structural forces' were present in influencing the services you received (or observed)? Would you class the service as 'residual', 'institutional', or 'social development'?

3. The assimilation of Aboriginal peoples was, until recently, a social policy objective. What was the rationale for an assimilationist policy and why is this idea now rejected? How do the Aboriginal values expressed in Crowfoot's article differ from traditional 'liberal' social welfare values?

4. Of the issues noted in Box 1.3—health system, education, taxes, unemployment, poverty, government spending, national unity—which do you believe should receive the greatest attention from Canadian leaders? Why? Are there other important issues that this report on a poll did not mention?

Notes

1. William G. Watson, John Richards, and David M. Brown, *The Case for Change: Reinventing the Welfare State* (Toronto: C.D. Howe Institute, 1995), 1.

2. Bob Mullaly, *Structural Social Work*, 2nd edn (Toronto: Oxford University Press, 1997), 78. Mullaly writes from the socialist viewpoint, which he divides into two different forms, social democracy and Marxism. He agrees (p. 65) that liberalism has been the defining force in Canadian social welfare and that this book has a liberal point of view.

3. Patricia M. Evans and Gerda R. Wekerle, eds, *Women and the Canadian Welfare State: Challenges and Change* (Toronto: University of Toronto Press, 1997), 22.

4. For an introduction to the range of contributions that feminism is making to the development of social welfare services, see Carol Baines, Patricia Evans, and Sheila Neysmith, *Women's Caring: Feminist Perspectives on Social Welfare* (Toronto: McClelland & Stewart, 1991); Baines, Evans, and Neysmith, *Women's Caring*, 2nd edn (Toronto: Oxford University Press, 1998); *Canadian Social Work Review*, Special Issue, 'Women and Social Work: Celebrating Our Progress' 10, 2 (Summer 1993).

5. Josephine C. Naidoo and R. Gary Edwards, 'Combatting Racism Involving Visible Minorities', *Canadian Social Work Review* 8, 2 (1991): 212.

6. Strater Crowfoot, 'Leadership in First Nations Communities: A Chief's Perspective on the Colonial Millstone', in R. Ponting, ed., *First Nations in Canada: Perspectives on Opportunity, Empowerment and Self-Determination* (Toronto: McGraw-Hill, 1997), 323

7. H.L. Wilensky and C. Lebeaux, *Industrial Society and Social Welfare* (New York: Free Press, 1965), 145.

8. United Nations, *Universal Declaration of Human Rights* (New York, 1948), Article 31.

9. Senator David Croll, *Poverty in Canada: Report of the Special Senate Committee on Poverty* (Ottawa: Queen's Printer, 1971).

10. David Woodsworth, *Social Policies for Tomorrow* (Ottawa: Canadian Council on Social Development, 1971), 7–8.

11. See Bob Mullaly, *Challenging Oppression: A Critical Social Work Approach* (Toronto: Oxford University Press, 2002).

12. John Rawls, *A Theory of Justice* (Oxford: Oxford University Press, 1972), 60.

13. W.G. Runciman, *Relative Deprivation and Social Justice* (London: Pelican Books, 1972), 310.

14. See the first two editions of *Social Welfare in Canada* or any comparable text written before the 1990s.

15. John Rawls, *Political Liberalism* (New York: Columbia University Press, 1993), 60.

16. Will Kymlicka, *Multicultural Citizenship: A Liberal Theory of Minority Rights* (Oxford: Clarendon Press, 1995), 126.

17. Ibid., 81.

18. For a full discussion of the global economy, see Peter Dicken, *Global Shift: The Internationalization of Economic Activity* (London: Paul Chapman, 1992).

19. Gunnar Myrdal, *Beyond the Welfare State* (London: Duckworth, 1958), 119.

20. Robert Heilbronner, *Capitalism in the Twenty-First Century* (Concord, Ont.: Anansi Press, 1992), 19.

21. James Ife, 'Localized Needs and a Globalized Economy', in Bill Rowe, ed., *Social Work and Globalization* (Ottawa: Canadian Association of Social Workers, 2000), 54.

22. Ibid., 55.

23. Allan Cochrane and John Clarke, *Comparing Welfare States: Britain in International Context* (London: Sage Publications, 1993), show how each welfare state incorporates significant features of the national society in its benefits and organization.

24. Ibid., 253–5.
25. Michael D. Levin, ed., *Ethnicity and Aboriginality: Case Studies in Ethnonationalism* (Toronto: University of Toronto Press, 1993), 3–4.
26. For a fuller discussion of the issues of Aboriginal self-government and its relationship to social policy, see Andrew Armitage, *Comparing the Policy of Aboriginal Assimilation: Australia, Canada, New Zealand* (Vancouver: University of British Columbia Press, 1995).
27. For a fuller discussion of the issues of ethnonationalism and multiculturalism, see Kymlicka, *Multicultural Citizenship*.
28. Linda McQuaig, *The Wealthy Banker's Wife: The Assault on Equality in Canada* (Toronto: Penguin Books, 1993), 15 ff.
29. *OECD Economic Survey, 1994: Canada* (Paris: OECD, 1994), 44.
30. Grant Schellenberg, *The Road to Retirement* (Ottawa: Canadian Council on Social Development, 1994), 40 ff.
31. See Gloria Geller and Jan Joel, 'Struggle for Citizenship in the Global Economy: Bond Raters versus Women and Children', Seventh Conference on Canadian Social Welfare Policy, Vancouver, June 1995.
32. Eric Trist, *The Relation of Welfare and Development in the Transition to Post-Industrialism* (Ottawa: Canadian Centre for Community Studies, 1967), 12.
33. Wilensky and Lebeaux, *Industrial Society and Social Welfare*, 138.
34. Ibid., 140.
35. Alfred J. Kahn, *Theory and Practice of Social Planning* (New York: Russell Sage Foundation, 1969), 50.
36. John Romanyshyn, *Social Welfare: Charity to Justice* (New York: Random House, 1971), 380.
37. The Roeher Institute, *Social Well-being: A Paradigm for Reform* (North York, Ont.: The Roehr Institute, 1993), 40; emphasis added.
38. David M. Brown, 'Economic Change and New Social Policies', in Watson, Richards, and Brown, *The Case for Change*, 116.
39. Gary Teeple, *Globalization and the Decline of Social Reform* (Toronto: Garamond Press, 1995), 21.
40. Ramesh Mishra, 'After Globalization: Social Policy in an Open Economy', *Canadian Review of Social Policy* 43 (1999): 17–24.

PART II

Income Distribution:
Seeking Fairness

CHAPTER 2

The Redistribution of Income: Theory, Principles, and Resources

The first major objective of social welfare is to mitigate the inequalities in income and wealth that capitalism creates. As a result, the redistribution of money, goods, and services is a central function of social welfare.

This chapter introduces the main reasons why the Canadian social welfare system takes income from one person and gives it to another. Each of these reasons has implications for what is taken, who receives a benefit, and the terms on which benefits are received. Understanding the principles of the redistribution of income provides us with a way to examine current policies and services and to anticipate the effect of new or revised provisions when they are at the proposal stage.

Learning Objectives

1. To understand how the social welfare redistribution of income takes place in the context of a capitalist economic system and how that system affects the redistribution.
2. To understand the five principal arguments that have been made for welfare transactions and the way each affects the social welfare policy and services that are offered.
3. To understand the difference between a 'selective' and a 'universal' program and to consider four major problems associated with the receipt of some forms of social welfare provision, as well as the effect they have on beneficiaries.
4. To understand why working for welfare, 'workfare', is often advocated but never works.
5. To understand the role that the tax system and employment equity measures now play in the redistribution of income and why an expanded use of these is often regarded as desirable.
6. To understand the extent of the income distribution system and how it affects the lives of all Canadians.
7. To understand the changes in the Canadian commitment to social welfare that were made during the 1990s and how that commitment compares to that of other developed countries.

Redistribution as an Economic Institution

Redistribution serves the basic purpose of decreasing inequalities. People are able to obtain goods and services for themselves that they could not have afforded on the basis of their incomes or wealth. Redistribution contradicts the most basic tenets of 'market' economic ideology.

First, the market exchange is viewed as being a 'free' exchange while social welfare operates in the command economy. In the market economy, no one is forced to accept employment, to purchase particular goods, to give money or service to others. Instead, all decide which economic exchanges they wish to engage in and the totality of their 'free' actions establishes the values of the contributions of each. This ideology neglects the effects of monopoly, differences in knowledge of opportunities, etc.; it nevertheless remains a fundamental part of normal economic exchange expectations. In contradistinction, the welfare exchange is compulsory. The attempt to attain welfare purposes on the basis of the voluntary contributor and the independent, self-determining beneficiary failed in the nineteenth century.[1] Instead, social welfare in its origins was made compulsory, on the givers by taxation and on the beneficiaries in the form of either social rights or social sanctions carried out under the authority of the courts.

Second, the market exchange is viewed as being based on a quid pro quo. That is, there is a *real* exchange. The worker contributes labour and in return receives wages. The consumer uses money to obtain goods and services. The owner obtains a rent for another's use of his property. In each case, the exchange is a mutual one. In the case of welfare, however, no true exchange occurs. The more appropriate term for the transaction is 'transfer'. This basic affront to the values of economic ideology is one reason for the continuing demand that the able-bodied 'work for welfare'. Surely, it is thought, the community should get some positive contribution in return for the payments it is making.

Lastly, the market exchange in capitalist societies is fundamental to the creation of inequalities. The exchange is not, in fact, an equal one, but favours those who, through their position in the market, are able to create the terms on which others work and for this service obtain for themselves part of the return from others' labour. The labour market exchange is thus effectively a partial transfer of the value of workers' efforts to those who have control of economic processes of production or distribu-tion, possess real property or capital, or control the terms of trade. A major reason for the welfare transfer is to correct in part this unequal exchange and the poverty and inequality it creates. There are, however, limits. C.B. Macpherson draws to our attention the fact that:

> the offsetting transfer within the welfare state can never, within capitalism, equal the original and continuing transfer. This is fully appreciated by the strongest defenders of capitalism, who point out, quite rightly, that if welfare transfers got so large as to eat up profits there would be no more incentive to capitalist enterprises, and so no more capitalist enterprise.[2]

Thus the welfare transfer is always a secondary one in capitalist economic processes.

Much of the economic literature identifies social welfare as constituting a burden on economic processes, an item of unproductive expense the economy has to sustain. At best, social welfare is justified by the need to secure social stability. Welfare economics is the study of the application of economic theory to well-being. In welfare economics individuals are discouraged from maximizing their financial situation without consideration of the effects of their choices on others. Thus, those who are better off are provided with a reason to help the poor, as they derive benefits in such forms as a healthier general population, stronger workers, greater financial stability, and greater acceptance of those inequalities that remain.[3] However, this means that the disadvantaged only exercise influence to the extent that their lives impinge on the privileged. The welfare economics approach leaves open the possibility that the privileged may choose to use their resources to keep the poor away from them rather than correcting the underlying inequality. This formula for examining inequality is therefore clearly less powerful than the social justice formula, and it leads to different conclusions on the extent of equalities that should exist. In particular, it does not raise or answer the moral question as to whether the extent of poverty and/or inequality is just.

These views are shared by the socialist critics of the welfare institutions of capitalist societies, who see them as being 'a central element in the framework of repression under which men live in market-dominated societies . . . a historical freak between organized capitalism and socialism, servitude and freedom, totalitarianism and happiness'.[4] Recent socialist commentators have gone further, pointing out that this modest role for social welfare neglects:

> the possibility that capitalism without reforms might not spur a working class into revolution but instead simply reduce it to poverty, destitution and fear of itself—and thereby break its will to resist. Second, they take for granted that in times other than extreme crisis and social breakdown the working classes could be an effective opposition to a trained and disciplined modern army or police force. The evidence would strongly suggest otherwise.[5]

This example of socialist analysis leads to a discouraging conclusion. It also does not recognize the role of liberal values in contributing to where a specific balance is struck with capitalism between coercive social control and control through welfare measures of relief and accommodation.

Nevertheless, the analysis reinforces the important observation that there is nothing inherent in capitalism that supports social welfare. In each case the welfare transfer requires both ideological and political justification. The assertion of this justification has a direct effect on the form of social welfare programs and, hence, on the recipients of social welfare benefits. There have been five principal arguments used to justify the welfare transfer:

1. need
2. insurance against social risk
3. compensation for loss

4. investment in human potential
5. economic growth and stability.

Each argument in turn, when translated by legislation into a program, has a determining effect on eligibility criteria for program benefits. The effects of the need to frame the social welfare distribution of income within the capitalist economic discourse have also led to recurrent major discussion and debate concerning:

1. universal versus selective transfer mechanisms
2. stigma
3. work requirements and workfare
4. dependency relationships
5. how to maintain public support.

Five Reasons for Paying Social Welfare Benefits

1. Need

The concept of 'need' is a central one in social welfare thought and, indeed, in everyday life. Nevertheless, the concept has some subtleties worth exploring. Foremost of these is the distinction that must be drawn between 'needs' and 'wants'. 'Want' implies a purely private assertion by a person; 'need' adds the notion of necessity and hence obligation on the part of others to respond. However, the 'others' are free to allow or reject the need. Rejection in effect converts the alleged 'need' back to the category of being a 'want' because no one has agreed on its necessity or accepted any obligation. Allowing the 'need,' on the other hand, legitimizes it. Thus, 'needs' are subject to social rather than private or individual definition.

Where the justification for a program is the need of the intended beneficiaries, it follows that eligibility will be determined by whether or not the need exists; the simplest case is where a need is assumed to exist. This was the original basis for the universal, non-means-tested Old Age Security and Family Allowance programs.

Such programming, in its original form, no longer exists. Old Age Security continues as a 'demogrant', but benefits are subject to tax and clawback provisions of the Income Tax Act, limiting the receipt of benefits on the basis of income. Family Allowances have been terminated and replaced by the Child Tax Benefit.

The more typical approach to the determination of eligibility based on need is to conduct an inquiry or *needs test* into the individual's circumstances to determine whether, within the meaning given to 'need' by the program in question, need exists for this individual. Such inquiries are characteristic of public assistance, public housing, and student aid programs. The determination of need at the level of the individual inevitably requires consideration not only of his or her financial circumstances, but also of his or her dependencies. More need has to be recognized in the circumstances of a man and woman living separately than in the case of a man and woman living together because in the latter case they share a roof. The inquiry to determine need thus is necessarily extensive, involving the review of matters that most people treat as being their private affairs. Furthermore, an element of discretion is desirable in such reviews because of the variability of individual circumstances; one teenager might be expected to live in his parents' house as a dependant while for another this arrangement might not be appropriate. Discretion also increases the authority of the granting agency in the lives of the recipients.

A distinction is sometimes drawn between a *means test* and a needs test. The means test is perceived as being a more arbitrary form of the needs test in that attention centres only on the individual's resources, e.g., income, assets, etc., and not on his requirements. However, for the purpose of this discussion, the distinction is not an important or significant one. Both types of test involve a similar process to determine eligibility, and they have a similar impact on applicants.

A variation of the needs test is used where income alone is considered and assets are disregarded. An *income test* is used in the Guaranteed Income Supplement program for seniors. An income test is also applied where social welfare benefits are conveyed in the form of tax deductions or refundable tax credits. Examples are the deductions for pension plan contributions, medical expenses, child care, tuition fees, and disability, and for the refundable tax credits for the GST and the Child Tax Benefit. In these cases the annual income tax return is used to establish eligibility for these welfare benefits.

Finally, in some social welfare programs, the financial circumstances of applicants are not the most relevant aspect of need determination. Particularly where programs, such as probation and child protection, are thrust upon their recipients by force of law, the process to determine need becomes clearly one in which the society makes a judgement (a formal legal judgement) that the person is in need of special attention. A similar situation often exists in the admission process to such institutions as mental hospitals and children's treatment centres. The need of the adult or child is determined by an assessment process that seeks to identify the form of the risks to life or health, the alleged pathology, and whether aid can be given by the treatment centre. These tests are no less tests of need than the financial tests discussed earlier. Their distinguishing characteristic is that they use social-psychological rather than socio-economic criteria for the decision.

Needs tests of one form or another have characterized social welfare from its earliest origins in the Elizabethan Poor Laws. They remain a central feature of social welfare. In recent years their use has increased as a way to target social welfare programs more closely to the need of beneficiaries. In addition, there is a trend towards lowering definitions of need and tying them to minimum wage conditions, rather than raising the definitions to meet recognized poverty objectives. In following this path Canada is reintroducing the policy of 'less eligibility' into welfare administration. The policy of 'less eligibility' was defined by the British Poor

Law Commission of 1834 and basically said that a person or family on welfare should always receive less than the wage earned by the poorest paid independent labourer (see Box 2.1).

2. Insurance against Social Risk

The concept of insurance against social risks as justification for welfare transfers has been taken over from the ideology of the economic market, but with major changes. The market use of the concept of insurance implies that the chance of a foreseeable risk, fire, accident, or death is assessed. On the basis of the assessed chance, and on the value of the loss incurred, a premium is charged to all who wish to protect themselves. If the foreseen contingency occurs, the insurer pays a settlement to the insured. The system is usually a voluntary one (auto insurance is an exception) in that neither insurer nor insured is forced to enter into a contract. It is designed in such a way as to be financially viable or the insurer goes bankrupt. There are no welfare transfer functions in private insurance for, although some receive benefits that others have paid for, the deliberate intention is to group insured policy-holders according to the nature of their risk so that each pays a fair premium for the protection bought.

Social insurance uses some of these ideas but modifies them in significant ways to obtain a welfare transfer effect. The four best-known Canadian social insurance programs are Unemployment Insurance, the Canada Pension Plan, medicare, and hospital insurance. The principal ways in which social insurance differs from private insurance are as follows.

1. *Compulsion rather than free contract.* Government programs typically demand universal coverage. This ensures the maximum distribution of the risk and that no one will have to seek assistance from other government agencies because they decided not to seek insurance. It also prevents the growth of private-sector insurance plans offering reduced premiums to low-risk clients.

2. *Lack of 'group experience' ratings.* While private insurance plans seek to relate benefits and risk closely to the individual person's situation, government insurance plans typically average all risks. Payment of premiums thus becomes a form of taxation, not particularly related to the chance of the individual becoming a beneficiary, and thereby produces a welfare transfer effect between those at risk and those not at risk.

3. *'Subsidy' elements.* While private insurance plans have to be actuarially sound, government insurance plans have often contained provision for subsidies. Thus, until the 1990s, if unemployment exceeded some anticipated rate, the Unemployment Insurance fund was subsidized from general government revenue. As originally designed the Canada/Quebec Pension Plan contained an internal transfer from current contributors to current beneficiaries, the extent of which raised pensions to four times the level justified on the basis of contributions and fund investments.[6] This, too, was ended in the changes made to CPP/QPP in the 1990s. Removing these subsidy elements has had the effect of making social insurance more like private insurance. As such, it distributes risk between contributors but not between income classes. As a result social insurance ceases to be a way of dealing with long-term problems of inequality, serving to reinforce and retain, rather than reduce, class differences.

4. *Increased range of 'risks' accepted.* Unemployment is uninsurable as a 'private' risk, partly because it is difficult (as the Unemployment Insurance Commission is aware) to control persons who are 'unemployed' by choice and partly because the risk of massive unemployment, resulting from recession, would threaten any private scheme with bankruptcy. Social insurance accepts these risks because a social purpose is to be obtained by protecting people against unemployment. In practice, government underwrites payments, preventing bankruptcy of the plan and ensuring that beneficiaries receive their entitlements.

5. *Benefits/contributions relationship.* In both private and social insurance a record of the contributions of those covered is kept and benefits are paid in foreseen circumstances. Eligibility for benefits is created by having an acceptable contributions record and by the occurrence of the foreseen contingency. In these circumstances, the applicant's right to benefit is contractually assured. Hence, no inquiry into other aspects of his personal or financial circumstances is necessary. The difference from private insurance is that in social insurance an acceptable contributions record is determined by social policy rather than by actuarial considerations.

Social insurance has provided social welfare benefits on a contractual basis without the need for a review of individual or family circumstances. However, this has resulted in some unintended consequences that have attracted increased attention.

Regressive distribution of subsidies. For example, the Canada/Quebec Pension Plan provides a large subsidy to current beneficiaries. This subsidy increases with the beneficiaries' contributions, thus, those who have made higher contributions (and incomes) get the most benefit.

Lack of equity in coverage. Social insurance was developed as a response to two principal problems of industrialism: occasional unemployment and retirement income. An assumption was made that these were the problems of

---

Box 2.1 Less Eligibility

From the evidence collected under this commission, we are induced to believe that a compulsory provision for the relief of the indigent can be generally administered on a sound and well-defined principle; and that under the operation of this principle, the assurance that no one need perish from want may be rendered more complete than at present, and the mendicant and vagrant repressed by disarming them of their weapon—the plea of impending starvation.

It may be assumed, that in the administration of relief, the public is warranted in imposing such conditions on the individual relief, as are conducive to the benefit either of the individual himself or of the country at large, at whose expense he is to be relieved.

The first and most essential of all conditions, a principle which we find universally admitted, even by those whose practice is at variance with it, is, that his situation on the whole shall not be made really or apparently so eligible as the situation of the independent labourer of the lowest class. Throughout the evidence it is shown, that in proportion as the condition of any pauper class is elevated above the condition of independent labourers, the condition of the independent class is depressed; their industry is impaired, their employment becomes unsteady, and its remuneration in wages is diminished. Such persons, therefore, are under the strongest inducements to quit the less eligible class of labourers and enter the more eligible class of paupers. The converse is the effect when the pauper class is placed in its proper position, below the condition of the independent labourer. Every penny bestowed, that tends to render the condition of the pauper more eligible than that of the independent labourer, is a bounty on indolence and vice. We have found, that as the poor's rates are at present administered, they operate as bounties of this description, to the amount of several millions annually.

The standard, therefore, to which reference must be made in fixing the condition of those who are to be maintained by the public, is the condition of those who are maintained by their own exertions.

SOURCE: British Parliamentary Papers, 1834, vol. xxvii: *Report of the Royal Commission on the Administration and Operation of the Poor Laws*, 127, in Brian Watkin, *Documents on Health and Social Services: 1834 to the present day* (London: Methuen, 1975), 7–8.

all independent earners and particularly of heads of households. Benefits and conditions of receipt were generous as compared to benefits distributed on the basis of needs tests. At the same time other risks, for example, the risk of family separation or of chronic underemployment, were not considered. The result has been the creation of a two-tier income support system that works to the disadvantage of women.

> First, there are the benefits available to individuals as 'public' persons by virtue of their participation and accidents of fortune in the capitalist market. . . . Second, benefits are available to the 'dependants' of individuals of the first category, or to 'private' persons, usually women.[7]

System manipulation. Because benefits are determined by established eligibility conditions it is possible to extract benefits from social insurance by organizing one's affairs in order to qualify. For example, Unemployment Insurance benefits have been paid to workers in manufacturing during layoffs for refitting and to fishermen and loggers during periods of unemployment due to seasonal conditions. Provincial governments have introduced temporary employment programs that provide just sufficient employment so that those participating qualify for Unemployment Insurance. Lastly, individuals can organize their affairs to leave employment on terms that permit them to qualify for benefits. They can also maximize their income by retaining benefits while returning to work in the 'underground' economy.

All of these are examples of system manipulation to maximize benefits or minimize contributions. Thus, the existence of social insurance gradually becomes built into people's lives and plans in ways that were not foreseen or intended. Indeed, the incentives to maximize social welfare income will, in marginal situations, displace employment income because the social welfare income is guaranteed by government while employment income is not. These effects are of considerable concern to economists as they are seen as having raised Canada's unemployment rate and reduced the efficiency of the Canadian economy and hence its global competitiveness.[8]

Despite these criticisms social insurance programs remain a very important feature of the Canadian social welfare system. Social insurance programs offer the stability of long-term contractual relationships between citizens and government that can only be changed through change in the enabling legislation. In most of the European countries social insurance covers a wider range of needs than in Canada and offers more generous benefit levels (funded by higher contribution levels).[9] Public support for social insurance programs in Canada remains strong; hence, the objectives of reform are defined in terms of dealing with the criticisms listed above, rather than focused on replacing the programs as a whole or scrapping them.

3. Compensation for Loss

The concept of *compensation* as providing a justification for welfare transfers has also been taken over from the marketplace and from the British common law. Under common law if one suffers a loss through either the deliberate or careless act of another, one is entitled to sue and obtain compensation through the courts. Examples of the use of the concept of compensation in social policy include: (1) treaties and comprehensive settlements with Aboriginal peoples; (2) programs of compensation, for example, Workers' Compensation and victim compensation; and (3) court-ordered financial settlements for separated families.

Most of the historic treaties made with Aboriginal peoples contain provisions for goods, money, or services in return for the release of land for settlement or development. A lot of controversy surrounds this practice of compensation. The treaties were often entered into at times when Aboriginal communities were being overwhelmed, the terms of treaties were more often imposed than negotiated, and current conditions are very different from the historical ones. Nevertheless, the principle of a negotiated settlement between peoples as a way of providing compensation for rights they have lost and as a basis for their management of their own welfare has not been set aside. Indeed, it is in the process of being revisited as part of the exploration of how to provide Aboriginal peoples with an appropriate settlement of outstanding land and treaty claims and contemporary rights of self-government.

Workers' Compensation provides the clearest example of the use of the concept of compensation in establishing a major social program. The principle underlying the program embodies a historic compromise, first enacted in Canada in 1914 in Ontario, between the right of employees to sue for industrial injury and their need to prove employer negligence as a condition of receiving a settlement.[10] Workers' Compensation has stayed closer to its market roots than social insurance. Although the compensation contract is required of both employer and employee as a condition of employment and is thus not voluntary, other features of Workers' Compensation operate on market principles. Thus, insurance premiums are based on industry accident records; premiums are paid by employers and are not subsidized from general revenues; and benefits are tied to lost employment income rather than to need.

However, Workers' Compensation, like Employment Insurance (the name was changed in 1996), is under pressure due to changed conditions. The theory that industry premiums would pay for benefits assumed the continuity of industrial activity. When an industry declines or ceases to exist, the costs of compensation to its former employees become a charge on all employers. Also, the process of submitting and processing compensation claims is becoming more litigious, with increases in costs to both Workers' Compensation plans and claimants. Finally, the determination of the extent of injury

places physicians in the position of being adjudicators rather than patient advocates.

There has been some looser use of the concept of compensation in the establishment of specific programs devoted to population groups that have suffered some general types of disadvantage. Thus, part of the argument for special services for veterans is that their military service has resulted in an effective loss of earning power, seniority, etc., not to mention the specific losses resulting from identifiable injuries. In addition, in recent years there has been increased recognition of the right to compensation for victims of certain types of crime, e.g., sexual abuse while a child.

Court-ordered settlements as a basis for welfare remain the primary means whereby family dependency and welfare issues are settled. The continued dominance of a common-law tradition in this field is testimony to the lack of attention in social welfare to internal family relationships and risks. Women, of course, are the principal caregivers. As they have performed this role by choice or ascription rather than as employment, it has been free. The consequence of this gift of skill, time, and labour is that, on divorce or separation, the courts, too, attach no monetary value to caring work within the home. As a result, on divorce, men's incomes and women's incomes diverge sharply. Ross Finie, in *The Economics of Divorce*, shows that:

> in the first year after divorce after-tax family income declines to 0.72 and 0.45 of the pre-split level for men and women respectively. . . . Over one-third of the women . . . fall into poverty at divorce, compared to just 9 per cent of the men. Conversely, 34 per cent of the men escape poverty at the split, whereas the figure is just 16 per cent for women. Finally, poverty rates in the first year of divorce are 17 per cent for men and 43 per cent for women—2.5 times greater.[11]

Facts like these provide the substance to the feminist analysis of the way that patriarchy has acted through the welfare state to protect the position of men and to confirm the dependent position of women.

Court-ordered settlements are also becoming more common as means of compensating victims for abuse by social welfare institutions. This includes abuse in residential facilities and by caregivers who were under the supervision of welfare authorities. The abuse of children in Indian residential schools has led to a series of lawsuits involving both the federal government and the churches that operated the schools (see Box 2.2). Victims of forced sterilization practices, which were applied to mentally disabled people until the 1970s, have also sought and obtained court-ordered settlements to recognize the injustice imposed on them.

4. Investment in Human Potential

The concept of investment has been used relatively infrequently to justify welfare transfers. It was used in some discussions of the problem of poverty in which the problem was defined as one of underinvestment in the human resources of poor people. Thus, in its *Fifth Annual Review*, the Economic Council of Canada referred to a need for 'upgrading of human resources involved in combating poverty'.[12] The concept has also been used in a general way to support the relocation and retraining programs of the Department of Manpower and Immigration and the extensive subsidies provided to education programs.

There is now a renewed interest in these ideas spawned by the issue of Canada's competitiveness in the global economy. Courchene writes:

> My position is that we have no alternative but to remake Social Canada in a manner consistent with the emerging global economic order. Implicit in this is the assumption that, if we put in place an appropriate social and human capital infrastructure, then physical capital investment will be forthcoming. Moreover, the

correct way to view the demand side is that the global demands for Canadian products are potentially infinite if we can meet the test of competitiveness.[13]

An investment ideology results in programs designed to concentrate resources on those who will benefit most. This diminishes the degree to which the programs are responsive to need and thereby decreases their effectiveness as welfare transfers. Indeed, it is questionable whether there is any welfare transfer effect in some social programs, such as higher education, where the primary approach to eligibility for benefits is based on a human resource investment ideology and a competitive process to determine who will be beneficiaries. Thus, remaking 'Social Canada' on the principles of social investment runs the risk of allocating welfare resources to those with the greatest ability rather than to those with the greatest need.

5. Economic Growth and Stability

Finally, arguments have been advanced for welfare expenditures because such expenditures will themselves contribute to economic stability and growth. In the 1960s Samuelson[14] argued that welfare expenditures could be manipulated to increase total spending power in times of economic recession and thereby contribute to improved economic performance. A similar argument was advanced by Galbraith in *The Affluent Society*.[15] The post-war Family Allowance program was accepted partly because it was seen as a way of providing for greater stability of consumer demand and hence as an asset in avoiding the recurrence of the pre-war Depression. These ideas were the products of Keynesian[16] economic thought, which was predominant until the 1970s when it was displaced by monetarism. The English economist John Maynard Keynes advocated that government influence the economy through taxation and expenditure measures. Monetarism relies on control of the economy through money supply and interest rates (controlled by the Bank of Canada). Monetarism remains the dominant school of macroeconomic thought and government practice.

This review of the five approaches to justifying welfare transfers has treated them in the order in which they contradict market ideology. The greatest contradiction is present in the discussion of need; partial accommodations are made in the discussions of insurance and compensation; and full accommodation is obtainable in the discussion of investment and economic growth. The greater the degree of accommodation, the less the welfare transfer that is justified.

Five Recurring Welfare Transfer Debates

1. Selective vs Universal Transfer Mechanisms

A *selective* transfer mechanism is one in which beneficiaries are determined by individual consideration of their circumstances. All means tests, needs tests, contribution records, and the like are instruments of selectivity. A *universal* transfer mechanism is one in which beneficiaries are determined on the basis of some recognized common factor and without consideration of their individual circumstances. Examples of selective transfers are social assistance and

---

Box 2.2 Church on Hook for Abuse

One Canadian Anglican diocese may declare bankruptcy and a second is facing 'grave' financial difficulties as lawsuits over Native residential schools progress through the courts.

The Diocese of Cariboo is considering declaring bankruptcy after a judge recently found it negligent in the sexual abuse of a boy at a Lytton, BC, residential school nearly 30 years ago. Floyd Mowatt sued the diocese, the national church and the federal government for damages as a result.

Justice Janice Dillon of the BC Supreme Court found all three parties jointly liable for undisclosed damages. The church is responsible for at least 60 per cent of the award believed to be about $200,000. That figure does not include legal and court costs.

The Anglican Church still faces more than 200 lawsuits involving hundreds of plaintiffs. The Diocese of Qu'Appelle in southern Saskatchewan owes $134,000 in legal bills and will cash in some available trust funds to pay them off.

The Lytton judgment, handed down Aug. 30, presents a damning indictment of the church's role in allowing a man with no child-care experience free and unsupervised rein of the children in his care at St George's Indian Residential School.

It is the first decision involving residential schools and the Anglican Church. The church had not decided by press time whether to appeal the decision that held the federal government responsible for only 40 per cent of the damages. However, General Secretary Jim Boyles says the church will pay its share of the compensation now.

'The plaintiff has suffered abuse,' Mr Boyles said in an interview. 'The court has validated the claim and it's just and fair that he receive the compensation.' The amount of damages had been decided before the trial began in May 1998 but the parties agreed to keep the amount confidential.

The question before the court was not whether there was wrongdoing but who the employer was and who should pay the damages. Derek Clarke, a residence supervisor at St George's, sexually abused the plaintiff during the years 1970 to 1973. Mr Clarke had already been found guilty of abusing several boys in a criminal trial and is in jail.

The church argues in court that the federal government owned and administered the residence during the years the plaintiff was abused. But Justice Dillon said that although the government took over ownership of the residence, the church continued to run the day-to-day operations and hire staff.

SOURCE: Kathy Blair, 'Church on hook for abuse: Diocese may fold in wake of ruling', *Anglican Journal*, 8 Oct. 1999.

public housing. The one remaining example of a universal transfer is Old Age Security, which is now limited by the clawback provisions of the Income Tax Act whereby benefits above an income maximum are recaptured. Thus, for all practical purposes this once intense debate is over. The advantages of simplicity of administration, clarity of social rights, and lack of stigma that were the advantages of the universal transfer have lost out to the wish to target social welfare resources carefully and avoid providing Family Allowances or an Old Age Security to 'The Wealthy Banker's Wife'.[17]

2. Stigma

Stigma means the conferring of a negative repute or social status on the stigmatized individual and would appear to be endemic in social welfare programs. The degree of stigma generated by social welfare programs is much greater in needs-related programs than in those programs that compromise with market ideology by adopting a compensation, insurance, or human investment justification for their existence.

The effects of stigma are felt by the recipients of benefits through attitudes and stereotypes held by the public and reinforced by the media. Stigmatized persons are, unfortunately, second-class citizens. As such, they learn to expect that a variety of social conditions usually enjoyed by others, such as reasonably adequate income, will be denied. The recipients come to view their social situation as one that is deserved, if not personally, at least by other members of their class. Thus, it is typically found that stigmatized populations hold very negative stereotypes of one another. This, in turn, makes it difficult for them to work together politically to obtain change in the society around them.

Stigmatization has the effect of making recipients amenable to the idea that they should accept with gratitude whatever the society should offer them. Thus work, at whatever wages and under whatever conditions, should

be accepted. The stigma of welfare assists in maintaining a considerable population in low-paid and unattractive occupations. As the 1971 Senate Committee on Poverty and every other study since has found, a majority of the poor are in the workforce. The stigma of welfare helps to keep them there.

Furthermore, the stigma has the effect of providing a justification for a series of erosions of normal social rights. At the less severe end of a continuum of such erosions, stigmatization classifies the individual recipient as a 'client', with its presumption that the client should be changed through rehabilitation or work opportunity programs. In the middle of the continuum of erosions of citizenship rights are various administrative incursions into the freedom people normally enjoy. Thus, in the past, welfare recipients have been denied full freedom to spend their welfare transfer income according to their own judgement. They have been prohibited from owning a car, renting a telephone, or visiting a beer parlor.[18] If they offended these administrative policy guidelines, then the guidelines would be enforced by denying the recipient cash and by issuing vouchers to control spending patterns. In the severe part of the continuum are the extreme measures of depriving citizens the right to vote, requiring that they live in designated places (poor houses, jails, mental hospitals), subjecting them to physical mutilations (sterilization), and breaking up families (neglect proceedings under child welfare legislation).

At different and recurrent points in the history of social welfare programs, these 'social control' effects of stigma and the means to achieve them have been given explicit sanction in public policy. In recent years, for example, some provincial governments have set up 'snitch' lines where people can phone in to report those they suspect of welfare fraud. At other times, stigmatizing controls have been concealed but remain as implicit contradictions of aspects of the welfare ideal. The current climate of economic rationalism is accompanied by measures that are increasing the stigma of receiving benefits.

3. Work Requirements and Workfare

In the history of social welfare provision there is no concern older or more persistent than the controversial requirement that the able-bodied poor be set to work. In 1349 in the reign of Edward III welfare to the able-bodied was denied in the following manner:

> Because that many valiant beggars, as long as they may live of begging, do refuse to labor, giving themselves to idleness and vice, and sometimes to theft and other abominations; none upon the said pain of imprisonment, shall under the color of pity or alms, give anything to such, which may labor, or presume to favor them towards their desires, so that thereby they may be compelled to labor for their necessary living.[19]

The historian Karl Deschweinitz, in *England's Road to Social Security*, cites the Elizabethan Poor Law provisions regarding the able-bodied and comments:

> In this first specification of a program of work, nearly four centuries ago, appears the same mixture of purpose that has characterised the use of work in relief ever since. The Elizabethan lawmaker proposes work as training for youth, as prevention of roguery, as a test of good intent, and as a means of employment for the needy. In the background is the House of Correction with its threat of punishment.[20]

In a recent series of conservative social policy studies sponsored by the C.D. Howe Institute the editors refer to the case for workfare in the following manner.

> A work requirement as a condition among employables for receipt of welfare serves to provide a kind of 'social capital'—namely, the moral value of work. Erosion of the work ethic has potentially serious intergenerational effects by creating a culture of welfare dependency . . . in the end despite all the rhetoric, a work oriented welfare system has little to do with cost, especially in the short run. But it has everything to do with self-respect and the work ethic, and with the political legitimacy of our social programs.[21]

The case for and against workfare has its basis in the comparison between the situation of those who are working as opposed to those who are receiving social welfare assistance. Because social welfare programs recognize 'need' and need is based on household measures, there are always some people who are better off on welfare than working. When people receiving social welfare benefits return to work, the social welfare benefit they receive is usually reduced on a dollar-for-dollar basis above some minimum of, say, $100. This means that there is no incentive to work above the $100 amount until the recipient's income can exceed the total amount of the social welfare payment for which he or she is eligible. The result is known as the 'welfare wall', an incentive either not to work at all or to defraud the system by taking casual work that can be concealed. Many attempts have been made to solve this problem.

1. *Restricting benefits below the level of the lowest-paid independent worker.* As referred to earlier, this was the principle of 'less eligibility' adopted in the British Poor Law reform of 1834. It survived as a central feature of social welfare administration until the twentieth century and is now being reintroduced through changes being made in social assistance programs. It retains a work incentive for all. Until the 1990s attempts were made to raise wages and family incomes through minimum wage provisions. However, raising wage levels by government regulation had the perverse effect of decreasing the amount of work available, as employers substituted machines for workers, moved to lower-wage locations, or went out of business.

The problems of raising minimum wages to support minimum incomes have become more severe because of the changing nature of work in Canadian society and the relationship to the global economy.

2. *Expanding work opportunities at reasonable wage levels.* This approach is a variation on the first one. If the private sector does not provide a sufficient number of jobs at decent wages, then, it is argued, this should become a responsibility of government working in co-operation with community groups. Cases for this approach have been made under such names as 'social development' and 'community economic development'.[22] The problem with this approach is not so much with the concept but with the scale with which it would have to be applied and with the extent of the associated costs. These problems are most severe where there is long-term unemployment.

3. *Providing a financial incentive to all welfare recipients for any work that they do.* This approach has been the one most advocated in the social policy literature. Examples are provided by the 1988 *Transitions* report[23] of the Ontario government and by earlier proposals for social welfare provision based on a full integration with the tax system, often referred to as 'negative taxation'.[24] The problem with these proposals is that since some people will have to depend on the program for their total income, the lowest benefit paid must ensure a minimum

level of adequacy. In addition, the program has to be designed in such a way as to provide an incentive for any individual to work, usually set at 50 per cent of their earnings. This combination of conditions leads to programs that are excessively costly. Thus, if a poverty line of $20,000 per year is adopted for a family of four and if an earner is allowed to retain 50 per cent of his earnings, then income subsidies for families of four are extended up to the $40,000 per year income level (see Table 2.1).

In the early 1990s the Ontario government partially implemented the recommendations of the *Transitions* report but this achievement was reversed by the restrictive reforms implemented by the Conservative government of Mike Harris following the 1995 provincial election.

4. *Work incentive programs for those on welfare.* Some of the principles underlying the negative tax program, particularly the principle of a graduated approach to retaining earned income, have been incorporated into general welfare policy in the form of short-term incentive measures to ease the transition between welfare and work. During these transition periods the welfare recipient also retains such welfare benefits as support with child-care costs and full medical coverage. Welfare recipients are usually offered a right to choose for themselves whether or not they participate in such programs, although the right to choose not to participate is somewhat of an illusion, as welfare

Table 2.1 Family of Four: $20,000 Poverty Line, 50 per cent Rate of Reduction

| | Negative Tax Income | |
Earned Income	Reduced by 50% of Earned Income	Total
0	$20,000	$20,000
$10,000	$15,000	$25,000
$20,000	$10,000	$30,000
$30,000	$5,000	$35,000
$40,000	0	$40,000

benefits can be terminated by a refusal to take available work.

5. *Workfare.* Workfare makes work for the able-bodied on welfare a program requirement. The argument for workfare is that a low-income earner will choose welfare instead of work if both offer approximately the same amount of income. Adding a workfare requirement equalizes this situation and provides an incentive to the welfare recipient to look for and accept regular employment rather than sit back and live on welfare. Without a workfare penalty, it is also argued, there will be a continued incentive for people to switch from work to welfare, a buildup of long-term welfare use, an increase in intergenerational welfare use, the development of a welfare underclass, and a continued erosion of public support for welfare measures.

The use of a work requirement for able-bodied recipients has had a long history. In the operation of the British Poor Law, the requirement took the form of the 'workhouse test': assistance was only to be available through admission to a local workhouse where the poor would be 'set on work', usually hard and demeaning work that had to be undertaken at the workhouse. The argument in support of this condition was that the person who did not accept it was obviously not destitute and so did not need relief. The problems of this approach to administering social assistance were numerous. First, the requirement served to deter those who should have had support on the grounds of need, but lived in destitution rather than accept the workhouse conditions. Second, in times of increasing unemployment the system would break down as too many people came to the workhouse and asked for work. Third, the workhouse was an expensive institution to maintain and was not effective in keeping the costs of welfare down. The workhouse system was finally abandoned for these reasons.

The modern equivalent of the workhouse is workfare and it faces all the same problems.[25] Nevertheless, the attraction of a work test remains strong, particularly to conservatives.

4. Dependency Relationships

One of the more troubling debates on the effect of receiving welfare benefits focuses on the long-term 'dependency' effect that is alleged to result. Conservatives make this case against welfare measures in several ways. Conservative economists were convinced in the early 1990s that Canada's unemployment rate was raised by several percentage points and the mobility of its labour force reduced by the availability of Unemployment Insurance and social assistance.[26] This view led to the introduction of lower benefits for the unemployed and stricter conditions of eligibility.

However, the concern that welfare creates dependency is not limited to conservative economists. Patrick Burman subdivides the act of giving into five categories based on the relationships they create between program administrators and recipients: (1) moralistic giving, (2) bureaucratic subsidizing, (3) response to needs, (4) community development, and (5) anti-poverty activism.[27]

Moralistic giving is practised by groups like the Salvation Army and the St Vincent de Paul Society. Here the poor are thought of as morally weak, lazy, and authors of their own fate. This allows the giving institution and administrators to use them to demonstrate their moral superiority. The act of 'giving' conveys a moral benefit on the giver and at the same time places the receiver in the subservient position of being the beggar. It opens the door for 'moral improvement'. The ideal recipient is defined in terms of 'salvation', the rejection of any form of 'sin', and conformity to the values of the giver.

Bureaucratic subsidizing is exemplified by the Canada Employment Centre, welfare office, and legal aid. Here the recipient has a legal entitlement to benefit, but conditions exist and accessing the benefit requires that the recipient negotiate with a case worker who exercises discretion at a number of levels. One level is that of judging whether the recipient has in fact met eligibility criteria, such as 'looking for work' and fully declaring all sources of income. A second level involves discretion on the part of the worker as to who is seen and when they are seen. The 'client' who is difficult to deal with can be kept waiting, for example, and the paperwork on that individual's file can take longer to get done. In other words, the case-worker has several ways to reward subservience and to punish non-conformity.

Response to needs occurs when the case-worker who is professionally trained not to exploit the client relationship genuinely tries to be the client's advocate. The location for this work can be either of the previous two settings or it can be in an independent 'advocacy' agency. The difference from the earlier settings is the attitude of the caseworker in defining the giving relationship. Here there is an attempt to 'empower' and to inform the client of her/his entitlement and rights of redress and appeal. However, the basic relationships of power and class have not changed. The services delivered are as limited as under the other formulations and the client remains dependent on the case-worker.

Community development replaces these dependency relationships defined around the receipt of benefits with a relationship defined around community change. The ideal model is one in which, through local action, a co-opera-tive enterprise provides the income through whch the participants become independent. The problem of the model is the dearth of opportunities to fulfill the goal.

'Anti-poverty activating' is the name given by Burman to the structural social work objective of reforming the society that led to the creation of poverty in the first place. Central to this approach is the expression, 'Think globally, act locally.' Here the critique of capitalist society and institutions is a prominent feature and attention is directed first to achieving local-level reforms in working conditions, environmental issues, and equity matters. Beyond this there are longer-term objectives of seeking structural reforms in terms of world trade and globalization and of

joining with workers in other countries in addressing international poverty problems.

In the end many who are poor develop a sense of 'powerlessness' as they face what seem to be insurmountable obstacles that undercut their capacity for independence (see Box 2.3).

Burman draws four conclusions from his interviews with service recipients:

1. They are people with their own idiosyncra-sies and unique experiences, and we should reject any stereotypical conclusions about their relationship to welfare institutions.
2. 'Empathy' is not enough; welfare institu-tions should provide means for 'articulating the voice of the "others"'.[28]
3. Those with low incomes are not looking for handouts, but would rather have societal opportunities and infrastructural supports. In other words, they seek ways to merge with society as a whole, not ways that segre-gate or distinguish them.
4. An approach to poverty that ends with alle-viating misery falls too far short of the goal of reducing inequalities so that poverty is no longer a concern.

5. Maintaining Public Support

The welfare transfer is an institutionalized form of gift. The most positive and, for welfare ideals, most supportive reason for the welfare transfer is consciousness in sharing a common fate with one's fellow citizens. For this reason, positive approaches to the development of social welfare in modern society have sometimes occurred during or after times of war. The British and Canadian social welfare services were intro-duced following the experience of nations that had come to accept the principles of pooling and sharing during the emergency situations of World War II. In one of the most famous essays on the concept of the welfare state the British sociologist T.H. Marshall identified modern social security measures with the concept of citizenship.[29]

The paradox of social welfare transfers is that, de facto, they tend to destroy this sense of common cause. The effect of stigma on public support is to divide citizens into two separate social classes, the 'givers' and the 'receivers'. The givers are identified with industry, self-support, and beneficence, while the receivers are identified with laziness, dependence, and self-interest. The welfare transfer thus creates alienation and undercuts the basis of its own public support.

The transfer based on a shared citizenship is debased by the dynamic into a transfer based on the principle that those who are the givers are justified in expecting that the recipients conduct themselves on terms dictated to them. A transfer based on a gift thus becomes a transfer viewed as a means of social control.

The history of the development of social welfare programs has been marked by cycles in which high ideals are declared—the Welfare

---

Box 2.3 Delilah

Delilah is a twenty-eight-year-old black woman with a welfare income.

I feel that being poor is not just a physical reality; it's a state of mind at the worst. I am an individual person, part of a family, being forced to fit a peg or classification in a system that makes no allowances for individuality. Our needs as a family are not considered to any reasonable degree at all.

Financial aid workers often do not try to work with you within the confines of the system, your needs being totally unimportant to them. Often you are told that the worker has not time to deal with something, or that she doesn't know anything about it. Very rarely do you ever encounter anyone who makes an active effort to work with you and understand the individual needs of your family. Not all the blame should go to the system, but it's often hard to see where it should go when you are too hungry to think straight.

I personally am poor because the man who supports me is in jail for a crime that he did not commit but only had knowledge of, not a crime of violence or hate. Unfortunately, society could not find a way for this man to remain in the community and support his family while paying his debt to society. Now the taxpayers support him, paying for his room and board and his medical and dental bills in addition to supporting myself and my child, paying our room and board, our dental and medical, etc.

Poverty is a lack of understanding of people's needs, as opposed to wants. It begins on the most basic level with a mistaken assumption that we can exist on the basic social assistance rates. It is mistakenly assumed that you, the parent, can rent a decent place to live and provide a clean, bright, healthy environment with nutritious meals and clean clothes on the amount of money provided. People on welfare try harder and hustle more to care for their children, clean the house, and do laundry in the bathtub because there is not even enough money to go to the laundromat. It is hard when the mother is not receiving a proper diet. This could be changed by the people of the community working together with the government to set up realistic guidelines that we could work within. A clearer understanding of the needs of the people in the community can be obtained by asking them! A great deal of money need not be wasted setting up a committee of government employees to look into this matter—just ask anyone who has had to struggle to survive on basic subsistence rates. Given sixty days of daycare and a bus pass, I personally could get off and stay off welfare forever. But although this sounds like a reasonable request, it does not fall within their guidelines in my case, and so I will never get it. It's not as though I don't know what I need. God knows I have spent enough time just sitting in my house planning what I need to remove myself from this trap. I'm angry!!! They give me my cheque so grudgingly every month, as though it causes them physical pain to talk to me, but they hold me back and refuse to provide the things that I need to remove myself from this trap—the welfare trap.

SOURCE: Sheila Baxter, *No Way to Live* (Vancouver: New Star Books, 1986), 19–20.

State, the War on Poverty—followed by periods in which the ideals erode. In such periods the social welfare transfer is viewed as a 'burden' rather than as a desirable social expenditure. The form of this cycle in Canada is reflected in Appendix B. For example, the 1940s were a period of substantial reform and review, which contrasted with the failure and chaos of the 1930s and the indifference of the 1950s.[30] Likewise, the achievements of the 1960s and 1970s led, in some measure, to the conservative reaction of the 1980s and 1990s.

Transfers and Taxation

Although taxes do not directly result in welfare transfers they do have an effect on the redistributive process as a whole because they determine how income is retained and, hence, what the final distribution of income is. Thus, the graduated income tax has an effect on the distribution of income, making the post-tax income distribution more egalitarian than the pre-tax income distribution. This result is not a welfare transfer in itself; there is no direct 'gift' effect. However, the combined effect of the graduated tax and the welfare transfer changes the income distribution in a more egalitarian direction to a greater degree than would be achieved by the welfare transfer on its own.

A properly graduated taxation system (in which those with the highest incomes pay a higher percentage of their total income in taxes) is an important support to the goal of the redistribution of income in an egalitarian manner. Taken as a whole, the Canadian tax system does not achieve this ideal. The effective total tax incidence is remarkably even so that all income classes part with approximately the same fraction of their total income in taxes. This is a result of the fact that the progressive graduations of the income tax system are almost completely counteracted by the regressive impact of sales taxes, housing taxes, social insurance premiums, import duties, etc. In all of these indirect taxes, the poor pay a higher proportion of their income than those who are better off.

In addition, the tax system has been used to distribute some social welfare benefits in the form of refundable tax credits, as in the case of the Child Tax Benefit, and to recapture social welfare benefits from those above a specific income threshold, as in the clawback provisions affecting higher-income recipients of Old Age Security. In recent years, there has been a considerable amount of discussion of the advantages and disadvantages of expanding the transfer functions of the taxation system to such fields as child poverty and child-care costs. Finally, the income tax system also contains tax exemption provisions (tax expenditures), some of which have welfare purposes. The best known of these are the RRSP and registered pension plan deductions, which provide a financial incentive to taxpayers to make pension provisions for themselves.

The use of the tax system to assess eligibility for welfare benefits and to pay benefits has several advantages. Because all persons file tax returns the individual beneficiary of integrated programs does not have to make a separate individual application. In addition, benefits through the tax system are seen as social rights, eliminating any stigma associated with their receipt.

Employment Equity Measures

A more 'structural' approach to changing income redistribution in order to provide for a greater degree of income equality and income equity has come in the form of government employment equity programs. Statistics Canada reported that for 1993, women working in full-time employment earned 72 per cent of what men earned, an average annual income of $28,932 as compared to $39,433. The gap between men's and women's earnings can be partly explained at one level by differences of employment type and differences in length and continuity of labour force attachment. But these arguments cut little weight when reviewed through a feminist analysis that equates difference in employment type to a combination of valuing men's work more than women's and discrimination against accepting women candidates in traditional 'male' fields of employment. The argument about length and continuity of labour force attachment is also flawed because women often are compelled to leave the labour force for child-bearing and for most child and elder care. Thus the persistence of a gender wage gap is evidence of the operation of an economy that systemically discriminates against women.

The response to this analysis has taken the form of attempts to regulate employment practices to improve access for women to all occupations; provide proportionately higher increases in fields where women constitute the majority of workers; offer periods of leave for maternity and other caring roles under terms that permit women to maintain their jobs; expand daycare services; and introduce goals or quotas as a basis for affirmative action. A similar approach is also argued as needed for other groups, such as Aboriginals, visible minorities, and the disabled, who are not fully and equitably represented in the distribution of employment and income.

Employment equity measures are an attempt to deal with one problem of income distribution—systemic discrimination—at its source. Patricia Evans writes:

> there are several . . . lessons [that] grow in importance as the claims of social citizenship erode, along with public services and income support, while the pace of globalization and deficit cutting mount. First, it is essential to reassert the claims of women to paid employment, and to recognize that women's responsibility for caring for others will not be adequately compensated in the absence of labour force attachment. Second, that the claims to paid employment without a recognition of women's caring responsibilities are claims that only the most affluent of working

women will benefit from, and claims that the most vulnerable, single mothers, are likely to be entrapped by. Third, that the full exercise of women's citizenship requires an equitable division of unpaid labour, and that this goal may be the most difficult to achieve through public policy initiatives.[31]

Employment equity measures, in the absence of full employment at adequate wage levels, represent only a partial solution to the redistributive objectives of social welfare policy. This partial solution can become a trap in that the existence of such policies can be used to expand the boundaries of women's employability[32] and thus reduce benefits from the social welfare system and/or make them subject to workfare or other employment conditions.

The Extent of the Social Welfare Income Transfer System

The redistributive social welfare system, also known as the income security system, is a major fact of life for all Canadians. In 1997, 17 per cent of GDP was redistributed, either as direct expenditures or as tax benefits for social welfare purposes. Every person received a portion of his or her income from the system and for many the system was the main source of income.

The programs that first come to mind are familiar ones like Employment Insurance, the Canada Pension Plan, social assistance payments, and Old Age Security. These are certainly included. However, these programs must be viewed as only part of a still larger whole, which gives recognition to five added elements: (1) tax expenditures; (2) housing, health, education, and other service benefits; (3) employment goals and programs; (4) family care; and (5) charitable and voluntary activities.

1. *Tax expenditures.* Tax expenditures are decisions made by the government not to collect taxes. An individual's income is increased as

effectively when the state waives a right to collect taxes as it is increased when the state decides to provide a specific grant. Thus the personal exemptions for a spouse and for the first child under the Income Tax Act increase the income enjoyed by single-earner households of two or more persons. The effect is similar to that of a program of direct grants for dependants, except that the benefits of tax expenditures are limited to those who have a taxable income. Another example is the Registered Retirement Savings Plan (RRSP) tax deduction, whereby middle- and upper-income earners can save, tax-free, for retirement.

2. *Housing, health, education, and other service benefits.* Income is valued for what it permits the recipient to purchase. The provision of income is thus a means to an end. The direct provision of goods or services to recipients short-circuits this chain of events.

The provision of social housing illustrates the importance of this relationship. Those recipients fortunate enough to live in social housing pay a reduced rent or co-operative charge, with the difference between this amount and the development and maintenance costs of the project being paid for by government. They also benefit by being less subject to some of the risks that renters face in the private sector, such as inadequate accommodation, eviction, discrimination, and rent increases. If social housing was available for all who wished to live in it (as in some European countries), the income needs of the poor would be reduced. In Canada, however, the social housing stock totals 6.5 per cent of all dwellings, only about half of which is available with rents geared to income. This is much less than is needed to house all poor individuals and families.

Health services are another example of a benefit that in most cases is provided directly to recipients. Physician and hospital services are universally available in Canada, and as a result Canadians do not have to make provision through their employers, private insurance, or savings as they do in the United States. However, the coverage of health services in Canada does not always include drug costs, dental services, and health appliances. Consequently, some people have to look to other ways of meeting these needs.

Education is a third example. In Canada primary and secondary education is universally available at no direct cost to families. Higher education, on the other hand, is only partly funded by direct government payments to universities and colleges; the additional costs are covered by fees. Furthermore, the person pursuing higher education is, in most cases, not eligible for such programs as Employment Insurance and social assistance. As a result the government has developed a supplementary welfare (student loan) system for people seeking higher education who cannot afford to pay their education and living costs. These three examples demonstrate how the extent of the income security system is determined by the extent of the direct provision of services by government.

Debate as to whether need should be met by the provision of income or by the provision of goods and services has been dominated by concern, on the one hand, for the freedom of the recipient and, on the other, for the general social interest and for the equity that accompanies the distribution. Where income is given directly the recipients are free to make their own choices about their welfare. This maximizes the recipients' choice, provided of course that the total income given is sufficient to purchase the required services. The provision of goods and services involves a decision by government as to what goods and services are needed—and as to their standard. This form of subsidy decreases the consumer's freedom. However, goods and services rather than cash have been considered to be in the general social interest in the fields of primary and secondary education and for most medical care. Providing goods or services rather than income is inherently more efficient in terms of ensuring the ultimate receipt of the intended goods or services, and where costs are high, unpredictable, or unevenly distributed over the population the provision of goods or services rather than income may be the only route to ensuring their ultimate receipt. A problem for recipients and for the design of other social welfare measures is created where, as in the case of social housing, only some people receive the service; or, as in the case of some medical services and higher education, the coverage of the universal service is only a partial one.

3. *Employment programs.* The employment policies and programs of government are a third influence on income security. These are broadly of three types: (1) policies designed to affect the quantity and distribution of employment; (2) policies designed to set the terms of employment; and (3) policies designed to produce work incentives.

Until the 1970s full employment was a major objective of government policy. The goals of the 1973 income security review were to 'maintain a high rate of employment, price stability, an equitable distribution of rising income, and a reduction of regional economic disparities.'[33] These policy objectives did not prove to be compatible. In particular, economic growth and high levels of employment came to be seen as incompatible with price stability and an equitable distribution of rising income. In the 1960s, the commitment to full employment (variously defined as between 2 per cent and 6 per cent unemployment) was unambiguous. However, in the 1970s economic policies encountered difficulty in obtaining either full employment or price stability, and the commitment to full employment was weakened. In the 1980s, a 9 per cent national rate of unemployment and regional rates of 15 per cent were accepted, and the idea that government might itself be an employer of last resort was abandoned. In the 1990s Canada had, for a time, an 11 per cent national rate and regional rates as high as 25 per cent. Although politicians on the hustings retain the rhetoric of 'jobs, jobs, jobs', there are no formal goals for full employment. When and where they exist, high rates of unemployment make it impossible for some people who want to work to find work and have enormous implications for the size of the income security system.

The prohibition of child labour and the regulation of hours of work were some of the earliest efforts at social legislation resulting from industrialism. The provisions for equity in employment practice and freedom from harassment at work are some of the latest. These measures have a relationship to income security as they establish rules of justice and fairness for the workplace and protect employees from exploitation. Minimum wages ensure that employers cannot exploit employees' need for work. In some countries, such as Australia and France, minimum wage policies have been a central feature of the design of income security. Although wage legislation, from an income security perspective, has the deficiency of not recognizing family dependencies, this deficiency can be remedied by a combination of wage legislation and family benefits.

Occupational benefits, which include such services provided to employees and their dependants as subsidized housing, dental plans, life insurance, sports clubs, and occupational health services, are also relevant. All serve to reduce the needs that must be met by income. Access to these benefits is limited to those who are employed by major companies and/or in employment covered by well-established union contracts.

4. *Family care.* A fourth influence on income security is the extent of family care and the mechanisms of enforcement. These used to be more extensive than they now are—during the 1930s, the extended family was viewed as a network to be used first by the unemployed. In the post-war social welfare programs, workers, who were then principally men, were relieved of the need to look to the family for support when they became unemployed, disabled, or old, but women and children were recognized in this system as the dependants of men. Exercise of their social rights was through enforcing men to be responsible, re-enforcing the dependency of

women and children. These assumptions and associated program features remain in effect even though the social conditions that once supported them have changed. The result is a reinforcement through the income security system of family inequities by gender and age of recipient.

5. *Charitable and voluntary activities.* There has always been some charitable and voluntary relief. Agencies like the Salvation Army and the St Vincent de Paul Society have a long record of relieving destitution. To these long-standing efforts must be added the food banks that began in the 1980s recession. The growing prevalence of homelessness, the continuing process of tightening eligibility conditions for government programs, and the reduction in welfare benefits are all contributing to a new growth of charitable and voluntary activity as a last resort for those whose need is not otherwise met.

The Canadian Social Welfare Redistribution System

The total Canadian redistribution system is composed of the following cash programs:

Old Age Security
Old Age Security Guaranteed Income
    Supplement
Child Tax Benefit
Canada Pension Plan
Employment Insurance
Workers' Compensation
veterans' pensions
Canada Health and Social Transfer
provincial social assistance programs
on-reserve assistance for First Nations
post-secondary student loans

the following fiscal measures:

personal deductions
tax credits
retirement savings exemptions
tuition fee deductions
child-care expense deduction

medical and charitable expense deductions
GST rebate

the following goods or service programs:

hospital insurance
medicare
National Housing Act—social housing provi-
    sions
provincial shelter aid and rental subsidies
home maintenance and renovation programs
vocational training programs
legal aid
education

the following employment-related measures:

full employment policies
minimum wage legislation
occupational benefits
employment equity requirements

the following occupational welfare measures:

sports and recreational facilities
housing
pension and insurance plans
transport
cars
expense accounts
tenured employment statuses (amounting to
    a guaranteed income)

the following family care and dependency measures:

wives and children's maintenance legislation
unmarried mothers' legislation
elder and other home care provisions

the following voluntary and charitable measures:

food banks
shelters
soup kitchens.

The total amount of income provided through the redistributive system is enormous. Table 2.2 shows how the cost of major programs doubled between 1984–5 and 1994–5, reaching a total of more than $120 billion. Since 1995 changes in overall expenditures have become much more difficult to track. In particular, the repeal of the Canada Assistance Plan and its replacement by the Canada Health and Social Transfer resulted in the federal government ceasing to track data on either provincial social assistance programs or its contribution to them. This has led to a situation in which continued growth can be seen for those parts of the system where data remain available but, as the total of government expenditures of all types on social programs is falling, shrinkage must be occurring in concealed ways in parts of the system that are no longer tracked.

In 1993, when the Canadian government was concerned about the extent of the deficit and social expenditures were under critical scrutiny, the Caledon Institute of Social Policy publication, *Opening the Books on Social Spending*,[34] explored the background and reasons for the continuing growth of social spending. Going back to 1958–9, the earliest date when reliable and comprehensive data were available, and adjusting for inflation, the total increase was estimated at 800 per cent. Adjusting for the increase in the population reduced the increase to 500 per cent. As a percentage of the gross domestic product, social spending has grown from 8 per cent to 20 per cent. New programs from the 1960s and 1970s—the Canada/Quebec Pension Plans, the Guaranteed Income Supplement, the Canada Assistance Plan, medicare, Unemployment Insurance expansion, and the Child Tax Credit—accounted for much of the growth. In addition, benefits, particularly for the elderly, had improved as a partial but incomplete response to the issue of poverty. The period of program expansion and benefit liberalization had ended with the 1970s. Since then the pressure had been to restrict benefits and control costs, yet growth had continued. The Caledon Institute concluded that:

> Social spending in the 1980s and 1990s is being driven primarily by powerful demographic and economic forces—chief among them the relentless aging of the population and the deadly combination of periodic recessions (which create mass, lingering unemployment) and a fundamental restructuring of the economy, the latter emanating largely from global changes whose ramifications we are just beginning to fathom.[35]

These pressures remain and are seen in the continued growth of expenditures for the elderly. However, the enactment of the Canada Health and Social Transfer in 1995, along with restrictions on eligibility for Employment Insurance, has had the effect of insulating the federal government from part of this pressure and has transferred that pressure to the provinces.

Changes in Canada's Commitment to Redistribution in International Perspective

The repeal of the Canada Assistance Plan (CAP) in 1995 and its replacement by the Canada Health and Social Transfer (CHST) was a major change in Canada's commitment to social program spending and to income redistribution. The CAP had been introduced in 1966. Key provisions of the CAP included the following:

1. Provinces were reimbursed for 50 per cent of their social assistance costs.
2. Provinces were required to make social assistance available to everyone who was in demonstrable need.
3. Previous categorical programs for the elderly, mothers, disabled, and unemployed, among others, were consolidated into one framework simplifying administration and reducing the division of the poor into deserving and undeserving categories.
4. A work requirement for the receipt of welfare was prohibited.
5. Welfare services for 'prevention and removal of the causes of poverty' were included.

Table 2.2 Estimates of Government Social Security Programs in Canada, 1984–5, 1994–5, and 1999–2000 ($ billions)

	1984–5		1994–5		1999–2000	
Target Group	Federal	Provincial	Federal	Provincial	Federal	Provincial
Poor						
Canada Assistance Plan	4.1	4.1	7.3	9.3		Data not available***
Canada Health and Social Transfer					12.5	
Provincial tax credits*		1.6		3.0		
On-reserve assistance	0.2		0.7		1.1	
GST rebate*			2.8			
Social housing	1.1		1.9		1.9	
Families						
Child-care deduction*	0.1					
Child Tax Credit/Benefit*	1.1		5.1**		6.0	
Family Allowances	2.4		**			
Child tax exemption*	0.9	0.5	**			
Married exemption*	1.4	0.6	1.6	0.7	1.9	
Employment Assistance						
Unemployment Insurance	11.6		15.6		11.3	
Workers' Compensation		1.6		3.8		
Training programs	0.1	0.1	1.3	1.3		
Student loans			0.5			
Elderly						
Quebec/Canada Pension	4.4	1.6 (Q)	12.5	4.6 (Q)	18.7	5.4 (Q)
Old Age Security	8.3		15.8		18.0	
Guaranteed Income Sup.	3.1		4.4		4.9	
Veterans' pensions	0.7		1.2		1.3	
RRSP/RPP/tax benefits*	4.7	2.3	17.7	7.4	14.5	

*   Indicates benefits transferred through the tax system; total $40.2 billion.

**   The Family Allowance, Child Tax Credit, child tax exemption, and employment deduction were replaced in 1993 by the Child Tax Benefit.

*** The repeal of the Canada Assistance Plan and the introduction of the Canada Health and Social Transfer resulted in the federal government withdrawing from gathering this data.

SOURCES: *Report of the Royal Commission on the Economic Union and Development Prospects for Canada,* 1985, 772; Department of Finance, *Creating a Healthy Fiscal Environment* (Ottawa, 1994); Human Resources Canada, *Income Security Programs Statistics Book,* 2001, and estimates prepared by the author.

6. Provincial residency requirements were prohibited.
7. Appeal procedures were required.
8. Provinces had to account for their use of CAP funds, and public data on social assistance programs, including comparative interprovincial and multi-year data, were available.
9. Limits were established on earned income and assets.
10. A concept of 'adequate' assistance was declared.
11. Provision was included for extending provincial programs to the Aboriginal community.[36]

The introduction of the CHST removed all these provisions except the prohibition of provincial residency. The CHST merged federal spending in support of health care and higher education with welfare expenditures and at the same time reduced the total amount available to the provinces. The result has been seen in a general reduction in the Canadian commitment to redistribution and to the goals of equity and equality.

While these changes were being made in the federal commitment to social assistance programs, the Canadian government was also reducing its commitment to Unemployment Insurance. Through the renamed Employment Insurance Act (1995), contribution requirements in terms of hours worked were increased; benefit periods were reduced; benefits for workers who had left a previous job voluntarily were denied; penalties for 'frequent use' were introduced; the proportion of a person's income replaced by benefits was reduced; and unemployment funding was freed to be used as earnings supplements. The effect of these changes was to reduce the support that the program provided to seasonal workers and to lower-paid workers in marginal employment. This corresponded to the conservative agenda that favoured the 'restructuring' of the Canadian labour market to encourage lower wages and more part-time employment.[37]

When the changes made in Canada are compared to other developed economies both major similarities and differences are apparent. Table 2.3 shows that all OECD countries reduced their social program expenditures during the 1990s. However, the reduction in Canada of 9.6 per cent was much higher than the average of 5.2 per cent, and the effect of the reduction was to drop Canada from eighth to fourteenth place in the rankings.

Changes, 1940–2002

The concepts behind the redistributive objectives of the post-war welfare state were clear. The objectives were framed in the context of the capitalist, industrial society and of a family unit with a male 'breadwinner' and a female 'homemaker'. The system aimed to protect such a family unit from five major threats to its economic well-being:

1. *Unemployment.* To support income levels during periodic recessions and layoffs, there was Unemployment Insurance.
2. *Family dependencies.* As wage income did not recognize differences in family size, Family Allowances were paid for each child in the home.
3. *Old age and disability.* To provide for an income in old age or following disability there was a basic pension, Old Age Security, and a social insurance plan, the Canada/Quebec Pension Plan.
4. *Illness.* Through a combination of hospital insurance and medicare everybody was assured of the basic resources to provide for medical attention when needed.
5. *Industrial injury.* To protect the worker against the risk of industrial injury there was Workers' Compensation.

For risks that lay outside this social safety net there were the needs-based provincial social assistance programs. Although these ideas were present in the literature in the 1940s, it was not until the 1960s that they were fully enacted.

The first attempt to move beyond this framework came in the late 1960s and early 1970s and was spurred by the realization that, despite these provisions, poverty persisted. The objective was to provide a guaranteed annual income that would encompass all the risks, other than illness and industrial injury, and that would replace the social assistance programs. The attempt failed.

A second attempt to move beyond the original framework came with the first post-1975 wave of financial restructuring and the rise of a new conservatism. The objective here was to make the social welfare transfer system smaller and more focused on need, while encouraging individuals to make private provisions for themselves. A partial dismemberment of the 1960s social welfare system followed. Family Allowances were replaced by an income-tested Child Tax Benefit. Old Age Security was 'clawed back' from higher-income earners through the tax system. On the other hand, RRSP and pension tax exemptions were raised to encourage private saving for old age.

A third attempt to move beyond the original framework, based in the feminist social movement, was occurring at the same time. Attention here was directed to the familial assumptions of the post-war welfare state and particularly the assumption that women would be 'dependants'. The objective was to add to, and modify, the

Table 2.3 Changes in Program Spending, 19 OECD Countries, 1990–1999

Country	Maximum % of GDP in 1990–4	Year	Maximum % of GDP in 1995–9	Year	% Change
Australia	34.0	1993	30.5	1999	−3.5
Austria	49.5	1993	46.1	1998	−3.4
Belgium	46.1	1993	43.6	1998	−2.5
Canada	46.0	1992	36.4	1999	−9.6
Denmark	57.4	1994	52.5	1999	−4.9
Finland	59.5	1992	45.6	1999	−13.9
France	51.0	1993	49.3	1997–8	−1.7
Germany	45.6	1993	44.3	1998	−1.3
Greece	41.1	1993	40.4	1996	−0.7
Ireland	34.4	1994	28.1	1999	−6.3
Italy	44.9	1993	41.0	1997–8	−3.9
Japan	34.4	1994	34.0	1997	−0.4
Netherlands	45.6	1992	39.3	1998	−6.3
Norway	54.9	1992	45.5	1997	−9.4
Portugal	39.1	1993	38.2	1995	−0.9
Spain	41.6	1993	35.0	1999	−6.6
Sweden	66.9	1993	53.5	1999	−13.4
United Kingdom	43.2	1992–3	36.9	1999	−6.3
United States	31.1	1992	27.3	1998–9	−3.8
Average	45.6		40.4		−5.2

SOURCE: John Richards, *Now That the Coat Fits the Cloth: Spending Wisely in a Trimmed-Down Age* (Toronto: C.D. Howe Institute, 2000), 3.

redistributive system to provide equity of treatment to women. There have been some successes, for example, an increased attention to employment equity and a provision to divide pension assets equally between men and women on divorce or separation, but other major goals, such as a comprehensive child-care system and a commitment to equity throughout the redistributive system, have not been achieved. Other groups whose distinct relationship to Canadian society had not been recognized in the earlier formula, including Aboriginal peoples, refugees and recent immigrants, and gays and lesbians, also advanced claims for a more equitable redistributive system.

A fourth movement away from the original framework took place in the mid-1990s. This was spurred by a combination of changed industrial and financial conditions (the global economy) and internal fiscal constraints (the deficit). The objectives—a smaller and less inclusive system—were similar to those of the second attempt but the pressures for change were now framed in terms of the global economy and external economic forces rather than as conservative ideological convictions. From a conservative perspective, this attempt was successful. The federal government reduced its exposure to social welfare costs,[38] and Canada's commitment to the redistribution of income and to the goals of equity and equality was weakened. When financial conditions improved in the late 1990s and the federal government had a surplus, it allocated this surplus to debt and tax reduction as the conservatives had always wanted. From the perspective of social justice the result is disaster.

Additional Readings

Thomas J. Courchene, 'Towards the Re-integration of Social and Economic Policy', in G. Bruce Doern and B. Bryne, eds, *Canada at Risk? Canadian Public Policy in the 1990s*. Toronto: C.D. Howe Institute, 1991, 125–48. This essay presents the conservative view of how social welfare policy needed to be changed.

C.B. Macpherson, 'The Real World of Democracy', *Massey Lectures, 4th Series*. Toronto: Canadian Broadcasting Corporation, 1965. This work provides a good historic statement of the classical liberal arguments for using social welfare policy to redistribute income.

C.B. Macpherson, *The Rise and Fall of Economic Justice and Other Papers*. New York: Oxford University Press, 1985. Chapter 1, 'The Rise and Fall of Economic Justice', provides an excellent statement of the ideas that have shaped the concept of economic justice, along with a prescient sense that their expression in the modern welfare state may be short-lived.

Alan Moscovitch, 'The Canada Health and Social Transfer: What Was Lost', *Canadian Review of Social Policy* 37 (Spring 1996): 66–74. Moscovitch details the changes that were made when the conservative arguments were incorporated into public policy and the Canada Assistance Plan was replaced by the Canada Health and Social Transfer.

John Richards, 'The Social Policy Round', in Richards and William Watson, eds, *The Case for Change*. Toronto: C.D. Howe Institute, 1994, 31–97. This is another conservative presentation of the changes that were seen as needed in Canadian social welfare—changes that were largely implemented by Canadian governments in the 1990s.

Study Questions

1. Examine the student loan program as a form of social welfare. What influence do you see from any of the six principal arguments referred to in this chapter as rationales for distributing income? What provisions are there in the student loan program for 'work requirements'? Why is

the program a 'loan program' rather than a 'grant program'? Is there a stigma associated with receiving benefits (and the obligation to repay them)?

2. How is 'employment equity' affecting social welfare? What changes have been made and what changes might be anticipated for the future?

3. Review the changes that were made in Canada's social security programs in the 1990s from the perspective of your reading of Richards's 'The Social Policy Round' (see above). Discuss the extent to which you agree (and disagree) with these changes.

Notes

1. The minority report of the British Poor Law commissioners of 1909–13, produced by Adrian and Beatrice Webb, foresaw that compulsion was essential to social security. For a full account, see Karl Deschweinitz, *England's Road to Social Security* (London: Oxford University Press, 1943).

2. C.B. Macpherson, 'The Real World of Democracy', *Massey Lectures, 4th Series* (Toronto: CBC, 1965), 48.

3. The welfare economics theory for determining the size and direction of the welfare function was outlined by Pareto, who based his consideration on the rule that 'the test of a socially beneficial redistribution is that it should be voluntarily undertaken', contradicting one of the fundamental principles of welfare thought. For a full discussion, see Robert Pinker, *Social Theory and Social Policy* (London: Heinemann, 1971), 116.

4. Herbert Marcuse, *One Dimensional Man* (Boston: Beacon Press, 1966), 52.

5. Gary Teeple, *Globalization and the Decline of Social Reform* (Toronto: Garamond Press, 1995), 22.

6. Newman Land, Michael Prince, and James Cutt, *Reforming the Public Pension System in Canada* (Victoria: Centre for Public Sector Studies, 1993).

7. Carol Pateman, 'The Patriarchal Welfare State', *Defining Women: Social Institutions and Gender Divisions* (Cambridge: Polity Press, 1992), 223–45, as cited by Patricia Evans, 'The Claims of Women: Gender, Income Security, and the Welfare State', in *7th Conference on Canadian Social Welfare Policy: Remaking Canadian Social Policy: Selected Proceedings* (Vancouver: Social Planning and Research Council of B.C., 25–8 June 1995).

8. See Thomas Courchene, *Social Canada in the Millennium* (Toronto: C.D. Howe Institute, 1994), 45, 58 ff.; also John Richards and William Watson, eds, *Unemployment Insurance: How To Make It Work* (Toronto: C.D. Howe Institute, 1994).

9. Allan Cochrane, John Clarke, and Sahron Gewirtz, *Comparing Welfare States*, 2nd edn (London: Sage, 2001).

10. Terrance J. Boygo, 'Workers' Compensation: Updating the Historic Compromise', in John Richards and William G. Watson, eds, *Chronic Stress: Workers' Compensation in the 1990s* (Toronto: C.D. Howe Institute, 1995), 96 ff.

11. Ross Finie, 'The Economics of Divorce', in John Richards and William Watson, eds, *Family Matters* (Toronto: C.D. Howe Institute, 1995), 122–3.

12. Economic Council of Canada, *Fifth Annual Review* (Ottawa, 1968).

13. Courchene, *Social Canada*, 163.

14. Paul Samuelson, *Economics* (Toronto: McGraw-Hill, 1966).

15. J.K. Galbraith, *The Affluent Society* (London: Penguin Books, 1958), 238–44.

16. John Maynard Keynes was the economic architect of the government response to the Great Depression of the 1930s. In *The Means to Prosperity* (1933) and *The General Theory of Employment, Interest and Money* (1936) he developed the position that the role of government was to stabilize the market economy through a fiscal policy that combined deficits in times of depression with surpluses in boom times. While governments widely adopted the idea of deficits, none showed the ability to produce the balancing

surpluses. For an account of Keynesian thought and its relationship to the Canadian welfare state, see Cy Gonick, *The Great Economic Debate: Failed Economics and a Future for Canada* (Toronto: James Lorimer, 1987).

17. The wealthy banker's wife was often referred to in the media to parody the provision of Family Allowances to all. For a postscript to this lost debate, see Linda McQuaig, *The Wealthy Banker's Wife: The Assault on Equality in Canada* (Toronto: Penguin Books, 1993).

18. See Margaret Hillyard Little, *'No Car, No Radio, No Liquor Permit': The Moral Regulation of Mothers in Ontario, 1920–1997* (Toronto: Oxford University Press, 1998).

19. England, Edward III, *The Statute of Laborers*, 1349.

20. Deschweinitz, *England's Road to Social Security*, 27.

21. John Richards and William Watson, eds, *Helping the Poor: A Qualified Case for Workfare* (Toronto: C.D. Howe Institute, 1995), xxiii.

22. See Marilyn Callahan, Andrew Armitage, Michael Prince, and Brian Wharf, 'Workfare in British Columbia: Social Development Alternatives', *Canadian Review of Social Policy* 26 (1990): 15–25.

23. Ontario Ministry of Community and Social Services, *Transitions: Report of the Social Assistance Review Committee* (Toronto, 1988), ch. 6.

24. For a full discussion, see Christopher Green, *Negative Taxes and the Poverty Problem* (Washington: Brookings Institution, 1967); H.W. Watts, 'Graduated Work Incentive: An Experiment in Negative Taxation', *American Economic Review* 49, 2 (May 1964); Arnold Katz, 'Income Maintenance Experiments: Progress Towards a New American National Policy', *Social and Economic Administration* 7, 2 (May 1973); John Richards and Aidan Vining, 'Welfare Reform: What can we learn from the Americans', in Richards and William Watson, eds, *Helping the Poor* (Toronto: C.D. Howe Institute, 1995), 1–36.

25. Eric Shragge, *Workfare: Ideology for a New Under-Class* (Toronto: Garamond, 1997).

26. Christopher Green, Fred Lazar, Miles Corak, and Dominique Gross, *Unemployment Insurance* (Toronto: C.D. Howe Inistitute, 1994).

27. Patrick Burman, *Poverty Bonds: Power and Agency in the Social Relations of Welfare* (Toronto: Thomson Educational Press, 1996).

28. Ibid., 186.

29. T.H. Marshall, *Class, Citizenship and Social Development* (Garden City, NY: Anchor Books, 1965).

30. For an extended treatment of the cyclical nature of social welfare concerns in the United States and their relationships to the society, see F.F. Piven and R.A. Cloward, *Regulating the Poor: The Functions of Public Welfare* (New York: Vintage Books, 1972).

31. Evans, 'The Claims of Women', 28.

32. Callahan et al., 'Workfare in British Columbia', show how this has happened in relation to workfare expectations of single mothers.

33. Canada, *Income Security for Canadians* (Ottawa: Queen's Printer, 1971), 11.

34. Ken Battle and Sherri Torjman, *Opening the Books on Social Spending* (Ottawa: Caledon Institute of Social Policy, 1993).

35. Ibid., 13.

36. Alan Moscovitch, 'Canada Health and Social Transfer: What Was Lost?', *Canadian Review of Social Policy* 37 (1996): 66–75.

37. Cindy Wiggins, 'Dismantling Unemployment Insurance: The Changes, the Impacts, the Reasons', *Canadian Review of Social Policy* 37 (1996): 75–84.

38. John Richards, *Now That the Coat Fits the Cloth: Spending Wisely in a Trimmed-Down Age* (Toronto: C.D. Howe Institute, 2000).

CHAPTER 3

Canada's Record:
Redistribution, Poverty, and Programs

The contribution being made by social welfare programs to the social welfare policy objectives of reducing poverty and increasing income equalities in Canada is examined in this chapter. Unfortunately, progress towards these objectives is, at best, very uneven, and for some groups the situation is one of increasing inequality.

Learning Objectives

1. To understand how poverty is defined and the composition and location of those groups most affected by poverty.
2. To use the Statistics Canada low-income cut-off lines as a means of measuring progress, or lack of progress, towards the objective of a more equal Canadian society.
3. To examine Canadian income redistribution programs and see where they are succeeding and failing.
4. To understand the changes made in Canadian redistribution programs in the 1990s and their effect on those living at low-income levels.
5. To understand the impact of poverty and social assistance on Aboriginal communities.

Redistribution Objectives

The official view of the objectives of Canada's redistribution system is provided by the opening paragraph of the government of Canada's 1994 discussion paper on social security:

Canada's social security system is a hallmark of our nation. Through it, we have defined ourselves as a country that aspires to give our children the best possible start to life, to enable all Canadians to meet their basic needs, and their families to live in dignity. It is a system dedicated to supporting the most vulnerable of our society, while creating opportunities for all Canadians to improve their lives. Social security embodies the values of justice, tolerance and compassion that mark our country.[1]

The ground-level view is provided by Kim Harvey, a 24-year-old who grew up with neglect, abuse, and poverty from the time her father left when she was a toddler:

'I have nothing. . . . I will never—ever—have children unless I'm in a position to make sure that they would not be on welfare—ever. I'd rather have an abortion first'. . . . Seven years after striking out on her own, Harvey is back where she started—a short subway ride, yet a world away, from the glittering towers of downtown Toronto. It's a bleak and often boring existence, surviving on the $65 a month left after paying the rent on her two-room flat.[2]

The truth is that although government documents often applaud the redistributive system, the reality of the system and its achievements is far removed from the rhetoric.

Specific objectives for the system as a whole, or for its parts, are not to be found, perhaps because if they were available the lack of achievement would be more apparent. The 1973 social security review provided one of the better statements:

> First, the social security system must assure to people who cannot work, the aged, the blind and the disabled, a compassionate and equitable guaranteed income.
>
> Second, the social security system as it applies to people who can work must contain incentives to work and a greater emphasis on the need to get people who are on social aid back to work.
>
> Third, a fair and just relationship must be maintained between the incomes of people who are working at, or near, the minimum wage, the guaranteed incomes assured to people who cannot work, and the allowances paid to those who can work but are unemployed.[3]

Although this statement did not define what was viewed as being 'a compassionate and equitable guaranteed income' or 'a fair and just relationship . . . between the incomes of people who are working . . . the guaranteed incomes,

. . . and the allowances paid to those who . . . are unemployed', these goals provide a basis from which the present redistributive system can be evaluated. Such an evaluation needs to take account of (1) poverty, (2) equity, and (3) employability.

Poverty and Poverty Lines

The Senate Committee on Poverty (1971) was the first body to provide a definition of poverty.[4] The Committee developed a series of poverty lines and then used them to establish objectives for the income security system. Following the work of the Senate Committee, Statistics Canada developed a series of 'low-income cut-offs' (LICOs) that vary by size of community. The LICOs are calculated from the results of Statistics Canada's survey of consumer expenditure. As spending on necessities falls as income rises, 'low income' is defined as the income level at which people on average spend more than a fixed percentage of their total income on the necessities of food, clothing, and shelter, plus 20 per cent. In 1971 'low income' was defined as spending more than 70 per cent of total income in this manner. This percentage was reduced as taxes on low incomes increased, thereby decreasing spending power. It now stands at 54.7 per cent. Table 3.1 shows the LICO values as of 14 September 2001.

Table 3.1 Statistics Canada Low-Income Cut-Offs, 2000, by Household and Community Size

Size of Household	500,000+	100,000–499,999	30,000–99,999	Under 30,000 Urban	Rural
1 person	18,371	15,757	15,648	14,561	12,696
2 persons	22,964	19,697	19,561	18,201	15,870
3 persons	28,560	24,497	24,326	22,625	19,738
4 persons	34,572	29,653	29,448	27,401	23,892
5 persosn	38,646	33,148	32,917	30,629	26,708
6 persosn	42,719	36,642	36,387	33,857	29,524
7 persons	46,793	40,137	39,857	37,085	32,340

SOURCE: National Council of Welfare Web site, updated 14 Sept. 2001.

The Statistics Canada LICOs are the most widely used standard for judging the extent of poverty in Canada, but by no means are these the only way to determine poverty levels. For some time after the work of the 1971 Senate Committee, its poverty lines were regularly updated and were used as a standard. In addition, the Canadian Council on Social Development developed a standard based on the extent of inequality in Canada. The CCSD 'lines of income inequality' are based on the premise that a 'typical' three-member Canadian family should not have to live on an income of less than half the income of the average Canadian family. Thus, the CCSD line is not a measure of poverty but a measure of inequality, reflecting the fundamental social welfare objective of decreasing inequalities.

Social conservatives have criticized all of these methods for establishing low income definitions on the grounds that they are not real measures of poverty, which, they argue, should be defined in terms of the minimum cost of paying for the bare necessities of life. This 'market basket' of goods approach has been used by the Fraser Institute to develop a separate (conservative) series of poverty lines. The Montreal Diet Dispensary has also had a long record of using a similar approach to defining poverty in Montreal. Table 3.2 compares the results of these different approaches to defining poverty.

The effect of using the Fraser Institute poverty lines to calculate the extent of poverty in Canada is substantial, reducing the number of people judged to be in poverty by 75 per cent. However, setting a poverty standard at Third World subsistence levels does not serve the purpose of measuring progress based on the social welfare value of limiting inequalities; rather, it is a way of disguising the disturbing fact that the number of people in poverty, as measured by the Statistics Canada LICOs, has been growing.

Since 1973, Statistics Canada has maintained an annual count of the number of Canadians whose household incomes fall below the low-income cut-offs. Table 3.3 shows both the total number and the rate for people in poverty as a percentage of the total Canadian population. The table shows that the total number of people in poverty has increased steadily, and although the percentage of Canadians in poverty fell from 1973 to 1981, since then it has increased, and all the gains made for families in earlier years were lost during the 1990s. These figures are based on total family income, which includes both market income from employment and investments and redistributed income from social welfare programs. The depth, severity, and duration of poverty have also been increasing, with most of this increase felt by individuals under 65 and family units with children.[5]

Table 3.2 Low-Income and Poverty Lines, 1994

Low-Income or Poverty Line	Family Size			
	Single	2 persons	3 persons	4 persons
Senate	13,300	22,190	26,620	31,050
Stats Canada: cities of 500,000+	16,609	20,782	25,821	31,256
CCSD	13,770	22,950	27,540	32,130
Montreal: basic needs	8,600	–	13,660	15,890
Fraser: Ontario	7,556	10,696	14,037	17,542

SOURCE: David Ross, Richard Shillington, and Clarence Lochhead, *The Canadian Fact Book on Poverty* (Ottawa: Canadian Council on Social Development, 1994), 12–24.

At the same time as the number of people in poverty has been rising, incomes have become less equal. This trend affects the lower middle classes as much as it does those who are in poverty, as the relative share of total income of the highest income earners has grown at the expense of all others. Table 3.4 shows this trend by comparing income 'quintiles'. An income quintile shows the percentage of total income that a 20 per cent segment of the population has at its disposal. It also shows the percentage of 'market' income, that is, income derived from work or investments, as well as 'total' income,

which also includes government transfer payments.

Table 3.4 indicates that 'market' income for people in the lowest two income quintiles has been falling rapidly. The fall in 'total' income has been less severe than in market income because government transfer programs have cushioned the fall. However, the replacement has not been complete, with the result that the number of people in poverty has continued to increase and the reliance on government programs to prevent a more severe increase in the numbers of people in poverty has grown. Table 3.5 shows that

Table 3.3 Number of Persons in Poverty (000s) and Rate (%)

	Singles		Families		Total	
Year	No.	Rate	No.	Rate	No.	Rate
1973	767	40.2	701	13.4	3,269	16.2
1981	940	37.5	721	11.3	3,339	14.0
1989	1,101	34.4	786	11.0	3,489	13.5
1997	1,663	39.6	1,175	14.8	5,222	17.5

SOURCE: David Ross, *Canadian Fact Book on Poverty*, (Ottawa: Canadian Council on Social Development, 2000), 47.

Table 3.4 Family Income Shares and Sources, 1981, 1989, and 1997

	Percentage Share		
Source of Income for Income Quintiles	1981	1989	1997
Market Income			
Lowest	3.5	3.0	2.1
Second	12.3	11.4	10.1
Middle	18.7	18.0	17.7
Fourth	25.3	25.1	25.8
Highest	40.5	42.4	44.3
Total Income			
Lowest	6.9	7.0	6.8
Second	12.9	12.6	11.9
Middle	18.4	17.7	17.4
Fourth	24.1	23.7	24.0
Highest	37.7	39.1	40.0

SOURCE: Ross et al., *Canadian Fact Book on Poverty*, 58.

government transfer income accounts for 90 per cent of total income for people in the lowest income quintile and for 34.4 per cent of income for those in the second quintile.

For most low-income people, other than seniors, market income means income from employment. In the 1960s and early 1970s Canada was confident that it could have a high rate of employment and a high-wage economy. In 1974 the minimum wage plus Family Allowances was sufficient to bring a family of three to the poverty line. However, since the 1970s there has been a continuing decline in minimum wage standards. Table 3.6 indicates this decline, the effect of which, coupled with the increase in part-time work, has meant that minimum wages have ceased to be a tool for keeping the income of lower-income Canadians above poverty levels. This is an example of how the pressures of globalization undermine low income earnings, as the reason for the fall in minimum wage levels most frequently given is Canada's need to have labour costs that are competitive in the context of the global economy (and the North American Free Trade Agreement).

The figures for poverty and income we have discussed so far are average figures for all Canadians. They give a good idea of the overall trends but they also mask major differences that

Table 3.5 Incomes before and after Government Transfers, 1997

Market Income Quintile	Average Market Income	Average Transfer Income	Average Total Income	Average Disposable Income	Tranfer Income as % of Total Income
First (bottom)	1,311	11,876	13,096	12,897	90.0%
Second	14,834	7,788	22,623	20,559	34.4%
Third	32,623	4,923	37,546	31,496	13.1%
Fourth	53,687	3,330	57,017	45,316	5.8%
Fifth	100,228	2,301	102,529	76,146	2.2%

SOURCE: Ross, *Canadian Fact Book on Poverty*, 130.

Table 3.6 Annual Minimum Wage Income by Province, 1976 and 1998–9 (1998 $)

Province	1976	1998/9	% change
Newfoundland	10,825	10,920	6.2%
Prince Edward Island	14,607	11,232	-23.1%
Nova Scotia	10,825	11,440	11.2%
New Brunswick	15,165	11,440	-24.6%
Quebec	17,253	14,352	-16.8%
Ontario	15,835	14,248	-10.0%
Manitoba	16,724	12,211	-27.0%
Saskatchewan	17,040	12,211	-28.3%
Alberta	16,502	12,008	-27.2%
British Columbia	18,257	14,872	-18.5%

SOURCE: Ross, *Canadian Fact Book on Poverty*, 93.

occur due to gender, age, family type, ethnicity, ability, and location.

Gender

In every age category women are more likely to be poor than men (Table 3.7). The gap is smallest between men and women in the prime working years of ages 35–54, rising for younger women and for older women. Overall, the ratio of women to men in poverty was 1.33:1 in 1993, exactly the same as it was in 1982. If one looks at change in the ratio for different years there seems to be a pattern whereby the ratio rises during periods of prosperity and falls during periods of recession. In other words, men do better during the good times than women.

Seniors

Keeping the income of most seniors above poverty lines has been the great success story of Canada's response to poverty. Table 3.8 shows this achievement. The rate of decrease in poverty among seniors has been dramatic; nevertheless,

in 1998, 629,000 remained poor, including a disproportionate number of older women. The increase in poverty among seniors between 1995 and 1998 shows, too, that this achievement should not be taken for granted.

Children and Families

The poverty of children is the poverty of the families to which they belong. Table 3.9 shows the slide of more and more children into poverty. The single-mother families are particularly vulnerable. For children in single-mother families, poverty is normal. Although two-parent families do better, there are still many of them in poverty, with more children in total than in the single-mother families. Poverty undermines the children's education, health, and expectations of living in a just and fair society.

In 1989 the Canadian House of Commons declared in a unanimous resolution 'to seek to achieve the goal of eliminating poverty among Canadian children by the year 2000'. Table 3.10 indicates the dismal failure to achieve this goal, with the poverty rate for children rising in every

Table 3.7 Poverty Rates by Age and Sex, 1993

Sex	18–24	25–34	35–44	45–54	55–64	65–74	75–84	85+
Men	16.7	15.8	12.7	10.4	14.0	14.3	14.0	17.3
Women	23.6	19.9	13.8	12.1	18.5	20.2	31.3	35.6

SOURCE: National Council of Welfare, *Poverty Profile 1993 (Ottawa, 1995)*, 33.

Table 3.8 Poverty Trends, People 65 and Older, 1980–1998

Year	Poor Seniors	All Seniors	Poverty Rate
1980	731,000	2,177,000	33.6%
1985	669,000	2,473,000	27.0%
1990	554,000	2,873,000	19.3%
1995	572,000	3,379,000	16.9%
1998	629,000	3,599,000	17.5%

SOURCE: National Council of Welfare, *Poverty Profile 1998* (Ottawa, 2001), 14.

province except Saskatchewan in the period to 2000.

Furthermore, Canada's achievement ranks poorly when compared with that of most other industrialized countries. Table 3.11 shows that Canada does not do well in keeping children out of poverty, being similar to the United Kingdom and the United States but far below the achievements of most European countries.

Aboriginal Peoples

Detailed data on the extent of poverty among Aboriginal peoples are difficult to obtain.

Income data on Aboriginal peoples on reserve are not gathered by Statistics Canada as part of its annual income survey, leading to a major understatement on the extent of poverty in Canada as a whole. *The Canadian Fact Book on Poverty 2000* provides a comparison of poverty data between Aboriginal and non-Aboriginal people by province, as shown in Table 3.12. However, even this comparison may understate the full extent of Aboriginal poverty as it is based on the 1996 census, which was probably not completed by a disproportionate number of the poorest Aboriginal people, both on reserve and homeless in urban areas.

Table 3.9 Families with Children under 18 Living in Poverty, 1980–1998

Year	Poor Couples, under 65 with children	All couples under 65 with children	Poverty Rate	Poor Single Parent Mothers under 65	All Single Parent Mothers under 65	Poverty Rate
1980	286,000	3,040,000	9.4%	183,000	318,000	57.7%
1985	334,000	2,950,000	11.3%	227,000	362,000	62.5%
1990	285,000	2,973,000	9.6%	255,000	421,000	60.6%
1995	394,000	3,134,000	12.6%	323,000	565,000	57.2%
1998	319,000	3,062,000	10.4%	314,000	580,000	54.2%

SOURCE: National Council of Welfare, *Poverty Profile 1998,* 18–19.

Table 3.10 Children in Poverty by Province, 1997, Rate and Per Cent Change Since 1989

Province	Number of Poor Children	Poverty Rate	Rank Order	% change since 1989
Newfoundland	30,000	22.8%	10	0
Prince Edward Island	5,000	14.9%	1	0
Nova Scotia	48,000	22.4%	9	41%
New Brunswick	34,000	20.1%	6	10%
Quebec	334,000	20.5%	7	30%
Ontario	538,000	19.9%	5	118%
Manitoba	60,000	22.1%	8	11%
Saskatchewan	50,000	19.5%	3	-8%
Alberta	117,000	16.0%	2	2%
British Columbia	174,000	19.6%	4	78%

SOURCE: Canadian Council on Social Development, *Report Card on Child Poverty in Canada 1989–1999* (Ottawa, 2000).

Visible Minority Status

As for Aboriginal peoples, data on the extent of poverty among visible minorities is not readily obtained because the Statistics Canada income survey does not record minority status data. The data that do exist have been gathered through the 1996 census and show poverty rates for visible minorities that are less severe than those shown for Aboriginal people (see Table 3.13) but substantially higher than for the non-visible minority and non-Aboriginal population.

Table 3.11 Poverty Rates among Children, Luxembourg Income Study, 1979–1999

Country	1979–83	1984–7	1988–93	1994–9	Rank Order 1994–9
Australia	14.0%	13.1%	14.0%	14.1%	8
Belgium	n.a.	3.4%	3.1%	3.8%	4
Canada	13.9%	13.6%	13.5%	13.9%	7
Finland	n.a.	2.9%	2.5%	3.2%	3
France	6.3%	6.5%	7.5%	5.6%	5
Germany	3.2%	6.4%	4.4%	8.7%	6
Italy	n.a.	10.8%	9.6%	19.5%	10
Netherlands	2.5%	3.6%	4.1%	n.a.	n/a
Norway	3.8%	3.8%	2.7%	2.7%	1
Sweden	3.9%	3.0%	2.7%	2.7%	1
United Kingdom	8.5%	9.9%	16.7%	16.2%	9
United States	18.5%	22.9%	21.5%	22.7%	11

SOURCE: Ross, *Canadian Fact Book on Poverty*, 144.

Table 3.12 Poverty Rates among Aboriginal and Non-Aboriginal Peoples, by Province, 1995

Province	Aboriginal Poverty Rate	Non-Aboriginal Poverty Rate
Newfoundland	27.5%	21.2%
Prince Edward Island	30.0%	15.2%
Nova Scotia	32.1%	18.7%
New Brunswick	42.7%	18.9%
Quebec	37.0%	23.3%
Ontario	36.2%	17.5%
Manitoba	52.2%	18.1%
Saskatchewan	53.1%	15.5%
Alberta	43.9%	17.5%
British Columbia	42.1%	19.0%
Canada	43.4%	19.3%

SOURCE: Ross, *Canadian Fact Book on Poverty*, 75.

Disability

Again, data on the incomes of people with disabilities are only available from the census.

Using a definition that defined disability as a long-term condition that limits activity at home, at work, at school, or in other activities, the census found that 2.8 million Canadians, or

Table 3.13 Poverty Rate by Visible Minority Status, by Province, 1995

Province	Visible Minority Status, Poverty Rate	Poverty Rate, All Other Groups
Newfoundland	24.3%	21.4%
Prince Edward Island	28.0%	15.1%
Nova Scotia	37.9%	18.1%
New Brunswick	34.2%	18.9%
Quebec	52.2%	21.5%
Ontario	34.3%	14.6%
Manitoba	31.3%	19.7%
Saskatchewan	29.9%	18.0%
Alberta	31.9%	16.9%
British Columbia	35.9%	17.6%
Canada	35.9%	17.6%

NOTE: Under the Employment Equity Act, members of visible minorities are those, other than Aboriginal persons, who are non-Caucasian in race or non-white in colour. Statistics Canada, *Census Definitions* (Ottawa, 2002).
SOURCE: Ross, *Canadian Fact Book on Poverty,* 77.

Table 3.14 Poverty Rates by Disability Status, by Province, 1995

Province	Disability Status, Poverty Rate	Non-Disability Status, Poverty Rate
Newfoundland	30.3%	20.5%
Prince Edward Island	26.1%	13.9%
Nova Scotia	28.7%	17.2%
New Brunswick	31.5%	17.3%
Quebec	41.2%	22.0%
Ontario	27.3%	16.5%
Manitoba	32.6%	19.1%
Saskatchewan	26.9%	17.3%
Alberta	29.3%	17.2%
British Columbia	29.8%	18.4%
Canada	30.8%	18.4%

SOURCE: Ross, *Canadian Fact Book on Poverty,* 76.

about 10 per cent of the population, had a disability. The overall poverty rate for persons with disabilities was 30.8 per cent, with women (33.1 per cent) having a higher rate than men (28.2 per cent). Poverty rates for persons with disability by province are shown in Table 3.14.

Table 3.15 Poverty Rates (Post-Tax Income) by Province, 1999

Province	Families		Individuals		All Persons	
	Number	Poverty Rate %	Number	Poverty Rate %	Number of Poor Persons	Poverty Rate %
Newfoundland	17,000	10.9	22,000	39.3	77,000	14.2
Prince Edward Island	2,000	6.0	5,000	26.5	11,000	8.4
Nova Scotia	24,000	9.4	40,000	30.0	113,000	12.2
New Brunswick	19,000	8.5	21,000	24.0	76,000	10.1
Quebec	216,000	10.4	433,000	36.7	1,084,000	14.7
Ontario	224,000	7.0	384,000	26.6	1,119,000	9.6
Manitoba	30,000	10.0	48,000	20.0	151,000	13.8
Saskatchewan	18,000	6.7	35,000	22.8	91,000	9.3
Alberta	61,000	7.6	128,000	29.4	334,000	11.4
British Columbia	110,000	10.2	163,000	26.8	513,000	13.1
Canada	723,000	8.6	1,280,000	29.0	3,569,000	11.8

SOURCE: National Council of Welfare, *Poverty Profile 1999* (Ottawa, 2002), Table 2.24.

Table 3.16 Poverty Rates for Selected Cities, 1995

City	Poverty Rate	City	Poverty Rate
Canada, All Persons	17.5%		
St John's	23.5%	Windsor	19.6%
Halifax	24.6%	Winnipeg	24.3%
Saint John	27.1%	Saskatoon	22.8%
Quebec City	34.1%	Regina	18.3%
Montreal	41.2%	Edmonton	26.0%
Ottawa	28.3%	Calgary	20.6%
Toronto	27.6%	Vancouver	31.0%
Hamilton	27.6%	Victoria	25.1%

SOURCE: Ross, *Canadian Fact Book on Poverty*, 78.

Location

Table 3.15, which indicates poverty by province in 1999, shows that the proportion of people in poverty is more similar in the different provinces than one might expect. However, poverty is concentrated in inner-city areas, with all major central city areas having poverty rates higher than the overall average rate, as shown in Table 3.16.

Poverty and Social Welfare Income Redistribution Programs

The role of Canada's social welfare income distribution programs in combatting poverty can best be seen by looking at their effectiveness in meeting the needs of seven social groups:

- seniors
- employable adults
- disabled adults
- children and families
- students
- the poor
- on-reserve Aboriginal peoples.

The programs are organized in two tiers. The upper tier consists of programs available as social rights. They are primarily directed to one or other of the first five groups and they are made available as a grant, social insurance, government compensation plan, loan, or tax benefit. The lower tier consists of the provincial and Indian Affairs social assistance and related programs, focused on the poor, that provide benefits on a discretionary basis following an individually administered needs test. Programs in the upper tier are *institutional* programs, as access to them is considered to be a normal part of life in Canadian society. Programs in the second tier are *residual*,[5] as access to them is based on need alone and presumes that the recipients have failed in some way to look after themselves. There is greater stigma associated with the lower tier.

Seniors

The needs of seniors are addressed by five programs:

- Old Age Security
- Old Age Security Guaranteed Income Supplement
- Canada and Quebec Pension Plans
- provincial supplementary benefits
- retirement savings provisions of the Income Tax Act.

1. *Old Age Security.* Old Age Security was introduced by the federal government in 1952. The elderly were defined initially as persons over 70; subsequently, the age level for receipt of benefit was lowered to 65. The program is

Table 3.17 Federal Old Age Security and Guaranteed Income Supplement Benefits, Compared to Poverty Lines, 1974, 1985, 1995, and 2001

		1974	1985	1995	2001
Single Person	Poverty Line	2,780	8,850	13,300	18,371
	OAS/GIS	2,247	7,356	10,296	11,264
	% poverty line	81%	83%	77%	61%
Couple	Poverty Line	4,620	14,750	22,190	22,964
	OAS/GIS	4,288	11,298	16,680	18,847
	% poverty line	92%	76%	75%	82%

NOTE: For years to 1995, Senate Committee poverty lines have been used, but for 2001 the Statistics Canada LICO for cities over 500,000 has been used as updated Senate Committee values are no longer available.

administered by Human Resources Canada. The level of benefit is set at $442/month (October 2001). The value of benefit is adjusted to inflation from a base figure of $100/month, established in 1973.

Old Age Security covers all Canadians. Immigrants require a minimum 10 years' residence in Canada to qualify for any benefits and 35 years of residence to obtain a full Old Age Security payment. Old Age Security income is taxable and is 'clawed back' from persons with annual income (2001) over $55,309.

The number of seniors eligible for Old Age Security was 700,000 in 1952 when the plan started. It rose to 1.5 million by 1970 and in 1995 exceeded 3 million. By the year 2005 it will be 5 million. Because of the growth in the number of recipients the amount paid has also increased, from $2 billion (in constant 1993 dollars) in 1952, to $8 billion in 1974, and to $18 billion in 2000.[6]

2. *Old Age Security Guaranteed Income Supplement and Spouse's Allowance.* The Guaranteed Income Supplement program was introduced by the federal government in 1966 as part of a comprehensive series of reforms affecting the income security of the elderly. The reforms included changes in the age of eligibility and the benefit of Old Age Security, and the introduction of the Canada Pension Plan. The total effect of these changes was intended to protect all elderly persons from poverty. A Spouse's Allowance was added in 1976 to provide support to persons between 60 and 65 who are married to people 65 and older.

Benefit levels under GIS vary with the recipient's income. The maximum benefit (October 2001), paid to those with no income other than Old Age Security, is $526/month for single persons and $342/month for each member of a couple. The value of the benefits is adjusted automatically to offset inflation. Benefits are not subject to tax but additional income results in GIS payments being reduced by 50¢ for each $1 received. Assets are treated only to the extent that they produce income.

For the single person who is entirely dependent on Old Age Security and GIS the maximum annual amount is $11,624; for a couple the total amount is $18,847. The value of these benefits in relation to poverty lines is seen in Table 3.17, which shows that, by themselves, they are not adequate to protect seniors from poverty, and that the proportion of poverty-line income they cover has been falling. However, because many seniors have other sources of income, including the Canada Pension Plan, the number of GIS beneficiaries (1.2 million) and the amount paid, in constant 1993 dollars ($1.3 billion), have increased only slightly since the program was introduced. The number of beneficiaries of the Spouse's Allowance program (100,000) and payments ($400 million) have also remained constant in recent years because of improved private and CPP/QPP pensions.

3. *The Canada Pension Plan and Quebec Pension Plan (CPP/QPP).* The Canada Pension Plan and the associated Quebec Pension Plan were introduced in 1965. The two plans are compatible with respect to contributions and benefits. The Canada Pension Plan is administered by Human Resources Canada and the Quebec Pension Plan by the government of Quebec. Both are social insurance measures covering several types of long-term contingency. They are most widely known for their retirement pension provisions but also provide benefits at death, widowhood (including orphan's benefit), and severe, prolonged disability. Full retirement benefits are payable at age 65, with a reduced benefit available from age 60. Benefit levels are adjusted to account for inflation.

Benefit levels under the CPP/QPP are based on contribution level (for all categories of benefit) and on the number of years in which contributions were paid (for disability and retirement benefits). Contributions are based on earnings. The contributor originally paid 2.5 per cent of annual earnings and the employer pays a similar amount. This level of contribution was not adequate to cover the benefits that were paid and the total contribution level of contributor and employer was raised to 5.85 per cent in 1998 and increases annually to 9.9 per cent in 2004. The ceiling (2001) on earnings for contribution purposes is $38,300. For the person who has made maximum contributions since the plan's introduction and who retired in 2001, the retirement pension was $775/month. Retirement pensions are subject to tax, with the first $1,000 being exempt. For nearly all couples the combination of full CPP/QPP benefits with other government programs becomes sufficient to ensure that their total income exceeds poverty lines.

CPP/QPP cover all employed (including self-employed) persons, but the long-term unemployed and the unemployable are excluded. The CPP recognizes women who leave the workforce to care for children six years of age and under by treating child-care years as 'dropout' years, reducing the total years needed to obtain maximum benefits. Where there is separation or divorce, benefit entitlements are 'split'.

4. *Provincial supplementary benefits.* A number of provinces supplement these federal payments with a variety of programs. Some of these are based on need, some are tied to housing costs, while others cover some health-care costs, such as drug prescriptions, not covered by health insurance on a universal basis for all seniors. The number and variation of these programs are such that the full detail cannot be provided here. The result for seniors is an additional level of protection from poverty.

5. *Retirement savings provisions of the Income Tax Act.* Total contributions and benefits under the Canada/Quebec Pension Plans have been kept low on the assumption that private and occupational plans will provide a third level of pension benefit for Canadians. Government support for the third level of pension benefits is provided by Registered Retirement Savings Plan (RRSP) deductions and Registered Pension Plan (RPP) deductions. The assumption is that this third level will close the gap between public plans that provide a poverty-line level of income

and the level of retirement income necessary to maintain the standard of living enjoyed during working years.

The amounts that can be contributed as tax deductions to RRSPs and RPPs were raised substantially beginning in 1991 and are now 18 per cent of income to a maximum of $13,500. To make this full payment the taxpayer needs a taxable income of $75,000. Furthermore, interest on RRSP and RPP savings accumulates free of tax. Eventually, tax is payable on these funds, but not until they are withdrawn. It is difficult to know what level of pension would be payable on the basis of the contributions now being made as this will vary with years of contribution and level of income. However, the value of the deductions to taxpayers (the tax expenditure by federal and provincial governments) is substantial—$21 billion in 1999–2000.

The tax deductions claimed rise with the taxpayer's income for three reasons. First, the amount that can be deducted rises with income; second, Registered Pension Plans are only available from major employers and governments, who also offer better wages; third, low-income earners do not have the cash to make even those contributions for which they are eligible. As a result, RRSPs and RPPs are a tax-supported benefit plan that provides its greatest benefits to upper-income earners.

Seniors: Conclusions

Programs for seniors were reviewed during the 1990s as part of the federal government's social security review. The changes made did not alter the basic role of the different programs. A proposed change that would have based the clawback of OAS on household rather than individual income was introduced, but this proposal was withdrawn due to a combination of senior citizen opposition and improvement in the government's financial situation. The largest change was the increase in contribution levels for the Canada/Quebec Pension Plans. The change was needed to ensure the continued financial viability of the plans. Prior to the decision to raise contribution rates to the 9.9 per cent level, estimates of the amount needed to ensure financial viability had been higher, one estimate putting it at between 13.7 and 16 per cent.[7] The decision to go to the 9.9 per cent level protects the plans for the next few years but will probably need to be re-evaluated. Funding pensions through contributions also has the effects of increasing the tax burden on lower-income earners and making it more expensive for employers to hire them. Both effects make it more difficult to keep the current generation of wage-earners out of poverty.

Employable Adults

The needs of employable (but temporarily unemployed) workers are met by three programs:

- Employment Insurance (including training provisions)
- resource industry adjustment programs
- provincial programs for employable adults.

1. *Employment Insurance.* Employment Insurance (EI), originally called Unemployment Insurance (UI), was introduced in 1940 and has been revised several times. A major revision of the Act in 1970 expanded UI to all wage- and salary-earners, increased benefit levels, increased the period for which benefit could be obtained, decreased the minimum period of employment needed to qualify a wage-earner for benefit, and included maternity and sickness benefits for the first time.[8] EI is administered by Human Resources Canada. Payments to the unemployed are provided through the Unemployment Insurance Account, which receives revenue from the contributions of wage- and salary-earners and from employers. Prior to 1990 there was also a contribution from the federal treasury. This was then eliminated and the account is now expected to balance over the business cycle. As a result, contributions from employers and employees rose following the

1991–2 recession to cover increased benefit payments. More recently they have been decreased as the fund accumulated a surplus with higher levels of employment in the late 1990s. The Unemployment Insurance Act was revised and renamed the Employment Insurance Act in 1995.

Benefit levels from EI are based on contributions. Employees contribute 2.25 per cent of earnings to an annual amount of $1,330 (2000). Employers provide 3.15 per cent of earnings through a payroll tax. Maximum benefits (as of October 2001) are paid to a person who has worked a minimum number of qualifying hours scaled to the level of his/her contributions. The minimum number of qualifying hours varies with the regional unemployment rate. Where the regional unemployment rate is under 6 per cent, 700 hours of work (approximately 20 weeks of full-time work) are needed to qualify for benefits. Where the unemployment rate exceeds 13 per cent, 420 hours of work (approximately 14 weeks) are required to qualify. There are also special qualification provisions for Fishing Benefits.

The maximum benefit payable is $413/week (October 2001) and the maximum time that benefits can be received varies from 36 weeks in areas where the unemployment rate is less than 6 per cent to 45 weeks in areas where it exceeds 10 per cent. The benefit period for sickness and maternity coverage is 15 weeks. The annual income at the maximum benefit rate is $21,476/year or approximately the amount needed to bring a wage-earner with one dependant to the poverty line. This annual income is proportionately lower than that which used to be provided. For example, in 1974, maximum benefits were adequate to bring a wage-earner with two dependants to the poverty line.

Unemployment Insurance was originally designed with the experience of the 1930s and 1940s and with the industrial business cycle in mind. It assumed that there would be periodic increases and decreases in employment and unemployment as the economy went from periods of expansion to periods of pause or contraction. It also assumed that the individual worker was powerless to do anything about these changes. As a consequence it was thought that the costs, in lost income to workers, should be shared among all workers and employers. This view of Unemployment Insurance did not take account of seasonal work, different unemployment patterns in different industries, structural problems, as when an industry disappears, or decisions by applicants to tailor their behaviour so as to maximize benefits. The reforms undertaken in 1995 when EI was introduced were designed to deal with these perceived problems.

Since 1989 there has been some use of EI funds to support worker retraining, particularly in areas where there are structural employment problems. To the employees of industries considered to be in permanent decline, EI offers a period of benefits but it does not in any way address the problem as to where recipients will work when benefits expire. The concern with structural adjustment and long-term employment problems is not a new one. As early as the 1960s there was concern that workers were not suitably trained for the jobs that an increasingly automated and technical society provided. The Department of Manpower and Immigration was created in 1965 to respond to this perceived problem. The department's brief to the Senate Committee on Poverty stated:

> The primary goal of the Department is to contribute to the attainment of economic and social goals for Canada by optimizing the use, quality, and mobility of all manpower resources available to the country. Thus the policies and programs of the Department are essentially economic in character.[9]

The programs developed from this mandate served to screen the most qualified and educable workers, provide them with job opportunities and/or employment, and hence generally aid the operation of the labour market. These are not unimportant functions but they inevitably constitute an institutional creaming function that tends to leave unserved those who are least competitive. There is also evidence that even individuals who are singled out for employment (and/or training) are not necessarily the recipients of any increase in income. André Reynauld, chairman of the Economic Council of Canada, explained in 1973 why an increase in the supply of skilled workers does not lead to any change in the income distribution:

> Put simply, the explanation is that wages and salaries are fixed for given tasks, and the best workers get the jobs. Workers thus compete for *jobs*, not wages. From the point of view of the employer, the best workers are those who can be trained for the job at the minimum cost. If, for example, the supply of university graduates increases, they simply displace non-university graduates with no impact on the distribution of incomes.[10]

This view of the operation of the government training programs suggests that they provide a subsidy to employers and industry and often duplicate training functions that individuals or industry would perform themselves. Opinion on the effectiveness of such expenditures and on the merit generally of a major government role in training remains divided. Courchene makes the argument for a major role: 'Training and skills development is not a panacea, but it is surely a critical part . . . of making the transition from a resource-based mentality to a human-capital or knowledge-based mentality.'[11]

The case against such a role is based on the reality that the people who are unemployed tend to be older or unskilled and the results of training have not been substantial enough to warrant the cost. Lazar, another labour economist, concludes his argument:

> Putting more money into training when the economy is operating with a high degree of

slack will prove ineffective. . . . Bad jobs should be attacked directly, through full employment and industrial policies. Using UI funds to expand training programs will do little, if anything, to correct the structural defect of bad jobs. Moreover, training will do little to transform unstable workers into stable ones.[12]

The Canadian Labour Congress has also opposed the use of EI funds for training, seeing this as a diversion of dollars that should be available to support incomes through EI benefits.

2. *Resource industry adjustment programs*. In addition to EI benefits, workers in devastated regions have, from time to time, received benefits where there are massive losses of employment. The payments to farmers who were not able to sell grain and to Atlantic fishery workers when the groundfishery was closed in 1993 are examples. These programs have faced the same problems that accompany the EI role in structural adjustment. It has been difficult or impossible to design a program that provides for an effective adjustment. A cushion can be provided that mitigates and delays the full income loss, but this is far less than the programs have promised.

3. *Provincial programs for employable adults*. These programs form part of the second tier of redistributive programs and are discussed later in the chapter. They are mentioned here as a reminder that the full response to employment problems is fractured between the federal and provincial governments and between the EI and social assistance programs. Any change in one affects the other. Any reduction in benefits through EI increases the costs of provincial social assistance programs. Any training program that operates for the exclusive benefit of EI claimants does so at the expense of making it harder for those on social assistance to compete for the same jobs.

Employment Programs: Conclusions

The changes made in UI/EI through the 1990s social security review were substantial. The program was changed from having major social objectives to one in which economic considerations were much more prominent. However, the changes that were implemented were substantially less than those that conservative economists had proposed. These would have split the program into two separate programs, one for people who experience temporary, infrequent unemployment, and a second, lower benefit program with income testing and training requirements for those who were frequent users.[13] Some proposals would have gone further and merged UI/EI with provincial social assistance programs. The reintroduction of 'Fishing Benefits' in the context of the federal election (2000) also showed that the Liberal government was prepared to recognize uses of the plan that had strong electoral support, whether or not they satisfied economic criteria. The greater emphasis on economic considerations, and the resulting restrictions on benefits, did result in an increase in use of provincial social assistance programs, and with it, an increase in poverty for unemployed individuals and families.

Persons with Disabilities

Canada has no overall framework for social justice for persons with disabilities and, unlike for seniors or the unemployed, has never devoted resources to build one. Instead, four unco-ordinated programs may, but more often do not, provide income security to persons with disabilities. The programs are:

- Workers' Compensation
- Canada/Quebec Pension Plans
- tax benefits for disabled persons
- provincial social assistance programs for unemployable people.

1. *Workers' Compensation*. Workers' Compensation programs are typically administered by semi-independent commissions reporting to a provincial Minister of Labour. Levels of benefit

under Workers' Compensation vary by province. A typical level of benefit is 75 per cent of pre-tax salary up to a maximum. The maximum level of benefit varies, with an average of $32,000/year (1995). This could bring a family of four to the poverty line, but many beneficiaries do not obtain maximum benefits. Benefits for widows and children are less adequate and, although these are now aided by the Canada Pension Plan, there are no provisions for integrating and co-ordinating the two. Unlike most other social benefits, Workers' Compensation payments are not taxed. As a result, in some cases, workers are better off receiving compensation than working.

Coverage under Workers' Compensation is required of all employers beyond a minimum size. But there are gaps in coverage. The self-employed represent one such gap. In addition, there are gaps at the individual level. The worker who undertakes duties not usually in his or her line of work, such as the office worker who assists with moving heavy equipment, may lose protection if injured in such an instance. The process of determining eligibility, particularly in cases where the results of injury are not immediately apparent, can be lengthy and contentious. Benefits can be refused to the recipient who rejects medical advice and, say, refuses to take treatment that could lead to a return to employment. Benefits are also lost, or reduced, when the person is considered to be fit for work of some sort, whether or not there is actual work available. Enforcement of these conditions has become much more difficult as unemployment has become more prevalent. It has also become more difficult as the process of establishing and maintaining eligibility has become the subject of litigation between claimants and Workers' Compensation authorities.

A basic problem of Workers' Compensation as a program for disabled persons is that it only recognizes disability that is the result of employment conditions. Most persons with disabilities are not covered.

2. *Canada/Quebec Pension Plan benefits.* The CPP/QPP provides a maximum benefit of $935/month with an additional $179/month for each dependent child. To qualify for disability payments the recipient must satisfy contribution requirements and be permanently and completely disabled. Benefits are lost if the person returns to work. Benefits are taxable but can be held at the same time as Workers' Compensation payments for the same disability.

As with Workers' Compensation, a basic problem of the CPP/QPP provisions for disability is the eligibility requirement. Persons who have never been employed, or whose work has led to few contributions, have no means of establishing the contribution record necessary to obtain benefits. A further problem is the outdated notion of disability, which does not recognize the contribution that persons with disabilities can make. Receiving benefits requires a withdrawal from the labour force rather than integration into it.

3. *Tax benefits for disabled persons.* The Income Tax Act permits persons with disabilities to claim a tax credit of $4,293 (2000) and medical care, including attendant allowance costs, within prescribed limits. These allowances provide some recognition of the costs of disability for persons with taxable income.

4. *Provincial social assistance programs for unemployable people.* These programs form part of the second tier of redistributive income programs. All needs not met by Workers' Compensation and the disability provisions of CPP/QPP affect the need for and the costs of provincial social assistance.

Persons with Disabilities: Conclusion

Proposals for persons with disabilities did not form a prominent part of the mid-1990s social security review. This is partly because their relationship to fiscal issues was slight and partly because equity issues were not prominent in the review. This has left several issues that need to be dealt with to ensure that Canada has more equitable programming for persons with

Box 3.1 Disability in the Labour Force: Barriers and Solutions

. . . In October 1998, the federal government released *In Unison: A Canadian Approach to Disability Issues,* a vision paper intended as a blueprint for promoting the full citizenship and full participation of Canadians with disabilities into all aspects of society. *In Unison* relies on three main building blocks: disability supports, employment, and income.

Even before *In Unison* identified employment as one of the building blocks of full citizenship, persons with disabilities understood its importance in their lives. With one of the lowest rates of participation in the labour force and one of the highest rates of poverty in Canada, women with disabilities are well aware of the advantages of having employment. The research presented here shows that much more work is needed in order to reach the goals outlined by the *In Unison* document.

poverty rate stood at 45.4 per cent—nearly five times higher. Women with disabilities who worked part-time for a full year had a poverty rate of 21.1 per cent, while those who worked either part-time or full-time but for less than 49 weeks had a poverty rate of 28.4 per cent.

Similar patterns of correlation between poverty rates and employment activity are found among women without disabilities and men with or without disabilities. Overall, women in Canada with disabilities experience higher rates of poverty than do women without disabilities, however, the gap between the two groups narrows considerably when they have similar work patterns. While employment alone will not put women with disabilities on an equal footing with either men with disabilities or women without disabilities, these findings suggest that it would go a long way towards improving their overall economic situation.

Disability is a strong indicator of poverty

The connection between disability and poverty is clear. In 1995, 36.2 per cent of women aged 15 to 64 with disabilities in Canada were poor, compared to 18.5 per cent of women without disabilities. In Ontario, the poverty rates were slightly lower: women with disabilities had a poverty rate of 31.6 per cent, compared to 16.4 per cent for women without disabilities. A similar pattern was observed among men. In 1996, the national poverty rate for men with disabilities was 34.1 per cent, compared to 15.6 per cent for men without disabilities. Again, men in Ontario fared slightly better, with respective poverty rates of 29.7 and 13. 6 per cent.

Labour force activity and poverty

As would be expected, there is an enormous difference in poverty rates between women with disabilities who are not employed at all and those who have full-time full-year employment. . . . [T]he poverty rate in 1995 for women with disabilities who were employed full-time full-year in Canada was 10.2 per cent; among Canadian women with disabilities who were not employed at all, the

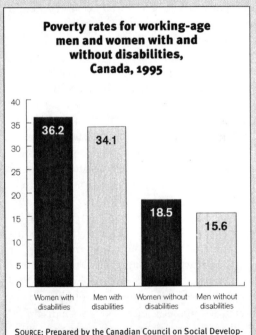

Poverty rates for working-age men and women with and without disabilities, Canada, 1995

Women with disabilities: 36.2
Men with disabilities: 34.1
Women without disabilities: 18.5
Men without disabilities: 15.6

SOURCE: Prepared by the Canadian Council on Social Development using data from Statistics Canada's 1996 Census.

SOURCE: Gail Fawcett, 'Disability in the Labour Force: Barriers and Solutions', Canadian Council on Social Development, *Perception* (Dec. 1999): 7.

disabilities. Proposals that need consideration include those put forward by the Council of Canadians with Disabilities and the Roeher Institute.

The Council of Canadians with Disabilities has argued against programs that treat people differently because of the cause of disability. This group calls for:

> integrated systems, not separate systems. . . . If we are designing new programs in Canada, let's ensure within the design access for all people within the program, rather than design parallel streams, which have kept people with disabilities separate from their neighbours and the mainstream of Canadian society.[14]

Adopting this proposal would lead to the introduction of a new federal/provincial program structure that would recognize disability, rather than separate those with disability into different categories depending on whether the cause of disability was a workplace accident, took place after a CPP/QPP contribution record had been established, or met neither of these criteria.

The Roeher Institute has proposed the establishment of a 'Canadian Disability Resource Program'.[15] The purpose of such a program would be to offset the costs of disability and to ensure access to disability-related supports for all disabled persons, regardless of the cause of their disability. The introduction of such a program would lead to treating the costs of disability equally for all Canadians regardless of their income. This would be much more equitable than the current situation in which, for most persons with disability, poverty is required to obtain benefits. Separating the costs of disability from other living costs could also bring the relationship between persons with disability and all other social programs into the mainstream. At present, many programs maintain separate provisions for persons with disability to ensure access.

In 1998 the federal and provincial governments took the first step towards recognizing the inadequacy of Canadian policies for persons with disability in a paper entitled *In Unison: A Canadian Approach to Disability Issues*,[16] but action to deal with the inadequacies has not followed (see Box 3.1).

Children and Families

Since the termination of Family Allowance payments in 1992, all child and family benefits are provided through the tax system. They are:

- the Child Tax Benefit and associated provincial programs
- the GST credit
- the child-care allowance
- the child and married exemptions.

1. *The Child Tax Benefit and associated provincial programs.* The Child Tax Benefit was introduced in 1992 following the ending of the Family Allowance and the child tax credit. The program has been revised many times, most recently in 1997 when the present two provisions, the 'Basic' and 'Supplement', were introduced. In addition, many provinces have similar programs of their own, which in some cases are administered along with the federal program. Table 3.18 lists the current programs. Four features of these programs need to be noted.

- *The level of benefits.* The Statistics Canada LICOs estimate the cost of keeping a first child out of poverty is $5,000–$6,000/year depending on location and the cost of subsequent children is $3,500–$4,000/year per child. In terms of monthly payments this means a payment between $300 and $500 per month per child. Judged by this standard the amounts of benefits provided are totally inadequate to the task of keeping Canadian children out of poverty.
- *The income levels for eligibility.* These are universally low, with most benefits being discontinued before family income reaches the LICO poverty lines. As a result these

benefits have no marginal effect on keeping families close to the poverty line above it.

- *Different benefits for working parents.* These minor variations are supposed to offset some of the costs of employment for low-income parents, but given the ludicrously small amounts it is hard to see how they would have this effect.
- *Full deduction from provincial social assistance benefits.* Without exception, these payments are deducted from the amounts that parents are eligible to receive from provincial social assistance programs. The result is that for all recipients of provincial social assistance, there is no net benefit from these programs.

2. *The GST credit.* The GST credit is available to low-income individuals and couples as well as to families with children. The value of the GST credit is $207/year for the first two members of a household and increases by

$109/year for each additional child. Benefits begin to be reduced when family income exceeds $26,991/year.

3. *The married and equivalent-to-spouse personal exemptions.* A federal tax credit of 17 per cent of $6,754 can be claimed for a non-working spouse or for the first child or other dependant living with a single person. The total value of this credit varies with the tax rate in each province but approximates $1,700/year. The exemption is not refundable.

4. *The child-care expense deduction.* This can be claimed on the basis of receipted child-care expenses up to $10,000/year for children with a disability, $7,000/year for children under the age of seven, and up to $4,000/year for children up to 14 years old. Because this benefit takes the form of a deduction from taxable income it has most value to upper-income earners.

These four measures, of which only the first two are targeted to the poor, constitute one of the weakest social policy responses to family

Table 3.18 Child Tax Benefits per Month

Name of Program	Earned Income Needed To Qualify	First Child	Second Child	Third or Subsequent Child	Income at which Benefit Reduction Starts
Canada Child Tax Benefit: Basic	0	93.08	93.08	99.58	$32,000
Canada Child tax Benefit: Supplement	0	104.58	87.91	81.66	$21,744
Alberta Family Employment Tax Credit	$3,500	41.66	41.66	0	$25,000
British Columbia Family Bonus	0	10.25	26.00	31.91	$20,500
British Columbia Earned Income Benefit	$3,500	50.41	33.75	27.50	$20,921
New Brunswick Child Tax Benefit	0	20.83	20.83	20.83	$20,000
New Brunswick Working Income Supplement	$3,750	20.83	20.83	20.83	$16,744
Newfoundland Child Benefit	0	17.00	26.00	28.00–30.00	$16,744
Northwest Territories Child Benefit	0	27.50	27.50	27.50	$20,921
Northwest Territories Workers' Supplement	$3,750	22.91	29.16	29.16	$20,921
Nova Scotia Child Benefit	0	37.00	53.73	60.00	$16,000
Saskatchewan Child Benefit	0	20.83	37.83	43.83	$15,921
Yukon Child Benefit	0	25.00	25.00	25.00	$16,700

need that can be found in Western developed countries (the United States has no program at all). In most countries, a family allowance or its equivalent is a cornerstone of the redistributive system, providing a major fraction of the total income of poorer families.[17]

Children and Families: Conclusions

Program changes made during the 1990s provided purely token recognition that one in five children lives in a poor family (for single-parent families headed by the mother the ratio is two in three). In 1989 the House of Commons passed a resolution seeking 'to achieve the goal of eliminating poverty among Canadian children by the year 2000'.[18] Strong arguments for better support to poor families with children were made by such bodies as the Caledon Institute[19] and the National Council of Welfare, and some conservative labour market economists also argued for improvements in this area. The support from the conservatives was based on (1) a recognition that child poverty undercuts the education and labour force readiness of the next generation of workers,[20] and (2) the fact that a stronger program of child benefits, along with other measures, would reduce the disincentives to leave 'the welfare trap'.[21] However, the response of the Canadian federal and provincial governments to achieve the commitment made by Parliament in 1989 fell far short of what was needed. One social policy analyst, Bridget Kitchen, concluded that:

> Child poverty has become a mainstream issue. It has been put on the political agenda. Everybody is against child poverty. The idea of national [and provincial] child benefits has political appeal. It allows them [governments] to appear to be doing something to help poor children, to reform their welfare programs and receive federal money. To actually improve the material circumstances of poor children, the federal government would have to spend billions of dollars more than it is currently doing. It would require the same type of serious fiscal

commitment that was given to fighting the deficit. . . . The amount that the federal government actually has allocated is not nearly enough, even as a down payment to seriously begin the fight against child poverty.[22]

Unfortunately for poor children, this inadequate approach has given the impression of change without the substance. Token programs have been introduced, while the number of children in poverty and the depth of their poverty increased during the 1990s (see Box 3.2).

Students

Students in post-secondary education are supported in their studies by the Canada Student Loan (CSL) program and related provincial programs. Post-secondary education is a provincial responsibility but the history of federal support for university and college education is a long one, including direct grants to universities (1951), cost-sharing agreements with the provinces (1966), and, from 1977 to 1996, block funding to the provinces under the Established Programs Financing Act (EPF). Direct student aid began as early as the post-war veterans' programs; the current form of the student loan program was introduced in 1964. The CSL and related provincial programs share many features with other redistributive social welfare programs. Living allowances are similar to the poverty levels defined by the Senate Committee and considerably higher than the survival levels defined by the Fraser Institute. In practice, because of payment caps and other limits within the student loan program, many students do not receive the full benefit of these allowances. Eligibility for the CSL program follows a test of income and assets.

Student loans are distinguished by the admission and diligent study requirements of the program. They are also loans rather than outright grants. However, the loans are interest-free and require no repayment during periods of study. In addition, loan remission is provided

Box 3.2 Report Card on Child Poverty in Canada, 1989–1999

'We should essentially establish the elimination of child poverty as a great national objective, not unlike what we did with the case of the deficit.' Minister of Finance Paul Martin, 19 Nov. 1998

Child Poverty – a social measure

Campaign 2000 believes that the discussion about child and family poverty in Canada focuses on how to equalize life chances for children. Poverty is a social measure, well beyond a tally for the basic survival needs of children and their families. Campaign 2000 and others reporting on poverty most frequently use the Statistics Canada Low Income Cut-Off (LICO). While Canada has no official poverty line, Statistics Canada has noted that the LICO [indicates that] . . . more than 55 per cent of [family] income [is spent] on food, clothing, and shelter. When surveyed Canadians regularly report that the LICO is reasonable.

In 1989, about 1 out of 7 children was poor, by 1997, 1 child in every 5 is poor. Since 1989, 463,000 more children became poor. Canadians find this situation unacceptable and have repeatedly expressed their desire for governments to take the leadership needed to improve life chances for children.

Child poverty grew to a record high in the 90s as Canada experienced a deep recession and high unemployment. As a result, the child poverty rate hit a high peak in 1993. As the decade ends the unemployment rate is decreasing and the child poverty rate has started to go down.

Poor families fall deeper into poverty during the 90s

While the rate of child poverty is beginning to go down, poor children are deeper in poverty. The average poor family lives $8,265 below the LICO. This is defined as the depth of poverty. The depth has steadily grown since 1989.

What has happened since 1989?

The number of –

Poor Children	↑ 49%
Children in families with income less than $29,000 (in constant 1997 dollars)	↑ 48%
Children in families experiencing long-term unemployment	↑ 16%
Children in working poor families	↑ 44%
Children in families receiving social assistance	↑ 51%
Poor children in 2-parent families	↑ 45%
Poor children in lone-parent families	↑ 61%

And, the rate of –

Low birth-weight babies (1989–96)	↑ 5%
Infant mortality	↓ 14%

Children in Canada Living in Poverty

Year	Number	Rate
1989	936,000	14.4%
1990	1,106,000	16.9%
1991	1,212,000	18.2%
1992	1,266,000	18.8%
1993	1,484,000	21.3%
1994	1,362,000	19.5%
1995	1,472,000	21%
1996	1,498,000	21.1%
1997	1,397,000	19.8%

Depth of Poverty in Canada 1989–1997

Low Income Cut-off

1989	1993	1996	1997
$7,428	$7,828	$8,231	$8,265

Average poverty gap (constant 1997 dollars)

SOURCE: Prepared by Canadian Council on Social Development using Statistics Canada's Survey of Consumer Finances, 1997 microdata files.

NOTES:
1. Poor children are those living in families whose total income before taxes falls below the Low Income Cut-off (LICO) as defined by Statistics Canada. Numbers in 1989 use 1996-base LICO and numbers for 1997 use 1992-base.
2. Child is defined as a person under the age of 18 living with parent(s) or guardian(s).
3. All measurements reflect change between 1989 and 1997 unless otherwise identified.
4. Statistics Canada data exclude those on First Nations reserves; those in the Yukon, Northwest Territories, and Nunavut; and children living in institutions.

Source: Canadian Council on Social Development, Campaign 2000, 'Report Card on Child Poverty in Canada 1989–1999'.

above specific levels of indebtedness and on performance conditions, including evidence of 'personal responsibility'. These features make student loans an alternative means of personal support to other redistributive programs. The cost, in interest forgiveness, loan remission, and bankruptcy relief of the Canada student loan program is estimated at $500 million per year.

There is concern that rising fee levels for post-secondary education may result in the student loan program becoming less and less adequate to cover the costs of post-secondary education. In addition, repayment problems are becoming more severe as students have greater difficulty finding employment and total amounts of indebtedness rise. It is less clear how these concerns will be addressed. If Canada were to adopt some other features of the social policy proposals that are being discussed, for example, the disability and child and family provisions, there would be an immediate and positive effect on the need for student loans and on the extent of indebtedness incurred by students. The preferable way to meet student need, and to ensure equity of access to higher education, is through the same equity measures that all Canadians deserve to have.

The Poor

The programs for the poor form the second tier of the income security system. For many Canadians they are the true safety net. Programs at this level operate on a definition of need. Any person or family whose need is not met in any other way is eligible to receive a payment. Thus, for practical purposes, programs at this level define the conditions of poverty under which many Canadians live. There are six programs at this level:

- provincial programs of social assistance
- social assistance for registered Indians
- work incentives and workfare
- veterans' allowances

- enforced dependencies
- food banks and soup kitchens.

The provincial programs of social assistance establish a policy framework within which the other programs at this level operate. Veterans' allowances provide relatively generous support but receipt is restricted to an aging and declining number of people. On-reserve assistance for Indians, since 1968, has been administered under policies that parallel the policies in the province in which the reserve is situated. Administration of on-reserve social assistance is by band and tribal council authorities, which are an important part of the structure of Aboriginal government.

Provincial Social Assistance
Social assistance is the contemporary inheritor of the 'poor law', 'relief', 'dole' tradition of income security. As such, it has a long history and no firm beginning point (unless we go back to the Elizabethan Poor Law of 1601).

Canadian social assistance programming was influenced from 1966 to 1996 by cost-sharing agreements between federal and provincial governments under the Canada Assistance Plan (CAP). The CAP brought a uniformity of approach to social assistance, which before then had consisted of a series of different programs.[23] The CAP permitted the federal government to enter into agreements with provincial governments whereby the provinces were reimbursed for 50 per cent of their social assistance expenditures. This relationship began to change in 1991 when a 5 per cent limit was placed on the annual amount that CAP payments could be increased to the provinces of Alberta, British Columbia, and Ontario. The effect of the limit was particularly severe on Ontario, which by 1995 was receiving an estimated $1.8 billion less than it would have under the 50 per cent formula. In the 1995 budget the federal government gave a one-year notice that as of 31 March 1996, the CAP would be withdrawn and replaced by the Canada Health and Social

Transfer (CHST) and the Human Resources Investment Fund (HRIF). The CHST provides for a federal financial transfer to the provinces for health, post-secondary education, and welfare costs. The amount to be transferred is established by a formula that includes tax points and fixed dollar amounts. However, the amount was reduced from that which would have been available under earlier federal-provincial cost-sharing arrangements by $2.5 billion in the 1996–7 and by $4.5 billion in 1997–8. The HRIF consolidated support for measures related to

Table 3.19 Welfare incomes by Province and Family Type, 1999

Province	Income Type	Single Unemployable	Disabled Person	Single Parent, One Child	Couple, Two Children
Newfoundland	Social Assistance ($)	1,102	6,940	11,316	12,064
	Total Income ($)	1,341	8,717	13,924	16,317
	% Poverty line	9%	59%	70%	56%
PEI	Social Assistance ($)	5,316	7,116	9,277	13,786
	Total Income ($)	5,515	8,442	11,670	17,799
	% Poverty Line	38%	59%	60%	62%
Nova Scotia	Social Assistance ($)	4,734	8,568	9,865	12,586
	Total Income ($)	4,573	8,809	12,558	16,633
	% Poverty Line	31%	60%	63%	57%
New Brunswick	Social Assistance ($)	3,168	6,696	8,772	9,828
	Total Income ($)	3,367	6,899	12,319	15,170
	% Poverty line	23%	47%	62%	52%
Quebec	Social Assistance ($)	6,024	8,712	8,341	10,243
	Total Income ($)	6,223	8,851	12,957	15,000
	% Poverty Line	37%	53%	57%	45%
Ontario	Social Assistance ($)	6,240	11,160	10,789	13,378
	Total Income ($)	6,822	11,759	13,704	18,130
	% Poverty Line	41%	70%	60%	55%
Manitoba	Social Assistance ($)	5,352	7,157	8,941	12,867
	Total Income ($)	5,551	7,061	11,375	17,919
	% Poverty Line	33%	49%	50%	50%
Saskatchewan	Social Assistance ($)	5,540	7,140	8,253	11,713
	Total Income ($)	5,739	8,384	11,877	17,590
	% Poverty Line	39%	57%	59%	60%
Alberta	Social Assistance ($)	4,746	6,384	9,019	13,774
	Total Income ($)	5,023	7,061	11,375	17,919
	% Poverty Line	30%	42%	50%	54%
British Columbia	Social Assistance ($)	6,046	9,252	10,548	12,396
	Total Income ($)	6,330	9,593	13,661	17,830
	% Poverty Line	38%	57%	60%	54%

SOURCE: National Council of Welfare, *Welfare Incomes 1999* (Ottawa, 2000), 14–15, 25–6.

employment and, here again, the total was less than that earlier available.

Each province sets its own level of social assistance payments and, in setting the level, takes account of other statutory benefits that recipients receive from either the provincial or federal government. This total level of statutory income is the true minimum income available to Canadians. Table 3.19 shows this variation and compares the total income level for each household type to the relevant poverty line.

The percentage of the poverty line achieved varies from a low of 9 per cent to a high of 70 per cent, with the typical payment being in the 50–60 per cent range. These levels show no progress towards the goal of reducing poverty (see Table 3.20). Indeed, the trend in the 1990s is towards lower percentages of the poverty line being covered by social assistance and associated payments.

Where higher levels of support for overcoming poverty have occasionally been achieved, for example, under the Bob Rae NDP government in

Ontario in the early 1990s, subsequent governments reduced the coverage and turned the clock back to the earlier percentages. The onset of conservative-type welfare reform was delayed in BC by an NDP government, but it came with the election in 2001 of the Campbell Liberal government.

Social assistance programs provide higher benefits for individuals who are considered unemployable. However, these benefits are limited to the individual affected and the amounts paid for other members of the household are calculated using the basic rates. For some groups of recipients it has also become more difficult to be considered unemployable. In particular, women with children at home have been increasingly defined as employable rather than unemployable,[24] thus reducing the benefits they receive and exerting pressure on them to join the labour force.

Social assistance programs often offer supplementary health benefits for recipients who are considered unemployable or who are in

Table 3.20 Minimum Social Security Payments and Poverty Lines, 1973, 1985, 1993, and 1999

	1973			1985			1993			1999		
	Payment	Poverty	%	Payment	Poverty	%	Payment	Poverty	%	Payment	Poverty	%
BC	3,840	5,740	67	8,561	14,750	58	13,345	20,945	64	13,661	22,768	60
Alberta	3,736	5,740	65	9,560	14,750	66	11,281	20,945	54	11,375	22,768	50
Sask.	3,696	5,740	64	9,504	14,750	65	12,093	18,398	66	11,877	20,130	59
Man.	3,744	5,740	65	8,025	14,750	61	11,386	20,945	54	11,375	22,768	50
Ontario	3,896	5,740	68	9,949	14,750	67	16,790	20,945	80	13,704	22,768	60
Quebec	3,242	5,740	56	8,801	14,750	60	12,607	20,945	60	12,475	22,768	53
NB	3,260	5,740	57	7,611	14,750	52	10,150	18,398	55	12,319	20,130	61
NS	3,192	5,740	56	8,774	14,750	59	12,080	18,398	66	12,558	20,130	63
PEI	3,153	5,740	53	9,439	14,750	64	12,773	17,973	71	11,670	19,450	60
Nfld	2,880	5,740	50	9,239	14,750	63	12,986	18,398	71	13,024	20,130	70

SOURCES: Poverty lines: Senate Committee Report, adjusted for inflation to 1973 and updated in 1985; National Council of Welfare, 1993. Social assistance rates for 1973 from 'Working Paper on Social Security', 1973; rates for 1984 from collected data; rates for 1993 from National Council of Welfare. Minimum social security payments consist of social assistance rates, plus Family Allowances, plus child tax credit or basic Child Tax Benefit. Poverty lines and rates for 1973 and 1993 are for a three-person unit; poverty lines and rates for 1985 and 1999 are for a two-person unit. Payment data for 1999 are from National Council of Welfare, *Welfare Incomes 1999* (Ottawa, 2000).

receipt of benefits for periods longer than a year. For the longer-term recipient there are also discretionary grants for such items as appliance replacement costs, school supplies, and unusual hardships. These supplementary benefits serve to ease the situation of those who have to use social assistance for long periods. On the other hand, they increase the contact with the social assistance system and tend to establish a dependent relationship on it.

Benefits from social assistance cannot usually be accumulated with any other form of income. If, for example, a beneficiary has a small disability pension, its value is simply deducted from the amount of social assistance for which the person is eligible. In addition, there are strict limits to the assets a person may have while obtaining social assistance. Employment income, too, is sharply limited, usually by a fixed amount—typically $100 or less. Beyond that amount social assistance income is reduced at rates that can be as high as 100 per cent and that are never less than 50 per cent. The result is an income disincentive to leave social assistance for employment and an incentive to conceal income by working in the 'hidden' economy. The disincentive to work, along with the loss of supplementary benefits that follows, constitutes what is known as 'the welfare wall'.

Coverage of social assistance is broad but discretionary. It is broad in that there are no exclusions from coverage in the way that social insurance programs exclude persons who do not satisfy defined criteria. This leads to social assistance programs supporting all those persons whose need is not met by other income security programs (persons unemployed for more than one year; persons disabled but not severely disabled; unemployed older persons who are not yet 65, etc.). Coverage is discretionary because no person is assured a right to a specific benefit level. Instead, his or her circumstances are examined and assessed by the administering agency, which then makes a judgement as to whether 'need' exists. Subject to limited rights of appeal that vary from province to province, the agency's judgement is final. This power is used to enforce a variety of types of dependency (e.g., on a separated or divorced spouse); to require specific types of training; and to require the beneficiary to take any available low-paid or unattractive work.

The stigma that accompanies receipt of social assistance is severe. The transfer is not assisted by appeal to the principles of universality, insurance, or compensation. Surveys of public opinion indicate uniformly negative attitudes towards social assistance recipients, often in the form of the 'welfare bum' stereotype. The effects on recipients are seen in their adoption of alienated attitudes and lifestyles. For most, these take the form of shame, concealment, or chronic depression. For some, they take the form of petty crime and vulnerability to exploitation (prostitution, shoplifting, delinquency).

Social assistance programming is a *bête noire* to the advocates of a fairer and more just redistributive system because it visibly exhibits the failure to obtain the ideals of social welfare. Nevertheless, social assistance programming has proved very durable. Its durability is a product of its flexibility and of the lack of coverage by other programs for very common types of risk. The government of Canada recognized these problems in 1970:

> social assistance will probably remain the least acceptable type of income security payment. Because of this, income security policy should try to minimize the extent to which social assistance is used. Through the development of the guaranteed income, and social insurance programs, reliance on social assistance will be gradually reduced.[25]

This goal has never been fulfilled. As long-term unemployment has increased so has the number of Canadians who have no other choice but to use this last line of defence against lost income. Over the years the numbers in receipt of benefits have continued to grow. In 1974 benefits were being received by approximately 1.2 million Canadians monthly; by 1985 approximately 1.9 million were in receipt; and by 1993 benefits were being provided to 2.9 million. This number fell with economic recovery and with welfare cutbacks in the late 1990s, but in 1999, 2.3 million were still numbered as recipients.[26]

Work Incentives and Workfare

It is important to differentiate work incentives from workfare. All provincial social assistance programs contain some work incentive features and these are supported by the National Council of Welfare:

> The National Council of Welfare feels that it is fair to require some effort on the recipient's part towards self-sufficiency whereever possible. Job search and training requirements have always been a condition of eligibility for employable welfare applicants. But we also feel that welfare rates should be based on the cost of a reasonable basket of goods and that recipient households should receive the full amount. Paying decent welfare rates and improving incentives to work by increasing earnings exemptions is sound social policy. Cutting benefits is not.[27]

Work incentives usually take the form of 'exemptions' from the social assistance earning policy that requires that income be deducted from the social assistance payment at a rate of 100 per cent. A typical policy would provide for the complete exemption of the first $100 of earnings, plus 25 per cent of additional earnings.

Workfare is defined by the presence of a work requirement for the receipt of welfare. This takes the form of a mandatory requirement to report for work (or training), accept work as assigned, and a penalty if these requirements are not met. The penalty can be a reduction in the welfare rate paid that can be as high as 100 per cent. As a result of conservative welfare reforms

made during the 1990s most provinces now have some form of workfare program for some social assistance clients. Table 3.21 shows the major characteristics of some typical programs, some of which do not fulfill the full definition of workfare, although they may be presented politically as if they did, as part of a 'get tough on welfare recipients' approach to policy.

Enforced Dependency Programs

Enforced dependency income security programs operate in close relationship to the social assistance program. A person is considered not to be 'in need' if he or she has an enforceable dependency. Such programming affects two principal groups, youth and women with dependent children.

Youth, meaning persons between 14 and 18 years of age, can be held ineligible for social assistance on the grounds that their parents can, or should, support them; in practice, a considerable degree of administrative discretion is exercised. Refusing benefits, of course, does not immediately lead to the young person living with his or her parents. Instead, young people may subsist, for example, as homeless street people by panhandling, shoplifting, or prostitution.

Women with dependent children can usually assert a claim against the children's father, on the basis of either legal status (e.g., Wives and Children's Maintenance Act) or presumed natural paternity (e.g., various Acts with respect to putative fathers). In either case, the woman has to lay a charge in Family Court. The charge is then pursued by a variety of collection agencies. Collection procedures have been gradually improved through reciprocal, interprovincial enforcement procedures and through automatic deduction-at-source policies.

Nevertheless, this part of the income security system continues to have major problems. Amounts of court-ordered support payments are often inadequate, even to social assistance levels. As the woman is supported in part by social assistance, the payment reduces the payment to her from the provincial government by an amount equal to that which she gets from her former partner. The woman gains nothing for her effort in pursuing collection. In addition, payments are only collectable where the man is in stable employment. Hence, stability is penalized and moving from job to job encouraged.

Since the 1990s there has been a general tendency towards stricter enforcement of these and similar conditions for the receipt of social assistance. These have been directed towards both reducing the number of people who are eligible for benefit and reducing the cost of benefits for those who are.

Table 3.21 Selected Workfare Programs

Program name	New Brunswick Works	Quebec Social Aid: employment programs	Ontario: Work for Welfare	Alberta: welfare employment programs
	(1992)	(1991)	(1997)	(1995)
Work requirement	5-month job placement, education and training program	Participation in one of three placement programs	17 hours/week on 'community improvement projects'	Participation in Alberta Community Employment or Employment Skills programs
Penalty for not participating	None (allegedly)	$100/month	Disqualification for benefits	Administrative harassment
Target groups	Social assistance recipients with the following charactersitics: on assistance for 6 months, grade 7–12, little previous work experience	Able-bodied employable single applicants under 65	New applicants classified as employable	Employable applicants
Participation rate	Pilot program	Low—37% refused to participate, and of those who agreed to participate less than half were placed	Not known	Not known
Success rate	17% not on social assistance (1995)	Success defined as 27% not on social assistance	Not known	Not known

SOURCE: Eric Shragge, *Workfare: Ideology for a New Under-Class* (Toronto: Garamond, 1997). Table constructed from data in source by author.

Food Banks, Shelters, and Soup Kitchens

The food banks occupy a distinct symbolic position in the income redistribution system, for they developed as part of the response to the recession of the early 1980s and the first moves to downsize government. To conservatives they confirm the hypothesis that voluntarism is alive and can fill gaps in the welfare system, but to most social welfare advocates they are symbolic of the failure of the state to provide adequate income security policies (see Box 3.3). The primary users of the food banks are people on social assistance and Employment Insurance.[28]

The shelters and soup kitchens operated by voluntary charitable and religious organizations are the last line of the redistributive system. Although they originated outside the government system, most now contract their services to the provincial social assistance programs. These resources provide some respite for the increasing numbers of homeless people who do not qualify for social assistance because they lack an accepted identification document and/or a permanent address.

The Poor: Conclusions

The 1990s were not a good time to be poor. Benefits were reduced, work requirements were introduced, and eligibility criteria were tightened. Life also became bureaucratically more complex as government programs multiplied and benefit conditions became harder to access and understand. The number of people who were classed as poor initially rose, and then in the latter part of the decade this number fell, although less than it had risen. Participation in the reduction was also very uneven, with the number of children in poverty continuing to increase. It is also apparent that inequality and the depth of poverty increased for those who remained on welfare. The level of participation of First Nation communities is of particular concern, with social assistance benefits, and accompanying poverty, defining the 'normal' conditions of life on many Indian reserves, as we shall see in the next section.

Social Assistance on Indian Reserves

The social assistance program on Indian reserves has been separate from that for other Canadians since the country was founded. In the nineteenth century and first half of the twentieth century relationships with the Indian population were conducted on a colonial model. Indians were not provided with full citizenship. Under Section 91(24) of the Constitution Act, 1867, the federal government was given jurisdiction over 'all matters' related to 'Indians and land reserved for Indians'. For Indians, the Indian Act of 1876 consolidated all law related to them, replacing the citizenship rights that other Canadians enjoyed. The Indian Act was (and is) a colonial statute. Indian agents were appointed for each Indian community to administer the day-to-day relationship between Indian people and Canada. Most normal rights of citizenship were denied to status Indians—those registered under the Indian Act. They could not vote, were denied traditional forms of government, could not employ legal counsel, and could not receive benefits from social programs. The Indian Act also defined who was, and who was not, an Indian, and established reserves where Indians were permitted to live. An Indian could apply to be enfranchised and, subject to satisfying the Indian agent that he was able to be a Canadian, could become a citizen. In some circumstances, such as marriage of an Indian woman to a non-Indian, serving in the armed services, or becoming a member of an established profession, Indians were deemed to have passed the test and were 'enfranchised' whether they wanted to be or not.

For those who remained 'on reserve' there was no equivalent of social assistance. Instead, the local Indian agent had discretionary powers of 'relief', which usually took the form of 'rations' provided through a local store. Cash assistance was not given. The result of this system was a level of poverty, deprivation, and oppression that went far beyond what any other

Box 3.3 BC Governments Must Not Leave Problem of Hunger to Food Banks

The current decline in financial donations to the Greater Vancouver Food Bank is cause for grave concern. It has rightly been picked up by the media and the public is being asked to meet the shortfall in food and funds. The moral imperative of the community to support our hungry fellow citizens should go without saying.

At the same time, as a community, we need to understand that behind the food bank issue lies a profound crisis in social policy: the collapse of Canada's social contract, now further imperiled in BC by provincial government cutbacks.

Over a 20-year period food banks here in BC and across the country have become an entrenched and institutionalized second tier of Canada's social assistance system. In March 2000 they were nationally feeding 726,902 people a month. In BC, during the same month, 85 food banks and 170 emergency food agencies assisted 75,987 people with their food needs, of whom nearly 40 per cent were children. Since 1984, as the incidence of hunger has grown in BC, the number of food banks has nearly doubled.

These numbers are astounding in a country as wealthy as Canada and whose federal budget is still in surplus. Yet they are likely an underestimate of the numbers of hungry Canadians. The recent National Health Population Survey (1998–9) reported that over 10 per cent of Canadians, or an estimated 3 million people, were living in food-insecure households. These included people who both worried about not having enough money to buy food and those forced to compromise their diets.

Food banks clearly perform a much-needed and worthwhile charitable function. Yet we mustn't be lulled into thinking they are solving the problem. The sad reality is that food banks run out of food, cannot guarantee nourishing diets, and have to turn people away. The evidence from numerous studies over a 15-year period indicates that food

banking is unable to solve the problem of hunger.

The goal of food banks is to meet emergency food needs as best as they can, not to deal with the underlying causes of poverty and hunger. Their dilemma is that the charity they provide is shielding governments from the extent and severity of the problem and allowing attention to be distracted from adequate income, employment, and social programs.

At the root has been the withering away of Canada's post-World War II social contract based on commitments to full employment/economic growth, universal social programs, and an adequate social minimum. The abandonment of this contract has been characterized by the downsizing and downloading of government; cuts to welfare benefits and entitlement; inadequate employment benefits and minimum wages; an increasing reliance on charity and the community to address problems like hunger and homelessness; and the demise of the Canada Assistance Plan in 1996.

Before we can solve the problem of hunger, British Columbians need to determine a new social contract for the province. This will not be achieved by our current government's insistence on pushing through a reform program that will only create greater social inequality and deprivation.

What is needed is a coming together of labour and corporate interests, communities, and the state. Perhaps this is a naive suggestion given the divisive and volatile nature of BC politics, but surely it is [in] no one's interest—rich or poor—to permit such widespread hunger to exist.

Graham Riches is Professor and Director of the School of Social Work and Family Studies at the University of British Columbia, and a research associate with the Canadian Centre for Policy Alternatives.

Source: Graham Riches, Canadian Centre for Policy Alternatives—BC, press release, 17 Jan. 2002.

Canadian experienced. Bridget Moran, a social worker in Prince George in the 1950s, gave this account of what she observed.

> All the tools of prevention (of child neglect) were controlled by the Indian Agent, an employee of the federal government, and were dispensed by him. . . . In the 1950s and early 60s, my colleagues and I dreaded these mandatory forays to reserves. In villages like Stony Creek, we came face to face with poverty such as we had never seen before. Sad to say, when the natives pleaded for food or clothing, we were helpless. We could do nothing but explain jurisdictions. 'We can not help you!' we would say. 'We work for the provincial government and it is the federal government who looks after you. You should see the Indian Agent and get him to help you.'[29]

After World War II, prompted by a number of reports that pointed out the failures of this colonial-style regime for Indians, the federal government amended the Indian Act to extend to Indians all provincial laws 'of general application' in a province (Indian Act, s. 88, 1951). When the Canada Assistance Plan was passed in 1966, the federal government included fiscal provisions to share the costs of social welfare services to Indians with the provinces. However, with the exception of Ontario, and with the exception of child protection services, the provincial governments have chosen not to accept this offer of jurisdiction. The result has been an impasse in jurisdictional authority for welfare, education, housing, and health, with the federal government refusing to legislate and the provincial governments refusing to extend services. This void has been filled on a non-legislative basis by two alternative sets of provisions: (1) direct federal services, and (2) First Nations self-government provisions.[30]

For social assistance services the federal government has adopted a policy through which it provides assistance for registered Indians in accord with the same set of policies that are in effect in the province in which the application is received. These policies continue to apply, even though in most cases local Indian bands or tribal councils accept responsibility for service administration. The percentage of bands administering the social assistance program rose from 88 per cent in 1989-90 to 95 per cent in 1999–2000. There are some important advantages to this pattern of administration but there are also disadvantages. The advantages are:

1. Indian applicants can apply for benefits to the local Indian band office where they will deal with staff, often other Indians, working under the authority of their own elected band councillors.
2. The provision of services in this way has allowed bands to develop their own staff and to provide employment and careers to their members.

The disadvantages of this way of providing social assistance are:

1. The policies under which assistance is given are decided by the province in which the application is received. As the province has no responsibility for services to Indians it has no interest in the effects of its policies, no feedback mechanisms, no commitment to consultation, and no responsibility or accountability for their results.
2. The support mechanisms that provinces develop to assist local staffs apply policies, for example, employment supports and access to daycare service, are not available to Indians and in many cases cannot be replicated in the context of band administration and on-reserve programs.
3. The administering band jurisdictions are often small and conflicts of interest between political, administrative, and client roles cannot be avoided. Rights of appeal and review are difficult to provide and staff-client relationships are problematic for both.

4. Although this form of administration is sometimes represented as a step towards self-government, it is very hard to see how one can lead to the other. In fact, its form is really neo-colonial, with direct colonial administration being replaced by a locally appointed administrative staff whose position in the community is secured principally by their allegiance to local political leaders and by their conformity to externally set policies.

Concern as to the effects of social assistance on the Indian community has been expressed on many occasions. The Royal Commission on Aboriginal Peoples noted:

> In public testimony and research studies, many Aboriginal people say that they detest and feel diminished by the atmosphere of passivity that has settled upon some of their communities as a result of the welfare economy. . . . The effects on physical health and morale if living in hopeless poverty are a concern to health advocates as well as to Aboriginal people. Yet social assistance itself is a form of legislated poverty.[31]

Box 3.4 Testimony: Welfare and the Aboriginal Community

Social financial assistance is the most destructive force on our heritage. Our people do not want to be part of a welfare state that looks after them from cradle to grave. If the social financial assistance can be transferred to First Nations, we can begin to develop our people, or at least provide employment which will make each individual feel like they are a productive member of the community.

> Elizabeth Hansen
> Councillor, Inuvik Native Band
> Inuvik, Northwest Territories, 5 May 1992

Welfare is a number one problem of (Inuit) society today, although it might be seen as a solution to the need of those that are unemployable. . . . My father-in-law, when he first heard that welfare was to be introduced in the North, he shuddered that this solution will not create a long-term solution that is acceptable, but it will create a great dependency where no one else will get out of it. He has been right ever since. Social programs that work are good, but these social programs should not be used to create dependency.

> Charlie Evalik
> Economic Development Facilitator
> Cambridge Bay, Northwest Territories,
> 17 Nov. 1992

In our community, a significant number of residents contribute economically through trapping, fishing, and hunting. All these economic activities are potentially productive and renewable but only if the ecology is not disrupted and is properly managed. The damming and flooding required by hydroelectric projects in Saskatchewan has caused severe impacts on the ecology. In fact, as time passes, these harsh effects have intensified to the point where 90 per cent of the main income earners in our First Nation communities have lost their employment, and are required to rely on social assistance.

> Peter Sinclair
> Mathias Colomb First Nation
> Thompson, Manitoba, 1 June 1993

There are many Indian people who get up in the morning and look for jobs. The first stop is usually at the Band Office, but there are no jobs, or limited jobs. The next stop is at the local employment office. Once there, they are reminded that they do not have the training or education to apply for these jobs. The last stop will be at the social assistance office. Without much hope for becoming financially independent, they become part of the forgotten Indian people. They are lost in the process.

> Linda Chipesia
> Whitehorse, Yukon, 18 Nov. 1992

SOURCE: *Report of the Royal Commission on Aboriginal Peoples,* vol. 3, *Gathering Strength,* 170–1.

The percentage of Indians on reserve receiving social assistance is also very high. The Royal Commission on Aboriginal Peoples found that, while the rate of social assistance use for the general population in 1991 was 8.1 per cent, the rate for Aboriginal people off reserve was between 22.1 and 24 per cent and the rate on reserve was 41.5 per cent.[32] Throughout the 1990s the number of social assistance on-reserve beneficiaries continued to rise, from a monthly average of 110,202 in 1989-90 to 151,737 in 1999–2000.[33]

It is difficult to see how this situation is going to change. The on-reserve Indian population continues to grow and few reserves offer sufficient employment opportunities to permit work to replace welfare. For some, leaving the reserve offers a personal solution. For others, there are the local employment opportunities that the Indian band provides. But for many, dependence on social assistance has become a continuing way of life.

Social Housing

Social housing occupies an anomalous position in relationship to all other redistributive programs. Program costs, in excess of $4 billion, are committed to a fixed investment in buildings rather than to providing payments directly to people. Social housing became a major thrust of federal housing policy following the 1964 National Housing Act amendments. However,

the program was operated under a series of differing federal-provincial agreements that were conceived and managed in response to changes in housing conditions and costs as these occurred from time to time. Politics also was a significant factor because housing projects served a symbolic role, providing visible token evidence of government concern and action. The result is a varied group of projects linked to programs that seemed relevant in their time but that now seem less so. Fallis,[34] on whom I have drawn in this section, provides an overview of the origins and use of social housing (Table 3.22). In this housing stock only rent geared to income (RGI) units are relevant to the redistributive objectives of social policy. Tenants in these units typically pay 25–30 per cent of their income for rent. Other occupants in the same buildings pay rents or co-operative charges determined by market conditions or by building construction, mortgage, and operating costs.

Social housing forms about 6.5 per cent of all accommodation and 16.3 per cent of rental housing. RGI social housing forms about half of the total. The other half is occupied by modest- and upper-income earners, of whom half are seniors. Fallis comments:

> From a social policy perspective, I believe the most damning criticism of social housing is that about half of social housing units are occupied by middle- and upper-income house-

Table 3.22 Social Housing Stock, Canada, 1993

Program	No. of units	RGI units	Ownership
Limited dividend	40,000	none	private
Public housing	206,000	all	public
Non-profit/co-op (pre-1978)	81,000	minority	non-profit and co-operatives
Non-profit/co-op (1978–85)	143,000	minority	public, non-profit, and co-operatives
Non-profit/co-op (post-1985)	65,000	majority	public, non-profit, and co-operatives

SOURCE: George Fallis, 'The Social Policy Challenge and Social Housing', in Fallis et al., *Home Remedies: Rethinking Canadian Housing Policies* (Toronto: C.D. Howe Institute, 1995).

holds. These households most certainly would be living in decent housing accommodation without any assistance. In many cases the level of assistance is shallow; however, in other cases . . . the level of assistance is large. . . . There are two answers. The first is that assistance to middle-income people is necessary to achieve income mix in social housing buildings. . . . The second is that the long-term goal was to assist in providing housing for all modest-income households.[35]

From 1994 to 2002, no additional federally funded units have been added to the social housing stock. Meanwhile, the increase in poverty during the 1990s was accompanied by a parallel increase in the number of people who cannot afford adequate housing, which rose from 1.2 million households in 1991 to 1.7 million households in 1996. Not surprisingly, families on social assistance comprise a high proportion of these situations, with lone-parent participation in some social housing projects being as high as 87 per cent of all tenants.[36] A combination of rising rents and low levels of rental construction by the private sector have contributed to this problem, particularly in areas of economic growth. Outright homelessness has also become more evident, not only for single people, but also for family units.[37] In response, in 2001 the federal government proposed a capital grant for any builder of new rental units, subject to the condition that the provinces provide similar support. The objective would be to stimulate construction of 12,000–15,000 new rental units annually.

Conclusion

Canada's redistributive system was weakened during the 1990s. Poverty increased and a clear federal commitment to reducing poverty was lost. At the same time, programs for seniors were retained and reformed to ensure their long-term viability. A commitment to combat child poverty was given, but the resources to fulfill the commitment were not adequate to the task. Conditions of receipt of benefits were made more stringent and bureaucratic complexity was increased. The very high levels of social assistance (and poverty) for First Nations living on reserve is of particular concern. The use of the more than $120 billion annual commitment to income security programs changed during the past decade, with more of these resources applied to seniors and less proportionately to families and children. During the 1990s Canada's social security system had a high political profile and changes were made, usually in a form approved by conservatives. The goals of a social welfare system dedicated to reducing inequalities became more distant.

Additional Readings

Rosemary Popham, David Hay, and Colin Hughes, 'Campaign 2000 to End Child Poverty: Building and Sustaining a Movement', in Brian Wharf and Michael Clague, eds, *Community Organizing: Canadian Experiences*. Toronto: Oxford University Press, 1997, 248–72. Campaign 2000 to End Child Poverty was the major focus of liberal advocacy and lobbying during the 1990s. This account outlines the campaign and its goals.

Marcia H. Rioux, *The Canadian Disability Resource Program: Offsetting Costs of Disability and Assuring Access to Disability-Related Supports*. Toronto: Roeher Institute, 1994. Rioux demonstrates what an alternate, and more comprehensive, vision for income services and support services to persons with disability could look like.

David Ross, *The Canadian Fact Book on Poverty*. Ottawa: Canadian Council on Social Development, 2000. This work is a mine of information and sources, and serves as a useful reference source. It is also required reading for anyone intending to comment on poverty in Canada.

Eric Shragge, *Workfare: Ideology for a New Under-Class*. Toronto: Garamond Press, 1997. Shragge (pp. 17–34) provides a good overview of what the introduction of workfare means for social welfare policy in Canada.

Study Questions

1. Canada had an objective of eliminating child poverty by the year 2000. We failed. What do you think are the principal reasons for our failure?

2. Benefits for single employable people are often set at very low levels. Why is this so and what can be done about it?

3. Is there a way to provide benefits to Aboriginal peoples that does not exacerbate the problems that have come from their internal colonization?

4. Redistribution programs for persons with disabilities seem to have no common purpose or rationale. Examine and assess the proposals made by the Roeher Institute and the likelihood of their adoption.

5. What is meant by 'workfare'? Why do you think such programs have a high political profile?

Notes

1. Human Resources Development Canada, *Improving Social Security in Canada* (Ottawa, 1994), 7.

2. Sandra Rubin, 'If I have children, I'll raise them very differently', *Victoria Times Colonist*, 17 Apr. 1994.

3. Canada, *Working Paper on Social Security in Canada* (Ottawa: Queen's Printer, 1973), 17.

4. David Ross, *The Canadian Fact Book on Poverty*. (Ottawa: Canadian Council on Social Development, 2000), is the source for the following summarized discussion of Canadian poverty lines. Students interested in a full and definitive discussion should read David Ross's monograph.

5. The terminology of institutional and residual forms of welfare was introduced in Chapter 1. It is based on the work of Wilensky and Lebeaux, *Industrial Society and Social Welfare* (New York: Free Press, 1965).

6. Ken Battle and Sherri Torjman, *Opening the Books on Social Spending* (Ottawa: Caledon Institute, 1993), 15; updated to 2000 from Canada, *Annual Financial Report 2000–01* (Ottawa: Ministry of Finance, 2001), 11.

7. Thomas J. Courchene, *Social Canada in the Millennium* (Toronto: C.D. Howe Institute, 1994), 69–70.

8. Canadian Welfare Council, *Unemployment Insurance in the '70's* (Ottawa: Queen's Printer, 1970).

9. Department of Manpower and Immigration, Brief to the Senate Committee on Poverty, 1968, First Session, No. 10, p. 372.

10. André Reynauld, 'Income Distribution: Facts and Policies', speech to The Empire Club, Toronto, 1 Feb. 1973.

11. Courchene, *Social Canada*, 162–3.

12. Fred Lazar, 'UI as a Redistributive Scheme and Financial Stabilizer', in John Richards and William Watson, eds, *Unemployment Insurance: How To Make It Work* (Toronto: C.D. Howe Institute, 1994), 82.

13. Human Resources Development Canada, *Improving Social Security in Canada* (Ottawa: Ministry of Supply and Services, 1994), 45–6.

14. Council of Canadians with Disabilities, 'Submission to the Standing Committee on Human Resource Development', Ottawa, 9 Mar. 1994, as excerpted in *Canadian Review on Social Policy* 34 (1995): 74.

15. Marcia H. Rioux, *The Canadian Disability Resource Program: Offsetting Costs of Disability and Assuring Access to Disability-Related Supports* (Toronto: Roeher Institute, 1994).

16. Canada, *In Unison: A Canadian Approach to Disability Issues* (Ottawa: Human Resources Development Canada and Social Union, 1998).

17. Shelley Phipps, 'Taking Care of Our Children', in

John Richards and William Watson, eds, *Family Matters* (Toronto: C.D. Howe Institute, 1995), 203–11.

18. Hansard, House of Commons Resolution, 24 Nov. 1989.

19. Ken Battle and Leon Muszynski, *One Way to Fight Child Poverty* (Ottawa: Caledon Institute, 1995).

20. W.G. Maynes, 'Child Poverty in Canada: Challenges for Educational Policy Makers', *Canadian Review of Social Policy* 32 (1993): 13–28.

21. Nancy Naylor, 'A National Child Benefit Program', in Richards and Watson, eds, *Family Matters*, 227; Courchene, *Social Canada*, 324.

22. Bridget Kitchen, 'The New Child Tax Benefit: Much Ado About Nothing', *Canadian Review of Social Policy* 39 (1997): 65–73.

23. See Dennis Guest, *The Emergence of Social Security in Canada* (Vancouver: University of British Columbia Press, 1985), 155–9, for an account of the evolution of the CAP.

24. Andrew Armitage, Marilyn Callahan, Michael Prince, and Brian Wharf, 'Workfare in British Columbia', *Canadian Review of Social Policy* 26 (Nov. 1990): 15–25.

25. Canada, *Income Security for Canadians* (Ottawa: Queen's Printer, 1971), 28.

26. National Council of Welfare, *Welfare Incomes 1999* (Ottawa, 2000), 68.

27. Ibid., 60.

28. For a fuller discussion of the role of food banks, see G. Riches, 'Feeding Canada's Poor', in J. Ismael, ed., *The Canadian Welfare State* (Edmonton: University of Alberta Press, 1987); G. Riches, *Food Banks and the Welfare Crisis* (Ottawa: Canadian Council on Social Development, 1986).

29. Bridget Moran, *Stoney Creek Woman Sai'k'uz Ts'eke: The Story of Mary John* (Vancouver: Tillicum Library, 1988), 8.

30. Hugh Shewell and Anabella Spagnut, 'The First Nations of Canada: Social Welfare and the Quest for Self-Government', in John Dixon and Robert P. Scheurell, eds, *Social Welfare with Indigenous Peoples* (London: Routledge, 1995), 1–53.

31. Canada, *Report of the Royal Commission on Aboriginal Peoples*, vol. 3, *Gathering Strength* (Ottawa: Supply and Services Canada, 1996), 166–76.

32. Ibid., 168.

33. Canada, Department of Indian Affairs and Northern Development, *Basic Departmental Data, 2000* (Ottawa, 2001), 41.

34. George Fallis, 'The Social Policy Challenge and Social Housing', in Fallis et al., *Home Remedies: Rethinking Canadian Housing Policies* (Toronto: C.D. Howe Institute, 1995), 1–50.

35. Ibid., 37.

36. Steve Pomeroy, *Towards a Comprehensive Affordable Housing Strategy for Canada* (Toronto: Caledon Institute, 2001), 3–4.

37. Canada Mortgage and Housing Corporation, *Children and Youth in Homeless Families: Shelter Spaces and Services* (Ottawa: CMHC, 2001), Research Highlights, Social Economic Series, 80.

PART III

Building Communities

CHAPTER 4

Community and Social Welfare: Theory, Principles, and Resources

Social welfare has a strong and continuing base in the expectations we have of our community. The concept of community is the second major component of social welfare. Together, the concepts of redistribution and community provide a foundation for the development of social welfare.

Learning Objectives

1. To understand why 'community' is a central objective of social welfare.
2. To understand 'community' as a living concept with many different forms.
3. To be able to distinguish six community functions of social welfare and the effect each has on social welfare policy and services.
4. To recognize the relationship between diversity in all its forms and community in social welfare policy and services.
5. To be able to recognize and respect the demand of Aboriginal peoples for community self-governance.

The social welfare services are a clear expression of our concern for each other, but many different motives underlie this concern. Each of these motives affects the provisions that are made. Sometimes the results further the objectives of social welfare policy and sometimes they detract from them. This chapter distinguishes these different arguments for community social services and their effects on the services that are delivered.

The Concept of Community

The concept of community can have many different meanings. One meaning is geographic. Most of us have lived in several geographic communities. Each had a distinct character and each implies for us a set of relationships and memories that are an important part of our life experience. A second meaning is functional. Through work, sports activities, ethnic association, religious commitment, and political activity we participate in communities that are defined less by geography than by function. Each of these also has a distinct character and is an important part of our life experience. In both geographic and functional communities we have the dual roles of contributing to the community and receiving from the community. Both types of community also provide the external context for our personal worlds of friendship, partnerships, and family relationships. Our participation and membership in community give meaning to our lives and are essential in our general health and well-being.

Social welfare policy is directed towards sustaining and promoting community relationships, for through these relationships the values of concern for the individual, diversity, and faith in democracy can be fulfilled.

Boulding, writing in 1967, saw that part of the distinctive meaning of social policy is found in its concern for the integrity of life.

If there is one common thread that unites all aspects of social policy and distinguishes it from merely economic policy, it is the thread of what has elsewhere been called the 'integrative system.' . . . The institutions with which social policy is especially concerned, such as the school, family, church, or, at the other end, the public assistance office, court, prison, or criminal gang all reflect degrees of integration and community. By and large, it is an objective of social policy to build the identity of a person around some community with which he or she is associated.[1]

The Roeher Institute indicated the continued commitment to the importance of community in its commentary on the concept of 'well-being' in 1993.

Individuals cannot obtain well-being by themselves. They do so in the context of the communities they belong to—geographic communities, as well as communities defined by common interest, language, culture, gender and other characteristics. Through institutions of education, government, media and culture, communities can transmit values and traditions to their members. They provide the language and ideas that people use to express what they want (Kymlicka, 1989) and the resources people need to participate and be included in society.[2]

Another way of defining the function of community in social welfare is to say that social welfare functions to mitigate the anomie and alienation that result from the materialism of urban, capitalist society. Brian Wharf and Michael Clague, in *Community Organizing* (1997), provide many examples, drawn from 30 years of community work in Canada, of these principles at work. They conclude:

In our view, the caring capacity can be created and nourished in many Canadian neighbourhoods and communities only if they are supported by progressive federal and provincial socio-economic policies. While some communities (like the Amish) are isolated from the rest of the world and manage to be caring places, their culture and style of living is vastly different from those that characterize Canadian communities. Most Canadian communities require support from senior levels of government, which have the mandate to redistribute income and wealth equitably and develop universal programs in education, health, and social welfare.[3]

Thus the two parts of the social welfare agenda, redistribution and community, are not separate from one another but directly connected, each needing the other to fulfill the objectives of social justice.

Urbanization, Capitalism, and Community

In understanding the role of social welfare and local social services in Canadian communities we need to consider the impact of urbanization and capitalism. Population movements in Canada during the past century have been dominated by migrations towards central Canada and towards the West, by a rural-to-urban migration, and by a continuing international migration to Canada's urban centres. First Nations, too, have increasingly participated in the rural-to-urban migration. The combination of these trends has made urban growth the dominant reality throughout Canada, but with the pace of growth varying between different metropolitan areas. The urban growth process is the product of Canada's economic development, initially as an exporter of commodities, then as a manufacturer, and now as a series of service centres. The by-products of this growth have been seen in the identification of a common set of problems, including poverty, housing, congestion, environmental decay, and social unrest.[4] Table 4.1 indicates the growth of selected Canadian cities.

The identification of these features of urban life as problems is testimony to the lack of congruence between the realities of urban living and the ideals that are held. Thus the reality of urban living is that the majority of contact between people is impersonal, either random in that strangers pass one another in a crowd or functional as where people meet at work. Neither form of contact is in accord with the ideal that people should know and understand each other. The reality of bringing large numbers of people together is that their competition for available space will result in the poverty of some and the gain of others. The reality of their diverse backgrounds and expectations is a disruption of their familiar patterns. The reality of asking that their young people learn to live in this new environment is conflict between groups and between generations.

Capitalism offers nothing that mitigates these tensions. Indeed, the emphasis on personal gain and materialism exacerbates them. All the great analysts of capitalism have been pessimistic about the social order it creates. Adam Smith foresaw the 'moral decay' of the working class; Marx found optimism, not in capitalism, but in the working class liberating itself from capitalism; Keynes saw that capitalism could acquiesce to a world of injustice, inequalities, and unemployment, from which he saw it being rescued by government; and Schumpeter argued that the culture of capitalism corroded values as a by-product of the continuing process of creating 'perennial gales of creative destruction'.[5]

Community is the antidote to these pessimistic conclusions, for it is through community that a human response to social problems is conceived, organized, and provided. The American sociologist C.W. Mills saw the connection between 'private troubles' and 'public issues' in the following way:

> Troubles occur within the character of the individual and within the range of his immediate relations with others: they have to do with the

Table 4.1 Population and Percentage Change in Population for Selected Metropolitan Areas, Canada, 1941–2001 (population in thousands)

	1941	1951	1961	1971	1981	1991	2001
Halifax	99	134	183	222	277	321	359
Montreal	1,216	1,504	2,156	2,743	2,828	3,127	3,462
Toronto	1,002	1,264	1,942	2,628	2,998	3,893	4,682
Winnipeg	301	357	476	540	584	652	671
Calgary	112	156	290	403	592	754	951
Vancouver	394	562	790	1,028	1,268	1,602	1,986
Percentage Change in Population Since Last Census							
Halifax	25.5	35.8	37.3	21.3	24.7	15.9	11.8
Montreal	12.1	23.6	43.3	27.2	3.1	10.5	10.7
Toronto	11.2	26.2	53.6	35.3	14.1	30.0	20.2
Winnipeg	2.4	18.1	33.4	13.5	8.1	11.6	2.9
Calgary	8.1	39.7	85.8	38.9	46.9	26.6	26.1
Vancouver	16.5	42.7	40.6	30.1	23.3	26.3	23.9

SOURCES: Leroy O. Stone, *Urban Development in Canada* (Ottawa: Dominion Bureau of Statistics, 1967), 278; *Census of Canada,* 1981, 1991, 2001.

self and with those limited areas of social life of which he is directly and personally aware. . . . A trouble is a private matter: values cherished by an individual are felt by him to be threatened.

Issues have to do with matters that transcend these local environments of the individual and the range of his inner life. They have to do with the organization of many such milieux into the institutions of an historical society as a whole. . . . An issue is a public matter: some value cherished by publics is felt to be threatened.[6]

Brian Wharf, in his commentary on case studies of social movements and social change in Canada, recognized the role of community in transforming personal troubles into public issues. The case studies that Wharf discusses—the women's movement, the First Nations movement, and the labour movement—show how this community dynamic works.[7]

In the context of globalization the concept of community takes on new meaning, as James Ife explains, as 'a deliberate strategy to counter globalization and to provide a grounding for human experience, or as a simple reaction to a world that is apparently moving beyond the control of ordinary people'. Ife continues:

There are several indications of such a trend. One is the increase in communitarian solutions. . . . Another is the insistence of Green political theory that ecologically sustainable answers to environmental problems lie with local action and community-based organizations. A further indication is the continuing interest in community-based structures such as alternative currency schemes, self-help groups and local action campaigns. A much more concerning trend, which also indicates localism, is the development of militia-style groups and extremist isolationist political parties as a reaction to globalization and to people's apparent loss of control over life choices. . . . It is important to note that despite

the erosion of community, which has been caused by 200 years of industrial capitalism, the idea of human community remains attractive and powerful. It is seen by many as the ideal basis for some form of culturally diverse and politically pluralist post-industrial society, in direct contrast to the perceived universality and uniformity of the globalized world.[8]

Diversity

Recognition of the importance of diversity in the contexts of social welfare and community has only come recently. The conceptions of community that initially guided the development of the welfare ideal were in response to industrialism and urbanization but did not recognize the importance of culture and differences of historical experience. They had a pastoral, bucolic emphasis that suggested the welfare function was trying to fill a rural, small-town void. Mills wrote:

In approaching the notion of adjustment, one may analyze the specific illustrations of maladjustment that are given and from these instances infer a type of person who in this literature is evaluated as 'adjusted.' The ideally adjusted man of the social pathologists is 'socialized.' This term seems to operate ethically as the opposite of 'selfish'; it implies that the adjusted man conforms to middle-class morality and motives and 'participates' in the gradual progress of respectable institutions. If he is not a 'joiner,' he certainly gets around and into many community organizations. If he is socialized, the individual thinks of others and is kindly towards them. He does not brood or mope about but is somewhat extrovert, eagerly participating in his community's institutions. His mother and father were not divorced, nor was his home ever broken. He is 'successful'— at least in a modest way—since he is ambitious; but he does not speculate about matters too far beyond his means, lest he become a 'fantasy thinker,' and the little men don't scramble after the big money. The less abstract the traits and fulfilled 'needs' of the 'adjusted man' are, the more they gravitate toward the norm of independent middle-class persons verbally living out protestant ideals in the small towns of America.[9]

This 1941 conception was silent on women, ethnic origin, race, and ability, let alone sexual orientation. It allowed no place for diversity. It reflected a society in which dominance by patriarchy, European ethnic origins, able-bodied white people, Protestantism, and heterosexuality were assumed. This once dominant view of the community ideal had a pervasive influence when the community institutions of the social welfare state were then in their formative period. The child welfare field provides many examples. McIntyre notes that:

women's private mothering, maintenance and caring for their own family members were transferred, through moral reform and rescue work, to 'mothering on a national scale' (Ursel, 1992: 71) that included public caring for the poor, disadvantaged and the neglected. Protection of the family, however, included reproduction, the promotion of motherhood, and the defence of a patriarchal sexual code.[10]

The imposition of cultural and racial dominance was particularly severe on First Nations communities throughout Canada. The goals of Canadian Indian policy were, and some would say still are, 'protection, civilization and assimilation'.[11] For more than 100 years, first through the use of residential schools, then through the provincial child welfare systems, the mission was to remake the next generation of First Nations people in the image of the European settlers.[12]

The translation of these rural, patriarchal, racist, and culturally dominant expressions of the community 'ideal' into public policy was directed towards the goal of integration—the establishment of one social community in which, nominally, differences would play no part in public policy but that was actually characterized by a suppression of differences. In Canada, Quebec was always regarded as an exception, but even in regard to Quebec there has been a continual and unsatisfying struggle to distinguish those matters in which Quebec should have its own institutions and policies and those in which it has to accept the institutions and policies of federal Canada. The 1995 referendum campaign provided many examples, with both Quebec and the federal government advancing competing claims to be in the better position to provide social programs.

The integration view of the role of community in social welfare policy seems out of place and time in the Canada of the twenty-first century, in which diversity is increasingly recognized and applauded. The social movements, as Wharf indicates,[13] are having, and have had, a major influence on our understanding of the community 'ideal' and on its translation into social policy. Thus, the conception of community now most widely held is 'diverse' or 'pluralist', with the existence of many communities recognized and the dominance of no single community ideal over others considered acceptable. Furthermore, the communities are seen in a dynamic relationship to each other, both producing changes in the whole and protecting those institutions and activities that are critical to their own presence and growth. First Nations are therefore acting as a collective community to obtain recognition as Aboriginal peoples with rights based in their presence on the land at the time of European settlement. Among those rights is the right to self-government, which also serves to strengthen and perpetuate a continued Aboriginal presence as a separate series of independent societies within Canada. The repatriation of the Canadian Constitution and the proclamation of the Charter of Rights and Freedoms in 1982 confirmed the importance of the language rights, personal rights, and Aboriginal rights that are the foundations for recognizing diversity and establishing pluralism.

Despite these changes in the community ideal, which are being introduced gradually into social welfare policy, one should not underestimate the continued ideological and institutional presence and influence of earlier forms of the concept of the community.

Community Functions of Social Welfare

Roland Warren provided a useful analysis of community functions that distinguishes the different ways in which the concept of community influences social welfare. The principal community functions are:

1. production, distribution, and consumption
2. socialization
3. social control
4. mutual support
5. social participation.[14]

1. Production, Distribution, and Consumption

The economic functions of community used to be thought of as purely marketplace transactions outside the scope of social welfare. This was never entirely the case. In First Nations communities, for example, the economic functions of community were always integrated with the social functions. Justa Monk of the Carrier-Sekani people describes his life as a boy in the 1950s in British Columbia.

> Until the road was built the people of Portage and Tachie lived in almost complete isolation. Our survival depended on boats, sleighs, horses, fish nets, traps, guns and the medicine we found in the forest. If we had to make it to the outside world, my people knew that the trip would be long and that there would be much hardship and danger too.[15]

At the time, however, such a life was seen as primitive by the Canadian government and social welfare was seen as having a role, through the residential schools, in providing Indian youth with a way of leaving the reserve and integrating into the general economy.

In the past decade, when the general economy has come to mean the global economy, there has been a growing realization that this economy may never provide the opportunities for work that a community needs. Nozick makes the case for 'sustainable community development' in the following manner:

> I recently heard an economics professor being interviewed on TV say that we must accept the disappearance of 'uneconomic communities' as a fact of modern life. Fishing villages, rural towns, are a thing of the past. . . . Community is not seen as having any inherent value worth preserving apart from economics. Furthermore there is no recognition that people have resources and means within their communities and regions to meet many or most of their needs. . . .
>
> What is needed is an approach which integrates economic, ecological, political, and cultural development as part of a strategy which has the revitalizing and reclaiming of community as its primary aim. I call this 'sustainable community development'. The goal is to: a) build communities that are more self-supporting and that can sustain and regenerate themselves through economic self-reliance, community control and environmentally sound development; and b) build communities that will be worth preserving because they are grounded in the life experiences of people who live in them, and in the natural history of specific regions.[16]

Community is thus seen as a means through which people can organize their collective affairs to regain control of their lives from the capitalist global economy. Community economic development works within the market economy. It utilizes all the processes of capitalism except that the endeavours are owned by the community and are in a developmental and non-exploitive relationship to the community.

2. Socialization

Socialization has always been seen as a major community function and social welfare services help 'individuals, through learning, [to] acquire the knowledge, values and behaviour patterns of their society and learn behaviour appropriate to their social roles.'[17] This sphere of social welfare activity is not only a dominant focus of much work with children but is present in such fields of practice with adults as home support and homemaker services and counselling.

The original view of how these socialization functions were performed began with consideration of the role of such primary institutions as the family and the church and the ways they have traditionally provided the means for individuals to learn mutually acceptable patterns of behaviour. This view now requires substantial modification to recognize: (1) the role of culture and ethnicity in providing a variety of models of socialization, all of which need to be accorded an equal degree of legitimacy in our social policies; and (2) the role of social groups in providing alternate paths to adulthood that have often not been recognized by traditional systems. Examples are provided by gay and lesbian culture and by feminist models of social relationships.

Beyond these community institutions are the roles being played by such established formal organizations as schools, children's treatment institutions, and alcohol and drug abuse services. Here, too, one sees the influence of the social movements in establishing new organizations to provide, for example, services for the victims of rape and sexual assault, family violence services, transition houses, and AIDS prevention and counselling services. The First Nations movement offers support to persons through band and tribal council offices, friendship centres, and a growing network of specialized social agencies. The recent immigrant and refugee communities are served by a network of community and religious agencies that have the objective of assisting immigrants and refugees with the processes of arrival, establishing citizenship, and settlement.

Social welfare organizations performing these functions can be further distinguished by how they act as agents of socialization. The terminology of prevention developed by Kahn[18] assists in such a classification.

Primary prevention. At the primary preventive end of the continuum are the declared educational services, for example, family life education, sex education, drug information, language training, anti-racist workshops, and AIDS prevention. These services are distributed broadly to the community as a whole and the case is increasingly made that they should be established parts of the socialization all young people receive through their inclusion in the curricula of school systems.

Secondary prevention. At the secondary level of prevention are social utility services, such as daycare and homemaker services; recreational services such as those provided by Boys Clubs, which are intended to meet the needs of potential problem populations; mental health counselling services; services to the parents of handicapped children; support and advice to victims of sexual abuse; advocacy in dealing with immigration authorities; and advice, guidance, and support with substance abuse problems. The distinguishing feature of this secondary level of socialization services is that individuals or families seek the services on their own initiative.

The services at the primary and secondary levels of prevention may be provided for geographic communities by public or private agencies or may be provided by ethnic or interest group communities for their members. These changes cumulate in the trend towards the recognition of the diverse, plural nature of the community.

Tertiary prevention. Beyond these primary and secondary socialization services are the tertiary services where the law is used to make the receipt of service mandatory on specific populations, e.g., child protection services, correctional services, and the committal aspects of mental illness services. However, with the addition of these mandatory powers to force services on people, it would appear that the emphasis on social control is sharply increased. Thus, although these services also perform socialization functions, they are discussed under the heading of social control.

3. Social Control

The inclusion of the concept of social control is more controversial. Yet social control is an inescapable function of all communities. Socialization, the process of learning acceptable behaviours, takes one only so far. If socialization fails, or if the community is threatened, all communities take protective measures by expelling threatening members, restricting their opportunity to threaten others, and sanctioning their behaviour. Social welfare participates, too, in these social control functions of community; social control being defined as the 'process through which a group influences the behaviour of its members towards conformity with its norms'.[19] The means used to obtain social control may be classified with respect to the type of power used: physical, material, or symbolic.

> The use of a gun, a whip or a lock is physical since it affects the body; the threat to use physical sanctions is viewed as physical because the effect on the subject is similar in kind, if not . . . in intensity, to the actual use. Control based on application of physical means is ascribed as *coercive* power.
>
> Material rewards consist of goods and services. The granting of symbols (e.g., money) which allow one to acquire goods and services is classified as material because the effect on the recipient is similar to that of material means. The use of material means for control purposes constitutes *utilitarian* power.

> Pure symbols are those whose use does not constitute a physical threat or a claim on material rewards. They include normative symbols, those of prestige and esteem; and social symbols, those of love and acceptance. . . . The use of symbols for control purposes is referred to as *normative* or *social* power.[20]

Coercion. The most coercive social control agencies, the military and the police, are generally regarded as outside the orbit of social welfare (although some aspects of police work, for example, youth work, are similar in form and intent to the practice of social agencies). Throughout its history, however, social welfare has been associated with various total institutions—residential schools, jails, mental hospitals, workhouses, and the like—that are testimony to the coercive social control functions of social welfare. In addition, social welfare has been the principal agent of social control dealing with relationships within the family, including, in child protection work, the authority to remove children from their parents.

There is a high degree of ambivalence with respect to the use of coercive power for social welfare purposes. The record of the use of coercive power for social policy purposes shows that it is open to tremendous abuse. Nazi Germany referred to its policies of genocide towards Jewish people, gypsies, the mentally handicapped, and homosexuals as being social policies. Canada and other Western countries engaged in the sexual sterilization of handicapped people. Canada used the residential school system for 100 years in an attempt to eradicate First Nations culture by preventing the transmission of language and traditions between generations. More recently, children have been taken from First Nations communities and then placed for adoption without consent, often in the United States, as a way of changing the course of their lives.[21] Until Criminal Code prohibitions were repealed in 1975, gay men could be harassed and prosecuted because of their sexual orientation. The aftermath of these examples of the use of coercive power for social control purposes continues to affect all these populations in the form of increased rates of imprisonment, mental ill health, alcoholism, suicide, sexual abuse, and family violence. These effects linger long after the original policy and its purposes have been abandoned.

On the other hand, the right of individuals to protection from their fellows cannot be denied, nor can social welfare agencies dissociate themselves from the effects of social control measures on the populations singled out for sanctions. The sensitivity to authority that comes from perspectives other than the dominant patriarchal one increases the ambivalence with which the use of coercive authority is regarded.

Callahan develops a feminist view of the situation of women who have had their children apprehended because of neglect and concludes:

> In any model, the so-called crime of neglect should simply disappear from the child welfare statutes. Instead, child welfare statutes could be reframed to define the caring services to be provided. . . . If chronic neglect is primarily a matter of poverty, frequently the poverty of disadvantaged women, then it should be dealt with as a resource issue rather than as a personal, individual problem. If situational neglect occurs, such as the abandonment of children, then such problems can be dealt with by providing care and resources to the children.[22]

Similarly, the report by the Aboriginal panel that reviewed child welfare legislation in British Columbia decided to recommend community healing rather than imprisonment for youthful community members who committed sexual abuse.[23]

Utilitarian power. The use of utilitarian power for social control purposes also produces some ambivalence, but it is much more acceptable than coercive power. In the examples given above of recommended changes of practice

from feminist and First Nations perspectives, services are substituted for coercion. Usually there is some negotiation with clients around such services and hence influence is exercised through the process of negotiating the terms and conditions under which support is given. A similar social control effect occurs in the behaviour of social agencies dealing with problems of substance abuse. For example, the use of medication programs, e.g., methadone treatment, places such agencies in the situation of trying to obtain social control over people seeking services by utilitarian means. In children's institutions, mental health facilities, homes for the elderly, and other institutional settings, rewards and sanctions often take the form of giving or withholding incidental items, privileges, and the like.

The institutions that use utilitarian power for social control are usually regarded as social welfare institutions and social workers frequently comprise a key component in their staff.

Normative power. Normative or social power would appear to be the most acceptable form of power to social welfare enterprises. The most pervasive use of such power is found in the way social welfare enterprises ascribe status to their service populations. The symbolic ascriptions used—'on welfare', debtor, addict, neurotic, etc.—all have stigmatizing consequences. Social welfare agencies obtain change in service populations partly by their power to ascribe such statuses and then symbolically to remove them when the process of rehabilitation is complete. This use of normative and social power for social control purposes represents the point at which social control functions blend with socialization functions.

The difference in the degree of acceptability to social welfare values of the three types of power is related to the alienating characteristics of the use of power for social control purposes.

> The use of the coercive power is more alienating to those subject to it than is the use of

utilitarian power, and the use of utilitarian power is more alienating than the use of normative power. Or, to put it the other way around, normative power tends . . . to generate more commitment than utilitarian, and utilitarian than coercive.[24]

Unfortunately, Canadian society exhibits social tensions and destructive behaviours we do not know how to control fully by normative or utilitarian means. Hence, coercive power remains essential. Nevertheless, the thrust of welfare values is towards the least possible use of coercive power for social control purposes. Part of the case that was made for maintaining a stronger, and more costly, social welfare system in Canada than in the United States was that Canadians want to avoid the pervasive sense of violence and the attendant policing presence that characterize the cities to the south.

4. Mutual Support

It is to the mutual support function of community that social welfare must appeal for resources. Mutual support is organized at three major levels: charitable gifts, taxation, and self-help. The charitable approach came first and still continues. It appeals directly to the feelings of concern and of *noblesse oblige* that, it is hoped, people have for those who are less fortunate. The taxation approach came second and was necessitated by the scale of the community social provisions that were needed and by the advantages of providing services to recipients as social rights based in citizenship rather than as supplicants dependent on charity. The self-help approach was always present but has come increasingly to the fore in the development of new services in the period from the 1970s to the present. The self-help, mutual-aid approach is based in the application of community development principles by oppressed and under-served groups. The social movements of women, First Nations, gays and lesbians, the disabled, the visible minorities, social housing co-operatives,

and other such groups are all examples of the power of self-help.

The self-help groups are also an important response to the inherently alienating and anomic nature of the urban community, the capitalist market, and bureaucracy. The major social agencies developed through the tax base have led to bureaucracies that are themselves alienating, thereby contributing to the problems they hoped to combat. The establishment of efficient but impersonal federated fundraising mechanisms for charitable purposes has had a similar effect on some aspects of charity organization. Bureaucracy poses a threat to the mutual support function of social welfare by eroding the sense of common community identity necessary to mutual support. Bureaucracy also depends on hierarchical power relationships, leading to the disempowerment of both line staff and consumers. The self-help groups provide a strong response to all these problems.

5. Social Participation

Social participation as a systemic function of community receives considerable moral support from the social welfare ideals of diversity and democracy. People *should* exercise a right to be heard and to participate in decisions that affect them. In the 1960s this thrust in social welfare thinking was endorsed in the American War on Poverty's Office of Economic Opportunity programs under the heading of 'maximum feasible participation'. A similar ideal was expressed in the social action goals of the Company of Young Canadians. The creation of the National Council of Welfare (1969), with representatives of the poor forming half the Board, was additional evidence of the search for means to allow the participation of consumers in the design and operation of social welfare.

The earliest connections were made between voluntary social welfare institutions and those of philanthropic means and high social status. Today we consider such an approach to be problematic, based as it is in a concept of social class that excludes the experience of much of the community. Similarly, although service groups provide a broad path to social participation to those community members willing to act personally for the collective good, these approaches also are flawed by the lack of opportunity to hear a clear consumer voice. There have been many attempts to extend this ethic further so that the consumers of social welfare services can make a contribution to their own social development and welfare. In some communities strong grassroots organizations have provided consistent means for the least advantaged citizens to make their views known and to participate by serving on agency boards, government councils, and similar participatory structures.

Early attempts to sponsor consumer participation by the state as part of social welfare revealed a complex relationship in which the community could function in a number of different roles in relation to the state, some of which were compatible with the interests of the state and some of which were not. Wharf and Clague[25] suggest that the relationship may take any one of five major forms:

1. agent of the state
2. partner with the state
3. campaigning against the state
4. independent of the state
5. challenging state institutions and values.

Agent of the state. In this role community is expected to implement plans conceived by the state. Examples would be the off-loading of government programs to local communities, with or without adequate funding as part of a planned program of cutbacks, and the expectation that the community will form itself into a series of groups to fulfill some government-conceived purpose, for example, improving community health. Andrée Demers and Deena White argue that this role leads to 'colonization of the community' as external authority leads to the creation of 'spurious' communities, lacking autonomy and maintained only by the compromising receipt of resources from the state.[26]

Partner with the state. In this role the community is more proactive. When a community group has been funded by government for a purpose that it initially conceived and campaigned for, it effectively becomes a partner with the state. Nevertheless, once government funding is provided the government becomes the senior partner in the endeavour and exercises a degree of control over the agency and its services. Examples include community services developed by women for sexual abuse victims, ethnic organizations that offer services to immigrants, and gay community groups that seek to help AIDS sufferers. Roxana Ng's careful dissection of funding relationships in an agency serving the immigrant community showed how the independence and autonomy of a community organization can be undermined once a funding relationship to the state is established.[27] However, the conclusion here is not that such relationships should be rejected, but that they should not be entered into naively. The community group that accepts funding should expect to have to defend its autonomy in order to protect the integrity of its relationship to the community it is serving.

Campaigning against the state. In this role the community acts, with and on behalf of the disadvantaged, as advocate, arguing for new and additional resources from the state. Examples would include the anti-poverty movement and the forceful role played by First Nation communities in asserting their right to manage their own affairs. There are limits to the compatibility between this role and the interests of the state. The following example from the early experiences of the Company of Young Canadians in the 1970s has features that many similar groups have experienced since.

The desire of the Canadian government to encourage participation at the grassroots is matched by its apprehension about the people who are animating the neighbourhood population.

The recent fervour over the Company of Young Canadians reflects this ambivalence, for the basic problem that emerged was not so much the adequacy of the CYC's performance as the uneasiness with which leaders in and out of government responded to the left-wing postures adopted by some of its members.[28]

Groups that organize demonstrations that embarrass authorities find that the objects of their attention complain through both bureaucratic and political channels. The granting agency comes under considerable pressure to curb the protest group's militancy. The granting agency yields to pressure reluctantly, but conditions are attached to the grant, such as different organizers, co-operation with local authorities, and no disruptive tactics. The social action group may then split into a moderate, funded group and a militant, unfunded faction. The subsequent internal quarrelling can easily destroy community respect and support for the group.

Experiences like this test a community group's solidarity. First Nations groups, organized around their Aboriginal roots and culture, find a heritage of pride and independence from which they can assert long-term goals for themselves as people. The feminist community, organized around common experiences of women, can also use that experience to maintain independence from the state. In the end the group has to be prepared to live without state funding rather than compromise its independence or it will die.

Independent of the state. In this role independent community organizations develop and control services with little or no interference from the state. Examples include projects undertaken on a co-operative basis, the determination that the First Nations and gay communities have shown in 'caring for their own', and some forms of community economic development. In each case there is a clearly defined and active community that has the capacity for independent action. This role is less confronta-tional and is idealized in the community development literature.[29]

Challenging state institutions and values. In this role the community directly confronts values that have been entrenched by the state. For example, heterosexism has restricted state recognition of gay and lesbian relationships and continues to exclude gays and lesbians from the benefits of social programs, and activist groups (and individuals) have confronted this exclusion by legal action and by celebrating gay and lesbian marriages. A second example is found in the challenge to corporate power and hegemony expressed by the demonstrators at World Trade Organization meetings that aim to exclude social issues from the global agenda.

Community and Diversity

As originally defined in social welfare thought and operationalized in the institutions of the welfare state, the concept of community was universal. Institutions developed in the context of Western industrialized societies were considered to have universal application. Alternative forms of care and social organization were considered primitive, to be replaced in due course by the welfare state forms. This formulation of the concept of community is recognized today as being an example of cultural and institutional racism. Thinking like this led to the 1951 changes in the Indian Act that were designed to transfer all welfare responsibility for First Nations to the provinces so Native peoples could have the modern welfare services that were being developed in the post-war era. This approach to policy was rejected by First Nation leaders, who sought an opportunity to develop alternative institutions of their own in the context of their own culture.

Recognizing the right of all members of the community to participate in the development of services that are attentive to their heritage has led to a continuing process of reform of the social services. Reform has taken several forms, of which the major ones are:

- the modification of policies and programs to be more attentive to cultural and historical differences;
- the development and administration of different policies and programs for different peoples;
- the financing of different programs serving different people;
- the development of autonomous institutions of self-government;
- the development of measures to deal with the problem of European racism.

Modification of policies and programs. This is the most basic claim that any sectional group can make and is essential to the accommodation of social justice and minority rights. The claims of gay and lesbian people for equality of treatment in matters of benefit and adoption are of this type, for they demand that policies and programs recognize difference (see Box 4.1). Similar claims are made by immigrant groups whose cultural needs were not recognized at earlier stages of Canada's social evolution, either because they were not there or because they were once the subjects of racist and cultural oppression. First Nations also made such claims when they sought release from the oppressive sections of the Indian Act that banned the potlatch and the sun dance. The case for change in these instances is based in an argument for equality that recognizes that majority groups establish cultural organizations in their interest and it is only just to allow a similar right to minorities of all types.

A supporting argument advanced by French Canadians, First Nations, Hutterites, and Doukhabors is that historic agreements were made at the time of settlement, giving them a right to be recognized in matters affecting the continuity of their communities and culture. For all these examples the claim being made is for inclusion in Canadian society and for social welfare provisions on terms that are non-discriminatory.

The development and administration of different policies for different peoples. The development of

different policies takes the subject of diversity a further step. Here the claim is not for inclusion but for separateness based on the recognition of difference. An example of such a claim is that made by First Nations for a separate justice system or for an independent mandate to organize and conduct their own child welfare programs. As Kymlicka points out, this is a more difficult claim for social policy because it requires the establishment of services that permit segregation and it raises questions regarding the rights of minorities within the groups seeking to establish separate policies. Should the protection of the Canadian Charter of Rights and Freedoms apply to the language rights of the English-speaking minority in Quebec? Should it apply to the gender rights of First Nations women? Should First Nations children be allowed to stay in non-Native foster homes if they so wish rather than be repatriated to the care of their people? If these and similar questions are answered positively then there are limits placed on the exercise of self-government and on the extent to which non-liberal expressions of diversity can be recognized. Kymlicka accepts these limits as a conclusion of his review of liberal values, citizenship, and diversity.

> These steps might include polyethnic and representation rights to accommodate ethnic and other disadvantaged groups within each national group and self-government rights to enable autonomy for national minorities alongside the majority nation. Without such measures, talk of 'treating people as individuals' is itself just a cover for ethnic and national injustice.
>
> It is equally important to stress the limits of such rights. . . . minority rights should not allow one group to dominate other groups; and they should not enable a group to oppress its own members.[30]

The financing of different programs for different people. The financing of different programs serving different peoples also poses some challenges.

As long as programs are equally available to all, they can be financed from the common tax base in which all share. This breaks down either when programs are not available to all or when all groups do not participate equally in paying taxes. In either case there is a tendency to see the specialized services being provided as the exclusive responsibility of the group that has sought them. The arguments for the majority paying for such services are that they represent a payment in compensation for past disadvantage, or that they represent a payment based on equality of treatment, or that they represent a payment due under the terms that government-to-government relationships were established. The first two arguments, compensation and

---

Box 4.1 Two Gay Couples Win Right to Adopt

Two lesbian couples have won a ground-breaking court challenge to Alberta's adoption law, paving the way for homosexuals to become the legal parents of their partner's children.

'We're elated,' said a 50-year-old woman whose adoption of her five-year-old stepson was approved yesterday in Court of Queen's Bench. 'This is an absolutely big justice issue for the sake of our children.'

Mr. Justice Peter Martin ruled that the two Calgary women are 'amply qualified' to become the legal parents of the sons they have raised since birth.

'I am also satisfied that these applications are in the best interest of the children,' Judge Martin wrote in his judgement.

The boys involved are aged 5 and 12 and were conceived by artificial insemination. Their step-mothers are the partners of their birth mothers.

The couples, whose names are protected by Alberta's Child Welfare Act, contested a section of the act dealing with step-parent adoptions.

The Alberta government fought the adoption application for about 18 months, but did an about-face six weeks before the trial and amended the act in May. But the amendment didn't specifically mention same-sex step-parents, and Friday's judgement clarifies that they now fit the definition.

Gaining legal status for non-biological parents has implications in several areas, including family health-care benefits, inheritance and custody in the event of death or relationship breakdown.

However, Julie Lloyd, a lawyer for the gay and lesbian advocacy group Equal Alberta, warned that same-sex couples may still have to challenge more than 60 pieces of provincial legislation to get all the same rights as heterosexual couples, including the right to the family health-care benefits.

'It's entirely unfair to put the burden on the lesbian and gay community to effect these changes, particularly since the courts have been so clear that the changes need to be put in place,' Ms. Lloyd said.

Hermina Dykxhoorn, president of the 5,000-member Alberta Federation of Women United for Families, predicted a storm of angry letters and phone calls to Alberta politicians in the wake of the judgement.

'This will be tried in the court of public opinion and most Albertans will be opposed to this,' she said. 'The definition of marriage and family must be protected.'

Psychologists who reviewed the two cases involving the Calgary boys, their parents and home concluded the children live in stable, secure, loving environments.

When told about the judgement, the five-year-old boy was ecstatic. 'Now we have a real family!' he shouted, springing into the air.

Representing the two couples, lawyer Gary Courtney pointed out the judge ruled that taxpayers will have to pay the $300,000 court costs of this case. 'This government seems to be unable or unwilling to recognize that they shouldn't be discriminating on the basis of sexual orientation,' Mr. Courtney said. He noted most other provinces prohibit discrimination on the basis of sexual orientation in the human-rights laws.

Quebec, Ontario and British Columbia have also amended other laws to remove discrimination against gays.

SOURCE: Carol Harrington, Canadian Press, 'Two gay couples win right to adopt', *Globe and Mail*, 27 Nov. 1999.

equality of treatment, both place the majority in control of deciding what is adequate compensation and what is equality of treatment. Only the last of these arguments, based on history and contract, is likely to provide a minority with independence of action.[31]

The development of autonomous institutions of self-government. Separate services with separate financial provisions are not possible without the development of autonomous institutions for governing them. Such institutions can take several forms. One form is established by appointing or electing a community board, as was done in Quebec with the establishment of community councils to manage all local social services. A second form occurs where responsibility is transferred to an already established community council or First Nations band or tribal council. A third form comes when an entirely new jurisdiction is recognized with full responsibility for the welfare of its members. An early example would be the constitutional powers for social policy that are held by the provinces. A modern example is found in the self-government provisions of the treaty made with the Nisga'a people of British Columbia (see Box 4.2).

Separation from the Canadian state is the final step in the development of autonomous institutions of self-government and is, in many ways, the most straightforward solution to the organization of different services for different people. Nor should it be seen as necessarily an extreme or hostile act. There is no reason to think that the example of Norway and Sweden, which separated in 1905 and have flourished since, should not be the example to which we should look. However, for many groups a territorial separation may not be possible. For those situations where separation is adopted as the way to recognize diversity, it will be important to attend carefully to minority community rights during the process of transition in order that each separate national state will recognize the minorities within its borders.

The development of measures to deal with the problem of European racism. The problems posed by European racism appear to be the most serious of all the issues faced in the development of plural social policies that recognize diversity. In most if not all of the countries of Western Europe and in the United States, racism undermines a common sense of community. In each case people of African or Asian origin can find that their opportunities are restricted because of the colour of their skin or the shape of their facial features. In Canada there have been numerous incidents of police violence against members of the black community, racist political parties begin to operate, and the social discourse is full of euphemisms for 'race', such as 'non-traditional immigrants' and 'visible minorities'. While the number of incidents of racism was small they seemed unusual and were often regarded as the results of personal bias. However, with rising numbers of vulnerable people and the increasing numbers of incidents, they can be seen to be based in European attitudes of racial superiority that are embedded in European culture. We cannot expect that these attitudes will be changed by a general policy of multiculturalism. Instead, clear anti-racist policies will increasingly be needed.

Neo-Colonial (Post-Colonial) Social Welfare Community Policy

The concept of 'colonization' can be used to examine the response of social welfare to the issues of diversity. The original response of ignoring issues of diversity and assuming European supremacy is a 'colonial' concept. In the application of this concept to the social services, issues of critical importance to a separate culture were decided independent of that culture. The resulting social services became primarily institutions of socialization and social control, lacking any recognition of the community values of mutual support and social participation. In this form they were an internal colonialism.

Most of the modifications of social welfare community policy discussed above can be classified as neo-colonial. In neo-colonialism, change from the original colonial structures becomes possible within limits. Responsibility for service delivery is transferred to formerly colonized groups but limits to their autonomy are maintained through financial controls and through setting boundaries to the exercise of autonomy. Post-colonialism operates in a middle ground between the earlier structures in which one society controlled another and the promise of a future society in which many societies coexist.

Neo-colonialism represents progress towards the final goal but not its achievement. Some Aboriginal writers are concerned that the achievements of the present could become the obstacles to change in the future. Taiaiake Alfred refers to the 'colonial mentality' that the present structures foster.

The colonial mentality (in Aboriginal leaders) is recognizable in the gradual assumption of the values, goals, and perspectives that make up the status quo. The development of such a mentality is almost understandable (if not

---

Box 4.2 Nisga'a Treaty More Than Symbols

The Nisga'a Nation has issued a citizenship card that under the new treaty reasserts their historic right to govern themselves—for many a source of pride.

But for Nisga'a language instructor Georgina Harris, the card is an embarrassment.

Ms. Harris, 63, still remembers when the federal government issued blue cards for Indians who were deemed responsible enough to be allowed to buy liquor.

'Once again, we're labelled,' she said. 'I know I'm an Indian. I don't need a card to tell me that I am.'

Nisga'a officials say the card is necessary for entirely practical reasons: They want to ensure that those claiming benefits are entitled to what they receive.

The wallet-size cards operate more like a grocery store membership than the citizenship card of an independent country.

With a card, a Nisga'a pays less for a licence to pick mushrooms or to register a property in the Nisga'a registry than do non-citizens.

Cardholders are entitled to buy a commercial fishing licence—for $25—and sell their catch. Nisga'a citizens are also eligible for a permit to hunt moose, mountain goats and grizzly bears on Nisga'a lands. But hunters are still subject to federal law and must also have a federal government firearms certificate before heading out into the woods.

Nisga'a citizenship is also required to be eligible to vote in local government elections.

However, citizenship is not required to serve on the health or education board. Nor is it a substitute for a passport, a driver's licence or even a health benefits card.

To qualify for citizenship, a person:
- Has a mother and father who were Nisga'a;
- Has a father whose parents or paternal grandfather's parents were Nisga'a;
- Has been adopted by a Nisga'a woman or by a Nisga'a man who had two Nisga'a parents;
- Is a native who marries a Nisga'a and has been accepted by a Nisga'a tribe as a member of that tribe in the presence of witnesses from other Nisga'a tribes at a traditional feast.

Despite the reference to family trees, Edward Allen, chief executive officer of the Nisga'a government, said citizenship is based on rights, not race. Those who have no Nisga'a blood in them can receive citizenship through adoption, he said. 'It's not according to bloodlines.'

So far, citizenship has been issued only to those officially recognized as Nisga'a by the federal government.

Nearly 4,700 have received the cards, which have a photo of the cardholder, a picture of the Nisga'a emblem and a listing of the holder's tribe, gender and birth date.

SOURCE: Robert Matas, 'Nisga'a treaty more than symbols', *Globe and Mail,* 26 Oct. 2001.

acceptable), given the structural basis of indigenous-state relations and the necessity for Native people to work through the various institutions of control in order to achieve their objectives. Native professionals, for example, find it hard to resist the (assimilative) opportunity structure created by the range of state strategies designed to co-opt and weaken challenges to the state's hegemony.[32]

True independence, an end to colonization, and the achievement of a plural society can only come through continuing to challenge the neo-colonial vestiges of colonial rule until they are no longer the dominant structures determining the nature of the relationship.

Community Governance

Community participation implies that there should be established and continuing means whereby communities can participate in the policy and management of the social welfare services they receive. The earlier charitable forms of organization achieved this goal for an elite comprised principally of community leaders who could assist in raising funds. The self-help groups obtain this objective through their own memberships. However, achieving this objective for government services has been difficult. Wharf, speaking of child welfare, summarizes the advantages of community governance.

> The first advantage of community governance is that it provides an opportunity for social learning—for citizens to gain some understanding of the complexities of child neglect and abuse and some appreciation of the impact of factors such as poverty and the lack of affordable housing. Second, community governance requires that communities *own* child welfare. Rather than being seen as the exclusive responsibility of a provincial bureaucracy that is supposed to solve all problems and is subject to severe criticism when it fails to do so, child welfare becomes a community

concern and challenge. Third, community governance allows for the possibility of tuning services to meet local needs, for experimenting with local innovations, and for involving citizens in a variety of voluntary activities. Fourth, community governance spells the end of large and cumbersome provincial bureaucracies.[33]

Despite these advantages, one can find as many examples of centralized, non-community-based systems of governance as one can find examples of systems that allow for local community input. Furthermore, in many instances local community governance structures have been introduced and then discontinued. The reasons for this failure to follow the community government values appear to be connected to the problems of bureaucratic organization and political control of the larger social service organizations.

Community Welfare and Community Health

Community welfare and community health are closely associated ideas. Public health has always been a major goal of public policy. Initially, establishing healthy communities was identified with issues of water quality, sanitation, and protection against the transmission of communicable disease. When these goals had been largely achieved, maintaining health was identified with public access to doctors, drugs, and hospitals. This was achieved through the introduction of hospital insurance, medicare, and provincial pharmacare or similar programs in the 1960s. This achievement resulted in a new attention to the meaning of 'health' as representing more than the absence of disease. Some of the health problems that remained, for example, substance abuse, eating disorders, violence, sexually transmitted diseases, road accidents, and environmental health conditions, had a social origin. Others were a product of unhealthy living conditions—e.g., the continuation of respiratory illness among people who were homeless or poorly housed, and the effects of chronic poverty—that required social rather medical intervention. Finally, community planning and services, rather than treatment, provide the most effective response to a series of medical problems. These include homecare services for the elderly, recognition of the effects of disabilities, non-institutional ways of providing for the needs of both the mentally handicapped and the mentally ill, and campaigns to reduce smoking.

As a result of these issues the concept of health as an objective of public policy has been expanded and health has been identified more and more with a lifestyle that contributes to the maintenance of health and communities that are healthy places to live.

The consequence is a convergence between the concepts of community welfare and health. The convergence is marked by overlapping interests of health and social agencies in all the examples provided above. The overlap raises new questions for community governance, too. Should communities have a health council and a welfare council, or should they have one body that provides a community government forum for both? Should budgets for health and social agencies be separate or should there be a way of recognizing that funding social services may be a more effective response to community problems than funding casualty departments? The overlap raises new questions, too, for the professions. Nursing and social work once seemed to have clear and distinct roles. These clear boundaries no longer exist as community care replaces hospital care and as conditions once defined as medical problems are redefined as social ones.

Canadian Community Social Welfare Systems

Social and community services surround us everywhere. While some are offered directly by governments, others are provided by non-profit organizations, both with and without government support, and still others are offered by private organizations working under contract for government agencies. These services are organizationally separate from the redistributive functions of social welfare but are directly related in two ways. First, changes in the extent and effectiveness of redistribution, and particularly increase in poverty, affect all their objectives and achievements. Second, funding for these services comes, in whole or part, from government and is under the same deficit-driven constraints as are the redistributive programs.

The current auspices of these services include organizations with:

1. an original philanthropic and charitable mandate, e.g., family services agencies, neighbourhood houses, Big Brothers/Sisters;
2. a government mandate:
   - provincial departments of social welfare or social development: e.g., social assistance, child welfare services, child-care services, and children's institutions;
   - provincial departments of health: mental health, family planning, substance abuse, etc.;
   - school boards and provincial government departments of education: special education, alternative schools, etc.;
   - federal and provincial justice departments: family court, probation, juvenile correctional institutions, etc.;
   - local government or non-profit social planning departments and health councils;
3. an Aboriginal mandate: friendship centres, band and tribal councils, Métis organizations, and independent Aboriginal organizations support a network of social services for Aboriginal peoples centring on seven principal functions:
   - social assistance and associated services
   - child welfare, child protection, and associated services
   - child-care services
   - elder and adult care

- substance misuse services
- social housing
- community economic development;
4. a mandate from an active social movement;
   - women's non-profit organizations, such as transition houses, rape crisis centres, abortion clinics
   - organizations for services to mentally handicapped people
   - organizations of persons with disabilities of all types
   - ethnic organizations and organizations of and for refugees and immigrants
   - labour organizations
   - seniors' organizations
   - non-profit community economic development organizations;
5. personal service or entrepreneurial organizations, e.g., marriage counselling, and some forms of daycare, child care, foster and group homes, home services, etc.;
6. a community health mandate.

Changes, 1940–2002

The application of the concept of community in the development of post-war social welfare services is, in retrospect, clear. In the 1940s Canada, along with other Western nations, was confident that a new and better society could be created and that community social services had a significant role to play. The new society would recognize the problems of industrialism, capitalism, and urbanization by developing an array of social services that would provide a means of social integration to deal with the anomie and alienation that was apparent. Services that had been provided on a charitable basis were established as government services, first on a residual basis to deal with immediate problems (during the 1940–50 period), but increasingly on an institutional basis as fundamental citizenship rights (1960–70). Towards the end of the 1970s an attempt was made by the federal government to consolidate this pattern through the establishment of an overall framework for financing

social services throughout Canada as part of the social security review. If it had succeeded it would have established an institutional commitment to community social services as a Canadian citizenship right. It failed, however, partly for financial reasons (the first wave of financial restructuring) but also because of provincial opposition to the further extension of federal authority. It is also possible that these government social services were beginning to be affected by the lack of informed community participation and by the alienation that their size and bureaucratization were causing.

At the same time as this consolidation of the federal framework was being planned there was the assertion of diversity claims that had been ignored. The 1970 Royal Commission on the Status of Women in Canada, the implementation in 1971 of the multicultural policy recommendation of the Royal Commission on Bilingualism and Biculturalism, and the rejection by First Nations of the 1969 White Paper on the Indian Act all indicated that diversity was the emerging issue for Canada's social discourse and hence for community social services. The assumptions of an earlier period concerning patriarchy, English-speaking dominance over other ethnic groups, and assimilation of First Nations had to be set aside. Community economic development also had its origins in this period in the 1973 Local Employment Assistance Program and the 1975 Community Employment Strategy.[34]

In the 1980s the claims of other groups to separate recognition became more apparent as visible minorities, the handicapped and disabled, gay and lesbian members of the community, and immigrants and refugees asked to be heard. The 1982 Canadian Charter of Rights and Freedoms provided important legal support to their claims. The changes begun in the 1970s also led to the development of new forms of community social service as the social movements went beyond criticizing the insensitivity of existing services by establishing services of their own. The development by feminists of sexual assault services and transition houses, the establishment by First Nations of child welfare services, and the establishment by the gay and lesbian community of AIDS-related services all indicate the strength of this trend. The 1980s were also the time when community social welfare activists began to take a serious interest in alternative forms of economic institution that offered the promise of development opportunities with greater community control while being less vulnerable to global economic influence. The concept of health was also broadened to a concern with community living conditions and social issues that defied medical intervention and required a community service response.

During the 1990s the trend towards pluralism in the delivery of community social services expanded and accelerated. The expansion was aided by the downsizing of government departments that occurred in every province. Often this downsizing led to new funding for alternative community service organizations. The development of Aboriginal community social services has been particularly striking. The services have grown much larger and carry a much wider array of service functions. They are now the predominant mode of providing service to Aboriginal peoples. The social service staffs in

Aboriginal communities have also grown in number and in professional and management capacity. In a broader context this growth is a major component of Aboriginal self-government.

The changes made in community social services are working deeper and deeper into the way our communities function and are a new and different expression of social welfare community objectives. There is no way back to a simpler society based on principles of integration into a single dominant Canadian society. Instead, the society is itself changing and must now deal with the conflict between the earlier concepts of community, dominated by established interests, and the new plural and diverse community. The community economic development movement offers an alternative approach for economic viability to that offered by the global economy. The healthy community movement offers an alternative to medical intervention as a means of ensuring personal well-being.

In the new century the community objectives of social welfare policy appear to be being achieved more fully than the redistributive ones. Horizontal equity between diverse social groups is increasing at the same time as vertical equity between income classes is decreasing.

Additional Readings

Ken Barter, 'Reclaiming Community: Shaping the Social Work Agenda', *Canadian Social Work* 2, 2 (Fall 2000): 6–18. This is a contemporary statement of the challenges faced by social work and related disciplines in putting into operation the concept of community today.

Gord Bruyere, 'Living in Another Man's House', *Canadian Social Work Review* 15, 2 (1998): 169–76. Bruyere provides an articulate account of his experience of social work education. The article illustrates how a concept of welfare developed in one society is inapplicable and irrelevant to another.

Will Kymlicka, *Multicultural Citizenship: A Liberal Theory of Minority Rights*. Oxford: Oxford

University Press, 1995. Chapter 8, 'Toleration and Its Limits', explores the relationships of tolerance and respect that are necessary in a society that respects diversity. It also suggests that there are limits to tolerance.

C. Wright Mills, *The Sociological Imagination*. New York: Oxford University Press, 1959. The classical statement of the relationship between private troubles and public issues, which has played a central role in establishing the community functions of social welfare, is found on pp. 1–15 of this seminal work..

Roxana Ng, *The Politics of Community Services: Immigrant Women, Class and the State*. Halifax:

Fernwood, 1996. This 100-page monograph is required reading for all who work, or are interested in working, in community social services. It carefully dissects the day-to-day work of a community agency and shows how an agency's relationship to the state permeates its affairs.

Study Questions

1. What are the strengths and weaknesses for social welfare policy of the concept of community captured in the reference from the C. Wright Mills article cited in the text?

2. Is social control an accepted goal of social welfare? If so, what is the role of the social services in setting and policing limits to individual and collective behaviour?

3. How is the concept of diversity affecting how we think about community? What effect is this change having in the way that social services are organized and managed?

4. Are there limits to our tolerance of cultural diversity within the general Canadian community, and, if so, who has a right to decide where those limits lie?

Notes

1. Kenneth Boulding, 'The Boundaries of Social Policy', *Social Work* 5, 12 (Jan. 1967).

2. Roeher Institute, *Social Well-Being: A Paradigm for Reform* (Toronto: Roeher Institute, 1993), 41, citing Will Kymlicka, *Liberalism, Community and Culture* (Oxford: Clarendon Press, 1989).

3. Brian Wharf and Michael Clague, eds, *Community Organizing: Canadian Experiences* (Toronto: Oxford University Press, 1997), 321.

4. See N.H. Lithwick, *Urban Canada: Problems and Prospects* (Ottawa: Central Mortgage and Housing Corporation, 1970).

5. Robert Heilbronner, *Capitalism in the Twenty-First Century* (Concord, Ont.: Anansi Press, 1992), 95–100.

6. C. Wright Mills, *The Sociological Imagination* (New York: Oxford University Press, 1959), as cited by Brian Wharf, *Social Work and Social Change in Canada* (Toronto: McClelland & Stewart, 1990), 9.

7. Wharf, *Social Work and Social Change*, 12.

8. James Ife, 'Localised Needs in a Global Economy: Bridging the Gap with Social Work Practice', *Canadian Social Work*, Special Issue 2, 1 (2000): 56.

9. C. Wright Mills, 'The Professional Ideology of Social Pathologists', *American Journal of Sociology* 49 (Sept. 1942): 175–6.

10. Ewan McIntyre, 'The Historical Context', in Brian Wharf, ed., *Rethinking Child Welfare in Canada* (Toronto: McClelland & Stewart, 1993), 19, citing Jane Ursel, *Private Lives, Public Policy: 100 Years of State Intervention in the Family* (Toronto: Women's Press, 1992).

11. John L. Tobias, 'Protection, Civilization, Assimilation: An Outline of the History of Canada's Indian Policy', *Western Canadian Journal of Anthropology* 6, 2 (1976): 13–29.

12. For a full account of a policy that had its origins in British imperial objectives, see Andrew Armitage, *Comparing the Policy of Assimilation: Australia, Canada and New Zealand* (Vancouver: University of British Columbia Press, 1995).

13. Wharf, *Social Work and Social Change*, 144 ff.

14. Roland Warren, *The Community in America* (Chicago: Rand McNally, 1963).

15. Bridget Moran, *Justa: A First Nations Leader* (Vancouver: Arsenal Press, 1994), 13.

16. Marcia Nozick, 'Five Principles of Sustainable Community Development', in Eric Shragge, ed.,

Community Economic Development (Montreal: Black Rose Books, 1993), 18–20.

17. Warren, *Community in America*, 174.

18. Alfred J. Kahn, *Social Policy and Social Services* (New York: Random House, 1973), 139–42.

19. Warren, *Community in America*, 177.

20. Amitai Etzioni, *Modern Organizations* (Englewood Cliffs, NJ: Prentice-Hall, 1964), 59.

21. Armitage, *Comparing the Policy of Assimilation*, 116.

22. Marilyn Callahan, 'Feminist Approaches to Child Welfare', in Wharf, ed., *Rethinking Child Welfare*, 204.

23. British Columbia, *Liberating Our Children: Liberating Our Nations* (Victoria: Ministry of Social Services, 1992), 107; see recommendations, ibid., 96-9.

24. Etzioni, *Modern Organizations*, 60.

25. Wharf and Clague, eds, *Community Organizing*, 301–25.

26. Andrée Demers and Deena White, 'The Community Approach to Prevention: Colonization of the Community?', *Canadian Review of Social Policy* 39 (1997): 13.

27. Roxana Ng, *The Politics of Community Services* (Halifax: Fernwood, 1996).

28. Ben Lappin, *The Community Workers and the Social Work Tradition* (Toronto: School of Social Work, University of Toronto, 1970), 167.

29. Wharf and Clague, eds, *Community Organizing*, 306.

30. Will Kymlicka, *Multicultural Citizenship: A Liberal Theory of Minority Rights* (Oxford: Oxford University Press, 1995), 194.

31. See Armitage, *Comparing the Policy of Assimilation*, 239–40.

32. Taiaiake Alfred, *Peace, Power, and Righteousness: An Indigenous Manifesto* (Toronto: Oxford University Press, 1999), 70.

33. Wharf, ed., *Rethinking Child Welfare*, 224.

34. Ken Watson, 'A Review of Four Evaluations of CED Programs: What have we learned in two decades?', in Burt Galloway and Joe Hudson, eds, *Community Economic Development* (Toronto: Thompson Educational Publishing, 1994), 134.

CHAPTER 5

Canada's Record:
Community Welfare
and the Social Services

This chapter applies the role of community in Canadian social welfare described in the previous chapter to the main types of Canadian community social services. These services provide most of the employment for direct service workers in the human services, for example, social workers, child and youth care workers, counsellors. As a result the issues have a direct relationship to working conditions for line workers in the human services.

Learning Objectives

1. To understand how government social services are organized.
2. To understand how Aboriginal social services are organized and their dual relationship to both Aboriginal and non-Aboriginal governments.
3. To understand the role of social movements in the organization of social services and their dual relationships to their members and to government.
4. To understand why social service co-ordination is needed and the different ways through which it can be achieved.
5. To understand the impact of contracting on social service organizations.
6. To understand the need for internal agency policies to protect clients and workers from abuse.

Community Social Services

Social and community services surround us everywhere. Some of the services are directly provided by an elected government, most often the provincial government. Other services are provided through such groups as community boards and contracted social service agencies and individuals. Contracts expand the way in which government control is exercised while separating responsibility for service delivery from responsibility for policy. In the case of Aboriginal social service organizations there is often a dual responsibility to Aboriginal and non-Aboriginal governments. A similar, but less developed, relationship is found where autonomous social movements develop social services and then seek government funding.

Government social services are offered primarily by provincial governments, with federal and municipal governments performing limited roles. The government social service system has not been developed as a whole; rather, each service has distinct historical origins, usually defined around a social problem and a social intervention designed to manage the problem.

Provincial Government Social Services

The principal provincial government social services in most provinces are:

- social assistance
- employment placement services
- child welfare services
- child-care services
- youth corrections services
- mental health services
- substance abuse services
- adult and elderly care services

1. Social Assistance

Social assistance social services have been developed around the social assistance income security program and are administered by either municipal or provincial government departments. Expansion of such services was one of the major objectives of the Canada Assistance Plan, which, in contrast to earlier cost-sharing arrangements with the provinces, included provision for the federal government to provide 50 per cent of the costs of 'welfare services'. Welfare services included casework, home-maker care, daycare, and community development.[1] The objectives of these services through the CAP was broadly stated as being 'the lessening, removal or prevention of the causes and effects of poverty, child neglect or dependence on public assistance'. Coverage of social assistance social services has been limited to people on the social assistance income security program and those whose income falls below poverty lines. In some provinces, for example, Alberta, these services are organized as separate preventive services while in others they are provided alongside the social assistance payment program.

The result of making social services available to the poor has not provided an effective strategy to deal with poverty. However, social assistance has become an important form of support for those who need and qualify for it. In particular, social assistance has been the means through which community services for persons with disabilities, including the mentally handicapped, have been developed. The link between these services and social assistance has been criticized on many occasions. Advocates for persons with disability have criticized the link as they consider that persons with disability should have access to the support services they need as a right, not contingent on financial need. Conservative critics of social assistance have been concerned that the link constitutes a barrier to people leaving welfare for independent employment because the loss of these benefits, when the recipient no longer qualifies for social assistance, acts as an incentive to remain eligible.

As a result of the value that these services have as social supports, there has been recurrent interest in separating the social assistance service and income programs and developing the services in their own right. The Senate Committee on Poverty advocated such a separation by removing all responsibility for income security to the federal level of government while leaving the provinces to provide social services, supported by a revised and expanded CAP. The federal income security review of the 1970s considered a similar proposal. The repeal of the CAP and the introduction of the CHST in 1995 opened the way for provinces to again review the relationship of these services to social assistance, as the direct funding link between these services and the CAP was broken. However, no province has undertaken a full review, anticipating perhaps that breaking the relationship would lead to an expanded demand for services.

2. Social Assistance Employment Placement Services

Employment placement services cover a wide range of rehabilitative services designed to assist the employable social assistance recipient re-enter employment. The services include:

- job clubs
- funded short-term work placements
- assisted child-care services
- short-term training programs
- 'workfare'-type programs

The services keep pressure on employable social assistance recipients to remain focused on finding a job and are seen as necessary to offset the concern that social assistance programs create dependency. Their effectiveness is open to question. As Marilyn Callahan points out, these programs seem to be conducted more for the political posture they represent than for any tangible benefit that can be discovered for the unemployed.[2]

3. Child Welfare Services

Child welfare services were developed initially in urban centres by Children's Aid Societies, supported by organized philanthropy.[3] In most provinces, this pattern was replaced by government services in the sixties and seventies when government support to Children's Aid Societies reached up to 95 per cent of their budgets. Government child welfare services are now usually provided by provincial departments of social welfare and operate alongside, but separate from, the same department's social assistance programs. Child welfare services also were included under the cost-sharing provisions of the CAP, now replaced by the CHST.

When the child welfare services were included in the cost-sharing provisions of the CAP it was expected that these services would be broadly defined and would be part of a general anti-poverty service strategy. This has never been achieved. The objectives of child welfare services have been to ameliorate or correct a series of specific problems, including child abuse, child neglect, and other parenting problems. Indeed, during the 1990s this focus narrowed to concentrate specifically on the investigation and prevention of child abuse. This narrowed view, from child welfare to child protection, has been precipitated by a combination of media attention and judicial review of the child welfare services. The results have included a concentration on 'risk assessment' technologies, a very difficult blame-ridden work environment for social agencies and social workers, and

rising child protection caseloads and numbers of children in care.[4] The focus on child protection has been challenged in three different ways.

One challenge came from looking at child welfare services from an institutional perspective. This approach recognized the difficulty experienced by *all* families in fulfilling their child-care functions in society. An institutional response to child welfare problems takes the form of a broad array of supportive family services—family life education, daycare, homemaker services, family counselling services—that would be made available to parents as social rights.[5]

A second challenge comes from the experience of First Nations with the child welfare system. Following the closing of the residential schools in the 1960s, provincial child welfare services were extended to Indian reserves. The experience was particularly harsh. By the late 1970s, 40 per cent of all children in care in the western provinces and in northern Canada were from First Nations, yet First Nations children comprised only 5 per cent of children.[6] First Nations resisted and challenged the loss of their children, and began to organize child welfare systems for themselves based in their own experience and culture.

The third challenge has come from the feminist social movement and has centred on the experience of mothers who have had their children apprehended because of neglect. Callahan writes:

> The more disadvantaged the mother or caregiver, the more disadvantaged is the child. This is the crux of the argument. The unequal status of women has two principal consequences for children: they are more likely to live in poverty and suffer the results because their mothers cannot earn sufficient wages and they are at greater risk of violence and sexual abuse because their mothers cannot protect them from likely offenders.[7]

By looking at the experience of women as caregivers and service providers, Callahan comes to the conclusion that the problem of neglect should be framed as a problem of poverty and dealt with by supporting women with practical services, not framed as a problem of inadequate parenting to be dealt with by taking children away as a form of punishment. In a recent commentary on the direction of child welfare policy, Karen Swift writes:

> I argue that the purposes of current child welfare policy have little to do with producing safety for children. Rather, they serve to intensify class and gender divisions, and are in keeping with the neo-liberal agenda operating in all policy arenas. These policy directions, I argue, will mean substantially increased surveillance of both the clients of child welfare services, who are mostly poor women, and the front line workers, mostly women, hired to protect children. At the same time, discussion of real and serious problems facing families involved with protection services will continue to be ignored and delegitimized as irrelevant to child safety.[8]

4. Child-care Services

Up to the 1960s less than 20 per cent of women with children were in the labour force and the prevailing view was that women with small children should be at home. The need for government-supported child care was placed on the social agenda by the 1970 Royal Commission on the Status of Women, which identified the increasing number of women who were entering the workforce. In 1984 the *Report of the Royal Commission on Equality in Employment* said unambiguously:

> Child care is not a luxury, it is a necessity. Unless government policy responds to this urgency, we put women, children and the economy of the future at risk. Considering that more than half of all Canadian children spend much of their time in the care of people other than their parents, and that more than half of all parents need child care services for

their children, social policy should not be permitted to remain so greatly behind the times.[9]

The need for expanded child care continued to increase. In 1986, the federal Task Force on Child Care[10] recommended a comprehensive child-care and parental leave system that would be implemented through new federal-provincial cost-sharing agreements. In 1988, the child-care deduction was introduced as part of the budget, providing some income tax relief for the child-care costs of middle- and upper-income parents. In the same year the Canada Child Care Act was introduced. By this time, 65 per cent of mothers with children worked outside the home, including 57 per cent of mothers with children under three.[11] The Canada Child Care Act was never passed. The bill was not adopted by the time Parliament was dissolved for the 1988 federal election, and neither it nor any alternative was introduced after the election. The objective at the time was to support an additional 200,000 subsidized child-care spaces. This would have led to a doubling of the existing subsidized spaces, then numbering 243,545 and serving 13 per cent of the children needing care. Since 1988, thought of federal legislation and action has waned with each passing year. In 1995 the passage of the Canada Health and Social Transfer Act, along with the decrease in federal funding, appeared to bring the pursuit of a national child-care strategy to a dead end. Quebec, alone among the provinces, introduced a comprehensive child-care policy and program in the early 1990s. The child-care debate, and the failure to act, demonstrated the problems of the social services in the 1980–2000 period. The federal government failed to act on a central issue of equity affecting primarily women and children, and the provinces, with the exception of Quebec, failed to fill the gap (see Box 5.1).

5. Youth Corrections Services

The development of correctional services for youth can be dated from the Juvenile

Delinquents Act of 1908. The Act was revised several times and then in 1984 was replaced by the Young Offenders Act, which abolished the general status of 'delinquency' in favour of the more precise status of 'offender', defined by the Criminal Code. The Young Offenders Act is a federal statute, part of the Criminal Code of Canada, and provides, in effect, for a series of court procedures and court dispositions for persons between the ages of 12 and 18 that are different from those applicable to adults. The Act also decriminalized behaviour for children under 12 by withdrawing authority for criminal proceedings.

All aspects of the administration of the Young Offenders Act are provincial. Family courts, probation services, and institutional facilities are all operated by the provinces.

Box 5.1 Good Child Care Harder To Find: Study

Almost two million Canadian children are cared for regularly by someone other than their parents. But only one in five receives care in a regulated setting like a daycare centre or after-school program, according to a new study.

With demand increasing, finding good care is harder than ever, as the number of child-care spaces in many provinces—particularly those that are subsidized—is actually dropping or remaining stagnant, the Canadian Council on Social Development says in a report being released today.

'Despite broad public support for child care, trends in the 1990s have been contrary. Child-care services have experienced erosion, fragmentation and disparity,' according to the State of Canada's Children.

For example, since 1992 the number of regulated child-care spaces in Alberta has fallen by almost 5,000. And, between 1995 and 1998, the Ontario government cut its spending on child care by more than $70-million. The exception is Quebec which, in the past three years, has added 100,000 new daycare spots and doubled its budget.

In its annual report card, the CCSD calls on Ottawa and the other provinces to embrace the Quebec model, which features universal, regulated $5-a-day care for all children under the age of 13, including pre-school daycare and before and after-school care. The Quebec approach is lauded as a holistic, coherent system that stresses early childhood development and supports parents while they work or study.

The provinces spend just over $1-billion annually on child care. There were 516,734 regulated spaces in Canada in 1998, according to the Childcare Resource and Research Unit of the University of Toronto. That works out to one space for every 10 children.

Marcel Lauziere, executive director of the CCSD, said that when the first ministers meet next week in Quebec City, the so-called children's agency should be front and centre in their discussions. 'The findings of Progress 2000 show that our kids can't wait,' he said.

Among some other highlights of the study:

* Public spending on education is declining relative to the gross national product.
* University tuition fees jumped by 125 per cent during the 1990s.
* There are 50 per cent more poor children today than in 1989.
* More than 40 per cent of all food-bank users are under the age of 18.
* The national crime rate has fallen for six consecutive years.
* There are dramatic declines in the number of young people dying in car crashes.

The report concludes that, overall, families and children are paying for the cutbacks of the 1990s, notably in health care, education and social services. The CCSD also argues that governments and business largely take families for granted and that many public policies are woefully outdated.

SOURCE: André Picard, 'Good child care harder to find: study', *Globe and Mail*, 25 Jan. 2000.

These services tend to fall across major established lines of provincial departmental bureaucracy, causing the development of a variety of administrative patterns. The Juvenile Court is usually administratively responsible to the provincial Attorney General. On the other hand, some of the resources needed by a service to juveniles are obviously child welfare services (foster homes and children's institutions). The result is that while in some provinces the probation service is established within the Attorney General's department, in other provinces it is established within the provincial Department of Social Welfare and in still others it works directly for the Juvenile Court.

The primary objective of juvenile correction services, as might be expected, is even more clearly focused social control than is the case with child welfare services. The central function of juvenile corrections has been to control and rehabilitate adolescents adjudged 'offenders' by the courts. The implicit theory behind this function has the following features: the community cannot overlook criminal behaviour; if the offender can be caught, he should be punished and reformed; however, the punishments contained in the Criminal Code are too severe and overlook the importance of growth and change in young people's lives. Thus, flexibility is needed in the measures that can be taken, which include discharging offenders to parents, probation, and children's institutions.

At the core of the problem of youth crime are a small number of brutal acts that endanger the life or health of other persons. These, indeed, cannot be overlooked, and most eventually appear before the court. They are surrounded by a much larger number of offences involving property (shoplifting, joy-riding in a 'borrowed' car, etc.), disturbance of the peace (noise late at night), and the use of alcohol or drugs. This second group of offences merges into an array of normal adolescent behaviours. In fact, to have committed one or more of the offences at some time or other can be considered sociologically normal behaviour. However, political and public concern with the Young Offenders Act and with youth corrections in the 1990s centred on the fact that children under the age of 12 could not be prosecuted and on the maximum sentence of three years that could be imposed under the Act. Both concerns reflected a 'law and order' orientation to youth and to social problems reflecting the dominant conservative social policy agenda.

The result is seen in the proposed Youth Criminal Justice Act (2001). Jim Hackler writes that the purpose of the new law appears to be to appease those who want to 'get tough'.

> This has never worked in the past, nor will it in the future. Those who think that punishment is the solution will never be satisfied. . . . Holding parents accountable sounds good. Many of the judges I interviewed said that when they came to the bench, they were determined to make parents responsible. They changed. A single mother has a teenager in trouble and three younger kids at home. Her boss is annoyed because she misses work to go to court. It creates financial hardship. The appointments she tries to keep with various bureaucracies make life even more miserable. Should the judge throw her in jail because her teenager is delinquent? . . . The simple-minded notion of holding parents responsible simply ignores the struggles of many parents dealing with difficult children.[12]

6. Mental Health Services

Mental health services include a variety of major independent programs brought into association with each other in the 1960s and 1970s. These included the operation of the large mental hospitals that are the inheritors of the asylum tradition of mental illness segregation; the work of independent medical practitioners in office-based practice who seek to modify behaviour by counselling and drugs; the community-based mental health clinics that had been developed from the earlier child guidance clinics; the psychiatric wards within acute-care general hospitals; and the independent and largely volunteer-operated services provided by such organizations as the Canadian Mental Health Association. In all provinces major mental hospitals have been closed and most treatment of mental illness is now performed in the community. This change was encouraged by the availability of new forms of drugs that allowed behaviours to be controlled in the community; the demands of parents and support groups for accessible services; professional preference for treatment in the community rather than institutionalization; concern for the civil rights of persons institutionalized on the basis of a medical diagnosis; and cost considerations. In the past two decades cost considerations, particularly the high per capita costs of institutional care, have been a driving consideration in a continued trend to community care.

Mental health services have been organized under a number of governmental auspices, including departments of health, departments of mental health, and departments of health and social welfare. These services were not covered by the Canada Assistance Plan, which tended to separate them administratively from child welfare and social services. The objectives of this complex of services are not easily stated. As with the residual child welfare and juvenile correction services, a core phenomenon, severe mental illness, requires specific forms of medical intervention. Beyond that core phenomenon, there is a much more diffuse arena in which behaviour can be labelled by using the terminology of mental illness (depression, anxiety, or character disorder), or it can be viewed as a by-product of the societal condition. If someone is destitute and alone, it is not surprising to find that person also anxious and depressed. For the core phenomenon, the objectives of mental illness services are clear enough. For the more diffuse surrounding phenomena, the mental health objectives are not at all clear. The 1991 BC Royal Commission on

Health Care and Costs noted that:

> while some mental illness may not be preventable, countering the effects of poverty, poor housing, physical and sexual abuse, the lack of meaningful employment and the abuse of drugs and alcohol is as important as medical treatment in the management and social integration of the mentally ill.[13]

If the definition of mental health is broadened to include all efforts to improve social life and deal with social problems, the name becomes increasingly inappropriate. Mental health, with its implications of a known or knowable set of 'normal' behaviours, is not an appropriate way of addressing the problems of political alignment, power, and change. Mental health services addressed to helping the poor cope with inequality can serve to sustain an unjust social order in which the mental illnesses of the rich (greed, avarice, and delusions of wisdom) are untreated. The concept of mental health, with its inevitable connection to the prestige and status of the medical profession, tends to lead to the devaluing of the contributions of laypersons and of other professions. Finally, mental health, with its tendency to organize reality on a health-to-illness continuum, has particular problems when used as a planning or developmental base.[14]

The trend towards community care has meant that considerable numbers of people who might have been hospitalized, or indeed who are hospitalized for short periods, are present in the community. Community mental health clinics with specialized nursing and social work programs have been developed to provide some community support to the mentally ill. The 'Lifeline' programs of the Canadian Mental Health Association serve a similar function. These services have expanded and continue to expand as community rather than institutional care objectives are pursued.

The people who receive these services in the community are more than often also in receipt of social assistance or are homeless and receive limited support from shelters, food banks, and soup kitchens. Others receive help from child welfare or correctional services. Thus, these community social services frequently overlap with each other and struggle with one another over how to share the responsibility of providing service or distributing the blame of failure.

7. Substance Abuse Services

Substance (alcohol, drug, tobacco) abuse services are usually organized and supported by ministries of health. Substance abuse is not only a major health problem but also a major social problem both to personal relationships and at work. Estimates of the financial consequences of substance abuse vary widely, but the costs of alcohol abuse alone are placed in the range of $10-$20 billion a year.

The prevention of substance abuse has increasingly been seen as being first and foremost a public health social problem rather than a medical treatment or law enforcement problem, although both these latter strategies have a role to play. The substance abuse services through ministries of health deal principally with public education and treatment, but they also have a policy and advisory role in the regulation of consumption and law enforcement. At the community level public education takes several forms, including general public education, school programs, and programs aimed at specific populations, such as the elderly, employee groups, and ethnic groups including First Nations, in each of which substance abuse has unique characteristics. Treatment, too, has increasingly been developed so as to work closely with community groups and other social supports both in the workplace and outside it.

8. Adult and Elderly Care Services

Adult and elderly care services have been developed by the provinces, each reflecting a particular history. Common features of the services available now include:

- assessment and case management services
- meals-on-wheels
- homemaker services
- home nursing care
- community physiotherapy and occupational therapy
- adult daycare
- respite care
- group homes
- long-term care residential facilities
- chronic-care units/hospitals
- assessment and treatment centres and day hospitals.[15]

These services sit across the boundary between the health and social services—some provinces administer them through health ministries while others oversee these services through social service ministries. Regardless of ministry responsibility the trend has been towards community rather than institutional services. Generally, too, services in these categories for the elderly are made available in Canada without a financial 'needs' test and with service charges set at a level that can be afforded on minimum incomes. The services represent a form of 'institutional' social welfare provision, contrasting with the 'residual' form of services for children and families. Services for adult persons with disabilities have been less well developed, more usually taking the form of the 'residual' social assistance social services described above.

Federal Government Social Services

Generally, the federal government is much less active than the provinces in the social services field, although the citizenship and immigration service is an important exception. The principal federal government social services are:

- citizenship and immigration services
- veterans affairs

1. Citizenship and Immigration Services

Since World War II Canada has had nearly 8 million immigrants. Currently, 4.5 million Canadians are 'foreign born' and constitute some 16 per cent of the Canadian population. Immigration continues at an annual rate of around 250,000 persons, constituting about 0.7 per cent of the Canadian population. The Canadian Department of Citizenship is also responsible for the Immigration and Refugee Board, which has the often controversial responsibility of adjudicating claims for refugee status. Given the negative publicity that has accompanied the refugee determination process it is important to see this work in the context of Canada's immigration policies as a whole. Refugee claimants approximate 25,000 persons annually, of which in 1997, for example, 40 per cent were accepted. Thus, the vast majority of immigrants to Canada enter through the mainstream immigration program.

Settlement services and support to community agencies offering settlement services are an important part of the responsibility of the citizenship and immigration service. Delivering these services through community agencies and, where possible, with the co-operation of the provinces is seen as serving the objective of the effective integration of immigrants into Canadian society.[16]

2. Veterans Affairs

The primary mandate of the Department of Veterans Affairs has been services to the veterans of World Wars I and II and the Korean War. As a result the services now available are principally for seniors. A veterans affairs mandate for services to peacekeeping ex-servicemen has not been developed.

Municipal Government Community Development and Social Planning Agencies

To this point, the social agencies that have been mentioned have been primarily case- and problem-oriented. Even the occasional reference to supportive services, such as daycare, has basically been within a vision of stable social institutions that need outside resources to meet their objectives. Community development and social planning agencies are directed to intervention at a different point in the symbiotic relationship between a community and its members—community governance. The community as a whole, not the members as individuals, is the target for intervention.

Community development had its origins in the processes through which economic development was introduced in post-colonial (so-called underdeveloped) societies in the post-war period. However, the first applications of community development in Canada were during the 1960s and focused on issues of social policy, particularly issues related to the 'War on Poverty'. Initial use was by organizations such as the Company of Young Canadians. Target groups were Aboriginal peoples and the poor. Community development work was largely initiated by government, although in some centres voluntary social agencies employed community development workers. The initial enthusiasm for community development was substantially dampened by a cyclical effect in which successful community work led to organized groups who expressed their own ideas as to what services they needed and who were critical of the services they were getting. Threatened by such challenges to existing services, the funds for community development work were often cut back or withdrawn.

The first social planning councils were organized in the 1960s, usually within the voluntary sector of social service activity. Their initial role was to identify need and suggest ways in which need might be served by voluntary social agencies. These activities were seen as helpful to the fundraising and allocating activities of Community Chests. In that the voluntary agencies were but part of a larger whole, it was inevitable that the studies of social planning councils also had to deal with the government sector of social service, if for no other purpose than to establish a frame of reference for the voluntary sector. The role of social planning councils was thus broadened. In recognition of the contribution to planning that was being made, some cities (Vancouver and Halifax) established their own social planning departments. These early beginnings established the methodology and value of social planning as a support to community governance.

Michael Clague provides a full account of the ebb and flow of the relationship from the 1960s to the 1990s between the social services and social planning and community development.[17] In each decade the larger community context and provincial government policies have given the relationship a distinct character. It seems that the provincial social services need the relationship to community that social planning and community development provide but are very reluctant to give control to local community groups. Pulkingham comments on her own experience of a community development project in British Columbia:

> While the point of departure for community development is an explicit value-based perspective committed to the extension of democratic dialogue . . . community-based strategies nevertheless remain highly susceptible to manipulation which encourages a form of conservatism and protection of vested interests that equals the more blatant social pathological approaches which individualize social problems.[18]

Despite these reservations, the need for a forum for community governance is beyond dispute. If the goal of the social (and health) community-based social services is social justice, then they cannot do their work in isolation from the communities they serve. Without the reality of continuing contact they become internally oriented and focused on their own bureaucratic problems. However, when they become more oriented to social control than to social justice, the voice of community often becomes an embarrassment as social agencies become part of the structure that upholds discrimination.

First Nation On-Reserve Social Services

Social services for First Nations on reserve have been developed independently of other government services and have characteristics of their own. Until the 1940s social services for First Nations were entirely under the control and management of the federal Department of Indian Affairs. For the most part social services were non-existent. There were two exceptions. The local Indian agents were empowered to distribute 'relief', often in the form of food rations, and Indian children could be required to attend residential schools. The residential school was much more than an educational institution. Initially it was intended to prepare young Indians for assimilation and Christian citizenship, but by the 1940s it had also become a general welfare resource for the care of children who in the view of local Indian agents were not being competently cared for by their parents.

The separate nature of welfare institutions on Indian reserves attracted attention during the 1946-8 hearings of the Special Joint Committee of the Senate and House of Commons Appointed to Consider the Indian Act. In a joint presentation to the Committee by the Canadian Welfare Council and the Canadian Association of Social Workers the argument was developed that Indian people should enjoy the same services available to other Canadians. This included the family and child welfare services provided by the provinces. In summary:

> the brief said that 'the practice of adopting Indian children is loosely conceived and executed and is usually devoid of the careful legal and social protections available to white children,' and as wards of the federal government,

'Indian children who are neglected lack the protection afforded under social legislation available to white children in the community.' The practice of placing children in residential schools was also condemned. . . . The brief concluded that the best way to improve the situation was to extend the services of the provincial departments of health, welfare and education to the residents of reserves.[19]

The argument presented in the brief was accepted by the Joint Committee and led to changes in the Indian Act. In 1951 the Act was amended and provision was made for the operation of provincial health, welfare, and educational services on reserves, under the terms of agreements to be negotiated with the provinces. However, except in Ontario, these negotiations could not be completed successfully. The other provinces all held to the position that services to Indian children and families were a federal responsibility. As a result, services were only extended where the federal government agreed to pay 100 per cent of the costs. As each province had its own ideas about extending services to Indian families and children, the services that were available also differed. The result was seen in the 1970s as constituting:

> an incredible disparity in the quantity and quality of child welfare programs available to status Indians from one province to another. In some instances there are disparities within a province. This myriad of differing policy approaches results in unequal treatment of Indian children across Canada.[20]

Among the disparities were the following:

- Outside Ontario, social assistance social services were not available on reserve as they were provided under the terms of the Canada Assistance Plan and only Ontario agreed to make a 50 per cent contribution to their cost. All other provinces insisted on 100 per cent reimbursement.

- Child protection services were available on reserve because the federal government was willing to pay 100 per cent of the cost of apprehensions, foster care, and adoption costs. However, the full range of child welfare services developed by provinces, particularly the preventive and home support services, were not available. The inevitable result was that apprehension of children became the principal form of on-reserve child welfare service.
- Provincial child-care services were not available on reserve.
- Youth correctional services were available on reserve under similar terms to child welfare service. The result was that there was an emphasis on incarceration rather than on community diversion.
- Provincial community mental health services were not available on reserve.
- Provincial substance abuse services were not available on reserve.
- Provincial adult and elderly care services were not available on reserve.
- Community development and social planning services by provincial or local governments were not available on reserve.

Opposition to the extension of provincial services to First Nation reserve communities came not only from the provinces but also from the First Nation communities, who saw the extension of provincial services as a step towards the goal of assimilation. The eventual complete assimilation of Aboriginal peoples has been the policy of the Canadian government since the passage of the Indian Act in 1876. In 1969 Jean Chrétien, then the Liberal Minister for Indian Affairs, tabled the policy document, *Statement of the Government of Canada on Indian Policy*, known as the White Paper. The White Paper called for the abolition of Indian reserves and of Indian status and the dissolution of the Department of Indian Affairs. Indians were to become full citizens and services to them were to be fully integrated with general community services. The White Paper policies were condemned by Indian leaders, and in 1971 these proposals were withdrawn and an end was declared to the policy of assimilation.

Since 1971 social service policy for Indian peoples has been caught between conflicting long-term goals. One long-term goal has been the establishment of Indian self-government, which has been pursued by the development of Indian band, tribal council, friendship centre, Métis, and independent Aboriginal organization capacity to provide services to Indian peoples. The second long-term objective is equality of service for all Canadian Aboriginal peoples— First Nations (Indian), Inuit, and Métis, both on and off reserve—and all other Canadian citizens. Whereas the first goal, self-government, has led to the development of many independent Aboriginal services, the second goal, equality, has limited their autonomy to providing approximately the same services that are available to other Canadians. As the services available to other Canadians are provided largely by each province, the model for service provision to Indian peoples has been one in which the services from Indian Affairs have been determined by provincial comparisons. As a result the services that are available are largely a copy of their provincial government counterparts. The principal services available are:

- social assistance social services
- child welfare services
- adult and elderly care services
- substance misuse services.

The impact of these services on First Nation communities is much greater than on the wider community because service use is much higher. The Royal Commission on Aboriginal Peoples reported a social assistance participation rate of 41.5 per cent for Indian persons 15 years and older living on reserve and 28.6 per cent for all Aboriginal peoples both on and off reserve. It also reported that the overall rate for Aboriginal children in care is 46 per 1,000 as compared to

less than 10 per 1,000 for non-Aboriginal children.[21]

Each of the services is also caught in internal contradictions that can be traced to the competing objectives of self-government and service equality. The social assistance program has not only led to high levels of dependency, it has also undermined community principles of collective support. Attempts to provide work incentives become meaningless where employment opportunities do not exist. The child welfare program has concentrated attention on the failure of the child's parents (often a single mother) while ignoring the capacity of the extended family and community to provide substitute care. The adult care program has sought to replicate provincial programs on reserve, ignoring the lack of licensing, lack of supervision, and lack of adequate professional support that the program requires.[22]

When one looks at the expansion of First Nation community social services there are some major areas of change, for example, the rapid development of First Nation child welfare agencies that occurred in the 1980s (Table 5.1) and has continued since.

But when one looks at the number of First Nations children in care and alternative child protection practice as indicators of improved social conditions, the picture is less encouraging. The number and percentage of First Nations children in care remains substantially higher than in population as a whole, and no evidence can be seen of any marked change in practice with the expansion of First Nations program administration (see Table 5.2).

The form of service produced through these contradictions has been neo-colonial. Neocolonialism was first observed in the former European colonies, which, once they acheived independence, continued to maintain social policies modelled after the policies of the former colonizing authorities. These policies were usually at variance with local needs and local culture, yet they persisted because indigenous social workers had been trained to apply them, because development agencies viewed them as 'modern' and hence deserving of support, and because indigenous elites in the post-colonial society had become familiar with them.[23]

There is wide recognition in First Nation communities that the Euro-Canadian model for the social services does not accord with that which would exist under self-government. The Royal Commission on Aboriginal Peoples argues for a fundamental refocusing of resources on the long-term goal of health and healing. However,

the most trenchant critique has come from the Mohawk writer and scholar Taiaiake Alfred in his critique of 'colonial mentalities' and 'co-optation', which he sees as threatening the independence and integrity of First Nations. He writes:

The colonial mentality is recognizable in the gradual assumption of the values, goals and perspectives of the status quo. The development of such a mentality is almost understandable (if not acceptable), given the

Table 5.1 First Nations Agencies Administering Child Welfare Programs

Year	BC	Alberta	Manitoba	Ontario	Quebec	Atlantic Region	Yukon
1981–2	1(1)	1(1)	2(9)				
1982–3	1(1)	1(1)	5(34)				
1983–4	1(1)	2(10)	6(59)		1(1)	3(3)	
1984–5	1(1)	2(10)	6(59)		3(5)	6(6)	
1985–6	1(1)	2(10)	6(59)		5(7)	9(21)	
1986–7	2(14)	3(15)	6(59)	1(14)	5(13)	11(23)	1(1)
1987–8	2(14)	3(15)	6(59)	4(56)	7(15)	11(23)	1(1)
1990–1	2(19)	3(15)	7(60)	7(84)	7(15)	11(20)	1(1)

NOTE: The first number in each instance indicates the number of child welfare agreements. The second number (in parentheses) indicates the number of Indian bands that are included.

SOURCE: Department of Indian and Northern Affairs, *Basic Departmental Data* (Ottawa, 1996).

Table 5.2 First Nations Child Care, 1969–70 to 1998–9

Fiscal Year	Number of Full Years of Child-in-Care Payments Made by DIAND	Number of On-Reserve Children under 16	Percentage of Children in Care
1969–70	4,861	94,368	5.1
1974–5	5,817	96,960	6.0
1979–80	5,820	94,414	6.2
1984–5	3,887	97,586	4.0
1989–90	4,178	105,992	3.9
1994–5	5,124	128,609	3.9
1998–9	5,985	136,415	4.4

SOURCE: Department of Indian and Northern Affairs, *Basic Departmental Data* (Ottawa, 1996), 52; (2000), 41.

structural basis of indigenous-state relations and the necessity for Native people to work through the various institutions of control in order to achieve their objectives. Native professionals, for example, find it hard to resist the (assimilative) opportunity structure created by the range of state strategies designed to co-opt and weaken challenges to the state's autonomy.[24]

Indian leaders and elders have also expressed their concern at present achievements. Speaking at an Assembly of First Nations child welfare conference in 1989, Chief Antoine of the Coldwater Band (BC) made a plea 'to eradicate the abuse—sexual, physical, and mental—we tend to foist on our children.' He said that this process would call for clear and honest recognition of the extent of the problem itself, as well as an acknowledgement that 'the support systems, either in place or being proposed by senior levels of government, are not readily accessible by our members, or [are] designed not to be accessible to our on-reserve population.' Antoine explained that investigations into the extent of sexual abuse in his community revealed 497 cases of physical and sexual abuse and 49 cases of incest. He talked about the life-long scars the abuse had left on both the abusers and victims, noting that 'we have to acknowledge and own the damn problem.' Since Health and Welfare Canada has failed to fund programs to help heal the situation, he added, 'we have to look inside our own resources to equip our front-line workers with the skills and information they need to cope with the problem. . . . We have to heal the abusers and the victims.'

At the same conference Lavina White of the Haida Nation said: 'I stand before you and our Creator to speak on behalf of those who cannot speak for themselves . . . I speak on behalf of the forgotten children in the urban areas.' White talked about the need to repatriate adopted children in urban centres back to their home communities, even though the whole concept of reserves was destructive. 'We have to think as nations', she said. 'We have to think of things holistically.'

White called for a national First Nations declaration that 'we're going to take care of our own children.' But she cautioned against taking information and statistics to government or the media, which end up using that information against First Nations people. For the media, she said, the approach must be that 'we're dealing with the problems we have, and they are alien to us.' White also talked about the need for self-government and the prophecies of a time when First Nations will govern themselves: 'If we move toward governing ourselves, we can look after our children.'[25]

The services developed for and by Aboriginal peoples are caught between two cultures, two governments, and two differing accountabilities. Although assimilation is no longer the explicit policy, it continues to be applied in its neo-colonial form. Some observers see reason for hope that progress towards a more genuine form of self-government is possible from within the constraints that neo-colonialism creates. Leslie Brown, Lise Haddock, and Margaret Kovach note that child welfare practice is different in many ways in the First Nation community they studied—in community responsiveness, respect for elders, incorporation of traditional practice, community empowerment, and the intimate knowledge of community events and people that comes from direct service. They conclude:

The delegation model is based in neo-colonialism. It is founded on the notion of 'giving' authority to deliver child welfare services, rather than recognizing First Nations people's inherent authority to care for their own children. Further it imposes a way of thinking about and practicing child and family services that is based on mainstream concepts, beliefs and practices. While allowing for some adaptation to accommodate culture and promote community empowerment, it doesn't challenge the fundamental beliefs that construct concepts of child protection. Is delegation wrong? Not entirely. It provides a mechanism for community empowerment. It ensures that there are Cowichan people involved in the administration and delivery of child and family service in their community and this is a huge improvement. However, it is a mechanism that maintains, rather than relinquishes, power and control. It is about working inside a box constructed by someone else.[26]

These major changes in First Nations social services and the federal policy of supporting self-government are challenged by social conservatives, who remain the advocates of the policy of assimilation. The concluding commentary by John Richards in the C.D. Howe Institute monograph, *Market Solutions to Native Poverty*, re-argues the case for ending the 'special status' provided by reserves and the Indian Act, seeing a future in Indians leaving the reserve and integrating into urban communities.[27] David Frum, a regular columnist for the right-wing *National Post*, argues for the complete reversal of First Nations policy (see Box 5.2).

Social Movement Community Services

The development of separate services by First Nations, albeit within the constraints of mainstream service forms, is only one particular example of a broader trend towards community-based service development and delivery by social movements. Other major contributors to this trend include the feminist movement, ethnic and immigrant organizations, the associations for the mentally handicapped and other persons with disabilities, and the gay and lesbian communities. Each of these movements has approached the task of developing social services from the perspective of mutual support. The services developed are not for others' benefit; rather, they have been created for the benefit of the members of the social movement.

Such services are usually characterized by such features as:

- a clear statement of who is being served and why;
- an approach to staffing and working relationships that is egalitarian and expresses values important to the movement;
- a political mission to demonstrate to the community that the movement can and will act;
- a unifying ideology anchored in a structural analysis of the origins of the movement.

The following are examples of social agencies initiated by the feminists, visible minorities, gays and lesbians, and community economic development activists that can be found in most Canadian urban areas.

1. The Feminist Movement

There is, of course, no single feminist movement, but there is a central feminist experience of gendered differences and prejudice, and sometimes one of disadvantage and oppression. Beginning in the 1970s women took their analysis of the feminist experience a step beyond a critical review of social structures and institutions when they banded together to act on the basis of their experience and analysis. Major policy fields in which the feminist movement has established services include:

- spousal abuse, where transition houses for women and children have been developed as a means of obtaining shelter and protection from abuse and as a way to leave abusive relationships (see Box 5.3);
- sexual assault centres, where the victims of sexual assault can receive immediate advice and assistance and longer-term support and counselling;
- abortion clinics, where women's right to make reproductive choices is protected;

Box 5.2 Natives Condemned by Public Policy

Prediction: Two decades from now, the income gap between aboriginal and non-aboriginal Canadians will be substantially wider than it is today. The distressingly high rates of suicide and drug abuse on native reserves will rise higher still. Canadian Indians will be responsible for an even more disproportionate share of the country's crime than they are today. And the blame for each and every one of these malign trends will squarely fall on the very people who smugly consider themselves the aboriginals' best friends: The politicians who sign deals like the Nisga'a treaty, the bureaucrats who defend tribal governments against outside scrutiny, the judges who exempt aboriginals from Canadian law.

Over the past 30 years, these officials have created an elaborate system of lucrative racially based privileges for Canada's aboriginal minority. They can ignore hunting, fishing and logging laws. They avoid income and sales taxes. They will be released on a sort of quasi-parole for crimes for which a white would be sentenced to prison. They are admitted to professional schools with dramatically lower grades and test scores than those expected from the majority population. They can assert claims to their neighbours' property without proof or records. They receive handsome cash stipends from the federal government and many of them have been granted huge and valuable stretches of Crown land to exploit as their own. Employment laws oblige banks, airlines and public agencies to hire and make it difficult and dangerous to fire them. They have been permitted to tear up leases and contracts and rewrite them in their own favour. The authorities look the other way as they shake down oil and mining companies for payoffs, invade parks and blockade highways.

This system of special privileges victimizes non-aboriginals. But look at what it is doing to its theoretical beneficiaries.

While 68 per cent of the population as a whole is either working or looking for work, only 47 per cent of on-reserve Indians, 57 per cent of off-reserve Indians and 59 per cent of Inuit are working or looking for work. Nearly half, 41.5 per cent, of on-reserve Indians over the age of 15 received welfare in 1990.

Those natives who do work are nearly twice as likely as non-natives to have a government-created job: 7.8 per cent of Canadians as a whole work directly for the government versus 15.2 per cent of natives. The 2.8 per cent of the population that is native has created fewer than 1 per cent of Canada's businesses, and about three-quarters of these businesses have only a single employee.

As the Royal Commission on Aboriginal Peoples noticed in 1996, natives who do post-secondary study tend to avoid 'hard' subjects like science and technology: While some 1.5 per cent of non-native adult Canadians hold a post-secondary degree in engineering, for example, only 0.18 per cent of natives do. And not only are natives much less likely to finish high school or attend university than non-natives, but the pervasiveness of affirmative action at the university and post-university level means that the attainment of a degree by a native is a less reliable indicator of achievement than the attainment of the same degree by a non-native.

Underemployed, bored people succumb to temptation from drugs, alcohol, over-eating and other self-destructive behaviours. Indian Affairs nervously averts its eyes from the subject (reporting only that 62 per cent of aboriginal people perceive alcohol abuse as a problem for their community), but it does record other indicia of trouble. Native babies are twice as likely as non-natives to die in childbirth. The native 2.8 per cent accounts for 4.4 per cent of Canadian cases of AIDS. Natives are three times as likely to suffer diabetes (a disease exacerbated by obesity) as non-natives. Young natives are eight times more likely to kill themselves than non-natives. On average, natives die seven years younger than non-natives.

Natives commit a shocking proportion of the nation's crimes. Canadian crime statistics are not generally broken down by ethnicity, but Indian Affairs reports that in Calgary, natives are 4½ times more likely to commit a crime than non-natives; in Regina and Saskatoon, natives are 12 times more likely to commit a crime than non-natives.

Why do natives behave in these appalling and self-destructive ways? Well, look at the incentives they face. The larger society tells them by word and deed: You don't need to learn (because you'll be admitted to university anyway), you don't need to work (because you can live off welfare and land-claim royalties), you don't need to perform competently on the job (because you were hired to fill a quota), you don't even need to obey the law (because you will not be punished if you break it), and if your life then turns out badly always remember—everything that happens to you is somebody else's fault. If ever there were a formula for impoverishing, degrading and destroying a group of people, our present policy of handouts and special privileges is it. The more lavishly we pour forth those handouts, the more egregious the special privileges, the more powerful the incentives to self-destructive behaviour will become.

SOURCE: David Frum, 'Natives are condemned by public policy', *National Post*, 30 Oct. 1999.

- sexual harassment services, where women subject to discrimination and oppression in employment relationships can receive support and counsel in dealing with their situation and in seeking redress;
- social housing co-operatives sponsored by women's groups, where the first considerations in housing are security of tenure, support with child care, and a welcome to women and children.

Callahan indicates four particular ways in which women's services have 'come out on the side of the clients':

> First, individual organizations have focused on one specific aspect of women's oppression: violence toward women or sexual assault or reproductive rights. . . . Second, organizations have written their commitment to social change into their mission statements and have attracted those with devotion to this mission. . . . Third, most feminist organizations include a structural analysis in their day-to-day service with their clients. . . . Finally, some feminist organizations have developed umbrella organizations without service responsibilities but with a clear social change focus.[28]

The development of services by feminist organizations has involved struggle and contradictions, particularly with regard to fundraising and organizational form. Although some funds have been raised by voluntary donations, establishing continuing services has required support from both private and government funding agencies. The result is that the operation of the transition house, for example, takes precedence over confronting the funding body on other issues of women's oppression that are within its mandate. Taking money involves compromise; establishing services that require continuity of staffing leads to a gradual professionalization of helping relationships. A reduction of early emphases on mutual support usually follows. Joan Gilroy expresses this concern in her discussion of the women's movement:

> Within the women's movement it is fairly often observed that transition houses are becoming more like traditional social agencies and that this is a consequence of their government funding. Feminists who work in these houses or who serve on their boards and committees are faced with difficult choices. On the one hand, the service is needed and providing it requires government funds. On the other, seeking and obtaining government money means emphasizing the personal rather than the social and political nature of the practice.[29]

2. Immigrant and Refugee Agencies

Every urban community has immigrant and refugee agencies that principally serve the visible minority members of the community. Some of the activities of these agencies involve assisting immigrants to maintain and share cultural ties. Immigration support services are also an important continuing focus, particularly in the contexts of family member immigration and refugee claimants. Language lessons, translation services, cultural awareness courses, and employment placement services are often provided. In many cases these agencies also offer services to the general community, including anti-racist training and cultural awareness education to schools, social agencies, and government departments.

Roxana Ng, in *The Politics of Community Services*, provides a good account of the affairs of a community agency that serves immigrant women of colour by helping them find employment. The agency's original objectives were

---

Box 5.3 Battered women's shelters in Canada: Safety always top priority

'Shelters are safe.' That statement from Louise Riendeau was a sentiment expressed by feminists across the country after the murder of Ginette Roger at a women's shelter in St-Jean sur Richelieu, Quebec (30 minutes south of Montreal).

Riendeau, the co-ordinator of Le Regroupement provincial des maisons d'hébergement et de transition pour femmes victimes de violence conjugale, a coalition of 48 women's shelters and transition houses in Quebec, says her organization had to put out a very clear message. 'We don't want women to feel afraid to use women's shelters.'

Ginette Roger left her husband, Marcel Samson, and had been staying at Le Coup d'Elle shelter for a month. Shortly before 3:00 a.m. on June 11, Samson showed up at the shelter and kicked in the door. He asked a staff member where his wife was and when he didn't get the response he wanted, he went looking for her. When he found Ginette, he shot her seven times. He left the shelter, and later turned himself over to police.

Earlier that morning, the house Roger and Samson had shared for the past 20 years was set on fire; police suspect Samson of the arson.

The media and reported public response to Roger's death focused on the 'security' of transition houses and women's shelters, rather than on the systemic problem of male violence against women. Questions raised highlighted what the shelter could have (or should have) done to better 'protect' Roger—from steel doors to alarms—and not the fact that the day before she was killed, Ginette Roger told the staff at the shelter she did not feel safe returning home.

Eileen Morrow of the Ontario Association of Interval and Transition Houses (OAITH) counters that the safety and security of women are taken very seriously by transition houses and women's shelters. 'We work from women's experiences and women's needs,' says Morrow. 'We encourage women if they are nervous to speak to the shelter workers about the security measures. If she's not comfortable, she should tell the shelter workers what would make her feel safe.'

She adds that if an abusive man wants to assault or murder his wife or female partner, he is not likely to try anything at the shelter. 'A lot of abusers are aware that shelters have high security, and their tendency is to get the women out of the shelter,' says Morrow. 'In over 20 years of shelters in Canada, think of the hundreds of thousands of women who have used them, without incident.' *(In fact, before the murder of Ginette Roger, there was only one other time a woman has been killed in a women's shelter in Canada.)*

Riendeau says that the solution isn't to create walled compounds around women who come to shelters. 'We cannot make the shelters into prisons. Women have to be comfortable; it has to feel like their homes.'

Instead, she says, the focus must be on ending male violence against women. 'We make an appeal to everybody—individuals, institutions, government—to end conjugal violence, to teach children not to respond with violence, to help victims make their lives again, and to say "no" when they see violent behaviour.'

SOURCE: Agnes Huang, 'Battered women's shelters in Canada: Safety always top priority', *Kinesis* (July-Aug. 1999): 5.

modified as it received funding from Canada Manpower and as the number of women placed in employment became the measure of the agency's achievement and key to continued funding. Although the agency began with the objective of being the advocate of immigrant women, Ng found that:

> As a community agency receiving state funding, which was in turn generated as tax revenue, they felt they had to be 'fair' to the 'public', the taxpayers who included both clients and employers. . . . it was clearly stated that the agency had taken on the role of mediating between employers and clients, rather than acting strictly as an advocacy body for immigrant women. In entering into a working relation with employers, the agency had progressively organized its work to the requirements of capital, and had unwittingly adopted the standpoint of capital.[30]

The erosion of the agency's original advocacy goals, however, is not the whole of the story. By entering into closer relations with the state and with employers the agency acquired new forms of influence, including having some 'bargaining power' regarding the wages and working conditions of 'good' and 'reliable' workers; monitoring working conditions and supporting clients when they were the subject of unfair practices, such as unfair dismissal or failure to get paid vacations in a pay package; and providing workshops for clients on their employment rights.[31]

Ng concludes that state funding requires individual negotiation:

> I want to state emphatically, however, that is is impossible to have a formulistic approach to state funding. Funding programs and their requirements vary considerably. . . . In other words, the question of how to develop a viable economic survival strategy (while remaining faithful to one's intent and objective) can only be worked out practically in relation to the specific situation of a particular group.[32]

Finally, she advocates an awareness that achieving objectives of change also requires the use of other strategies:

> More seriously, in many forms of grassroots organizing, there has been a tendency to channel the majority of organizing efforts into state-funded services, to the exclusion of other forms of resistance. While state funding to community services is an indicator of the battles fought and won by grassroots community struggles, we should not forget that community struggles extend beyond the formation of service organizations funded by state programs. There are other terrains of struggles (e.g., mass protests, alliances with other movements such as labour movements) which are equally important and complement the advances made through state-funded community services.[33]

3. Gay and Lesbian Community

The AIDS epidemic, and the ambivalent early response of governments to it, had a major impact on the gay and lesbian community. In the early stages of the epidemic, homophobic reactions to the plight of victims were common. They were defined as having 'deserved' their fate. Government action to develop strategies to provide accurate information was slowed by resistance to the idea that homosexual relationships should be recognized in public policies. Even access to drugs and treatment was slowed by public resistance to 'pay for' victims' hospital and drug costs. Proposals to isolate victims from the community in quarantine and to require blood tests also showed how close public policy came to asserting a coercive response. The gay and lesbian community responded with services of its own.

> As early as February 1983, AIDS Vancouver was formed, and a month later the AIDS Committee of Toronto was set up. These groups were rooted in the gay and lesbian communities.

They were also the first to organize education and prevention campaigns, as well as being the source of social support for people living with AIDS. . . . These community groups formed a national association in 1985—the Canadian AIDS Society; by 1990, 31 ASOs (AIDS Service Organizations) belonged to the society. . . . Early in the crisis, ASOs in Canada resembled their US counterparts—they were volunteer organizations, financed mostly from private sources. Over time, however, several Canadian ASOs secured funding from municipal, provincial, and federal governments.[34]

4. Community Economic Development

Community economic development (CED) is the establishment by communities of self-sustaining economic enterprises that provide employment and operate in the market, but are owned and managed collectively (rather than by capitalists) and seek community welfare values rather than purely economic ones. CED is expanding rapidly and the boundaries of what constitutes CED are not yet defined. Marcia Nozick lists five major principles of this approach to welfare.

- Gaining economic self-reliance: reclaiming ownership of our communities.
- Becoming ecologically sustainable: developing green, clean, and safe environments.
- Attaining community control: empowering members of a community to make decisions affecting their community, workplace, and daily lives.
- Meeting the needs of individuals: looking after our material and non-material needs.
- Building a community culture: getting to know who we are.[35]

Gaining self-reliance for the local community is the antithesis of the community's existence being subject to the economics of the integrated global economy. It does not mean economic isolation from other communities. All communities interact with others, and the objective of CED is not a separate self-sustaining commune but a community that can work together and grow with social and economic objectives of its own, a community that is not rendered powerless by the anonymous and distant operations of banks and large corporations.

Becoming ecologically sustainable is another objective. Looking for ways to do business that are environmentally responsible is pursued as a moral objective, not merely as a response to government regulation. Nature is not seen as an infinite resource to be exploited and dominated. Instead, oneness with nature is recognized. The objective is to preserve the diversity of nature and of relationships with it, while conducting continuing economic enterprises.

Attaining community control includes ensuring that communities operate their own enterprises but also includes the development of co-operative and consensual models of ownership and management. In such models all community members—men, women, children, young and old alike—participate. Community economic development aims not to be hierarchical or patriarchal, with power and control in the hands of a few and all others being alienated and dependent.

Meeting the needs of individuals means recognizing that individuals constitute the community. Each person has unique needs to be met and unique contributions to make. This value is the antithesis of the way that urban communities isolate people and dissolve the bonds between individuals. Instead of dissolved bonds, new ones are forged and individuals are not abandoned. Such communities also attend to welfare and redistributive objectives through direct relationships between people rather than through the indirect and bureaucratic ones that constitute the formal organization of social welfare.

Building a community culture indicates a commitment to develop and sustain the ways of life that form our communities. Nozick refers to this objective as developing a 'community of communities' in which different groups, 'ethnic, religious, but also women's groups, arts groups, gay and lesbian groups', have their uniqueness respected and celebrated.[36]

Determining the extent of CED is not easy in such a rapidly developing field. In the early 1990s, prior to its termination, the National Welfare grants program of Human Resources Canada sponsored a series of studies of CED.[37] Lewis, in his 1993 survey of CED models, distinguished four principal types. (1) A 'growth equity' model focuses on building wealth-generating assets. Most of the examples of this model were in Aboriginal communities, which had 180 development corporations. Other examples were the non-profit housing development organizations that had been formed to develop and sometimes manage social housing. (2) A 'loan/technical assistance model' provided debt financing to individuals and to worker co-operatives, together with business development advice. Aboriginal communities owned 33 Aboriginal development corporations with loans of $100 million and additional capital commitments of $70 million. There were also 13 First Nations-controlled business development centres (BDCs). Outside First Nations communities there were 215 BDCs in communities with populations under 60,000. (3) A 'human resources and employment development' model focused on job readiness and skills, supported by outreach to communities to build opportunities. (4) A 'planning and advisory' model provided planning and technical assistance to a defined membership or geographic area. Examples included the services provided through First Nations tribal councils, community futures committees, and economic development commissions.[38]

Community economic development is sustained in small communities by the federal Community Futures program and by the work of provincial and municipal ministries and departments of economic development. In Aboriginal communities CED is supported by the Department of Indian and Northern Affairs.

Issues of Social Service Organization

The number of social services that exist in most communities is large. Each service has its own mandate, organization, sources of support, and politics. This complex of social services delivery systems is not without substantial merits, the foremost of which is the ability to provide some good services to clients. In addition, the separate services have provided clients with some choice of service; the client who did not like the services received from the child welfare agency might do better with the services received from a family service or mental health agency, and so on. The separate services have also provided independent foci for growth and political support; hence, their resources in total may be greater than could have been obtained by a unified approach. Finally, the independent services have provided the context for the development of specialized professional expertise.

Nevertheless, the existing array of major delivery systems has two major defects. The first is that the individual delivery systems often fail to provide the full range of service that a consumer needs. Each service is built around a particular sectional interest and most share a social problem/residual services approach to service design. As a result, service consumers may have to deal with several social agencies to obtain proper attention for their problems. The second defect is that, from the perspective of the community, the existence of a series of independent systems, serving overlapping populations, leads to many intersystem boundary problems. These include such major problems as frequent referrals, service gaps, and co-ordination problems, as well as competition for resources, professional rivalry, and excessive administrative costs. In response to these problems there has been a history of reorganization of the personal social services with the intent to find simpler and more economic means of service delivery.

Concern with this series of problems has been evident since the early 1960s. In one form or another, experiments, pilot projects, and service reorganizations have been one of the most familiar and recurring themes in the social services for the last 40 years. Unfortunately, it is difficult to point to examples of successful change that really made a difference for communities, social service consumers, or governments. Reviewing 30 years of experience in British Columbia, Michael Clague, a former executive director of the BC Social Planning and Research Council, concludes:

> The history of reform of human services in British Columbia over the past thirty years is a story of bold initiatives that fell upon political misfortune and half measures that were never fully developed. What is striking is that when one initiative falls out of favour, the next inevitably takes one or all of the same organizing premises: decentralization, coordination/integration, and local accountability/citizen empowerment.[39]

Because this history appears to have been one of repeated effort to achieve worthy objectives its major themes of co-ordination and integration require discussion.

Co-ordination

Co-ordination of services is essential where a client is accessing, or needs to access, more than a single service. At the most basic level appointment times need to be arranged that permit attendance and economize on travel time. However, the principal purpose of co-ordination is to ensure that service goals recognize all the facts and problems that need to be dealt with. Very often social agencies see only part of the client's problem. For example, the probation officer sees a youth who has broken the law and who has been before the court, while the substance misuse agency sees a youth who has a drug or alcohol problem; meanwhile, the child welfare agency sees a youth in rebellion against parents and perhaps driven to

despair. Clearly, the workers in these agencies need to talk to one another to sort out a common and achievable set of goals. To achieve this objective most community agencies work in collaboration with each other, with the more persistent and complex issues being discussed by inter-agency committees. Sometimes it becomes possible to share buildings so that working relationships between agencies can be achieved more readily. On occasion the sharing of buildings takes the more formal form of a community centre in which a number of independent agencies share physical facilities and such common elements between all agencies as reception, filing, and community liaison.

Between the larger agencies, co-ordination is often defined through establishing written protocol agreements. These agreements spell out how the agencies plan to work together and usually designate particular spokespersons for each agency so that there are clear channels of communication between them.

These necessary relationships are time-consuming and maintaining them often depends on goodwill and informal ties between participants. Consequently, there has been continued interest in achieving more formal relationships that would permit 'one-stop' shopping for clients and reduce administrative overhead costs and competition between agencies. These more systemic approaches to dealing with the issues of service co-ordination are also referred to as *integration*.

Integration and Major Reorganization

The case for major reorganization of children's services in Canada was first developed by the 1970 Commission on Emotional and Learning Disorders in Children (CELDIC),[40] which applied to children's services in Canada some of the principles that had been applied in the earlier (1968) comprehensive reorganization of British social services.[41] The CELDIC report proposed that social services be organized on a geographic basis, with a local service centre responsible to a community board as the primary place for service delivery. Quebec adopted the proposals through 1972 legislation that established local community service centres (LCSCs) as the first level of service delivery. Its emphasis was on prevention and support related to both health and social needs. For intensive services, the personnel in the LCSC made referrals to the other service units of the system—the hospital centre, the social service centre, and the reception centre. Each LCSC was seen as serving a designated geographic area. The intention was that services should be readily accessible; hence, an upper limit of a 30-minute travel time to an LCSC was sought. In population terms, urban LCSCs served a minimum population of 30,000, while rural LCSCs served a minimum population of 10,000.

The LCSC was governed by a board made up of: five persons, residents of the area, elected at an annual meeting; two persons, residents of the area, appointed by the Lieutenant-Governor (a measure to ensure that socio-economic minorities were represented on the board); one person elected by the professionals practising in the centre; one person elected by the non-professional staff of the centre; one person from the associated hospital centre; one person from the associated service centre; and the general manager of the centre (advisory capacity only). The function of the board was to identify needs, oversee services, and serve as a focus for community action.

After the opening of approximately 40 LCSCs in 1975, this march towards community control and service integration was halted because of professional and bureaucratic opposition—and the conflict and disruption such opposition occasioned. Control and direction were reasserted centrally through a budget and administrative process that distributed services to centrally defined target groups. The service philosophy changed to that of 'complementarity' between the LCSCs and other existing services. Quebec has continued to build on this service base. The result is a comprehensive approach to community social services that is not replicated anywhere else in Canada.

Attempts to produce a similar pattern in other provinces either have been less comprehensive, as with Alberta's municipally organized preventive social service departments, or have been rejected following political change, as in the case of British Columbia's Community Resource Boards. A review of this history, and of parallel and similar US experiments, has led to the conclusion that comprehensive attempts to reorganize the community social services are a largely wasted effort. Such efforts, moreover, distract attention from more fundamental problems, serving only to give the appearance of change without the substance.[42]

To this research conclusion we must now add that the development of First Nations and other social movement social services also raises a major question as to the desirability of the goal of seeking service integration. A major goal of the social movement social services is to reflect more adequately community diversity. This goal conflicts with the idea that a single form of service integration is desirable, even if it is achievable. As a result, co-ordination between social agencies at the working level emerges as the only practical course to meet social service consumer needs in a comprehensive manner.

Contracting

Since the 1980s there has been a strong trend by government agencies towards contracting for services rather than providing service directly. Many factors have contributed to this trend, including financial and organizational factors. Services can be obtained at lower costs on a contract basis from community agencies than by employing staff under government collective agreements. If services have to be reduced, this can be done more readily by the non-renewal of a contract than by laying off or relocating government staff. However, there are also more positive reasons for this trend. Contracting has become the main way in which the social movement social services have been expanded. Contracting for services with local community agencies ensures a degree of contact with the community that is rarely achieved in direct government service. The services provided tend to be less bureaucratized and more accessible, and for the community agencies the government contracts are an important source of revenue.

In nearly all communities, voluntary agencies such as family services and neighbourhood houses have now become partially or largely dependent on contracted work for government agencies. Initially, the approach to government-community agency contractual relationships was often in the form of a partnership. The contract terms were loosely drawn with the expectation that flexibility and accommodation on both sides of the relationship would provide best for the development of services to clients. However, the logic of contracting has tended to take over: service specifications have been clarified; cost savings have been sought; and contracting has come increasingly to mean competitive practices. The competitive practices that are required for contract negotiation have had many consequences for community social agencies and for their work. Entrepreneurial, negotiating, and management skills in obtaining contracts have become essential. The agency community has come to take on some of the features of an industry. The willingness to criticize government and government social agencies in public has been diminished.[43]

Although the initial contracted agencies were usually community-based non-profit corporations, entrepreneurial, profit-based companies have increasingly entered the field. Such companies have often come into being as a direct result of government staffing cuts. Indeed, the effect of such cuts has often been softened by offering the staff being severed the opportunity to contract for services with government. On the positive side, competitive contracting practices lead to increased clarity as to what service is being sought and a desirable search for

economy in providing the service. Achieving these objectives without sacrificing service quality requires that attention be given to the credentials and experience of those providing direct service to clients. Clear minimums must be stated in the tender documents. Attention must also be given in residential facilities to the expense parts of budgets necessary to provide for a healthful diet, recreation, and so on.

Despite the problems of delivering services through contract, the trend towards more contracting seems irreversible. Already, service contracts would appear to comprise half or more of all service expenditures, and the financial and management advantages to cost-conscious governments in pursuing contracting for service is limited, in the end, only by the need to retain legislative, financial, and some systems functions in government hands.

Internal Abuse Prevention

Social agencies are vulnerable to internal abuse. Their clients are often in severe distress, which can leave them open to manipulation. The agency's staff often contains a substantial number of volunteers or poorly paid service workers whose rights may not be well known or who may be vulnerable to intimidation or harassment. However, the fundamental reason that social agencies need abuse prevention policies is that they are organizations and, as such, are vulnerable to all the same problems as other organizations.

Social agencies work with vulnerable people, children, the elderly, the mentally confused, and the poor. All are not in good positions to know their rights or to assert them. Professional codes of behaviour have long recognized this problem in making it plain that the welfare of the client is the worker's first responsibility and by defining client exploitation as unprofessional conduct. Nevertheless, client exploitation by social agency staff occurs. The abuse of First Nations children in residential schools has been well documented. There has been a similar record of abuse in many residential services for children, including continuing instances of abuse of children in foster care. Measures to prevent abuse include the careful screening of staff and foster parents and clear reporting channels, preferably through an independent investigating agency where allegations of abuse occur.

The employment and seniority relationships between staff in social agencies are also open to abuse. Policies are needed to define harassment, whether based on minority status, sex, sexual orientation, or any other basis for discrimination. Conflicts of interest also require definition and defined remedies. Social agencies are often small and have the strength that comes from close community and personal relationships. These sources of strength can also leave the organization vulnerable to charges of nepotism, favouritism, and financial corruption, as the protections that size and bureaucratic process provide are not applicable.

Conclusion

Canada's community social services are an impressive expression of the social welfare commitment to community. In the main the services 'survived' the conservative financial pressures of the 1990s, but they were influenced by them. The approach to child protection became more punitive and more dominated by investigation and risk assessment methodologies. First Nations social services were expanded, but these expanded services had a neo-colonial form that replicated mainstream agency policies and practices, rather than being based in the historical experience and culture of Aboriginal peoples. Social movement social services also grew in importance and scope, but social movements found that the relationship with the state left them open to influence to serve the needs of the state over the needs of their constituencies. Attempts to reorganize the social services have continued, but there has been a growing realization that the problems with which the social services deal are not influenced by the way the services are organized. The growth of poverty and inequality has undermined the effectiveness of the social services and increased the need for them. Yet the services provided have been unable to offer any solutions to the problems of poverty or inequality.

Additional Readings

Andrew Armitage, 'Lost Vision: Children and the Ministry for Children and Families', *BC Studies* 118 (Summer 1998): 93–108. This article shows how government child welfare agencies were affected by rising poverty and by reviews of the death of children needing protection during the 1990s.

Marilyn Callahan, 'Feminist Community Organizing in Canada: Postcards from the Edge', in Brian Wharf and Michael Clague, eds, *Community Organizing: Canadian Experiences*. Toronto: Oxford University Press, 1997, 181–204. Callahan's article shows the complexity that social movements face as their search for ways to provide services encounters the funding requirements of the state.

Michael Clague, 'Thirty Turbulent Years: Community Development and the Organization of Health and Social Services in Brtisih Columbia', in Wharf and Clague, eds, *Community Organizing*, 91–112. Clague provides a full picture of the development and evolution of community social services under changing provincial government objectives and ideologies.

Hugh Shewell and Annabella Spagnut, 'The First Nations of Canada: Social Welfare and the Quest for Self Government', in John Dixon and Robert P. Scheurell, eds, *Social Welfare with Indigenous Peoples*. London: Routledge, 1995, 1–53. The authors provide a description of the development of First Nation on-reserve social services and a critical analysis of accomplishments.

Study Questions

1. Examine the auspices and funding of a community social agency with which you are familiar. What role does the board play in setting limits for services? What role does funding play in establishing limits? Who is in control of the organization, the board or the funding body?

2. What happens when a client needs services from more than one community organization? How have social agencies sought to provide better services to multiple-need clients?

3. Visit a Native Friendship Centre or Indian band office, introduce yourself, and inquire about the services they provide. What makes these services different from those provided by non-First Nations governments and community agencies?

4. Why is it argued that community governance makes for better social services and what stands in the way of achieving this goal?

5. Select one community social movement and show how it has affected the availability of social services in your own community.

Notes

1. Canada, *Canada Assistance Plan* (Ottawa: Queen's Printer, 1965), s. 2(m).

2. Marilyn Callahan, Andrew Armitage, and Brian Wharf, 'Workfare in British Columbia: Social Development Alternatives', *Canadian Review of Social Policy* 26 (Nov. 1990): 15–25.

3. For an account of the development of child welfare in Canada, see Ewan McIntyre, 'The Historical Context of Child Welfare in Canada', in Brian Wharf, ed., *Rethinking Child Welfare in Canada* (Toronto: McClelland & Stewart, 1993).

4. Andrew Armitage, 'Lost Vision: Children and the Ministry for Children and Families', *BC Studies* 118 (Summer 1998): 93–108.

5. Andrew Armitage, 'The Policy and Legislative Context', in Wharf, ed., *Rethinking Child Welfare*, 53.

6. Andrew Armitage, 'Family and Child Welfare in First Nations Communities', in Wharf, ed., *Rethinking Child Welfare*, 147 ff.

7. Marilyn Callahan, 'Feminist Approaches: Women Recreate Child Welfare', in Wharf, ed., *Rethinking Child Welfare*, 182.

8. Karen J. Swift, 'The Case for Opposition: Challenging Contemporary Child Welfare Policy Directions', *Canadian Review of Social Policy* 47 (2001): 59.

9. Canada, *Report of the Royal Commission on Equality in Employment* (Ottawa: Ministry of Supply and Services, 1984), 192.

10. Status of Women Canada, *Report of the Task Force on Child Care* (Ottawa: Ministry of Supply and Services, 1986).

11. National Council of Welfare, *Child Care: A Better Alternative* (Ottawa, 1988), 3.

12. Jim Hackler, Department of Sociology, University of Victoria, 'Brief on Proposed Criminal Justice Act', presented to Senate Legal and Constitutional Affairs Committee, 24 Oct. 2001.

13. British Columbia, *Closer to Home: The Report of the British Columbia Royal Commission on Health Care and Costs*, vol. 2 (Victoria, 1991), C-73.

14. See, for example, Michael Boyle, 'Children's Mental Health Issues', in Laura Johnston and Dick Barnhorst, eds, *Children, Families and Public Policy* (Toronto: Thompson Educational Publishing, 1991).

15. Marcus Hollander, 'The Cost-effectiveness of Community-Based Long-Term Care Services for the Elderly Compared to Residential Care: A British Columbia Perspective', Ph.D. thesis (University of Victoria, 1999), 11.

16. G.C.J. Van Kessel, 'The Canadian Immigration System', Ottawa: Citizenship and Immigration Canada, address to the International Conference on Migration, Baden, Austria, 26 Nov. 1998. Available at: <www.cic.gc.ca/english/refugee/kessel>.

17. Michael Clague, 'Thirty Turbulent Years: Community Development and the Organization of

Health and Social Services in British Columbia',
in Brian Wharf and Michael Clague, eds, *Community Organizing: Canadian Experiences* (Toronto:
Oxford University Press, 1997), 91–112.

18. Jane Pulkingham, 'Community Development in
Action: Reality of Rhetoric', *Canadian Review of
Social Policy* 32 (1993): 29–42.

19. Patrick Johnston, *Native Children and the Child
Welfare System* (Toronto: James Lorimer, 1983),
3.

20. Ibid., 20.

21. Canada, *Report of the Royal Commission on Aboriginal Peoples* (Ottawa: Supply and Services,
1996), vol. 2, 801, vol. 3, 25.

22. Hugh Shewell and Annabella Spagnut, 'The First
Nations of Canada: Social Welfare and the Quest
for Self Government', in John Dixon and Robert
P. Scheurell, eds, *Social Welfare with Indigenous
Peoples* (London: Routledge, 1995), 1–53.

23. Stewart MacPherson, *Social Policy in the Third
World: The Social Dilemmas of Underdevelopment*
(Brighton, UK: Harvester, 1982), 143–63.

24. Taiaiake Alfred, *Peace, Power, and Righteousness:
An Indigenous Manifesto* (Toronto: Oxford University Press, 1999), 70.

25. Assembly of First Nations, *National Inquiry into
Child Care* (Ottawa, 1989).

26. Leslie Brown, Lise Haddock, and Margaret
Kovach, 'Watching Over Our Families: Lalum'u-
tul' Smun'eem Child and Family Services', School
of Social Work, University of Victoria, 2000,
unpublished paper.

27. John Richards, 'A Comment', in John Richards
and William Watson eds, *Market Solutions to
Native Poverty: Social Policy for the Third Solitude*
(Toronto: C.D. Howe Institute, 1995), 163.

28. Callahan, 'Feminist Approaches', 192.

29. Joan Gilroy, 'Social Work and the Women's
Movement', in Brian Wharf, ed., *Social Work and
Social Change in Canada* (Toronto: McClelland &
Stewart, 1990), 78 n. 28.

30. Roxana Ng, *The Politics of Community Services:
Immigrant Women, Class and State* (Halifax: Fernwood, 1996), 66.

31. Ibid., 87–91.

32. Ibid., 93.

33. Ibid, 94.

34. Guy Poirier, 'Neo-Conservatism and Social Policy
Responses to the AIDS Crisis', in Andrew
Johnson, Stephen McBride, and Patrick J. Smith,
eds, *Continuities and Discontinuities: The Political
Economy of Social Welfare and Labour Market
Policy in Canada* (Toronto: University of Toronto
Press, 1994), 139.

35. Marcia Nozick, 'Five Principles of Sustainable
Community Development', in Eric Shragge, ed.,
Community Economic Development (Montreal:
Black Rose Books, 1993), 20.

36. The similarity of these values to the liberal social
welfare values introduced in Chapter 1 is apparent.

37. National Welfare Grants, *Community Economic
Development Products* (Ottawa: Human Resources
Development Canada, 1995).

38. Mike Lewis, 'The Scope and Characteristics of
Community Economic Development in Canada',
in Burt Galloway and Joe Hudson, eds, *Community Economic Development* (Toronto: Thompson
Educational Publishing, 1994), 48–58.

39. Michael Clague, 'Thirty Turbulent Years: Community Development and the Organization of
Health and Social Services in British Columbia',
in Wharf and Clague, eds, *Community Organizing*, 109–10.

40. Commission on Emotional and Learning Disorders in Children, *One Million Children* (Toronto:
Leonard Crainford, 1970).

41. United Kingdom, *Report of the Committee on
Local Authority and Allied Personal Social Services*
(London: HMSO, 1968).

42. Brian Wharf, 'Organizing and Delivering Child
Welfare Services: The Contributions of Research',
in Joe Hudson and Burt Galloway, eds, *Child
Welfare in Canada: Research and Policy Implications* (Toronto: Thomson Educational Publishing,
1995), 7.

43. Josephine Rekart, *Social Services and the Market
Place* (Vancouver: Social Planning and Research
Council of British Columbia, 1995).

PART IV

The Political and Ideological Context

CHAPTER 6

Social Welfare:
Power, Politics, and Organizations

This chapter examines the political context of social welfare in Canada. Figure 6.1 provides an overview of what will be considered here. Canadian social welfare policy is influenced by many different political actors, including some that act at an international level. The overall picture is one of multiple sources of power with the state's ability to play a balancing role weakened by globalization and other international relationships.

Learning Objectives

1. To understand how the Canadian state, Constitution, legislatures, courts, and bureaucracies act to determine Canadian social welfare policy.
2. To understand how the state is influenced by nine elites and organized interests, which have the power to affect how governments make Canadian social welfare policy.
3. To recognize how each of these actors has influenced policy and services.
4. To understand how the sources of influence are changing and how Canadian social welfare policy is being influenced by globalization and other structural forces that operate at an international level.
5. To think about how one's own energies and interests can best be applied to influencing Canadian social welfare policy.

Power and Social Welfare

Provision for social welfare, that is, the translation of welfare values into welfare programs, requires the exercise of power. The $120 billion redistributed annually and the expenditures on community social services evidence power in operation. Hundreds of thousands of civil servants, administrators, contractors, social workers, child-care workers, homemakers, and others are employed in social administration. They are a large industry and lobby group by any standard. Millions of Canadians depend on the social welfare system to pay their bills in whole or part. They, too, are a substantial vested interest and potential voting block. The social movements of feminism, First Nations, multicultural

and refugee organizations, and gays and lesbians also have political voice. This concentration of money and interests attracts the attention of all other major interests. Corporations, banks, the media, the courts, wealthy individuals, international economic and political organizations, organized labour, and politicians of all persuasions have interests of their own in the conduct of such a large enterprise because its affairs affect theirs. Power is the essence of social welfare and this chapter will deal with principal features of the way the organization of power in Canadian society affects social welfare. As such, it will deal principally with the operation of the Canadian state.

In the following discussion the concept of the Canadian state should be distinguished from the concept of a Canadian government. Canada possesses not one government able to exercise power over welfare but a multiplicity of governments—federal, provincial, and municipal. Furthermore, important powers are held by the courts and by the administrative bureaucracies created to oversee social provision. All of these are parts of the Canadian state. Only the state can organize resources on the scale needed for social welfare, and so the state and its politics determine the scope of social welfare and the direction of public policy. The dominance of the state in social welfare matters is also desirable. Social welfare involves the exercise of considerable coercive, utilitarian, and normative powers. It is a mark of civilized society that

coercive power is unified—which, in a democratic capitalist society, implies a state function. Further, establishment of social policy involves decisions and moral choices. It is desirable that these decisions and choices at policy, program, and administrative levels are accountable to the society. This is achieved through the state exercising major authority over social welfare.

The interested parties in social welfare and their interaction with the state are shown in Figure 6.1. The state provides a forum in which the different parties interact and the means whereby decisions are made. For these reasons, all students of social welfare have to concern themselves with the way the Canadian state works.

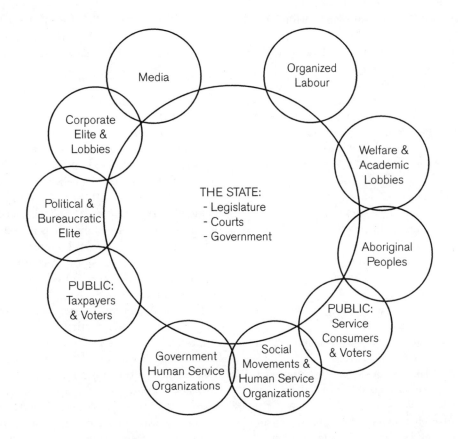

FIGURE 6.1 Social Welfare in Canada: The Political Map

The Canadian State and Constitution

The Canadian state is a federal state, the Constitution of which provides formal sanction for the existence of a federal government and 10 provincial governments. Power for social welfare functions is divided between the federal government and provinces. In specific terms the British North America Act, now incorporated into the Canadian Constitution as the Constitution Act, 1867 (as amended), states:

91. It shall be lawful for the Queen, by and with the Advice and Consent of the Senate and the House of Commons, to make Laws for the Peace, Order and good Government of Canada, in relation to all matters not coming within the Classes of Subjects by this Act assigned exclusively to the Legislatures of the Provinces; and for greater Certainty, but not so as to restrict the Generality of the foregoing Terms of this Section, it is hereby declared that (notwithstanding anything in this Act) the exclusive Legislative Authority of the Parliament of Canada extends to . . .

    2. The regulation of Trade and Commerce.

    2A. Unemployment insurance.

    7. Militia, Military and Naval Service, and Defence.

    11. Quarantine and the establishment and maintenance of Marine Hospitals.

    24. Indians and lands reserved for Indians.

    25. Naturalization and Aliens.

    27. The Criminal Law . . . .

    28. The establishment, maintenance, and management of Penitentiaries.
        . . .

92. In each Province the Legislature may exclusively make laws in relation to matters coming within the classes of subject next hereinafter enumerated, that is to say,

    6. The establishment, maintenance, and management of public reformatory prisons, in and for the Province.

    7. The establishment, maintenance, and management of hospitals, asylums, charities and eleemosynary institutions, in and for the Province, other than marine hospitals.

    16. Generally all matters of a merely local or private nature in the Province.

94A. The Parliament of Canada may make laws in relation to old age pensions and supplementary benefits, including survivor's and disability benefits unrespective of age, but no law shall affect the operation of any law present or future of a provincial legislature in relation to any such matter.

This formal division of powers has been interpreted as providing to the provinces primary jurisdiction over social welfare. The combined effect of sections 91 and 92 resulted in the provinces having all the general powers in the field of social welfare that are not included in the specific list of federal powers included under sections 91 and 94A. This interpretation has been established as a result of the federal government seeking increased powers, certain of the provinces opposing such powers, and the issues of division of powers ultimately reaching the courts.

The role of the courts, and specifically of the Judicial Committee of the Privy Council in Great Britain, was seen when, in 1937, the federal Employment and Social Insurance Act was deemed ultra vires. In that instance the Attorney General for Ontario brought action against the Attorney General for Canada. The Supreme Court of Canada ruled 4 to 2 in favour of Ontario. Canada appealed to the Privy Council in London, which until 1949 was the court of final appeal for Canadian jurisprudence, and the judgement of the Supreme Court was upheld. In 1940, the legislative authority for unemployment insurance was obtained by the federal government through the adoption of a constitutional amendment specifying parliamentary jurisdiction (section 91, subsection [2A]).

Forewarned by this sequence of events, the federal government sought and obtained a constitutional amendment in 1951 giving it authority to make laws in relation to old age pensions (section 94A). This authority was extended in 1964 to cover survivors, disability, and supplementary benefits, allowing the introduction of the Canada Pension Plan. The power of the Parliament of Canada to make laws affecting social welfare has thus been limited by the Constitution and the courts.

There is one exception. The federal government has the exclusive power with respect to Indians and land reserved for Indians (section 91[24]). However, in 1951 the federal government introduced an amendment to the Indian Act (section 88) that has the effect of incorporating into the Act all provincial law that is not contrary to federal law. Thus, in matters of child welfare, where the Indian Act is silent, provincial child welfare laws govern Indians. Nevertheless, the situation of First Nations remains different from that of all other Canadians. The federal government remains the only government with financial responsibility and has the exclusive authority to legislate where it chooses to do so.

The principal reasons for federal powers over social welfare were stated by the government of Canada as part of the background preparation for the 1968 constitutional conference.[1] Dealing with income security measures, the reasons given were:

1. *Income redistribution.* The federal government asserted a role in redistributing income nationally, benefiting the populations of poorer provinces at the expense of the wealthier. Only the Parliament of Canada could provide for such redistribution, hence the need for federal powers.

2. *The sense of community.* The range of social welfare income security measures, such as Family Allowances (now the Child Tax Benefit), Old Age Security, and Unemployment Insurance, has been viewed by the federal government as contributing to a sense of national unity. Receipt of cash by persons is seen as one of the most tangible benefits conferred by a government. The federal government wishes to exercise this power.

3. *Portability.* The Canadian people move frequently between provinces. It is undesirable that benefits vary sharply between provinces. Such variations would tend to deprive some people of benefits they might have expected and hence would tend to impede the movements of people.

4. *Economic policy.* Because income payments made by the federal government affect the total demand for goods and services, they are a part of the means used by the government of Canada to stabilize the economy. Thus, the federal power over economic policy requires the exercise of welfare powers.

5. *Service equality.* In the field of social services, the federal government was prepared to concede a primary role to the provinces. However, a national interest was asserted in social services—that of ensuring a reasonable measure of service equality between provinces.

These goals reflected one of the central objectives of federal social policy, first asserted by the Royal Commission on Dominion-Provincial Relations (1940). The Royal Commission wrote its report in response to the economic chaos and misery that had resulted from the Great Depression of the 1930s. It was particularly concerned by the regional impact of the Depression, which had been most severe in the Maritime provinces and on the Prairies:

> Not only national duty and decency, if Canada is to be a nation at all, but equity and national self-interest demand that the residents of these

areas be given average services and equal opportunities,—equity because these areas may have been impoverished by the national economic policies which enriched other areas, and which were adopted in the general interest.[2]

To these earlier reasons for a strong federal role in social welfare, an additional one can be added. As a result of the establishment of a Charter of Rights within the Canadian Constitution, Canadians have been given constitutional assurances that require Canadian—implicitly federal—interpretation and administration. Language rights and provisions for freedom of movement are two such examples, the latter having the effect of rendering ultra vires a variety of provincial residency conditions that formerly restricted welfare rights.

These reasons for the assertion of a federal power with respect to social welfare are in no way peculiar to Canada. Indeed, the history of the development of social welfare programs throughout the Western industrialized world suggested, until the last decade, a general tendency towards the extension of the welfare powers of national governments. During the 1990s these classical arguments for a major national role were heard less often in Canada and other countries. The reasons for this include the federal deficit and the problems it created for the federal government to be able to perform the role it has sought. They include, too, a measure of disillusionment with the effectiveness of social policy in achieving its stated objectives, or disillusionment with the unexpected consequences of the achievements, for example, the apparent development of regional and personal forms of 'transfer dependency'. In addition, it seemed that governments had been influenced by the conservative critics of all social policy who consistently argue for a larger role for the capitalist market and for a smaller role for the state.

Distinctive to the Canadian experience has been the opposition of certain provinces to

federal authority and the effects of that opposition. The principal reasons given by certain provinces for seeking to ensure their control over social welfare include the following:

1. *Quebec.* The Quebec government is the leader of a 'distinct society' of French culture and language that is a minority society within Canada. The provincial government has thus sought to represent and develop French-Canadian society within the province of Quebec. Social policy has been viewed as playing a central role in the maintenance of French language and culture and has been referred to in each referendum campaign. Quebec therefore wants full powers over social policy for exactly the same national reasons that the federal government does. The separatist Parti Québécois would go further and assert that the history of federalism shows that this has not and cannot be achieved within federalism. They point to the Meech Lake Accord and the Charlottetown Accord as failed attempts to obtain the necessary powers. The Quebec federalists have used the same line of argument to oppose extensions of federal powers and to retain in as full a form as possible the provincial social policy powers that exist in the Canadian Constitution.

2. *Ontario, Alberta, and British Columbia.* The effect of the redistributive welfare function is that the wealthier provinces, specifically Ontario, British Columbia, and Alberta, provide funding to the poorer provinces and to the people who live in them. Sometimes the governments of Ontario, BC, and Alberta have accepted the federal argument that this transfer is a national necessity. On other occasions they have opposed the transfer and have sought to keep jurisdictional and financial responsibility for social welfare at the provincial level. This argument is being reasserted as the federal government cuts back its contribution to social welfare spending while seeking to maintain national standards. With the introduction of the CHST, the federal government stopped paying half the cost of social programs and of medicare. As a result the provinces have

increasingly questioned the federal right to set policy.

3. *Provincial diversity and politics.* Canada is the second largest country, geographically, in the world. The distinct regions and their distinct peoples have differing welfare needs and governments of differing political persuasions. At different times, different provinces have established precedents in programming, for example, the introduction of medicare in Saskatchewan in 1962, which would not have been possible if the provinces lacked jurisdictional power. On other occasions some provinces have wanted to offer more restricted services and expand the role of the private market. These initiatives can and have conflicted with federal policies, resulting in contradictory programs and policies. Within the administration of joint programs these political contradictions result in major conflicts and competitiveness between federal and provincial bureaucracies. The net result for both governments is usually a largely wasted effort, with public resources consumed in purely political competition.

4. *Administrative efficiency and accountability.* The effect of federal actions—in combination with provincial action—has been to produce major administrative burdens on both levels of government. Furthermore, the existing divisions of power obstruct the proper accountability of governments for the services they render by diffusing political accountability and transferring the forum for decisions from publicly elected legislatures to closed-door meetings between federal and provincial officials and politicians.

In addition to the provinces, the leaders of First Nations are also seeking to obtain recognition of social policy as an inherent Aboriginal jurisdiction. Like the Quebec government, they want to be able to use social policy as a means of developing and protecting their distinct identities. In the 1990s these arguments by provinces and First Nations worked in support of the federal government's own reasons for a diminished role in social welfare. With the end of the 1990s, however, the first of a series of federal budget surpluses was achieved. These surpluses provided the federal government with the capacity to play a more active role in social policy. Still, the other arguments for a less active role continue to apply.

The Federal Role

The existing federal role in social welfare has been built using five different policy and administrative mechanisms.

1. *Use of existing federal powers.* The federal government has made extensive use of those welfare powers it has been able to develop on the basis of the division of powers in the Constitution. Thus, a wide array of employment services and training subsidies has been developed on the basis of the powers of the federal government with respect to the economy and on the basis of the Unemployment Insurance amendment. The federal responsibility for the militia and for military service has been the basis for the organization of extensive welfare services for veterans. Similarly, the federal responsibility for Indians has been used, somewhat less comprehensively, in the development of welfare services for Native peoples. The federal responsibility for naturalization and aliens has been used to develop services for immigrants and also to provide support to multicultural activities under the general heading of 'citizenship' services. The federal responsibility for the criminal law and for penitentiaries has been used in the development of national parole services.

2. *Taxing and spending powers.* As a result of federal-provincial income tax agreements the federal government has exclusive income tax authority in all provinces except Quebec. Even in Quebec, where there is a separate provincial income tax, the federal government has its own income tax authority. Thus the federal government can make a tax expenditure or provide a refundable tax benefit.

The government of Canada has also assert-ed the right to make payments directly to individuals. Family Allowances, for example, were introduced in 1945 without constitutional amendment. However, while asserting this right, the government has introduced little legislation of this nature and has now withdrawn Family Allowances. Instead, constitutional amendments have been sought. This could be the result of apprehensions that, if challenged in the courts, such powers would not be upheld.

3. *Equalization payments.*[3] The principle of equalization is enshrined in the Constitution. The purpose of equalization is to ensure 'that provincial governments have sufficient revenues to provide reasonably comparable levels of public services at reasonably comparable levels of taxation'.[4] Equalization is a key federal-provincial program for social welfare, as it is designed to ensure that the revenue base for social welfare (and other government services) is similar in all provinces. Through payments made from the Equalization program and from the Canada Health and Social Transfer, Ontario, Alberta, and British Columbia (the wealthy provinces) received $1,108 per capita in 2001–2. Newfoundland (the poorest province) received $2,900 per capita, Manitoba, $2,061 per capita, and Quebec, $1,670 per capita.[5]

4. *Established Programs Financing and the Canada Health and Social Transfer (CHST).* Estab-lished Programs Financing was introduced in 1977 to replace cost-sharing in the fields of hos-pital insurance, medicare, and post-secondary education. Through EPF, tax points and cash were made available to the provinces in place of cost-sharing. (A tax point is the amount of money yielded by 1 per cent of income tax revenue in the province; no money changes hands with tax points; the province simply keeps a larger share of income tax revenues.) Originally, the tax points and cash were similar in amount, but with the imposition in 1982 of an overall ceiling on EPF transfers, the propor-tion of the payment in tax points rose and the amount paid fell. The introduction of the CHST

has delayed the point at which the cash portion of former EPF payments drops to zero by adding the former Canada Assistance Plan shared-cost payment to the EPF transfer, albeit at a reduced level. However, the decline in the federal finan-cial commitment to health and social policy continues, and with it there is a steady increase in provincial autonomy.

5. *Shared-cost programs.* Historically, shared-cost programs were the most important means used by the government of Canada to extend its influence over social welfare. A shared-cost program was one in which the federal Parlia-ment approved legislation permitting the payment of federal funds to provinces in support of provincial welfare programs. Such programs are also referred to as 'conditional grant' programs. Shared-cost programs had a significant effect on the use of provincial powers. To be eligible for cost-sharing, the province had to design a program that met federal requirements; elsewise, it would have to forgo the available program funds. As their elec-torates were already contributing to program costs in Canada as a whole through the federal taxes they were paying, the provinces were obliged to enter such agreements. To influence provincial priorities and programs, the federal government used cost-sharing extensively in this way throughout the post-war period until the 1980s. The Canada Assistance Plan, hospi-tal insurance, medicare, support for post-sec-ondary education, and the public housing provisions of the National Housing Act were all introduced as shared-cost programs. The result is seen in the development of a similar array of basic social welfare provisions throughout Canada.

The use of shared-cost programs did have problems, however. (1) The less wealthy regions and their provincial governments bene-fited less from such programming than the more wealthy regions whose provincial govern-ments could better afford the provincial contri-bution to program costs.[6] (2) Shared-cost programs had the generally undesirable effect of diffusing government accountability for social welfare programs. Instead of clear responsibility residing at either the federal or provincial level, it rested with both. (3) In addition, administrative, legal, and fiscal complexity compounded with each passing year. Governments at the provincial level used their resources to seek the widest possible cost-sharing, while at the federal level the definition of eligible expenditures was narrowed to restrain costs.

Despite these problems the CAP remained a shared-cost program as cost-sharing provided an assurance of federal participation in the unpredictable changes in welfare costs that accompany the business cycle and its differential impact regionally. The withdrawal of the CAP as a shared-cost program was done to allow the federal government to limit its exposure to these risks. With the conclusion of the CAP and the introduction of the CHST the use of cost-sharing is limited to social housing and some other minor activities. It would seem probable that cost-sharing for these programs, too, will eventually be ended.

The Social Union Framework Agreement

The Social Union Framework Agreement (SUFA)[7] is the most recent attempt (1999) of the federal and provincial governments to make a coherent statement of how they intend to work together in the field of social policy. The agreement has five sections. Section 1 is a reiteration of the jurisdictional responsibilities of the federal government and provinces and a commitment to respect them. Section 2 is a commitment to 'mobility rights', that is, transferability and reciprocity so that Canadians will not be penalized when and if they move from one province to another. Section 3 is a commitment to openness and accountability, which strikes many observers as ironic since the agreement was developed in a series of closed-door provincial and federal-provincial meetings that were neither open nor accountable. Section 4 is an undertaking by each of the governments to consult with the others before making changes in social policy and Section 5 is a commitment of the federal government to give a year's notice if programs are to be cut and not to introduce new initiatives without the agreement of the majority of the provinces.[8]

SUFA has been a source of disappointment to commentators from all parties to the social policy debate. From the perspective of those who would like to see progressive changes made in social policy, SUFA is an inadequate vehicle for the establishment of new programs.[9] From the perspective of conservatives, SUFA seems at best irrelevant and probably an obstacle to fundamental program review.[10] Aboriginal peoples were upset when SUFA was adopted because they were not involved in its formulation. The references to Aboriginal people in SUFA commit the federal government and the provinces to work with one another and with Aboriginal peoples, but the suspicion is that the federal and provincial governments will form a common front when dealing with Aboriginal people, rather than treat the Aboriginal national organizations as partners in the way advocated by the Royal Commission on Aboriginal Peoples.[11] Finally, Quebec, conscious of its jurisdictional independence, declined to be a signatory to the agreement.

The Influence of Electoral Politics

The influence of electoral politics on Canadian social welfare policies and programs is exercised within the context of the divided jurisdiction over social welfare between the federal and provincial governments. This division of jurisdiction affects the power of any government, federal or provincial, to pursue its policy aims. Thus, electoral politics does not have the same direct impact on policies and programs that can be expected in a unitary state.

For example, the election in 1963 of a Liberal government, headed by Prime Minister

Pearson and committed in its electoral platform to the establishment of the Canada Pension Plan, led to extensive federal-provincial negotiation. The federal government needed to secure a constitutional amendment to introduce the plan. To obtain this concession, changes in the original thrust of the government's intention were negotiated. These included the establishment of a separate parallel plan by the province of Quebec (the Quebec Pension Plan) and provision for the establishment of a pension fund that would be invested in provincial government bonds, providing the provinces with a dependable source of capital. The federal situation is basically the same today. The election of a Liberal government in the 1990s, headed by Jean Chrétien, seeking to contain and reduce federal expenditures led to extensive federal-provincial negotiations. New social policy initiatives are usually first canvassed at a meeting of federal ministers with their provincial counterparts.

The situation of a provincial government elected with a clear mandate for social reform is constitutionally clearer. However, the provincial freedom to act has been constrained by national program standards, as in the Canada Health Act, and by the detailed cost-sharing agreements under the CAP. The result has been that provincial governments for many years had to negotiate federal agreement for social program changes. The result was the development of federal-provincial policy on a consensual basis that moderated the effect of ideology on policy formulation. This is not to suggest that electoral politics are without influence on social welfare. It does imply that political compromise between governments of different political persuasions has been the characteristic route to change.

Further, the major federal political parties each made some contribution to building social welfare in the 1960s and 1970s, and in the 1980s and 1990s each participated in dismantling and restraining costs. Despite these modifying influences on the expression of a clear welfare ideology within the field of electoral politics, significant differences exist between the major political parties.

The New Democratic Party has been the most consistent advocate of social welfare in the Canadian political spectrum. The party's political statements, more clearly than those of other parties, have committed it to the welfare ideal of the redistribution of income, wealth, and power. When elected to office (in British Columbia, Saskatchewan, Manitoba, Ontario, and Nova Scotia), New Democratic governments have shown a willingness to introduce social welfare programs not legislated anywhere else in Canada or, indeed, in North America. An example of an initiative of this type was the enactment by Saskatchewan of a provincial medicare program in 1962. The effects of these initiatives have extended beyond the provinces in which they were enacted. The federal government has been co-opted to their support and other provinces have tended to establish similar provisions at later dates.

In the federal Parliament, in which the New Democratic Party has consistently held only a minority of seats, the party's spokespeople have been the advocates of social welfare programs. Long before Liberal or Progressive Conservative governments have introduced social welfare legislation, members of Parliament from the NDP and its predecessor, the Co-operative Commonwealth Federation, have brought the need of Canadians for such programs as pensions, medicare, housing, and income guarantees before the House of Commons.

These consistent long-term objectives have been challenged in the 1980s and the NDP has found itself in the position of an opposition party defending the status quo from government-initiated dismantling and restraint policies. When elected as a government the NDP has had to face the same revenue and expenditure problems that confront all Canadian governments. The result for NDP leadership has been difficulty in acting as they would wish in such areas as welfare rates and reform. Diana Ralph writes:

We asked anti-poverty activists in British Columbia, Saskatchewan and Ontario to comment on how the poor are faring under their respective NDP governments. While acknowledging small improvements, all three are disappointed by the failure of the NDP to make good on their commitment to challenge inequality and poverty and by their capitulation to the 'corporate agenda.'[12]

The Liberal Party can rightfully claim to have comprised the federal government when nearly all significant social welfare legislation has been passed by Parliament. They also formed the federal government for most of the post-war period: 1945–57, 1963–79, 1980–4, 1993– . Furthermore, committed Liberals spoke proudly of their party's record in the welfare field. Judy LaMarsh wrote of the Department of National Health and Welfare and of her being asked to be minister (1963–5):

> It is a department to a Liberal that is cherished indeed. Such greats in their time as Paul Martin and Brooke Claxton had served in that portfolio. To any Liberal, the subject matter dealt with in National Health and Welfare are 'gut' issues—basic to their whole philosophy of the role of Government in modern society.[13]

Although very significant social welfare programs were legislated by Liberal governments in the 1960s, the record of the federal governments led by Pierre Trudeau generally was one of rhetorical support for welfare ideals accompanied by increasing bureaucratization of welfare functions. Sometimes it seemed that the true beneficiaries were increasingly the service staffs rather than the needy groups within the society. The recent record of the Chrétien government has been one of managing the process of containing costs and reducing the federal presence in social policy.

At the provincial level, Liberal governments have shown various attitudes towards social welfare legislation. Some Liberal governments, such as the British Columbia Liberals under Gordon Campbell, have run against the welfare proposals of their New Democratic Party opponents. Other Liberal governments have established positions of leadership in the introduction of social welfare programs in their own provinces and in the influence they have brought to bear on the federal government. Liberal governments in Quebec have shared this emphasis. The comprehensive and substantial social reforms resulting from the Commission of Inquiry into Health and Welfare (the Castonguay-Nepeuv Report, 1971) are a good example.

During the years when the Progressive Conservative Party formed the federal government (1957–63, 1979–80, 1984–93), no major welfare programs were ever enacted. During the Mulroney government there was a general failure to match with action the early rhetoric proclaiming that 'social programs are a sacred trust'. The work of the Task Force on Child Care, the only significant social policy initiative that received serious consideration, did result in the introduction of legislation, but the legislation was never enacted. On the dismantling side of the equation, Family Allowances were replaced by the Child Tax Benefit in the first move towards replacing universal provisions with selective ones. A process of partial de-indexation was also put in place that means that inflation will continue to erode the value of federal social program benefits. Despite these early moves towards restraint, the Mulroney government failed to deal with the mounting problems of public expenditure and the deficit, allowing these long-term threats to social programs to grow unchecked. Given the neo-conservative emphasis of the 1980s and the enthusiasm with which Mulroney was a fellow-traveller of the right with US President Ronald Reagan and Britain's Margaret Thatcher, it is in fact surprising that there was not stronger federal leadership aimed at restraint and simplification. However, the Canadian federal Conservatives exercised great caution in the welfare

field, leaving it to the provincial parties to articulate and apply restraint. As a result the years
from 1984 to 1993 were largely wasted in incremental bureaucratic 'tinkering' with social programs by a government that did not appear to
treat matters of social policy as priority issues.
By the time the Liberals were elected in 1993
Canada was under heavy economic and international pressure to deal with its continuing
deficit problem. The opportunity for earlier preventive action had been missed.

Those provinces that have had Progressive
Conservative governments for extended periods,
such as Ontario, have shown cautious or negative attitudes towards social welfare programs.
Thus, the original opposition of Ontario to the
federal medicare program was not only based in
the province's desire to protect a field it viewed
to be part of provincial jurisdiction. It was also
an expression of conservative political philosophy. Despite the fact that at the provincial level
Conservative parties have held office more frequently than Liberal parties, it is not possible to
find examples of provincial Conservative parties
that have shown a strong commitment to welfare. On the other hand, it is not difficult to find
examples of Conservative parties that have
engaged in active anti-welfare measures, for
example, the 1993 Klein government in Alberta
and the 1995 Harris government in Ontario.
The opportunity for anti-welfare action by Conservative governments is being broadened by the
federal withdrawal from cost-shared programming.

The Canadian Alliance (formerly the Reform
Party) in western Canada and the Social Credit
in Alberta and British Columbia have expressed
a strong market orientation that has usually
resulted in opposition to social programs and a
willingness to engage enthusiastically in
restraint policies. The 1983 Social Credit Ben-
nett government in BC will long be remembered
for the reputation it established for cutbacks and
mass firings of civil servants. The rhetoric of
removing the state from areas of activity that
should be left to families and to charitable

institutions was later widely adopted by provincial governments, including especially the Klein
government (Alberta) and the Harris government (Ontario). The Alliance has also provided
a political home to social conservatism—opposing, for example, the expansion of social benefits
to gay and lesbian couples (see Box 6.1).

The Parti Québécois in Quebec has shown
an active concern for social policy issues. In the
1995 referendum campaign virtually all
women's and social services groups in the
province were in the 'Yes' camp. Federalism and
the conservative social and economic policies of
the 'rest of Canada' were critiqued and rejected
as stronger and more progressive social policies
for Quebec were seen as being made possible by
establishing a sovereign Quebec. On the other
hand, most business and conservative interests
in the province favoured maintaining the Canadian federation.

The Courts

The courts played an important role in the early
development of Canadian social policy in
upholding provincial jurisdiction and thereby
forcing the federal government either to seek
constitutional amendments or to influence,
rather than control, social policy through use of
the spending power. However, it was not until
the passage of the Charter of Rights and Freedoms in 1982 that the courts obtained the
authority they now have. The Charter requires
that the law and its administration be impartial
and free from discrimination. Social policy, by
contrast, is all about discrimination. Some
people receive benefits while others do not.
Some programs are only available to seniors
while others are only available to children.
Some relationships, for example, heterosexual
marriage, are recognized by the state, while
others are not. Some people, for example, Aboriginal peoples, have a special status. In these
many instances of discrimination, the courts
have to judge whether the discriminations in
social policy are 'reasonable'. The courts are not

a law-making body, nor do they control expenditures. The power of the courts lies in their ability to strike down legislation or prohibit administrative actions that cannot be justified as reasonable. They can, of course, also award settlements to persons who have been discriminated against. The courts are thus an important instrument of social change in such areas as women's equality rights, abortion, gay and lesbian rights, and mandatory retirement. At some future point they could be much more active than they have been so far and strike down many more social policy provisions. Courchene sees a possible role for the courts 'for creative destruction in the evolution of social policy'[14]—by which he means the wholesale removal of existing programs as discriminatory. Historically, however, the courts have not readily set aside the policy decisions of legislatures, so a wide use of the courts in striking down major social policy provisions seems improbable.

Box 6.1 Reform Opposes Same-Sex Benefits

The Reform Party plans to oppose extending benefits to same-sex couples, a move that political opponents say makes the party look intolerant as it seeks to transform itself into a new, broader-based movement.

Reformers decided at yesterday's weekly caucus meeting to oppose the bill unveiled by the Liberal government last week, saying Ottawa should also offer benefits to other cohabitants in dependent relationships, such as siblings.

Reform House Leader Chuck Strahl said yesterday that not offering benefits to other such couples offends the party's notion of equality. The bill allows same-sex couples to collect survivors' pension benefits and take advantage of certain tax incentives.

'We're going to oppose the legislation,' he said. 'This is geared specifically and only for people in same-sex relationships, people who are in a sexual relationship. What we've said is: Rather than just select out people based on conjugality, we should really examine the whole ideal of government benefits and who they should go to.'

However, opponents of the party said that not supporting the bill will paint the party as intolerant at a time when it is changing its policies to become the Canadian Reform Conservative Alliance.

'They may wind up impaling themselves on this particular issue,' said Peter MacKay, the Progressive Conservative House Leader. 'I see this as a question of financial equity and equality under the law.'

Nonetheless, Mr. MacKay said yesterday, the Tories are leaning toward holding a free vote on the matter and that there are also people in his caucus who have difficulty with the bill.

NDP member Nelson Riis said that insisting on extending benefits to other economically dependent groups is a smoke screen for many Reformers who oppose the bill.

'I think it confirms what a lot of people have suspected and that is that they are a very narrow-based, intolerant party that reflect a lot of the views out of rural Alberta,' he said.

Justice Minister Anne McLellan has ruled out for now the possibility of extending benefits to other couples. Doing so could add unwanted obligations (such as support payments) to individuals in such relationships.

However, not all Reformers said they are certain to vote against the legislation. Rahim Jaffer, whose Edmonton riding has a large number of gay constituents, says he hopes to survey residents and see how they feel about the bill.

Mr. Strahl conceded that the party's opponents may try to paint the new party as homophobic, but he noted that other parties also have difficulty with the bill. The Liberals, for instance, have at least six members who have indicated they may not support it.

SOURCE: Brian Laghi, 'Reform elects to oppose bill for same-sex benefits', *Globe and Mail*, 17 Nov. 2000.

Elites and Organized Interests

The Corporate Elite

In his analysis of social class and power in Canada in 1965, John Porter distinguished a series of elites: an economic elite; a labour elite; a political elite; a bureaucratic elite; and an ideological elite composed of the media, higher learning, and clergy.[15] In Porter's study the corporate or economic elite was defined by studying the boards of directors of 183 corporations that dominated the Canadian economy. He found a pattern of interlocking memberships and shared family ties, private school education, Anglo-Saxon origins, and a capitalist value system. Wallace Clement's analysis of the corporate elite in the 1970s found a similar pattern, with a tendency towards greater concentration of power and more ties to American and multinational capital.[16] Later works and studies have confirmed the existence of an elite comprised of Canadian business leaders and multinational corporate representatives that collectively own or manage the major capitalist enterprises that dominate the Canadian economy. This elite group has acquired greater influence through its participation in the global economy. The corporate elite and its small business allies can be viewed as being usually hostile, or at best tolerant, towards social welfare institutions. Porter wrote:

> The Chamber of Commerce and the Canadian Manufacturers' Association are together organized corporate capitalism, if not at prayer, at least in an intense passion of ideology. At meetings and in briefs to governments the way to salvation which is presented is through competitive free enterprise. All measures toward welfarism are seen as the road to ruin. Higher profits, higher incomes, and lower taxes to provide initiative at the top are seen as essentials to social progress.[17]

During the period when social programs were being developed, the effects of the economic elite's influence on social welfare appeared to lie principally in their power to delay or divert the extent of the welfare transfer. The egalitarian approach to taxation proposed in the *Report of the Royal Commission on Taxation* (1966) triggered a period of intense lobbying by economic interests seeking to protect incentives and productivity. The subsequent amended Income Tax Act (1971) led away from the egalitarian thrust of the original proposals. The influence of the economic elite on specific measures, for example, pensions, also appears to have been substantial. The introduction of the Canada Pension Plan was marked by the opposition of the Canadian life insurance industry. Judy LaMarsh provided an entertaining account of a group of insurance company presidents visiting her with the intention of persuading her not to proceed with the legislation:

> We had no real meeting of minds at all, although the discussion was polite enough, because I could not understand their bland assumption that we would renege on our election promises, and they could not make me see that it would be better all round, and less disruptive of business, if we just forgot the whole thing.[18]

However, the effects of this campaign remain. Judy LaMarsh herself pointed out that the Canada Pension Plan was designed with the expectation that private insurance plans would be 'stacked' over the government plan. This is another way of admitting that the government plan would provide a rather low level of benefit so that the interests of the private insurance industry would not be seriously hurt. In addition, the right of individuals to deduct life insurance premiums from their pre-tax earnings was retained, and subsequently the amount deductible was increased.

Since the 1970s the corporate elite has become more sophisticated and influential. It has supported the development of a significant research and policy analysis capacity. The Fraser

Institute, the C.D. Howe Institute, and the Business Council on National Issues have a substantial research, analytic, publishing, and lobbying capacity. The C.D. Howe Institute's Social Policy Challenge series, for instance, comprises 14 volumes covering every aspect of social policy reform from workfare to pensions, from Employment Insurance to the family, from demographics to Aboriginal policy. Although the Institute claims to present a diversity of viewpoints, the overwhelming authorship is by labour market economists who share the values of the corporate agenda. Other views that are published are introduced by the authors as 'dissenting' and are treated as marginal. The corporate agenda has also been reinforced through the ties that have been drawn between the agenda and the global economy. McQuaig indicates that the Canadian business community has sometimes looked for bad news on the Canadian debt and deficit as a way, presumably, of reinforcing an internal agenda of social policy restraint and reform.[19] Diana Ralph writes:

> The underlying goal is to 'harmonize' the Canadian labour force with the demands of the global market place. In other words, the reviews are not just another round of cuts. They are about destroying the whole notion of social insurance and social rights and replacing it with a draconian corporate model based on forcing workers to 'adjust' to Third World labour conditions. Both Liberal and Conservative federal governments (as well as provincial governments of all three parties) seem to have decided that the world economy globalization is inevitable and, for some, even desirable. Under threats of lowered credit ratings, and heavy pressure from corporate lobbies, they have all agreed to collaborate with business interests to help them stay afloat among the high stakes players of the international market place.[20]

The corporate agenda has been an open one, and in the 1990s it exercised a very strong influence on the restrictive changes in Canadian social policy that were then made. By the end of the 1990s writers for the C.D. Howe Institute, such as John Richards, could look back with some satisfaction at what had been accomplished:

> Ending Canada's quarter century of poor fiscal performance has been a complex exercise in reconciling inconsistent expectations across the country among interest groups about public spending and willingness to pay taxes. The reconciliation is not perfect and never will be, but relative to the early 1990s, it is much improved. Unfortunately, memories are short and current surpluses are an inducement for Ottawa—and those provinces that are in surplus—to return to former fiscal habits. The relevant warning is that those who forget the past are often condemned to re-live it.[21]

On the other hand, the radical form of the corporate agenda had not been followed. The influence of conservative thinking, aided by the corporate agenda, aided by international pressure, produced a reduction in Canada's program expenditures and a reduction in Canada's commitments to social policy and to the redistribution of income, but it had not ended these commitments. Nor was their end sought in the restated corporate position advocated by Richards. Early in the twenty-first century, the corporate elite should be seen as having the ability to influence deeply, but not determine, the direction of public policy.

The Political and Bureaucratic Elite

The political and bureaucratic elite are comprised of leading politicians, judges, and senior civil servants. The social background of this group is primarily upper middle class. Entry to its ranks formally depends on politics or merit, rather than money. However, Porter's analysis of the political and bureaucratic elite almost 40 years ago suggested that 'the underprivileged classes have never produced a political leader at the federal level.' One could have added that women were rare exceptions and ethnic origin was disproportionately Anglo-Saxon. Porter also found that Canadian politics was affected substantially by 'avocationalism' (political careers are interstitial in business or legal careers rather than being vocations in their own right) and by the fact that the complex structure of federalism tended to convert potentially partisan political issues into issues of administrative politics between bureaucracies. In turn:

> Avocational and administrative politics leaves the political system relatively weak as a system of institutional power. With a political elite of substantially middle class origins the dynamics of social class which give rise to conservative and progressive social forces have never worked themselves out within the political system. Perhaps it is from looking at their politicians that Canadians get the impression that their society is a middle class one. Neither the corporate elite, nor the very wealthy, have much to fear from middle class politicians. It is more likely that the politicians hold the corporate elite in awe.[22]

Dennis Olsen, writing about the early 1970s, found some changes, particularly more francophone presence. However, attitude changes were slight. The 'middle class state elite sees itself in alliance with business, or at least not in any fundamental opposition to its general interest.'[23] As a result, the bureaucratic and state elite are influenced relatively easily by the corporate elite and its agencies.

The political and bureaucratic elite are also sensitive to Canada's national standing in formal international assemblies. Canada has an established international reputation for living standards, social stability, human rights, support to the United Nations and other international agencies, relative openness to receive refugees, and peacekeeping. Canada maintains that reputation by support and adherence to United Nations conventions on such matters as

human rights (including the Convention on the Rights of the Child) and racism. United Nations conventions do not have the force of law, nor do they require member governments to operate social programs.[24] The most the United Nations can do is monitor compliance by publishing reports on the records of member states. Canada's record of treatment of Aboriginal peoples is an example of a field where Canada has been sensitive as to how its actions are viewed at the international level.[25]

The influence of international financial and economic agencies is also substantial. These agencies include the Organization for Economic Co-operation and Development (OECD), the International Monetary Fund (IMF), the World Trade Organization (WTO), and the World Bank. These agencies monitor the world's economies from differing perspectives and for different reasons. However, they share a common set of economic interests and ideologies. The OECD provides parallel analysis and data on the economies of 24 market economies, principally in Europe and North America. Its view of Canada's fiscal performance mirrors that of the corporate elite and of the C.D. Howe Institute. The 1994 edition of the OECD Canada survey contains a section on social programs. It concludes:

> Canadians were adversely affected by two major recessions and dislocation due to economic restructuring [a reference to NAFTA and to the global economy]. However, the current trend of expenditure on UI and social assistance cannot be sustained in the current fiscal environment. Furthermore, these programmes are no longer appropriately designed for current economic and labour market conditions. Indeed, they contain disincentives to work, which may contribute to a growing dependency on transfer income.[26]

Views held in the IMF and World Bank were similar. If Canada had had to turn to the IMF for support for the Canadian dollar, one would have expected that cuts to social programs would have been high on the list of items to be conceded as a condition of support, just as has been the case with all other countries that have had to turn to these agencies for financial support. Tester writes:

> The logic behind the structural adjustment programs applied to third world countries is deceptively simple. As a condition of receiving ongoing financial support, debtor countries have to accept terms laid on them by the IMF. These measures include: reducing the cost of government, especially by reducing the size of the public service; terminating government subsidies for food, fuel, and other essentials; devaluing the currency to control imports and increasing exports. . . . According to some reports, Canada has been secretly advised by the IMF to handle the Canadian economy in the same way . . . .[27]

The political and bureaucratic elite are sensitive to messages of this type. They would like Canada to have a good international financial report card, and, having achieved higher marks through measures introduced in the 1990s, these leaders are concerned not to again join the ranks of those countries seen as being without sufficient financial discipline. This leads to concerns that the Canadian political elite and bureaucracy may offer insufficient resistance to the international agenda of the World Trade Organization and other groups that view social policy primarily from the context of global economic policies (see Box 6.2).

The Media

Ownership of the media (with the exception of the CBC) is by the Canadian corporate elite and by international corporations. This ensures that the perspective of the corporate elite on policy issues is always maintained. It does not mean that the views of the elite are presented on every occasion and in every article. At the day-to-day

level of operation, journalists and editors have usually had freedom to operate and seek to present a broad array of points of view. However, it would be unusual for a major paper or television network to mount a sustained coverage of social policy issues from a pro-welfare perspective. (The *Toronto Star* is an exception in this regard.) On the other hand, all provide sustained coverage of corporate and business news, usually written from an informed and sympathetic position.

The National Council of Welfare's 1973 study, *The Press and the Poor*,[28] explored how the media treated poverty. The findings suggested that the media tend to maintain rather than alter contemporary attitudes towards the nature of poverty and social welfare. Several reasons for this tendency are suggested. The media are often monopolies—one-newspaper cities abound in Canada, for example. But the media are also expected to be responsible, to avoid the one-sided pursuit of partisan issues, and to present all sides of an issue. Where this task is done well, the result is to confirm existing understandings of issues. In addition, there are tendencies, not deliberate or malicious but inadvertent, to make media coverage of poverty shallow. These include the relatively 'unimportant' nature of the community involved, the control of most information by bureaucracies hostile to the disclosure of their internal affairs, and the tendency to view the situation of the poor in 'we-they' terms. Because of these tendencies, the media tended to reinforce existing stereotypes and misunderstandings. Given media ownership, it is not realistic to expect them to analyze closely or to play a critical role in interpreting issues contrary to the interests of their owners.

Marilyn and Karen Callahan (1997) found the same tendency to reinforce, rather than challenge, existing stereotypes present in the media's coverage of child welfare issues in the 1990s. The focus of the Callahans' work was the coverage by the *Vancouver Sun* of the death of Matthew Vaudreuil and the subsequent Gove

Box 6.2 The WTO and Globalization

It is critically important that Canadians and British Columbians understand that, despite the failure to establish a new negotiating round, the so-called Millennium Round, at their meetings in December [1999], the World Trade Organization is pledged to negotiate in the area of agriculture and services, a holdover from the previous round.

Negotiations in these areas threaten food marketing boards, the distribution of genetically engineered seeds and foods, and our public health and education programs by allowing private providers to offer services in these spheres on an equal footing with not-for-profit providers.

Moreover, the philosophy, structure, existing agreements and rules of the WTO are all still in place, including the profoundly undemocratic dispute-resolution mechanism. Bilateral and multilateral talks are continuing on a whole host of new regional agreements on trade.

Canada acts as a major proponent—indeed a cheerleader and bagman—for corporate-driven free trade and acts to frustrate public-interest law everywhere it can. Other than Finance, the Department of Foreign Affairs and International Trade has become the most powerful ministry in government.

Yet, in Seattle, the resistance of the over 70 developing countries to signing new agreements they had not been party to creating and the incredible civil society mobilization of around 50,000 people, will require change or the appearance of change in the WTO.

We have already heard from the US president calling for some labour and environmental considerations for any new trade rules and Canada's International Trade Minister Pierre Pettigrew calling for structural reforms.

Far more important has been the unexpected outcome of the UN Biosafety Protocol in Montreal which, for the first time, recognizes the precautionary principle as a valid means for nations to refuse the importation of [genetically engineered] seeds and foods, and gives, although ambiguous in its working, equality between UN public-interest law and trade laws administered by the WTO.

Again, criticism of the WTO and the globalization agency has been stinging at the UN Conference on Trade and Development in Bangkok, with the UN secretary general calling for a 'new deal' in global trade.

So what is at stake for civil society at home? First, there is the direct challenge to our national sovereignty and the powers of both provincial and municipal governments in their respective jurisdictions. It is the intention of the WTO agreements to bind all subnational governments, which does not depend on the acceptance of those governments.

Second, with social services on the table, as stated above, Canada's cherished social programs of medicare and publicly funded education, already threatened from within, are at risk of being wiped out or severely crippled by private, for-profit providers in these fields who must be offered the same subsidies or other advantages offered to not-for-profit providers. At the very least, the result would be a private system for the rich and a second-class system for the rest of us.

At the meeting of the WTO Assembly in Geneva on Feb. 7 it was agreed to move ahead on the privatization of social services with our own Sergio Marchi, former minister of international trade, heading up the negotiations. So it is now clear that Canada will actively participate in the dismantling of its own social programs now that it has already starved them through the withdrawal of funding.

Third, at the local and regional level, governments would no longer be able to provide incentives, subsidies or preferential treatment for local economic development, social or cultural priorities. Our labour, environmental and social standards would all be placed at risk through the invasion of transnational corporations operating under the protection of the WTO.

Saul Arbess is president of the Victoria chapter of the Council of Canadians.

SOURCE: Saul Arbess, 'WTO sticks to agency despite complaints', *Victoria Times Colonist*, 18 Feb. 2000.

Inquiry into Child Protection in British Columbia. After examining thousands of pages of transcripts from the inquiry and hundreds of articles they came to the following conclusions:

- The very first article, which stereotyped the mother as 'evil', caring more for herself and her boyfriends than for her child, set the tone of all that followed.
- The social workers were simple-minded and easily duped by the deceitful mother; they thought they could assess character but in fact were incompetent.
- What power the social workers did have was used to push around those they could in an attempt to ensure that their own interests were protected at all costs.

This stereotyped picture covered up a much more complex story of a mother who was herself a victim of abuse, handicapped, and a former child in care; of workers who took prudent actions while often lacking the working conditions and support that they should have had; and of an inquiry that found no evidence of concealment of information despite the intense pressure on careers and reputation that resulted from the inquiry. The *Vancouver Sun*, it seemed, ignored a multi-faceted attempt to understand a tragedy, preferring to provide its readers with 'a titillating story written as a serialized morality play'.[29]

Government Human Service Organizations and Program Beneficiaries

The establishment of social welfare policy objectives and programs has required the development of major administrative and service organizations. Indeed, the presence of such organizations is seen as a hallmark of modern society. These organizations have the task of translating the policies, values, and ideals of the welfare state into specific programs. They do the work of redistribution and provide the social services. On the one hand, they provide access to service, distribute benefits, and create special statuses; on the other, they deny access to service, maintain social control, and stigmatize their clientele. They are needed but they are rarely loved. In fact, '[t]he individual's loss of power to human service organizations is a fundamental characteristic of the welfare state.'[30] Whereas the elected governments are invested with the formal powers of the state, the actual day-to-day operations and the power that derives from that are held by the organizations that do the work. The billions of dollars and the thousands of civil servants and professional social workers involved represent a substantial interest in their own right.

The division of powers between federal and provincial governments has increased the power and influence of the organizations that deliver benefits and services, having the effect of removing political decision-making with respect to policy from elected assemblies to intergovernmental negotiations between federal and provincial bureaucracies. The career civil servant works within the context of existing social welfare programs. The day-to-day dealings necessary for the conduct of the large shared-cost programs required the maintenance of working agreements and relationships. Individuals involved shared similar backgrounds, usually in social work or public administration, participated in career patterns that move from provincial bureaucracy to federal bureaucracy, and shared similar values and goals with respect to social welfare programming. At one time, during the 1960s and 1970s, these organizational interests provided an enduring and consistent force for social welfare reform. However, this influence has been weakened at both federal and provincial levels by staffing policies that have focused on management expertise rather than social policy knowledge in senior staff, accompanied by policies of moving senior staff between ministries. Both sets of staffing policies have made it more difficult for civil servants to develop and maintain a progressive influence on social policy.[31] Nevertheless, the government service organizations provide what Courchene refers to as 'the inertial power of the status quo'.[32]

The power is established at two major levels: employees and beneficiaries. Both levels are broad enough to have an impact on elections, particularly in some constituencies and in areas of the country where the benefits of the regional redistribution that accompanies social welfare are strongest. There have been examples of successful political resistance to change in social programs, as when seniors opposed the de-indexation of Old Age Security proposed by the 1985 Mulroney government. The power of employees and beneficiaries to resist the changes that conservatives sought in social policy during the 1990s was recognized by the conservative Courchene, who wrote that 'these vested interests [employees and beneficiaries] are indeed powerful.'[33] The dominant corporate elite and their allies appeared to think that the inertial power of the status quo was the most likely reason they would not reach their goals in the 1990s of a radical pro-market restructuring of social welfare. This, more than anything else, led them to want to reinforce their arguments by referring to Canada's deficit problems.

> In the final analysis, it may well be wishful thinking on my part that the politics of social policy reform is do-able. But then the alternative is to run into the fiscal and financial 'wall' and to turn over the restructuring, in part at least, to agents outside Canada.[34]

In retrospect, the power of the social welfare organizations (and beneficiaries) to guard their own interests proved insufficient and the result was the series of deficit reduction budgets presented by Finance Minister Paul Martin, which had the effect of accomplishing a fiscal restructuring inside Canada without any need of international intervention.

In addition, a purely defensive posture in regard to social programs, allied with social service unions and professionals, was not attractive to many social policy advocates, who in many cases had spent a good deal of time criticizing programs for their policy shortcomings and for their bureaucratic administration. Diana Ralph wrote:

> The vision of fighting just to keep what we have is too narrow. People feel justifiably ambivalent about the social programs they use and pay for. It's hard to work up much enthusiasm for even the 'good old days' of the Welfare State. We wanted a just, equal, safe and humane society. We got inadequate, demeaning welfare, UI and Workers' Compensation. We wanted an end to violence against women, and we got underfunded shelters and rape crisis lines. We wanted an end to racism, and we got small grants to competing ethnic minorities to fight among themselves and blame all whites.[35]

Organized Labour

The role of organized labour in social welfare has been an uneven one. The Canadian Labour Congress, in particular, has been proud of its support of the process of social reform:

> In the deliberations of labour conventions since 1898 there have been changes, sometimes in subject matter, sometimes in emphasis; but there has always been a persistent theme of concern with social issues which affect all citizens. The trade union movement, from its beginning until the present, has seen itself as a spokesman for ordinary working people in those matters.[36]

Social welfare, however, has not been a central concern of labour in Canada, which has concentrated most of its attention on the basic processes of labour organizing and wage and benefit negotiation. Nor has organized labour been immune from the sexism and racism found in Canadian society generally and in social policy in particular. Carniol concludes his sympathetic treatment of the labour movement and social work by saying:

> Coming from a history of hostility from employers and the state, the labour movement has had an uphill struggle. In addition to being put on the defensive by dominant economic structures, trade unions had incorporated the sexism and racism prevalent in Canadian life. Only in recent years has the labour movement become inclusive of women and people of colour.[37]

In fighting for a 'family wage' and accompanying social policy provisions in UI and Workers' Compensation, the labour movement emphasized the financial dependency of women. Attention was primarily on the blue-collar industrial worker. The reality of the gender division of the labour force is that it now has two worker stereotypes—the male blue-collar worker and the female service worker—with a large wage differential between them. The single mothers in the service occupations are most vulnerable to living below the poverty line, whether employed or on social assistance, yet their cause has received less attention because women were assumed to be secondary earners rather than full labour force participants.

In turn, Canadian social welfare legislation has been less attentive to the relationship between social welfare and wages than in those Western countries, such as Australia, in which the labour movement has played a more substantial role in the development of minimum wages as a central feature of social welfare. Wage differentials between men and women are significantly less in Australia.

In the current unstable economic climate organized labour is primarily focused on job preservation and creation, particularly the preservation and creation of jobs in the manufacturing and public service sectors of the economy, where unionization has been highest and where job losses are reducing union memberships. As noted above, the stance of organized labour has not gone unnoticed by those who are proposing radical changes in social program employment terms. A secondary objective of labour has been to preserve the structure and benefits of the UI program. These objectives made organized labour a significant contributor to the defence of existing programs and benefits during the 1990s when these benefits were being cut back. In addition, in recent years organized labour has given attention to issues of women's equality and freedom from harassment or discrimination in the workplace.

The Academic and Religious Elites

Porter identified two additional elite groups, an academic elite and a religious elite. In 1965 Porter wrote that the academic elite contributed little to social criticism and had little impact on the society outside its walls in English Canada. French-Canadian higher learning appeared to have a more dynamic relationship with the society of which it was part. However, such writers as Marcel Rioux[38] and Yves Martin[39] or, indeed, Pierre Trudeau, concentrated their attention on nationalistic issues rather than on issues of social class and inequality. Neither the English nor the French tradition was thus particularly productive with respect to the development of a distinct Canadian welfare ideology. However, the isolation of higher learning from social welfare programs was not complete, and since 1965 there has been substantial growth in informed academic analysis of social welfare. One school of thought has been characterized by the concern for liberal values and the pursuit of social justice; a second has been characterized by Marxist and structural analysis of welfare; a third has been characterized by economic analysis. Each of these schools of thought has well-defined positions on the current issues of social policy. However, they do not cohere into a single position; hence, the overall effect of the academic elite is diminished.

The religious elite have also had a dispersed relationship to social policy. The influence of organized religion on electoral and regional politics has been substantial. On the Prairies, with the exception of Alberta, the Social Gospel of the Protestant churches, the agrarian populist sentiment, and the hostility to eastern business interests provided the context for the emergence of the one consistent supporter of welfare ideals in the Canadian political spectrum—the Co-operative Commonwealth Federation (now the NDP). The early leaders of the CCF-NDP, among them J.S. Woodsworth, Tommy Douglas, and Stanley Knowles, were drawn principally from the ranks of the clergy. The United Church, in particular, continues to be a source of progressive thought and action.

In Alberta the same social forces, combined with fundamentalist rather than Social Gospel traditions, provided the context for the development of the Social Credit Party, which has tended to support individualism rather than welfare collectivism. In Quebec, the Roman Catholic Church viewed itself as the protector of nationalism and to this end sought and obtained control over the institutions of health, education, and welfare. It was not until the second half of the twentieth century that Quebec began the task of secularizing its social institutions through legislation to make them responsible to state political processes, as is characteristic of Western industrialized societies.

Thus, although the impact of churches on social welfare in Canada has been considerable, the influence has not been in one direction but has rather contributed to substantial differences in approaches to social welfare between different regions of Canada. At the national level, no unified influence exists.

The Welfare and Academic Lobbies

The pro-welfare think-tanks at the Canadian Council on Social Development, the National Council of Welfare, the Caledon Institute, and the more recent (and more radical) Canadian Centre for Policy Alternatives provide an important research, analytic, and publishing capacity that matches the capacity of the conservative Fraser Institute and the C.D. Howe Institute. They are also part of a wider network of social policy advocacy that includes associated national organizations like the National Anti-Poverty Organization and End Legislated Poverty, professional organizations like the Canadian Association of Social Workers, local community social planning councils and similar organizations, and university departments of social work and social policy. The strength of this network is primarily intellectual. It has provided a stream of ideas as to how to improve social programs. The most recent product has been the focus on child poverty and the proposals for an expanded family or child benefit program. Some advocacy groups are also effective organizers of public demonstrations and protests. At one time, during the 1960s and 1970s, groups such as these had the attention of governments. Now they have to fight for attention against the dominant position established by the corporate elite and their organizations.

The Feminist and other Social Movements

The feminist social movement has been an important influence on social policy, particularly during the 1980s and 1990s, and its achievements in forging new social policy fields and establishing new services, particularly at the community level, are impressive. At the national level the Canadian Advisory Council on the Status of Women sponsored a series of studies on the relationship of employment, social policy, and poverty to women's situation in society.[40] The more militant National Action Committee on the Status of Women (NAC) has provided organizational support to protest actions against government restraint and reform proposals at both the federal and provincial levels. The NAC has also been a strong advocate of women in the refugee and immigrant communities and has opposed measures that make immigration more difficult or more dependent on payments.

An important contribution of feminism to social policy changes comes in the form of an expectation now that all social policy change will be subject to a 'gender lens' review. Such a review examines proposals from the perspective of their effects, positive or negative, on women and equity. Sumera Thobani, at the time the NAC president, provided the following account of how she raised the need for such a review with Finance Minister Paul Martin:

> 'What is the national interest? Patriarchy? Sexism?' She noted that NAC had held at least five meetings with Finance Minister Paul Martin and had asked him whether or not his department had conducted a gender analysis of the federal budget. 'Quite frankly, Ms. Thobani, our department does not have the capacity for doing that kind of analysis', she quoted him as saying. She added that 'any democratic government which is committed to the political participation of women has a responsibility to be funding that kind of work.'[41]

Other social movements, for example the gay and lesbian movement, also have notable accomplishments, both as service providers and as critics of existing services and advocates of change. Yet, from a political perspective, a weakness of the social movements is that they are based on organizing people on sectarian lines for sectarian purposes. Each movement seeks its own objectives and common agendas are difficult to establish, or, if formed, contain so many items that the agenda as a whole becomes overloaded with the specific issues of each group. How to unite the social movements in a common vision is of central concern to such writers as Brian Wharf,[42] Diana Ralph,[43] and Peter Leonard.[44] But until a solution is found the source of the strength of the social movements will also be a source of weakness. Individually, they can influence how social welfare changes or does not change, but they have little or no influence over the scope and resources of social welfare as a whole. Courchene and the corporate elite he speaks for appear to ignore them. One can read the social policy series of the C.D. Howe Institute from cover to cover without finding a social movement perspective seriously incorporated into a policy proposal. In most cases they are not even acknowledged to exist and, where they are, they are speedily discounted as 'special interest' groups and 'vested interests'.

Aboriginal Peoples

While most of the parties to the conflict on the future role and substance of social welfare are giving primary attention to specific program objectives and issues, Aboriginal peoples are concerned principally with jurisdiction. The Aboriginal encounter with social welfare has been oppressive and destructive of Aboriginal culture from its nineteenth-century formulation in the Indian Act, and in treaty negotiation, to its present expression in federal and provincial programs. From an Aboriginal perspective there is no virtue to be found in the loss of an independent way of life and the substitution of social assistance; no virtue to be found in the removal of children and their placement as foster or adopted children in non-Aboriginal homes; no virtue in having replaced the wisdom of elders by the wisdom of judges, lawyers, and social workers; no virtue in having introduced communities to alcohol and drugs and offered in return detoxification and counselling; and no virtue in generations of children going to residential school, only to return abused and poorly educated.

Poverty is everywhere in the Aboriginal community. However, a result of its prevalence is that it loses some of its power to frighten and obtain conformity to social norms. The Aboriginal community is by far the most militant of the social movements, and, along with the environmental movement, one of a few social movements prepared to defy courts and go to jail for political reasons.

The Aboriginal community is, of course, not a unified entity but a very diverse one. However, two major branches of Aboriginal political diversity are apparent. The first consists of the historic nations that constituted Aboriginal Canada at the time of settlement. These peoples have their greatest strength in the historic treaties and in the largely rural Indian reserves where they live and where their institutions of self-government operate. The separate interest of the individual nations is the dominant issue among these various peoples. The second branch consists of the urban Aboriginal populations, including the Métis people. More than half the total Aboriginal population now live in urban areas. In these areas intermarriage and class differentiation are prominent and the Aboriginal organizations that have been developed serve Aboriginal people as a whole rather than as separate nations. For urban Native peoples it is the collective interest that is dominant.[45]

The objective of Aboriginal militancy is control of social policy, that is, jurisdiction rather than specific reforms. Canadian governments at both the federal and provincial levels have indicated that social policy is 'on the table' for negotiations on Aboriginal self-government, but what this means has yet to be clarified. For the reserve-based First Nations it could mean something akin to provincial status for Aboriginal communities, but judging from the agreements made to date it would appear that this usually represents a neo-colonial form of self-management of programs conceived in the mainstream community and dependent for their resources on funds transferred from general taxation. For the urban community, it means simply that Aboriginal agencies will be treated like any other organized urban group. That is, Aboriginal urban service organizations will be supported and policies that recognize the existence of the Aboriginal community will be encouraged. Both sets of policies are a long way removed from the Aboriginal goal of policy independence and are

examples of what Augie Fleras refers to as 'institutional assimilation', which now replaces the 'cultural assimilation' of the 1960s and 1970s.[46]

In support of this policy, federal and provincial governments are also engaging in political action to co-opt the Aboriginal agenda and convert it into less militant and more acceptable forms. This includes vigorous suppression of the most militant groups, marginalizing their influence by ignoring their demands, funding the less militant Aboriginal groups, and conducting limited reforms, as in the management agreements. It is clear to most observers that these methods will not be sufficient to meet the policy recommendations of the Royal Commission on Aboriginal Peoples or the expressed aspiration of national Aboriginal organizations. Michael Prince and Frances Abele write:

> Our central argument is that the full realization of Aboriginal self-government will require significant revisions to fiscal federalism and some innovations yet to be identified. Existing fiscal arrangements are suitable for some First Nations, perhaps, but not for others. As self government arrangements evolve and the new institutions develop and adapt, it is becoming clear that the emerging 'system' for funding Aboriginal governments will be extremely heterogeneous, as are the emerging governments themselves.[47]

To this point, the commitment to decolonization has yet to be formed into an effective and functioning decolonizing administrative strategy. Meanwhile, there is a risk that the existing neo-colonial relationships will be consolidated and de facto will become the new Aboriginal reality, just as they have in the wider context of neo-colonial international relationships.[48]

The Political Process

There are two principal views concerning the distribution of power in society. The first is that power is concentrated in all societies in the hands of an elite.[49] The elite rulers of the society control all important decisions within the society, protect their own interests and power, and enjoy the benefits derived therefrom. In this view, power and the extent of the social welfare function are in the end determined by the corporate elite both within and outside Canada. Elections and electoral politics matter little, as the state and the elected politicians are, in truth, a front for more powerful elites that have the power to impose a regime of their choosing on Canada, whether the rest of the society wants it or not.

This view contrasts sharply with the pluralistic view of Western industrialized democracies—that they are characterized by a high degree of diffusion of power.[50] This diffuse or pluralist model suggests that society is organized into a series of competing interest groups. Each group is able to defend and to obtain some adjustments to its particular interests, and no group is in a position to impose unilaterally its interest on others. From this view the power of the corporate elite is regarded as significant but not overwhelming. The views of the corporate elite may have been dominant in the 1990s, but the interests of other groups also had to be considered. Governments remain in control of the political process and are not just puppets, fronting for corporate interests. Elections and electoral politics remain important. Looking back on the 1990s one can see evidence for both views. Governments did remain in control of the social policy agenda, but the influence of the different groups with an interest in social policy was not equal. The agenda was primarily determined by the corporate elite, aided by international relationships and by a compliant bureaucracy.

Redistribution, Change, and Social Class Considerations

The changes made in Canada's social welfare redistributive system in the 1990s have had different effects on the different social classes.

For the top 40 per cent of income-earners the present system provided few direct benefits, but those that it did provide, for example, RRSP and RPP pension provisions and the child-care deduction, were untouched by the financial restructuring of the 1990s. People in these income groups also receive benefits from the universal service systems, e.g., medicare and education, and, by a process of institutional creaming, receive the best of treatment from these systems. In the 1990s, with regard to the distribution of income, these groups more than held their own, capturing a larger share of pre-tax, pre-redistribution income. The next 40 per cent of income-earners, including most children and most seniors, draw some financial benefits from the upper tier of the redistributive system. Health and social services are very important components of their financial well-being. Although the programs are patchy and do not meet all needs, they are available as social rights and receipt of benefit is usually free of stigma. Programs at this level, particularly the UI and Workers' Compensation programs, came under critical scrutiny to make them 'more efficient', meaning lower or more restricted benefits, and, for UI as it was transformed to become EI, gave greater attention to labour market effects. Seniors succeeded in resisting attempts to reduce their program benefits. The OAS 'clawback' of benefits was not extended to treat couples' joint income and changes were made in the Canada Pension Plan to protect the ability to pay promised benefits. Thus, although there was some impact for the second 40 per cent of income-earners, in the main, the changes were modest and these groups can be said to have shown the ability to protect their interests in social welfare policy.

For the lowest 20 per cent of income recipients the redistributive system is the major, sometimes the only, factor in their incomes. The programs at this level serve a disproportionate number of women and children, persons with disabilities, recent immigrants, and most Aboriginal people. And here the most serious effects of the 1990s social welfare restructuring were felt. The federal role in maintaining national standards through the Canada Assistance Plan was removed. Benefits fell and inequality increased. Related social policies in areas like child protection policy became more punitive.

Could anything have been done to prevent this attack on the most vulnerable members of our community? A study of public support for social programs conducted in 1991 and 1992 by John Crane of the University of British Columbia found that there was more support than opposition for social programs.[51] Crane interprets his results to mean that the public would be willing to expand social programs and pay more for them. However, although there were more positive than negative responses, the largest response was often in the 'mixed' category (see Table 6.1), reflecting ambivalence, or even disinterest, rather than enthusiasm and commitment. Thus, the impact of class cleavages and electoral politics on social policy was uncertain, and one can see, in retrospect, that social welfare was vulnerable to the restrictions that were enacted.

Conclusion

The political image of Canada as a society in which differences of class and ethnic origin are ignored or concealed in public debate, as presented by John Porter in *The Vertical Mosaic* in 1965, remains largely true almost 40 years later. In the intervening years a period of expansion in social programming and an attempt to deal with problems of poverty were replaced by a period of retrenchment. Commenting on changes in social policy since Porter wrote, Julia O'Connor writes:

> In conclusion we can say with certainty that the welfare state in Canada contributes significantly to the amelioration of market and associated inequities and that this contributes to the achievement of social justice. However, these inequities are increasing over time, and, in the absence of a political commitment to address the increase, Canada is moving further away from the achievement of a just society characterized by a considerable degree of equality of condition or even of opportunity. This is exacerbated by the changing context within which the welfare state is operating in the 1990s relative to the 1960s.[52]

In the new post-deficit world of the early twenty-first century, social policy continues to face an uncertain political future. The conservative establishment continues to play a dominant role and its influence is not offset by any

Table 6.1 Satisfaction with the Number, Kinds, and Direction of Social Programs

Satisfaction	Number of Programs		Kinds of Programs		Direction of Programs	
	No.	%	No.	%	No.	%
1. Extremely Dissatisfied	7	5.6	4	3.2	10	8.4
2.	5	4.0	10	8.1	32	18.5
3.	14	11.3	30	24.2	50	15.1
4. Mixed	43	34.7	40	32.3	44	37.0
5.	29	23.4	33	26.6	19	16.0
6.	16	12.9	14	11.3	5	4.2
7. Extremely Satisfied	10	8.1	7	5.4	1	0.8

SOURCE: John Crane, *The Public's View of Social Programs* (Vancouver: University of British Columbia Press, 1994), 172.

political lobby of equal power. The Social Union Framework Agreement of 1999 is no more than a commitment of the provinces and federal government to work with one another. It fails to provide a statement of objectives that would attract public support and it fails to provide for the development of Aboriginal self-government. As each year passes, the development of a new public commitment to social justice seems less likely to occur.

Additional Readings

Marilyn Callahan and Karen Callahan, 'Victims and Villains: Scandals, the Press and Policy Making in Child Welfare', in Jane Pulkingham and Gordon Ternowetsky, eds, *Child and Family Policies: Struggles, Strategies and Options*. Halifax: Fernwood, 1997, 40–57. Marilyn and Karen Callahan show how the press tends to confirm stereotypes rather than challenge them.

Michael Mendelson, 'The New Social Union', *Canadian Review of Social Policy* 43 (1999): 5–6. This article critiques the Social Union Framework Agreement, Canada's latest attempt to clarify the relationship between the federal government and the provinces in the development of social policy.

Julia S. O'Connor, 'Social Justice, Social Citizenship and the Welfare State, 1965–1995: Canada in Comparative Context', in Rick Helmes-Hayes and James Curtis, eds, *The Vertical Mosaic Revisited*. Toronto: University of Toronto Press, 1998, 180–232. This essay applies John Porter's classic analysis of power and social class in Canadian society to the changes that had taken place in social welfare in Canada over the 30 years since Porter's book was published.

Michael J. Prince and Frances Abele, 'Funding an Aboriginal Order of Government in Canada: Recent Developments in Self-Government and Fiscal Relations', in Harvey Lazar, ed., *Canada: The State of the Federation 1999/2000*. Montreal and Kingston: McGill-Queen's University Press, 2000, 337–67. This essay discusses the funding mechanisms needed for the development of a more independent form of Aboriginal self-government.

Study Questions

1. Select a recent example of a change in social policy that you would regard as a change for the better and draw a political map showing who supported the change and who was opposed to it. Summarize the reasons each would give for their position.

2. Repeat the exercise above for a change in social policy that you would regard as a change for the worse.

3. Compare the examples you selected for questions 1 and 2. What common factors emerge in the roles played by different actors? Which tend to take clear positions and which tend to 'sit on the fence'? Where were final decisions made and who made them?

4. Think about your own position. What issues in Canadian social welfare policy do you wish to influence? What influence do you have now and how can you ally yourself with others to increase it? What longer-term actions, say, over the next five years, might you take to increase your influence?

Notes

1. Canada, *Income Security and Social Services* (Ottawa: Queen's Printer, 1969).

2. Canada, *Report* of the Royal Commission on Dominion-Provincial Relations (Ottawa, 1940), Book 2, 128. 'These areas' refers to the Maritime and Prairie provinces.

3. The next three federal-provincial funding and policy mechanisms are referred to by Courchene

as 'fiscal federalism'. For a much fuller and more technical account of how they work, see Thomas Courchene, *Social Canada in the Millennium* (Toronto: C.D. Howe Institute, 1994), ch. 4.

4. Constitution Act, 1982, section 36(2).

5. Department of Finance, 'Federal Transfers to Provinces and Territories', Department of Finance Web site. Accessed 3 June 2002.

6. For a general discussion of conditional grant mechanisms, see Donald Smiley, *Conditional Grants and Canadian Federalism* (Toronto: Canadian Tax Foundation, 1973).

7. Canada, *A Framework to Improve the Social Union for Canadians: An Agreement Between the Government of Canada and the Governments of the Provinces and Territories* (Ottawa, 4 Feb. 1999).

8. Michael Mendelson, 'The New Social Union', *Canadian Review of Social Policy* 43 (1999): 5–6.

9. Martha Friendly, 'Is this as Good as it Gets? Child Care as a Test Case for Assessing the Social Union Framework Agreement', *Canadian Review of Social Policy* 47 (2001): 77–82.

10. John Richards, 'The Social Union Framework Agreement: Disappointing and Irrelevant', *Canadian Review of Social Policy* 47 (2001): 83–8.

11. Michael Prince, 'Ready or Not? Hide and Seek Politics of Canadian Federalism, the Social Union Framework Agreement, and the Role of National Aboriginal Organizations', in Tom McIntosh, ed., *Canada's Social Union: Perspectives and Directions* (Regina: Canadian Plains Research Centre, 2002), 99–111.

12. See Diana Ralph, 'Anti-poverty Policy under NDP Governments,' *Canadian Review of Social Policy* 31 (1993): 63.

13. Judy LaMarsh, *Memoirs of a Bird in a Gilded Cage* (Toronto: McClelland & Stewart, 1968), 49.

14. Courchene, *Social Canada*, 206.

15. John Porter, *The Vertical Mosaic* (Toronto: University of Toronto Press, 1965).

16. Wallace Clement, *The Canadian Corporate Elite* (Ottawa: Carleton University Press, 1986).

17. Porter, *The Vertical Mosaic*, 306.

18. LaMarsh, *Memoirs of a Bird in a Gilded Cage*, 90.

19. Linda McQuaig, *Shooting the Hippo: Death by Deficit* (Toronto: Viking, 1995), 41–6.

20. Diana Ralph, 'Fighting for Canada's Social Programs', *Canadian Review of Social Policy* 34 (1994): 75–85.

21. John Richards, *Now that the Coat Fits the Cloth: Spending Wisely in a Trimmed-Down Age*, C.D. Howe Institute Commentary #143 (Toronto: C.D. Howe Institute, 2000), 45.

22. Porter, *The Vertical Mosaic*, 412.

23. Dennis Olsen, *The State Elite*, as quoted by Leo V. Panitch, 'Elites, Classes and Power in Canada', in Michael Whittington and Glen Williams, eds, *Canadian Politics in the 1990s* (Scarborough, Ont.: Nelson, 1990), 186.

24. Y.N. Kly, 'On the Meaning and Significance of the United Nations Convention on the Rights of the Child', *Canadian Review of Social Policy* 27 (1991): 66–73.

25. Andrew Armitage, *Comparing the Policy of Aboriginal Assimilation: Australia, Canada and New Zealand* (Vancouver: University of British Columbia Press, 1995), 229.

26. OECD, *Economic Surveys, Canada* (Paris: OECD, 1994), 114.

27. Frank James Tester, 'The Disenchanted Democracy: Canada in the Global Economy of the 1990s', *Canadian Review of Social Policy* 29–30 (1992): 132–57.

28. National Council of Welfare, *The Press and the Poor* (Ottawa: NCW, 1973).

29. Marilyn Callahan and Karen Callahan, 'Victims and Villains: Scandals, the Press and Policy Making in Child Welfare', in Jane Pulkingham and Gordon Ternowetsky, eds, *Child and Family Policies: Struggles, Strategies and Options* (Halifax: Fernwood, 1997), 40–57.

30. Y. Hasenfeld, *Human Service Organizations* (Englewood Cliffs, NJ: Prentice-Hall, 1983), 1.

31. Richard Splane, 'Social Policy Making in the Government of Canada: Reflections of a Reformist Bureaucrat', in S. Yelaja, ed., *Canadian Social Policy*, 2nd edn (Waterloo, Ont.: Wilfrid Laurier University Press, 1987).

32. Courchene, *Social Canada*, ch. 6.

33. Ibid., 197.

34. Ralph, 'Fighting for Canada's Social Programs', 78.

35. Courchene, *Social Canada*, 200.

36. Canadian Labour Congress, *Labour's Social Objectives* (Ottawa, 1973).

37. Ben Carniol, 'Social Work and the Labour Movement', in Brian Wharf, ed., *Social Work and Social Change in Canada* (Toronto: McClelland & Stewart, 1990), 137.

38. Marcel Rioux, *Quebec in Question* (Toronto: James Lewis and Samuel, 1971).

39. T.B. Bottomore, *Critics of Society: Radical Thought in North America* (New York: Random House, 1969), 113.

40. Canadian Advisory Council on the Status of Women, Brief presented to the Commission of Inquiry on Unemployment Insurance, Ottawa, 1986; CACSW, *Integration and Participation: Women's Work in the Home and the Labour Force* (Ottawa, 1987); CACSW, *Planning Our Future: Do We Have to be Poor?* (Ottawa, 1988); CACSW, *Women and Labour Market Poverty* (Ottawa, 1990).

41. Sumera Thobani, in *7th Conference on Canadian Social Welfare Policy: Remaking Canadian Social Policy: Selected Proceedings* (Vancouver: Social Planning and Research Council of BC, 25–8 June 1995), 25.

42. Wharf, ed., *Social Work and Social Change in Canada*, 144 ff.

43. Ralph, 'Fighting for Canada's Social Programs', 78–80.

44. Peter Leonard, 'Knowledge/Power and Post-modernism: Implications for the Practice of a Critical Social Work Education', *Canadian Social Work Review* 11, 1 (1994): 11–26.

45. Frances Abele and Michael J. Prince, 'Alternative Futures: Aboriginal Peoples and Canadian Federalism', in Herman Bakvis and Grace Skogstad, eds, *Canadian Federalism: Performance, Effectiveness and Legitimacy* (Toronto: University of Toronto Press, 2002), 231–2.

46. Augie Fleras and Jean Leonard Elliott, *The Nations Within* (Toronto: Oxford University Press, 1992), 225.

47. Michael J. Prince and Frances Abele, 'Funding an Aboriginal Order of Government in Canada: Recent Developments in Self-Government and Fiscal Relations', in Harvey Lazar, ed., *Canada: The State of the Federation 1999/2000* (Montreal and Kingston: McGill-Queen's University Press, 2000), 337–67.

48. Stewart MacPherson, *Social Policy in the Third World* (Brighton, UK: Wheatsheaf, 1982).

49. Gaetano Mosca, *Ruling Class* (New York: McGraw, 1939); Vilfredo Pareto, *Mind and Society* (New York: Dover, 1935).

50. R.A. Dahl, *Pluralist Democracy in the United States: Conflict and Consent* (New York: Rand McNally, 1967).

51. John Crane, *The Public's View of Social Programs* (Vancouver: University of British Columbia Press, 1994). The organizational sample was created to represent diverse points of view on social programs and included members from business, consumer, women's, and professional associations. Ibid., 10.

52. Julia S. O'Connor, 'Social Justice, Social Citizenship, and the Welfare State', in Rick Helmes-Hayes and James Curtis, eds, *The Vertical Mosaic Revisited* (Toronto: University of Toronto Press, 1998), 180–232.

CHAPTER 7

Social Welfare:
Ideologies and Research

This chapter examines more closely how ideology affects Canadian social welfare policy. The positions of the major ideological schools of thought are outlined along with the institutions through which they develop and organize their positions. Their contemporary influence on Canadian social welfare policy is compared.

Learning Objectives

1. To understand the influence of each of six major schools of thought (or ideologies) on Canadian social welfare policy.
2. To know the major institutions through which each of the schools of thought develops and disseminates its materials.
3. To be able to find examples of the work of each and critique them.

The systematic study of social policy is a field in which the principal academic participants represent the disciplines of social work, sociology, economics, political science, public administration, women's studies, and Aboriginal studies. These disciplines also have a shared discourse among them, through a shared literature and through periodic social policy conferences.[1] Within this discourse there are six discernible schools of theory and research, organized partly on ideological lines and partly on the social reference group with which participants identify. These are the *liberal, conservative, socialist (also referred to as Marxist), feminist, anti-racist,* and *Aboriginal* schools of thought referred to in Chapter 1. The differences between these schools is seen not only in different opinions about the origin and solutions of social problems, but also in the methods of critical inquiry, research, language, and knowledge base that each uses.

The Liberal School

The early products of the liberal school are synonymous with the work of the first social reformers who documented social problems and proposed pragmatic solutions to those problems. The results of their work were briefs to governments, submissions to charities, and similar activities. If homelessness was the problem, then shelters should be provided. If people were poor they needed jobs or money. If people were sick they needed health care. The approach was practical and the underlying assumptions were moral and reformist. The society in which the problems arose was taken as a given, capable of improvement by being made more fair, just, and equal. Facts on social problems were the principal contribution that could come from research. The facts were reviewed using liberal values, and conclusions and recommendations pointed the direction for change.

This school of thought and work remains a central feature of the study of social policy. The early data-gathering of reformers on such matters as poverty, employment, incomes, health, and housing conditions has been taken over by government service and statistical agencies as part of a government database. The resulting information on issues relevant to social policy is basically descriptive. Extensive demographic data, problem-oriented data, 'service output' data, and comparative data exist.

The Canadian census provides a typical major source of descriptive demographic data on population, age distribution, location, migration, income, housing, land use, employment, etc. The census is supplemented by extensive survey data developed by Statistics Canada and by provincial departments of vital statistics covering such continuing subjects as births, marriages, divorces, deaths, and epidemiological illness patterns. Furthermore, the meaning of these data is explored through monographs that indicate historical trends and provide comparisons between provinces and countries. The reasons for selecting some subjects for information-gathering while neglecting others are principally historical, influenced by specific requests and policy initiatives. The influence of a research and statistical establishment is also evident in the attention typically given in such data to issues of historical comparability. Data from the census and from statistical agencies represent an essential beginning point for the analysis of quantitative aspects of social welfare but are typically insufficient in detail to be of immediate utility in assessing social welfare programs or institutions.

Based on this work, Canada has developed ongoing data series that are essentially descriptive of particular social problems. The social problems chosen for the development of such series are usually those that have been of social policy interest. Typical examples of such series are poverty lines, unemployment rates, crime and delinquency rates, and the consumer price index. These 'social problem' series differ from general demographic data in that they are developed around some basic set of government policies and thus tend to have a normative thrust. For example, since the governmental concern with poverty in the 1970s, data have been gathered as a record of government progress, or lack of progress, in combatting the problem of poverty. Attempts to use these data to develop a

comprehensive set of social indicators have continued since that time. Some of this work has focused on specific subjects, such as the status of children, women, elderly people, and visible minority groups.[2] The best current example of a more comprehensive approach is the *Personal Security Index* published annually by the Canadian Council on Social Development.[3]

The third type of descriptive data, available in voluminous quantity, is the service output and service resource data typically published in annual reports by human service organizations. Internally within each organization there is extensive data-gathering, primarily for management purposes. This detail is usually not readily available for external analysis, but from it a more restricted set of annual statistics is developed to describe, in general terms, the type and quantity of the services. Thus, a daycare service will report so many 'child-days' of daycare; a counselling service will indicate the total number of clients seen and the average number of appointments; and a prison will indicate the number of persons admitted, incarcerated, and discharged. Such annual reports also often describe the cost of such services, the personnel by whom they were rendered, and the physical resources used.

Data from this source are by-products of the bureaucratic/professional social welfare establishment. When viewed in this way, such data can be seen as important, indeed essential, to the operation of existing social welfare institutions. However, such data are not oriented to overall priority analysis (they basically assume the priorities that have shaped their own development); they are not a good source of criticism of the institutions that produce them (the data basically serve the interests of the producing institutions and do not recognize the critical views or viewpoints of service consumers); and they present a unified view of the social reality based on one point of observation. Furthermore, this information is incomplete and uncoordinated. The output of smaller organizations, of which there are many, is difficult to assemble:

definitions of services vary, and it is usually impossible to know whether a small number of people are being served by many agencies or whether each agency is serving different people. Thus, understanding the collective impact of social agencies on social problems usually requires extensive, and costly, studies that begin with the consumer.

Comparative data between countries or provinces are also difficult to assemble because of differences of definition between jurisdictions and organizations. For international data the publications of the Paris-based Organization for Economic Co-operation and Development (OECD) are the best sources of information. Comparisons between jurisdictions are important for understanding the accomplishments and shortcomings of any particular jurisdiction in a broader perspective.

The social policies of a jurisdiction are complex constructions, each of which reflects the issues that were prominent when the policy was introduced. It is easy to confuse the effects of a particular policy with changes taking place in demography, economics, or culture and ascribe either undue efficacy or undeserved failure to policy differences. The scholar is also frequently too close to the policies to be studied to have an independent way of looking at them. He or she is usually a member of the society being studied and usually has an interest in the subject because of an association with particular views or proposed reforms. The comparative method provides a partial answer to the problem of perspective by laying one set of actions alongside another. As a result, one can see that they are similar in some respects and different in others. If the similarities are sufficiently confirmed in numerous examples, then it begins to be possible to ascribe some of the differences to conditions that are unique to a particular society. Joan Higgins, in her discussion of the comparative method, writes that 'Probably the most important reason for engaging in comparative research is that it encourages a distinction between the general and the specific.'[4]

The second reason for comparative analysis is that it assists in searching for new prescriptions for the conduct of social policy. Change begins in many ways, sometimes through limited and local actions,[5] often through state or national initiatives, and sometimes through international action. Regardless of the origins of change, the practical conduct of social policy is determined by the interface between client groups and the police, social workers, teachers, clergy, and volunteers who actually work with them. These people, clients and helpers, can in practical ways change their own situation and develop new ways of working together. Often these changes are suppressed in the name of existing policies, good order, and stable government, but sometimes they are allowed to grow and receive the formal endorsement of social policy authorities. These 'mutations' of social policy occur at different rates in different countries, depending on local conditions. Not all succeed; indeed, many can be expected to fail. However, all are of interest to the student of social policy who searches for new prescriptions for old problems. The comparative method can thus be an orderly search for examples of previously unknown or unused approaches, together with evidence of their effects.

Bodies like the National Council of Welfare, the Caledon Institute, the Canadian Council on Social Development, and the Child Poverty 2000 campaign, as well as a great number of policy advocates, take the basic social data developed by government agencies and service organizations and use it in making their arguments that government should provide more and better social welfare programs. The conclusions of the work of this school are usually specific and factual and are designed to promote improvement in welfare policies. A strong theoretical base is usually not apparent but there are underlying assumptions that approximate the commonly understood liberal values with which this book began. The reports often make it appear that the making of social policy is a matter of common sense once the facts are known.

A weakness, from both a practical and theoretical point of view, is that this approach has difficulty accounting for why its efforts have not been more successful. If Canada is a generous and liberal society committed to ending child poverty, then why does it not enact the measures that would bring child poverty to an end? (Perhaps because 'child poverty' is a well-meaning but fundamentally flawed concept that avoids a more central issue—poverty itself and the inequities that maintain it in all capitalist market societies.) From a more theoretical point of view, the major weakness of the liberal approach as described above is that it has taken too much for granted: capitalism; the nation-state; democracy; Western cultural supremacy; 'progress'; a patriarchal family model; and an assumption that the solutions provided by policy advocates will work. These assumptions have come under searching examination and analysis by the other schools of policy thought.

The Conservative School

The conservative (also referred to as neo-conservative or neo-liberal) school of thought and study also has a long history. In many ways it is truer to the principles of classical liberalism than the liberal school referred to above. These include an emphasis on the freedom of the individual, the freedom of the economic market, private ownership, and minimum government intervention. The role of government is, first, to protect those mechanisms that are essential to the operation of the marketplace, such as contracts and private ownership, and, second, to maintain public order by punishing crime and maintaining stability. This school of thought has always contributed significantly to the development of social policy. An early contribution was the 1834 British report on the operation of the Poor Law, which provided principles of eligibility and payment that continue to be applied in social assistance-type programs.[6] The thrust of this work has been to find ways to minimize the role of social welfare, justify the least possible public intervention, and carry out programs in ways that deter their use.

In the current period, proponents of this school like to think of themselves as deeply concerned with issues of social policy from a hard-headed but not hard-hearted perspective. The preface to Thomas Courchene's *Social Canada in the Millennium*, for example, proclaims that:

> Like the country he so obviously cherishes, Courchene is a fascinating mix of talents and interests. He is an economist with a heart, a subspecies that, despite what many people think, actually does exist. His professional credentials are impeccable. . . . The implacable logic of the economist's model persuaded him that the apparently perpetual poverty of Canada's poorer provinces may well be the result of generous federal transfers; these, he contends, encourage people not to move to other regions of Canada where they might do better.[7]

A characteristic of this model is that the economic market has the central place in both analyses and conclusions.

> Courchene sees the world with the clear unblinking focus that is modern economics' most compelling attribute: if you pay people who live in poor regions, they may stay there; if you provide generous unemployment insurance (UI), don't be surprised if unemployment rates rise . . . . These are the facts of life. . . . People do maximise and if we ignore that fact we are simply fooling ourselves.[8]

An example of the analysis provided by this school is contained in the 1994 volume in the C.D. Howe series on Unemployment Insurance. Christopher Green, a McGill University economist, examines the different unemployment rates of Canada and the United States. Earlier studies revealing the existence of a difference led to study of the reasons for the difference. Green analyses data on the use of Unemployment Insurance during the previous two business cycles, showing that the use of Unemployment Insurance *rises* in periods of economic expansion when one would expect it to *fall*. The reasons for this are alleged to be: 'the positive feedback of regional extended benefits . . ., the tailoring of market behavior to the parameters of the UI system . . ., and the "repeat user" syndrome'.[9] In other words, people are using the system as a support to their incomes. Use rises during periods of economic expansion as more people have enough contributions to qualify. Use also rises as people find out how to get the maximum benefit to which they are entitled, and repeat use rises as people become familiar with the system. Whether or not one concludes that the existence of these behaviours is a reason for changing the UI program depends on the values with which one has begun the discussion. To the conservative economist it is obvious that anything that diverts the worker's attention from accepting and continuing in a job, however poorly paid, means that the economy as a whole is not getting the benefit of that person's labour. As a result we are assumed to be collectively poorer and less competitive than other societies. Box 7.1 illustrates the application of conservative thought to the problem of poverty.

A major strength of this line of analysis is that it fits well with the anxiety that has been accompanying the restructuring of the world economy and Canada's place in it. The Canadian economy needs to be able to withstand international competition and Canadian workers have to be competitive with workers anywhere in the world. This line of argument always suggests lower welfare benefits, and thus costs, fitting well the need of governments to reduce total expenditures.

The development of evaluation models and experimental techniques, and their application to social policy issues, is another important activity of this school. The first major works of this type were undertaken in the United States in the 1960s during the War on Poverty. Later, in the 1970s, there was the negative taxation experiment in Manitoba, modelled on American experiments conducted in New Jersey, Seattle, Denver, and Gary, Indiana.[10] The central question for the negative taxation experiments was whether expanded welfare programs, particularly programs more available to the working poor, resulted in a decreased work effort. The experiments took three to five years to complete. The conclusion was that work effort was not decreased by a guaranteed income, at least not under the conditions in which the experiments were carried out. Left unanswered was the question as to whether work effort might decrease over longer periods or if the negative tax program was made available to all. In the end the Manitoba experiment had little effect, for by the time the results were known, social policy issues had lost priority on the agenda of governments and a decision not to proceed had already been reached on political and financial grounds.

In the 1980s and 1990s the conservative school of thought made important contributions to the development of cost-analytic techniques to social programming. These techniques include cost-benefit analysis, cost-outcome analysis, and planned program budget systems. These are the working tools of much day-to-day policy and program analysis conducted by government agencies, either internally or through contracts with consulting firms or individuals. The questions for this type of research are usually narrow and administratively oriented. How much will it cost to introduce a new system for administering benefits? How much could be saved by reducing welfare rates or what would be the cost of increasing them? What savings could be anticipated by contracting for services rather than providing them directly by government employees? These questions are posed and answered without reference to any general policy direction, yet, cumulatively, they have a substantial and continuing effect on the conduct of social policy, reinforcing a conservative approach to the use of resources and to habits of thought and action.[11] In the 1990s proponents of this school took the lead in the design and development of workfare programs.[12]

Finally, during the 1990s especially *social conservatives* increasingly critiqued social welfare systems and advocated traditional values. Like other schools of thought, social conservatives have many differences among themselves, but the following characteristics are most often present:

- Religious views and moral positions derived from religious views are taken seriously. Most commonly, the religious views are 'fundamentalist' Protestant or Roman Catholic, characterized by strong views on 'sin'

Box 7.1 Poverty Is Voluntary, So Let's End It

Poverty in Canada could be virtually eliminated in a generation. The policy prescription is easy. End welfare. Re-institute poorhouses and homes for unwed mothers.

That might seem like drastic action, rich in its potential for human tragedy.

Society would, rightly, reject the prescription, although over time it would virtually end the disease of poverty, which has afflicted humanity since the first cities arose.

Never before in human history has a person's future been less dependent on their past or family station. Never before in human history has society had the prosperity to offer comprehensive education to all citizens. Never before has society generated such wealth or such opportunity for everyone.

All the barriers people once faced—barriers that could pen people into poverty—have disappeared. Yet poverty has not disappeared, though its nature has changed.

Poverty seldom means deprivation of physical necessities as in the past. This is doubtless the first generation in human history where obesity is a real health problem for the poor. But poverty in a relative sense remains with us.

Why, in a world bounding with possibilities, do so many normal, healthy people make poor choices that lead to poverty? Why do so many young people give up on education? Why, even as unskilled adults, do they allow themselves to get trapped into a cycle of welfare and low-skill jobs, when dozens of training programs are available?

Why are others simply unable to hold jobs once they get them? Why do teenage girls have unpro-tected sex, when single motherhood is almost a certain route to poverty? Those are questions the policy reformer—or even the most radical social activist—needs to address before prescribing solutions to the poverty problem. Given all the opportunities each of us faces, poverty is now largely a voluntary choice.

That statement will infuriate many, but it remains true that virtually no one growing up in Canada need be mired in poverty as an adult. Individuals seldom make a clear-cut decision to be poor. Instead it is usually the collective weight of a number of decisions: play is more fun than study-ing; if I quit school and work I can have more money than any of my friends; not to mention all the difficult sexual choices teenagers face today.

Social welfare programs are invariably set up to help people with today's problems—welfare for a single mother who can't make ends meet without government assistance, employment insurance for a fisherman who needs help supporting the family during the off-season.

But the long-term consequences of those programs have seldom been thought out.

What happens as it becomes more acceptable socially and economically to be a single parent? What happens when the fisherman's son, instead of staying in school, decides to become a fisherman himself, subsidized by EI money, even though he knows the work leads to a dead end? The cycle of poverty is perpetuated through voluntary choice.

Fred McMahon is director of the social affairs centre of the Fraser Institute.

SOURCE: Fred McMahon, 'Poverty is voluntary, so let's end it', *Vancouver Sun*, 9 Aug. 2001.

and 'evil' and a literal interpretation of the application of scripture or church edict to everyday life. If, for example, homosexual relationships are found to be sinful in scripture, then there is no place for homosexuality in public policy and there should be no place for tolerance towards homosexuality in employment practices, school instruction, media entertainment, etc.

- Traditional family-centred policies are viewed as preferable. The traditional twentieth-century nuclear family—a married couple and children, with the mother preferably at home—is considered to be the cornerstone social institution of our society. All variations from this model—single parenthood, separation and divorce, blended families, and families with gay or lesbian parents—are considered to be undesirable. As a result the role of social policy should be to support traditional families and to discourage other family forms.
- Human life is sacred from conception to death. Thus, policies that permit abortion or euthanasia are abhorrent.[13]

Social conservatism is sometimes associated also with concerns about the ethnic and racial composition of society. Some social conservatives think that social life, ideally, should be with the members of one's own race or social group. This view is close to 'racism' and tends to be suppressed in most statements of social conservatism; nevertheless, it does resurface from time to time.

The Socialist School

The socialist school is also referred to as the Marxist or political economy school of policy analysis. Marx did not himself analyze the welfare state (it had not been developed when he wrote), but he was as concerned with the problem of poverty as were the liberal social reformers. However, while the reformers saw the problem of poverty as being one to be solved by knowledge and the application of values, Marx saw the problem of poverty to be the result of the oppressive way that economic processes were organized in capitalist society. Mishra writes:

> Under the capitalist mode of production the basic structural elements through which wealth and poverty are generated and reproduced are: private ownership of the means of production; production for profit; private property and inheritance; and the allocation of incomes and resources through the market mechanism. For Marx, these core institutions of capitalism and the underlying values constitute the very antithesis of a welfare society. Under capitalism incomes and life chances are distributed almost entirely through the impersonal market mechanism. . . . Coercion and competition rather than cooperation and solidarity lie at the root of capitalist social organization. For Marx, then, the values and norms of welfare cannot make headway in a society of this type.[14]

The Marxist analysis provides an explanation of why social welfare policies have not been successful; they have been carried out in a society in which continuing economic processes continuously undercut and undermine both the reforms themselves and the values on which they rest. Thus the Marxist is not surprised at the problems now faced by social welfare. Indeed, the more surprising event was that the welfare state was established at all. Nevertheless, once established, social welfare has been recognized as a sphere of activity distinct from capitalism that has required examination.

The analysis to which this perspective leads is historical, political, and theoretical. Economic and social processes are discussed in order to show how they contribute towards maintaining capitalism. Information on political contributions, elite relationships, and the ownership of major corporations and of the media, for example, is used to show how social control is maintained and fundamental social reform prevented. The history of social welfare programs is studied to set the expansion or contraction of programs in the general framework of capitalist economic and political processes. Piven and Cloward's *Regulating the Poor*[15] is an excellent example of this mode of analysis, purporting to show the relationship between welfare programs and the maintenance of public order and work incentives. Tester and Kulchyski, in *Tammarniit (Mistakes): Inuit Relocation in the Eastern Arctic 1939–63*, show how the process of introducing social welfare to the Inuit served larger Canadian processes of territorial control, resource development, and totalization (the cultural and institutional integration of minorities). The preface begins:

> The 1990s are witness to a fundamental reexamination of the Canadian liberal welfare state which developed following the Second World War. . . . there is a growing tendency to question whether the welfare state could ever achieve its stated ideal of equality, while respecting the diversity among Canadian citizens. Recent history also suggests that the welfare state has ultimately failed to act as an effective buffer against the excesses of capitalist enterprise. Social workers and others are coming to understand that the welfare state is not the benevolent purveyor of egalitarian and humanist values that it was once held to be. Rather, it is increasingly recognized as something quite different—a source of oppression and racism, a regime which, because of its structures and biases, has often discriminated against women, children, and other marginalised groups.[16]

Commentary from members of this school is more prominent in academic circles and in newsletters that circulate among members than in the mainstream press.

Despite the importance of this school as a source of analysis and academic criticism, it was not until the 1990s that the contribution of the school to the development of social welfare became apparent.[17] In part this was because its conclusions had often been pessimistic as to both the possibilities for change and whether any change short of an unachievable revolutionary one is worthwhile.

One application that gained adherents in the university schools of social work is the development of 'structural' social work. Mullaly provides an example of this approach in his discussion of social reform processes that work, first, 'within (and against) the system' and, second, 'outside (and against) the system'.[18] The structural social worker is always working 'against' rather than 'for' the system. The system is the capitalist state, including its social welfare services. Thus, 'structural social work practice comprises a simultaneous two-pronged approach: (1) to provide practical, humanitarian care to the victims and casualties of our patriarchal, liberal-capitalist society; and (2) to restructure society along socialist lines.'[19] By work 'within (and against) the system', Mullaly means all those social workers who are employed by government human service organizations. Mullaly provides strategies for this work, including getting service providers and users to recognize that the personal is political and to work towards empowerment, consciousness-raising, collectivization, and radicalizing the agency. The role of workers within the system is filled with contradictions and many are said to hold the 'belief . . . that they must become "guerrillas in the bureaucracy" and undermine the agency at every turn from their political underground position.'[20] Social workers working 'outside (and against) the system' are less caught in these contradictions because they can serve their employer and their clients simultaneously. Here, too, the struggle is not an easy one, as 'we, as North Americans, have been socialized into working and living in social institutions where hierarchy, specialization, and an overreliance on rules prevail.'[21]

Another application has been seen in the work of the Canadian Centre for Policy Alternatives (CCPA). The CCPA is a non-profit research organization that draws its membership from socialist academics, labour unions, churches, and other non-profit and co-operative organizations. Although some of its support is from liberals rather than socialists, it has positioned itself to the left of governments both federal and provincial. A major activity of the CCPA is the development of annual alternative budgets,[22] each of which has offered a different (and more socially just) approach to federal expenditure priorities. The CCPA also provides political commentary from a socialist perspective on current events (see Box 7.2).

A new and distinct branch of the socialist school is the 'postmodern' school. Postmodernism is a fundamental critique of the concept of the 'modern':

> The modern idea [was] of a universal, essential subject, common to all humanity, which has been at the core of socialist belief in the possibility of a worldwide political struggle as well as underpinning the Western drive to colonizing the Other in the name of single notion of 'Civilization'.[23]

Such a critique questions the possibility of constructing social justice and challenges all the programs of the welfare state that claim to have social justice as their goal. Postmodern writers are also influenced by the work of Michel Foucault, whose critiques of madness, punishment, and sexuality expose the cultural relativism within which ideas of the 'normal' are held and enforced.

> Postmodernity (and in this it differs from modernist culture of which it is the rightful issue and legatee) does not seek to substitute one truth for another, one life ideal from another. It splits the truth, the standards and

ideal into the already deconstructed and the about to be deconstructed. It denies in advance the right of all and any revelation to slip into the place vacated by the deconstructed/discredited rules. It braces itself for a life without truths, standards and ideals.[24]

Despite its sometimes obscure language, the postmodern school provides a fundamental challenge to the Western assumptions of a right to define the concept of welfare from within the experience of one society and then to export that view through colonialism and neo-colonialism throughout the world. The critique of welfare institutions developed by the postmodernists is searching but the conclusions tend to endorse an anarchy that would be a complete contradiction to the concept of a just and peaceful society.

The Feminist School

The work of feminists is pervasive in both the liberal and socialist schools of social policy but is not present in the conservative school. There are, of course, women contributors to the conservative school, but no conservative analysis is written with a critical consciousness of gender relationships.

The contribution of both liberal and socialist feminists to the discipline of social policy begins with critical awareness of the role played by the concepts of patriarchy, family, motherhood, and caregiving that were assumed in the establishment of social welfare policy.[25] These ideas were also connected to nationalism and, in a number of jurisdictions, particularly Quebec in Canada, to pro-birth family policies. The pro-birth policies were designed to encourage the continuity of both nation and race. Examples of these policies include the increased Family Allowance payment with family size that was a feature of Quebec's administration of Family Allowances, the 'bébé-bonus' that replaced it,[26] and the opposition to birth control measures in general and to abortion in particular.

Box 7.2   The Real Foes of Terrorism are the NGOs, Not the War-hawks

Why has opposing corporate globalization become such a politically incorrect activity in the post-Sept. 11 universe? Why have so many civil society groups become reluctant to continue their street demonstrations against the IMF, the World Bank, the WTO, and the other institutional agencies of corporate rule?

The answers are fairly obvious. The Western business and political leaders who have been promoting and exploiting free trade and other neoliberal policies for the past few decades were being challenged by the mounting worldwide opposition against their agenda. Their meetings had been disrupted, their plans delayed, their image tarnished. The horrific events of Sept. 11 gave them an opportunity to strike back at the protestors as well as at the first country singled out for harbouring terrorists. The protestors, of course, were hit with propaganda, not with bombs, but the effect—mentally and emotionally—has been devastating.

What the business and political elites did was to claim that the terrorists were in effect targeting capitalism as an economic system, and hence were attacking 'democracy', 'freedom', and 'globalization'. This interpretation of the Sept. 11 atrocity led inevitably to the charge that any individuals or groups who continued to disagree with corporate globalization were, knowingly or not, siding with the terrorists.

It's an absurd and unprincipled smear campaign, but, driven by the media and fed by public hysteria, it has the desired result. Most of the civil society groups that were spearheading the anti-globalization movement—at least those in the Western nations—have been intimidated. Many of their supporters have fallen away. Some have redirected their activism into a resurgent peace movement, but even the anti-war protestors are finding their 'patriotism' being questioned.

The bitter irony of these developments is that, prior to Sept. 11, the war on terrorism was being waged more effectively by the protestors. Since that date, those who have stifled the protests and replaced them with a vengeful military response are (unknowingly, one hopes) fuelling and strengthening the forces of terrorism. (I use the term 'terrorism' reluctantly, knowing that it can also be applied to some of the actions and policies of the United States and other Western nations, but in the absence of a more precise and appropriate term, let's for the moment apply it solely to the individuals and groups so designated by the US and its allies.)

To understand this basic fact—that it is the protest movement, not the war-hawks, who are fighting terrorism—one has to engage in another now politically incorrect exercise: examining the root causes of terrorism. Many analysts have traced its emergence to the Israeli-Palestine conflict, which is undoubtedly a significant factor. But even if that fierce dispute had never erupted, the resort to violence by some of the world's most miserable and dispossessed peoples would still have occurred.

The attacks on New York and Washington, as some of the more perceptive observers have noted, were acts of desperation, not of power. They were conceived and executed—ruthlessly and inexcusably—on behalf of the billions of people around the world who have been victimized by the globalization of corporate rule.

It would perhaps be an oversimplification to say that the war now being fought is a war of the poor against the rich, of the powerless against the powerful, the homeless against the well-housed, the hungry against the well-fed. But there would be an element of truth in that outlook, too. Undoubtedly, it is the suffering and deprivation of the world's destitute billions that have provided the breeding grounds for what the affluent West calls terrorism. People who have been condemned to lives of brutishness and pain are understandably angry when they see the resources of their countries diverted to enrich a privileged and pampered minority in North America and Europe. That anger will inevitably find an outlet.

Ed Finn provides commentary on public issues to the Canadian Centre for Policy Alternatives.

Source: Ed Finn, 'The real foes of terrorism are the NGOs, not the war-hawks', Canadian Centre for Policy Alternatives, press release, 25 Oct. 2001.

Patriarchal policies assumed women were dependent on men and were designed to reinforce the position of men as 'heads' of households. Examples include the 'man in the house' rule used in the administration of social assistance, whereby if a man lives with a woman then household income determines eligibility, and the assumption made in UI benefits that they should be adequate to support a family. In addition, many social agency policies were based on assumptions about the availability of women for unpaid 'caring' work in the home and in the community. Examples here include foster care policies based on payment only for the expenses of foster children, not the work of caring for them; the presumption that women are available to care for handicapped or elderly relatives; and the lack of a major commitment to child care.

Liberal and socialist (and radical) feminists[27] differ as to the solution to these issues in much the same way as there are differences between the liberal and socialist schools of social policy. The liberal approach is reformist. It begins with an examination of the sex-based assumptions and laws that have characterized social policy. All those policies that have assumed a difference of rights or entitlements between men and women need critical examination and reform. The biological difference between men and women must be recognized positively by measures to permit and support women in performing their biological role in reproduction, but this must be done in ways that do not lead to unnecessary sexual stereotyping. Thus, 'maternity' leave should be replaced by 'parental' leave, for although women bear children there is no need to assume that women alone can care for infants. All caring roles need to be recognized as work and need to be shared by both men and women.

The socialist and radical approaches attach more importance to structural factors, particularly capitalism (for socialists) and patriarchy (for radicals). The radical point of view sees women oppressed as a class by men as a class. The oppression takes the form of male control over sexuality and reproduction. The power is rooted in male aggression, violence, and militarism. For some radical feminists these are biologically determined.

> One solution for many radical feminists is political separation, that is, campaigning, organizing, working separately from men. A further step for some is personal separatism, living and having relationships with women only, not out of personal choice, but out of political choice. . . . The recreation, protection and provision of a 'women's culture' for the nourishment of women only, then, has become the mainstream of today's radical feminism and writing.[28]

The influence of radical feminism on social policy has been substantial. Action on a series of issues—rape, family violence, abortion, sexuality, and reproductive technology—has been either determined by radical feminists or deeply influenced by the positions they have taken.

Socialist feminists concentrate their attention on the connection between capitalism and patriarchy, particularly the analysis of women's role in reproduction as providing workers for capitalist exploitation. For socialist feminists the role of women is socially 'constructed' within capitalism rather than being biologically determined. For socialist feminists 'there can be no socialism without women's liberation, and no women's liberation without socialism.'[29]

Feminists from both the radical and socialist schools have also been at the forefront in the critique of the internal culture of social welfare organizations. Most welfare organizations, and all government human service organizations, have been structured by men. Consequently, their organization and functions are characterized by:

- male dominance rather than gender equality;
- competition and independence, rather than co-operation and interdependence;

- hierarchy;
- rational control and an emphasis on technology;
- a separation of private and public, which results in compartmentalizing experiences;
- a devaluing of subjective experience.[30]

Women thereby experience organizations differently from men. In the organization as a whole and certainly in its 'lower levels' of pay and status, women predominate, but they do not control the culture. At the management and executive levels men predominate and establish a culture in which being male is normal. On the other hand, being female causes problems regarding femininity, pregnancy, having caring responsibilities, dress, and harassment. To succeed in such organizations women are expected to 'behave like men' and become 'super women' with all the qualities of both genders.

The human service organizations established by feminists have sought to establish a democratic internal culture: all participate, including service users; decision-making is by discussion and consensus, rather than by hierarchical position and majority vote; leadership is agreed on and changeable, depending on the issues; terms of employment recognize caring responsibilities; all participants are safe from harassment. Achieving this vision has not been easy in the social movement service organizations and has been even more difficult in the government service organizations. Nevertheless, the goal of a more equal and democratic workplace for workers and service users represents an important challenge. If human service organizations cannot produce a more equal and equitable environment in their own sphere of activity, how can they expect to introduce these values to the wider community? If the transformation to a non-patriarchal or socialist society cannot be started somewhere, how can it be started at all?

The contribution of feminism to the discipline of social policy also includes the development and application of institutional ethnography as a research method. Institutional ethnography was championed by Dorothy Smith in order to develop a 'sociology for women'. Smith was concerned that sociology had developed a 'gender subtext' because 'it was thought, investigated and written largely from the perspective of men.' Men had written from their standpoint 'within the organizational order' while the experience of women had 'generally been outside the organizational order which governs contemporary advanced capitalist societies.' Institutional ethnography begins with the day-to-day experience of women, rather than with the 'defining issues and problems as they have been established in the currency of the discipline'. With a beginning point centred on the question 'How does it happen to us as it does?' Smith advocates a co-operative research method done with participants as a 'means of exploring and making public the social ground and organization of our common and divergent experience'.[31] The effect of Smith's approach is seen in the way that it makes visible the whole of women's lives and does not concentrate attention on the features of interest to researchers, managers, policymakers, or any other representatives of established authority.

When applied to social policy the effect of research conducted through this method is to open up a whole new territory for understanding women's lives that had been ignored in social policy research. Government social policy in all its forms has been constructed to maintain order and achieve common objectives. Smith points to the fact that the objectives of social policy have been largely the work of men and that the standpoints of both the liberal and conservative schools are those of an established ruling apparatus, particularly those of its managers. The vast majority of research is undertaken to explicate questions of either policy or management that are of interest to policymakers or managers. It is thus inevitable that the voices of those people who are not policymakers or managers are marginalized. In many cases they may not be heard at all; in others, their voices will have been filtered and distorted by the process of gathering and selecting the pieces that were deemed important. In all cases there has been some objectification of what are considered to be data. Children, men, women, lesbian, gay, black, First Nation—all have become statistics. Added up, compared, and analyzed, their individual experiences have been taken from them and turned into a product on the basis of which policy-makers can decide on a course of action and managers, acting for them, can distribute money, goods, and services.

Smith and other researchers using institutional ethnographic methods are making other buried voices heard, and what they have to say is different from the official rendering of events that has dominated the development of the discipline of social policy. An example of how some of these principles are being introduced is provided by Callahan, Lumb, and Wharf's 'Strengthening Families by Empowering Women':

> The objective of the project was to determine if a new and distinctive approach to child welfare could be developed using the following guidelines. (1) Women-centred; the project will be designed to address the concerns of mainly single-parent women as they see them. (2) Concerned with the economic as well as the social concerns of parents. (3) Focused on front-line workers. (4) Designed to involve clients, community workers and local residents in the development and delivery of the project and to expand opportunities for clients to work in groups together. (5) Developmental rather than prescriptive. (6) Focused on the process of change. (7) Designed to be replicated elsewhere and to inform policy development.

The study offered recommendations that would permit social workers and clients to work much more closely together in supportive rather than conflicting ways.

One finding from this study is overwhelmingly important: single women and their children make up a very large proportion of the child welfare worker's caseloads, yet they were not considered when developing child welfare policy and programs. Often investigations proceed, assessments are made and services are offered in the same way as if there were two parents. Single-parent mothers in this project argued forcefully that they have an enormously difficult job with few supports and resources. They want child welfare services to be reshaped to deal with their reality.[32]

The resulting service paradigm replaced the investigation of neglect by social workers with the empowering principle of co-operation between workers and clients in finding solutions to the problems faced by single mothers in caring for their children.

Although the application of institutional ethnography to social policy has been pioneered by feminists, the method can be applied by men or women and can be applied to assist in understanding the perspective of any and all social groups.

The Anti-Racist and Anti-Oppressive School

The anti-racist academic critique of social policy was developed principally in the United States and Britain. In the United States all discussion of social welfare has a racial subtext. American blacks are markedly worse off than whites: 'in 1990 the median income for white families was $36,915, for black families $21,423: 44.8 per cent of black children lived in poverty compared with 15.9 per cent of white children.'[33] As a result, blacks participate at much higher rates in all social welfare programs. Although the origins of modern American social policy are usually equated with the Depression and the New Deal, contemporary American social policy is dominated by questions of race. Racial judgements affect social policy in two ways: (1) directly, through the existence of outright prejudice against any measures that collectively take resources from whites and give them to blacks; (2) indirectly, as a result of the interaction between the general expectation that welfare users should be 'worthy' and the stereotype of blacks 'as irresponsible and as failing to try as hard as they could or should to deal with their problems'.[34]

In Britain the anti-racist critique of social policy was developed from the experience of the post-war Caribbean immigrants with the British welfare state. Despite its professed egalitarian values, the welfare state was in the forefront of dispensing unequal treatment to immigrants in housing, schooling, and policing. At first the reason was attributed to a lag in the responsiveness of welfare institutions to new problems. In time, measures were changed so that outright barriers to providing benefits to immigrants were removed and Britain began to think of itself as a multicultural society. However, as Britain and Western Europe go through their own processes of economic restructuring and integration into the world economy there is a growing tendency to look at imported labour of non-European origin as unneeded. Welfare resources used to maintain this labour pool are thus being 'wasted'. Immigration, it is claimed, should be stopped or, better still, reversed.[35] Fifty years after the initial importation of large numbers of Caribbean and East Indian workers, it is difficult to see the recurring pattern of discrimination as being based in any other factor than European white racism.

The anti-racist critique of social policy exposes the connections between racism and social welfare in both societies. In Canada the anti-racist critique informs the positions taken both by the First Nations and by visible minority social movements in their own criticism of their experience of social welfare. As with the feminist school of social policy analysis, there are anti-racist critiques of social policy within both the liberal and socialist schools but not within the conservative school.

The anti-racist critique begins by recognizing the importance of 'deconstructing' white racism. This means accepting the existence of white racism and understanding how social policy has worked to marginalize and oppress all people of colour, while upholding white privilege. The situation of First Nations provides the one example as the statute under which they are defined, the Indian Act, had an explicit racial base in European superiority in religion, culture, lineage, and genetics. The 'right' of the Canadian government to rule Indians was provided without question, for in European minds the superiority of the settlers and their institutions was established by God and proved by science through the work of nineteenth-century geneticists on the 'survival of the fittest'. In relation to visible minorities the Canadian experience parallels in some ways the British one. Immigration policy is seen as an economic tool, with people's social policy rights being subordinate to the extent to which their labour (or capital) is needed.

The approach of the liberal school to these problems is reformist. The institutions of social welfare need to be adapted so that all Canadians have equal access based on a common citizenship. The review of agency policies to ensure that they do not incorporate assumptions from European culture would be an example. The approach of the socialist school is more structural. White racism is seen as an entrenched set of attitudes that are growing as economic restructuring is proceeding. There is doubt in this school as to whether liberal reform will take place and a continued apprehension that explicit racial discrimination will come to the fore as it has in the United States and Britain.[36]

A recent development has been the expansion of the anti-racist school of thought into a more encompassing anti-oppressive school.[37] The term 'anti-oppressive' provides a link between emancipatory work against racism and emancipatory work against other forms of oppression, notably, gender, heterosexuality, ability, and age. There is a link here as well to the postmodern writers of the socialist school who are also concerned with how oppression occurs in society. Some Schools of Social Work have adopted anti-oppressive social work as an essential practice concept, as illustrated in Box 7.3.

The Aboriginal School

The development of a distinct Aboriginal school of theory and research is the achievement of Aboriginal leaders, writers, and social agencies. The earlier literature consisted of analyses and writing 'about' the Aboriginal experience of social welfare, and this literature, although important in raising awareness of social problems, was written from the perspectives of the mainstream culture and the various schools of analysis. An example would be the landmark 1983 study by Patrick Johnston on Aboriginal children in care.[38] Johnston's study has been extensively quoted and represented a turning point in the analysis and understanding of the impact of child welfare measures on Aboriginal peoples. Nevertheless, it was a report 'about' Aboriginal people, written from a 'liberal' perspective and sponsored by the 'liberal' Canadian Council on Social Development. It was not a report by Aboriginal people and it did not indicate the development of a distinct school of analysis.

The development of a specific Aboriginal approach can be seen in the Aboriginal writing of the late 1980s on social problems and social issues in the Aboriginal community. Much of this early writing was by Aboriginal women who exposed the problems of their own community and who were not satisfied by superficial (often liberal and well-meaning) attempts to explain away differences. Joyce Timpson, in her review of Native Canadian child welfare literature, writes:

> By the late 1980s, Canadian Native people removed the veil of political untouchability from child abuse and related problems.

Canada's first Native alcohol treatment and training facility, the Nechi Institute, proclaimed that no Native person was free from the effects of child sexual abuse. It exposed the taboos of abuse, whether by family or spiritual leaders, in a ground-breaking publication, *The Spirit Weeps . . . .* Native women have challenged the non-Native notion that cultural differences account for a higher rate of sexual abuse in their communities—a notion that has fed the denial of its existence . . . .[39]

The analyses of and literature produced by contemporary Aboriginal writers is based in the present experience of the new Aboriginal agencies as they confront the real problems of their people and communities. While contributions from the liberal, socialist, feminist, and anti-racist schools can be recognized in this work, distinctive features attest to the development of a new, separate, and independent analysis. Gord Bruyere, an Anishnabe and an Assistant Professor at the University of Victoria School of Social Work, wrote how his whole experience of being a student and teacher was analogous to 'Living in Another Man's House'.

> I was distressed by the possibility of being disrespectful by writing as if I were another outsider who was simply writing about Aboriginal peoples and their ways, rather than being an Aboriginal person trying to understand himself and his Aboriginal ways as best he could at that particular time. This was not an ethnographic study nor an exercise in metaphysics; this was about my life and my family's life and about Anishnabe people.
>
> I was not worried about the writing itself; I was worried about what people who read it would do with it. In essence I was afraid to be disrespectful of the elders and traditional teachers who are so giving of their knowledge and wisdom. I was afraid to 'capitalize' and to 'exploit'. I was also concerned about being complicit with others who would use what I had written in a way that was disrespectful to

Box 7.3 University of Victoria, School of Social Work Mission Statement (2000)

The emerging vision of the School of Social Work commits us to social justice, anti-racist, and anti-oppressive social work practices, and to promoting critical enquiry that respects the diversity of knowing and being.

Our **educational mission** is to prepare generalist social work practitioners skilled in critical self-reflection and in working with individuals, families, groups and communities. In particular, we endeavour to prepare First Nations social workers and child welfare practitioners. We emphasize structural, feminist, First Nations and anti-oppressive analyses.

Our **scholarly mission** is to share and create collective knowledge and understanding through engaging in critical enquiry and by supporting research and innovative curriculum development at the undergraduate and graduate levels.

Our **practice mission** is to act on social justice issues through community change initiatives and anti-oppressive social work. Our political and social responsibility is to participate in and reflect community experiences in all our efforts to challenge oppressive societal structures.

In all our activities, we aspire to create a supportive environment that promotes equality, respect, responsibility, curiosity, collaboration, flexibility, risk-taking and creativity. We support interdisciplinary collaboration. We seek to provide accessible and flexible social work education and we are committed to working across differences, such as gender, age, race, ethnicity, class, abilities and sexual orientation.

Anti-oppressive social work

The commitment to anti-oppressive (AOP) social work is a central concept of the new statement. The School's commitment to AOP is not presented as a fixed or finished ideology, indeed such an idea would be contrary to the fundamental concepts of AOP that demand that social work be taught and practised within a continuing critique. Central to the critique are the following elements:

1. Goals. A foundation commitment to anti-racism, the de-colonization of First Nations, and to radical and feminist critical thought are central to AOP.

2. Location. Each social worker (practitioner, teacher, student) must recognize their own social and political locations (for example, race, ability, sexual orientation, religion, etc.) and the relationship between those locations and their understanding and capacity (both positive and negative) as social workers.

3. Respect for knowledge from the margins. Because received social work knowledge, policy and practice are principally based in mainstream culture it are particularly important to support and create space in the core of our curriculum where knowledge from the marginalized constituencies and writers can be heard and theory and understanding can be developed.

4. Postmodernism. In AOP the assumptions of progress, Western cultural superiority, hierarchy, the legitimacy of authorities, binary thinking, etc., are the subjects of critical challenge and reappraisal. Power is recognized and reappraised as it relates to the individual, social and institutional.

5. Social and environmental respect and justice. A commitment to a broad concept of social justice is central to the development and practice of AOP. This includes, respect for the environment, a holistic approach to life, the principles of equality and equity, and the right to diversity in culture, sexual orientation, religion and ability. It also implies a commitment to act against unjust conditions.

6. Application to social work practice. AOP is a constructive critique of social work with the intent to reform practice and social policy and develop more just models for community and society.

SOURCE: University of Victoria, School of Social Work, *Application for BSW and MSW Accreditation 2001.*

Aboriginal peoples and their ways of knowing.[40]

The development of the Aboriginal school also poses a strong challenge to what has been referred to earlier as neo-colonialism in social welfare policy. When new programs 'for' Aboriginal people are derived primarily from the ideas of non-Aboriginal people 'about' Aboriginal people, one should not be surprised if the resulting programs are neo-colonial in form because their source remains vested in the colonial relationship. In contrast, Taiaiake Alfred writes:

> From the outside, the intensity of the crisis is obscured by the smokescreen of efforts to reduce the most obvious signs of social deprivation and increase the material wealth within Native communities. It is commonly thought that allowing indigenous people a reasonable standard of living will solve all their problems. But there is more to justice than equity. Of course indigenous people have a right to a standard of living equal to others. But to stop there and continue to deny their nationhood is to accept the European genocide of 500 years. Attempting to right historical wrongs by equalizing our material conditions is not enough: to accept the simple equality offered lately would mean forgetting what indigenous nations were before those wrongs were done. Indigenous people can not forget.[41]

Thus the new Aboriginal school of analysis represents a fundamental rejection of colonialism in all its forms and the pursuit of social justice 'by' Aboriginal people and 'for' Aboriginal people.

Auspices and Control of Research

Social welfare research is a complex and technical exercise. The resources needed in terms of money, manpower, and access to information

make research dependent on the establishments that dominate the social welfare enterprise. Thus, the liberal architects of social welfare and the conservative critics command most of the resources. They are both represented by substantial policy institutes, and governments conduct or sponsor research to extend and explore the perspectives they represent. In contrast, the socialist, feminist, anti-racist, and Aboriginal critiques of social welfare are largely academic exercises conducted in universities and rarely used directly in the actual business of establishing social policy. Leslie Pal provides an analysis of the Canadian policy research industry, one branch of which deals with the examination of social welfare policy.[42] Table 7.1 applies Pal's analysis to the social policy research field and provides an overview of how the research resources are organized.

The ascription of ideology to the various research units, government agencies, and university departments is admittedly stereotypical, as in each case one will find examples of dissenting work that provides an alternative voice to the predominant ideology. Most of the groups represented in the table now have Web sites and provide for the downloading of their research. Appendix C, Canadian Social Welfare Web Sites, provides a means of looking at examples of the research work of most of the research agencies referred to in this book and named in Table 7.1. The student is encouraged to visit their Web sites and look at their work.

The exceptions to this commitment to public access are the private-sector for-profit research organizations that provide a confidential service to their 'client'—usually a government agency.

The Nature of Social Policy Knowledge

The characterization of the discipline of social policy and the auspices of social welfare research developed in this chapter has given considerable attention to the purposes for which research is conducted and the major schools of inquiry. What has become of the positivist, scientific, concern with knowledge per se? The answer is that a positivist view of knowledge, free of considerations of value and politics, is not possible for social welfare policy analysis and research. In social welfare research and policy analysis, knowledge is always related to values and to the methodology by which it is produced. There is no such thing as value-free social welfare research. Given that social welfare values are themselves contentious, it is not surprising to find that social welfare research is politically and ideologically charged. Each of the major schools has developed methods of

Table 7.1 Social Policy Research Auspices and Ideology in Canada

School of Analysis	Government	Quasi-Government	Profit	Non-Profit	University
Liberal	Line departments of government: social services, health, women's affairs, Aboriginal affairs, etc.	Royal Commissions and task forces: Reproductive Technology, *Transitions* (Ont.), *Making Changes* (BC)		Canadian Council on Social Development Caledon Institute	Schools and Departments of Social Work and related disciplines
Conservative	Central agencies of government, e.g., treasury boards, premiers' offices, finance ministries		Consulting firms (Price Waterhouse, Coopers and Lybrand) and pollsters (Decima, Goldfarb, Leger & Leger)	C.D. Howe Institute Fraser Institute	Schools and Departments of Economics and Public Administration
Socialist				Canadian Centre for Policy Alternatives	Structural Schools of Social Work
Feminist				National Action Committee on the Status of Women	Schools and Departments of Women's Studies, Feminist Schools of Social Work
Anti-racist					Anti-oppressive Schools of Social Work
Aboriginal	Aboriginal governments and service organizations, e.g., child welfare organizations	Royal Commission on Aboriginal Peoples		Assembly of First Nations, Native Women's Association of Canada	Schools and Departments of Aboriginal Studies and Aboriginal educational organizations

SOURCE: Categories adapted from Leslie Pal, *Public Policy Analysis,* 2nd ed. (Toronto: Methuen, 1992), 71.

inquiry of its own that serve to expand the knowledge of social welfare that it regards as significant.

The impact of social policy analysis and research on policy and practice is also uncertain. First, there is the contention between the schools of policy development and research. Each provides its own stream of ideas and develops its own sets of proposals, frequently in conflict with each other. Second, research can be undertaken for a variety of reasons: to 'contain' social problems by diverting attention from immediate reform proposals and establishing a distance, in time, before reform is again on the public agenda; as a symbolic gesture, recognizing political alliances, past commitments, and good wishes; to establish social control over opponents by examining their weaknesses and harassing them in the process of inquiry; and to establish a veneer of objectivity that disguises conclusions already established on ideological premises. In all cases it is important to probe the auspices of research as well as the methodology before reviewing the results.

Third, research reports, even if accessible, are fundamentally produced by an elite for an elite. More frequently than not, information is couched in technical language and contributes thereby to a condition of social mystification. Findings are often inadequately translated into their meaning for application and so the general reader is left without a clear understanding of the implications of policy proposals. Finally, the use of language is also frequently confusing because each school has its own lexicon. Consider the phrase 'incentive to work':

- For the liberal this phrase means developing social programs so that people on social assistance have the opportunity to keep a substantial fraction of employment income.
- For the conservative it means a reduction in social welfare benefits accompanied by workfare measures.
- For the socialist this phrase confirms ideologically that the function of welfare is to maintain capitalist control over labour.
- For the feminist the phrase provides a reminder as to how incentives to work have been widened to include an increasing number of mothers with children, while simultaneously benefits to them are reduced and their poverty is perpetuated.
- For the anti-racist critique 'incentive to work' means developing policies under which blacks and immigrants can be forced to take work that no one else will.
- For the Aboriginal the phrase is a reminder of the absence of work opportunities in her or his own community, while simultaneously public criticism exists of Aboriginal unemployment and welfare dependency.

Meanwhile, most participants in the social policy process, whether service consumers, members of the public, media writers, or elected officials, operate from direct impressions and personal belief (affected in obscure ways by past inquiry). Conversely, those who operate in the 'elite' realm of research have no monopoly on knowledge. The methodologies of the disciplines and of inquiry not only bring precision; they also inevitably distort the varied state of human affairs by emphasizing patterns of similarity and consistency at the expense of individual variations and uniqueness. Each, in its own way, has self-fulfilling characteristics that confirm to the participants the correctness of their preconceptions.

Additional Readings

Examples of additional readings from writers of the liberal and conservative schools have been used frequently in earlier chapters (you may want to select some yourself for comparative study). The following readings are from the other four schools of thought.

Taiaiake Alfred, *Peace, Power, and Righteousness: An Indigenous Manifesto*. Toronto: Oxford University Press, 1999, 70–95. The reading begins with a dissection of how internal colonialism has led to neo-colonialism and concludes in a presentation of some of the challenges posed by self-government.

Patricia Evans and Gerda Wekerle, *Women and the Canadian Welfare State*. Toronto: University of Toronto Press, 1997, 3–27. In Chapter 1, 'The Shifting Terrain of Women's Welfare', the authors provide a liberal feminist overview of major issues for social welfare in Canada.

Lena Dominelli, *Anti-Racist Social Work*. London: Macmillan, 1988, 93–145. Dominelli, in Chapters 4 and 5 of this important work, provides an excellent example of anti-racist analysis as it applies to the everyday practice of social welfare organizations. Although Dominelli writes about race in social welfare in Britain, the form of analysis is equally applicable to all forms of oppression and to Canadian social welfare.

Bob Mullaly, *Structural Social Work: Ideology, Theory and Practice*, 2nd edn. Toronto: Oxford University Press, 1997, 99–137. In Chapter 7, 'Structural Social Work Theory', Mullaly shows how the different policy paradigms are divergent from or related to a structural or progressive approach to the development of practice and policy.

Study Questions

1. Take two articles written from different ideological positions on a similar subject and prepare a detailed comparison of their conclusions and reasons for their conclusions.

2. Select a policy paper written by a government agency and review it critically, writing as if it were for a newsletter of one of the main schools of thought discussed in this chapter.

3. Outline the challenge represented by Alfred's manifesto, *Peace, Power, and Righteousness*, to each of the other major schools of thought.

Notes

1. Every other year since 1983, the 'Conference on Canadian Social Welfare Policy' has been held. The latest was the 2001 conference held at the University of Calgary. The conference brings together academics from all the main university departments that have an interest in social welfare, researchers from the various lobby groups, and federal and provincial government representatives. Usually, politicians present key addresses at this forum. The papers presented are a good indicator of the current 'hot' subjects of discussion and are usually made available through the conference organizers. The conference is sponsored by the Ministry of Human Resources and Development Canada (HRDC).

2. Deborah Rutman and Andrew Armitage, 'Counting on Kids: An Overview of "State of the Child" Reports', *Canadian Review of Social Policy* 31 (1993): 3–30.

3. Canadian Council on Social Development, *Gaining Ground: The Personal Security Index, 2001* (Ottawa: Canadian Council on Social Development, 2001).

4. Joan Higgins, *States of Welfare* (Oxford: Basil Blackwell, 1981), 12.

5. Marilyn Callahan and Brian Wharf, *Demystifying the Policy Process: A Case Study in the Development of Child Welfare Legislation in British Columbia* (Victoria: University of Victoria, 1982). Callahan and Wharf trace the origins of reform to practitioner dissatisfaction at the resources and policies available to them, although in the end the practitioners' concerns are largely lost in senior-level political manoeuvres. In a similar vein, Asa Briggs, in an introductory essay in E.W. Martin, ed., *Comparative Development in Social Welfare* (London: George Allen and Unwin, 1972), 12, recognizes that 'local action has . . .

frequently preceded national action in the making of English social policy.'

6. Great Britain, *Report of the Royal Commission on the Administration and Practical Operation of the Poor Laws, 1834* (London: Queen's Printer, 1834).

7. Thomas Courchene, *Social Canada in the Millennium*, Preface by Thomas E. Kierans, John Richards, and William Watson (Toronto: C.D. Howe Institute, 1994), xv.

8. Ibid., xvi.

9. Christopher Green, 'What Should We Do with the UI System?', in Green et al., *Unemployment Insurance: How To Make It Work* (Toronto: C.D. Howe Institute, 1994), 10.

10. See Arnold Katz, 'Income Maintenance Experiments: Progress Towards a New American National Policy', *Social and Economic Administration* 7, 2 (May 1973).

11. Richard Splane, 'Whatever happened to the G.A.I.?', *The Social Worker* 48, 2 (Summer 1980).

12. John Richards and Aidan Vining, eds, *Helping the Poor: A Qualified Case for Workfare* (Toronto: C.D. Howe Institute, 1995).

13. Darrel Reid, 'You Better Get Used to Us', *Globe and Mail*, 23 Jan. 2002, A11.

14. Ramesh Mishra, *Society and Social Policy: Theoretical Perspectives* (London: Macmillan, 1981), 71.

15. Frances Fox Piven and Richard Cloward, *Regulating the Poor: The Public Functions of Welfare* (New York: Random House, 1972).

16. Frank James Tester and Peter Kulchyski, *Tammarniit (Mistakes): Inuit Relocation in the Eastern Arctic, 1939–63* (Vancouver: University of British Columbia Press, 1994), xi.

17. Sandy Wachholz and Bob Mullaly, 'Towards a Research Model for Structural Social Work', *Canadian Social Work Review* 14, 1 (1997): 37.

18. Bob Mullaly, *Structural Social Work: Ideology, Theory, and Practice*, 2nd edn (Toronto: Oxford University Press, 1997).

19. Ibid., 163.

20. Ibid., 182.

21. Ibid., 189.

22. See, for example, Canadian Centre for Policy Alternatives, *Healthy Families: First Things First.*

Alternative Federal Budget 2000 (Ottawa: CCPA, 2000).

23. Peter Leonard, *Postmodern Welfare: Reconstructing an Emancipatory Project* (London: Sage, 1997), xi.

24. Ibid., 15, quoting from Bauman, *Intimations of Postmodernity* (London: Routledge, 1992).

25. Fiona Williams, *Social Policy: A Critical Introduction* (Cambridge: Polity Press, 1989), xii.

26. The 'bébé-bonus' provides payments of $500 for the first baby, $1,000 for the second, and $8,000 for the third and subsequent babies born to Quebec mothers as an inducement to have children. The program is designed to combat the low annual birth rate of 1.6 births per 1,000 women of child-bearing age in Quebec. This rate is substantially less than the 2.1 per 1,000 necessary to sustain the existing population.

27. Williams, *Social Policy*, uses an expanded list of six distinctions within feminist critiques of the welfare state: libertarian feminism, liberal feminism, welfare feminism, radical feminism, socialist feminism, and black feminism. The distinctions have been shortened here in the interests of space. The reader is encouraged to look at Williams's work to see the full range of feminist criticism and contribution.

28. Ibid., 54.

29. Ibid., 57.

30. Wendy Weeks, 'Gender in the Social and Community Services: Implications for Management', *Human Services Management Network Conference* (Brisbane: Queensland University of Technology, Apr. 1992).

31. Dorothy Smith, 'Institutional Ethnography: A Feminist Method', *Resources for Feminist Research* 15, 1 (1986): 6–12.

32. Marilyn Callahan, Colleen Lumb, and Brian Wharf, 'Strengthening Families by Empowering Women', unpublished research monograph (University of Victoria, School of Social Work, 1994), iv.

33. See Andrew Hacker, *Two Nations: Black and White, Separate, Hostile and Unequal* (New York: Charles Scribner's Sons, 1992), for a host of statistics on black-white inequality in the United States.

34. Paul Sniderman and Thomas Piazza, *The Scar of Race* (Cambridge, Mass.: The Belknap Press of Harvard University Press, 1993), 113–14.

35. Lena Dominelli, *Anti-Racist Social Work* (London: Macmillan, 1988), 11.

36. K. Victor Ujimoto, 'Studies of Ethnic Identity and Race Relations', in Peter Li, ed., *Race and Ethnic Relations in Canada* (Toronto: Oxford University Press, 1990), 225–6.

37. See, for example, Bob Mullaly, *Challenging Oppression: A Critical Social Work Approach* (Toronto: Oxford University Press, 2002).

38. Patrick Johnston, *Native Children and the Child Welfare System* (Toronto: Lorimer, 1983).

39. Joyce Timpson, 'Four Decades of Literature on Native Canadian Child Welfare: Changing Themes', *Child Welfare* 74, 3 (1995): 525–46.

40. Gord Bruyere, 'Living in Another Man's House: Supporting Aboriginal Learners in Social Work Education', *Canadian Social Work Review* 15, 2 (1998): 169–76.

41. Taiaiake Alfred, *Peace, Power, and Righteousness: An Indigenous Manifesto* (Toronto: Oxford University Press, 1999), xv.

42. Leslie Pal, *Public Policy Analysis*, 2nd edn (Toronto: Methuen, 1992).

PART V

Conclusion

CHAPTER 8

The Uncertain Future
of Social Welfare

It is now time to think about the future of Canadian social welfare. The services and programs with which we are familiar are products of the twentieth century, but what will be their fate in the twenty-first century? What do we think of as successful and where are there lessons to be learned from what are now seen to be mistakes? How does each of the major schools of thought envisage the future of Canadian social welfare?

Learning Objectives

1. To know how each of the major schools of thought envisages the future of Canadian social welfare.
2. To be able to recognize major sources of strength in Canadian social welfare.
3. To be able to recognize major unsolved dilemmas in social welfare policy and the achievement of social justice.
4. To have an informed personal commitment as to how to work for social justice.

Changing Visions

Despite the cutbacks and restraint measures of the 1990s the resources committed to social welfare remain substantial. However, the use of resources has witnessed significant change as a result of budget decisions made by governments. These decisions have affected some parts of the system more than others. For example, Employment Insurance and social assistance, which support working people, were cut, while programs for seniors were exempted from cuts. The result is that social welfare itself has become a more conservative institution, more committed to upholding the class structure of the society than was apparent earlier. This is now the fourth edition of *Social Welfare in Canada*, which was first published in 1975. In each of the editions the liberal values of a more socially just and equal society have been central to the appraisal of social welfare policies and programs. In 1975 and 1988 the perspective

taken by this book was that of embracing the liberal value base but submitting the accomplishments, programs, and organizations to critical analysis. Significant changes towards the establishment of a more socially just society seemed achievable in 1975, but when the 1988 edition was printed progress towards this goal had been slight and the achievement of significant change seemed less close than in 1975. When the third edition appeared in 1996 Canadian social welfare policies were in the middle of a critical conservative reappraisal and changes to conform to the results of that appraisal were being proposed and introduced.

In the year 2002, as this is written, the results of the changes made in the 1990s are apparent and have been incorporated into social welfare policy. Social welfare policy appears now to be more stable, with change in policy no longer a government priority. Instead, there are new priorities: particularly, the 'war on terrorism' and the security and trade relationship with the United States occupy the federal government agenda. It is time to ask what has been accomplished as well as to speculate about what changes may come in the early years of the twenty-first century. From the past one thing is clear—the future is unpredictable and will not conform fully to any of the predictions that we make. Nevertheless, each of the major schools of thought does have a view about the future of social welfare.

The Liberal Vision

Looking back over the changes that have occurred since 1975 it is difficult for the liberal not to be disappointed by what has not been achieved and apprehensive about the future. First, there was the failure to achieve the objectives of a more equal society that were set as part of the 'War on Poverty' in the early 1970s. Then there was the development of an articulate and powerful conservative lobby that opposed welfare measures in the 1980s, along with the first restraints and cutbacks. In the 1990s the cutbacks became more severe, with the federal government as well as the provinces participating. The effects of the cuts made in the 1990s, especially for the most vulnerable, such as single mothers, children, and persons with disability, removed most of the gains that had been made since the 1960s. Rather than dealing with the problems of poverty and inequality at their source, social welfare policy has had increasingly to deal with the secondary effects of the failure to deal with poverty, such as child abuse, substance misuse, and homelessness.

A review of the major values that guided the development of the liberal position also suggests that progress has been at best uneven and that the guide to progress those values provided has become dated.

1. *Concern for the individual*. The changes in social welfare policy over the last decade have not been in accord with the value of 'concern for the individual'; instead, they have been driven by a private market-based concept of individualism. Individualism has meant an expectation of individual economic self-sufficiency, which has led to support for lower levels of social assistance benefits and to workfare-type programs. In addition, the focus on the individual now needs to be reinterpreted in the context of diversity. As originally used in liberal thought, the concept of 'equality' assumed that all individuals should be treated the same way. However, this sameness of treatment is now seen as imposing cultural practices that have not taken account of diversity. The phrase 'concern for' also has a paternalistic tone that suggests that someone, or some institution, knows best where the welfare of the individual lies.

2. *Faith in humanity*. Faith in humanity can be maintained but the original conception, with its expectations of personal fulfillment, now appears naive and overstated. The labour economists have been proven to be partly correct. Lower welfare benefits do lead to having fewer people on welfare (and to greater pressure and reliance on food banks and more homeless people). Children and other vulnerable people are abused and need protection. Faith in humanity needs to be set in the context of institutions that promote, encourage, and ultimately require good behaviour.

3. *Equity*. There has been progress towards the goal of equity. There is certainly more understanding and appreciation of the need to have equity between women and men, between Aboriginal and non-Aboriginal people, and of the need to regard sexual orientation as a private matter. However, the introduction of these principles into social welfare policy has been slower and more difficult than one might have expected and further changes will need to be made.

4. *Equality*. Here there has been little progress and what little progress was achieved in the 1970s was largely reversed in the 1990s. It is increasingly difficult to see how the operation of social welfare is contributing to greater equality. Data on the distribution of income point towards growing inequality. Rather than

contributing to equality, it appears that social welfare has assumed the role of stratifying poverty, with the elderly and other 'deserving' poor getting marginally better treatment than the young employable 'undeserving'. In the programs themselves social control objectives, such as deterrence against fraud, workfare requirements, and child protection 'risk' assessments, are increasingly prominent as the pursuit of equality is replaced by the management of inequality as the major goal.

5. *Community*. The social welfare focus on the integrity of community life remains important. Here there has been some progress towards replacing large centralized bureaucracies by more locally based community groups. As well, the community-based social movements have been the source of much new thinking about social welfare and have been a major source of change.

6. *Diversity*. Recognizing diversity was not a goal of social welfare as conceived in the 1960s. A start was made in recognizing it as a goal in the 1970s reports on multiculturalism and on the status of women and in the rejection by Aboriginal people of the 1969 White Paper. Since then there has been progress towards recognizing the importance of differences. As a result social policy must now balance the requirements of equity with the requirement to respect diversity.

7. *Faith in democracy*. A qualified faith in democracy is retained as no better system has yet been devised. However, confidence that governments can make autonomous national decisions about social policy has been weakened. It has become increasingly apparent that economic globalization has limited national autonomy and, with it, national ability to have independent social policies. Faith in parliamentary democracy has also been weakened as the partisan and bipolar nature of debate and voting processes lacks the flexibility needed to incorporate respect for diversity into social policy. As a result 'faith in democracy' needs to be interpreted in ways that provide for the continued expression of difference and for the development of consensus, rather than as a desire to establish ruling majorities.

The social programs developed on the basis of the liberal vision also have internal problems of their own. These include:

1. *Dependency*. Over time a process of 'normalization' in the receipt of social welfare benefits is understandable. The more people in the community who are beneficiaries, the more normal it seems to be one of them. The longer receipt goes on the harder it becomes to make changes. However, the way that benefits have been provided is also part of the problem. Social assistance has created one form of welfare trap because earned income has been confiscated, resulting in there being no incentive to earn. Employment Insurance, the Canada Pension Plan disability benefits, and Workers' Compensation have created another form of dependency relationship, providing benefit rights contingent on not working. The 'social safety net' was designed as a support system when other systems, particularly the economy, failed to provide a base level of income, but for some it has become a continuing and inadequate home.

2. *Stigma*. Social welfare programs stigmatize recipients and alienate taxpayers. Many of the programs promote the division of the community into classes. The classes are defined first by whether one is a beneficiary or a contributor, and secondarily by the type of benefit and the public view as to whether the benefit was 'deserved'. The result is a hardening of class distinctions rather than the creation of community solidarity.

3. *Imposition*. The welfare relationship tends to be paternal, patriarchal, moralistic, and colonial in form. Recipients are treated as requiring guidance. In programs like the social assistance program, expectations are imposed on recipients through a formal hierarchical relationship. The child welfare system attempts to protect children from neglect but ends up 'manufacturing bad mothers' as it shifts attention from the failure of social policy to the individual mother,

who it is assumed 'could' have acted differently.[1]

Taken together these criticisms cause doubt, even in the strongest supporters of social welfare, that the system can ever achieve all the values that inspired its construction. Instead, it seems that social welfare will achieve some of the values at the expense of others and become an established part of the status quo. In this role social welfare is a potent force in defining and upholding class distinctions among the poor and thereby creating a form of social stability. From an international perspective the social welfare systems of many developed countries already appear to conform to this model. Germany and Ireland are examples of social welfare systems where stability and conservation of the social order are major goals.[2] In some ways Canada appears to be joining this group; in other ways, for example, in public attitudes towards the poor, it is becoming more like the United States. The power of the original egalitarian liberal vision to guide the future development of social welfare in Canada has been displaced, at least for a time.

This is not to say that the liberal vision is dead. The vision continues to draw its strength from the pride that Canadians have in building a social order in North America that is safer and more just than that of the United States. The established liberal values with which this book began capture the essence of that difference. As Crane points out, solid majorities still support nearly all the existing social programs.[3] These values are reflected, too, in the public policy support given to maintaining benefits for seniors and, less effectively, in the campaign against child poverty. In federal and provincial government departments of health and welfare the liberal view continues to be held and the policy analysis institutions of the liberal school—the Canadian Council on Social Development and the Caledon Institute—continue to provide a steady stream of reports and analysis.

In the academic community the liberal position is also well represented. Rice and Prince[4]

provide a coherent contemporary statement of the liberal vision that emphasizes the need to: (1) recognize ecological limits; (2) 'rebuild' social policy; (3) renew the attack on poverty; (4) pursue international agreements that fully consider social policy; and (5) democratize the welfare state.

To begin, a contemporary social policy agenda must recognize that our resources are limited and our environment is fragile. The economy, nationally and internationally, must accept those limits and social welfare policy has to be based on a sustainable use of resources and a preservation of our environment.

Then, the role of social policy needs to be 'rebuilt' in the context of the new century to undertake the tasks that are now relevant to our contemporary world. Measures are required to maintain a just and fair society and to offset the 'social deficits' of capitalism. These measures include:

- strengthening the commitment to health care and 'healthy public policy';
- eliminating child poverty;
- developing a national child-care system;
- introducing fairer student loans;
- making a new commitment to affordable social housing;
- recognizing the rights of Aboriginal peoples, persons with disabilities, and gays and lesbians;
- making a renewed commitment to employment and fairer taxes.

The renewal of measures to deal with poverty is a central part of the liberal agenda proposed by Rice and Prince, who make a strong case for replacing (or supplementing) existing income security programs with an all-inclusive negative taxation program. This would provide a universal means of offsetting income deficits regardless of source and without the demeaning and controlling effects of social assistance programs.

As others have, Rice and Prince argue that the global reach of economic policy and corporate capitalism must be balanced by international social policies. These should include:

- global citizenship, ensuring all people the right to a decent life;
- the development of international links between social policy interest groups;
- the co-ordination of market regulatory activities;
- the institution of global forms of taxation;
- recognition that world social policy has to be diverse and plural and that Western policies cannot be imposed on the world through a new colonialism based on economic dominance.

Finally, it is recognized that the bureaucracies and government agencies of the welfare state were fundamentally undemocratic in form. Instead, the social movements and local communities should have the positions of ownership and control so that social welfare ceases to be an imposed institution and becomes more citizen-based.

The Conservative Vision

During the 1990s the conservative vision had a major impact on social welfare in Canada. It gained this position through a combination of events and ideas. The change taking place in the world economy through the globalization of economic activity and the revolution in information technologies was one such event. Courchene and other conservatives have argued that Canadians can participate effectively in the new economic order, but in order to do so Canada needs an appropriate set of social policies. He writes:

Canada, in the millennium, will be largely defined by its social infrastructure. As a working 'mission statement', as it were, I adhere to the notion that Social Canada's role is to provide for Canadians to develop and enhance their skills and human capital to enable them to become full participants in the emerging global/information society. . . . Canadians have made impressive postwar gains in social policy. . . . However, under the onslaught of what I have referred to as 'restructuring imperatives', our postwar achievements now hang in the balance. In order to maintain a distinctive, made in Canada social infrastructure, we have little option but to filter our long-standing values of fairness, sharing and equity through the new realities of fiscal restraint, globalization and the information revolution.[5]

A second event was the recurring financial deficits that Canada was facing in its public expenditures. By the 1990s there was an international consensus of financial opinion that Canada had a problem it needed to deal with. Both the Mulroney Progressive Conservative government and the Liberal Chrétien/Martin government adopted this point of view and set about reducing government program expenditures. This provided opportunity to conservatives to restate a long-standing opposition to social welfare in a form in which it appeared to provide the answers that were needed to the issues of the day, first to the problems of the deficit, second to maintaining economic productivity, and third to the disillusionment with the accomplishments of the liberal social welfare state. Although the conservative values are held by the corporate elite and are developed through its institutions, they derive their strength, too, from the meaning they give to common experiences of all people. As was said of the British Conservatives:

The strength of Thatcherism is its ability to ventriloquize the genuine anxieties of working-class experience. The declining economy and reduced living standards are explained by the expensive burden of public services as the economics of the State are reduced to the accountancy of the kitchen. . . . The ringing appeal to freedom has displaced any lingering enthusiasm for the musty attractions of social democracy, so readily identified with an enervating Statism.[6]

One indication of a shift in public attitudes was the election in Canada of Conservative provincial governments in Alberta and Ontario that espouse positions on social issues once seen as extreme. A second indicator was the increasingly conservative nature of Liberal government proposals, such as those made by Finance Minister Paul Martin in the 1995 budget. At the provincial level as well, some Liberal governments, for example the Campbell government in British Columbia, became ardent followers of conservative policies. Even provincial NDP governments have been converted to conservative policies during their time in power. Out of office the NDP sounded as if governments could continue to spend their way out of recession, and that the problem of the deficit was a capitalist plot to divert attention from the need for higher social spending. However, once they became governments they found themselves unable to act on their rhetoric to the extent that their supporters had hoped.

The conservative social vision has the strength on internal clarity. Individual action is favoured over collective solutions; privacy is valued over the intrusion of social workers; risk and entrepreneurship are valued over the privilege of either union tenure or civil service security; selectivity, keeping intervention and costs as limited as possible, is valued over universalism; market incentives to move away from the Atlantic provinces to Ontario and the West are favoured over regional policies to preserve communities; open competition is favoured over all forms of affirmative social action for women, Aboriginal peoples, visible minorities, or other marginalized groups; social integration through economic processes is favoured over all forms of separate community development; punishment of crime is favoured over structural change to reduce the causes of social alienation and crime.

In the post-2000 period moderate conservatives, conservatives 'with a heart' as Courchene and Richards would style themselves, want to hold onto some parts of the heritage of Canadian social policy and reshape it to what they consider to be the new imperatives. These include:

- respecting the principle of tax and expenditure coincidence (i.e., no more deficits);
- submitting the federal spending power to increased consensus from the provinces before Ottawa spends in areas of their jurisdiction (i.e., the Social Union);
- stabilizing federal and provincial government program spending as a share of gross domestic product over the business cycle (i.e., no proportionate increase in social program costs);
- realizing modest tax cuts, with Ottawa taking the lead (i.e., move towards greater inequality of after-tax income).[7]

Although this agenda may appear to offer little to social welfare, it is actually a moderate conservative position as it aims to protect the current level of social expenditure, which Richards regards as being part of *social capital*, defined by the World Bank as 'the informal rules, norms, and long-term relationships that facilitate coordinated action and enable people to undertake cooperative ventures for mutual advantage'.[8] The position suggests that social welfare should be limited to a role of supporting economic policy and providing social stability. It suggests that there is no place for new programs or for using social welfare as part of a deliberate policy of moving towards a more equal society.

The contextual issues to which the moderate conservative position draws our attention—the deficit, the global economy, and the information revolution—are all important. The values that it shares with liberalism of individualism, faith in humanity, and democracy produce, for liberals, some common ground. But even the moderate conservative vision does not recognize:

1. *Poverty.* There is a failure to acknowledge the seriousness of the problem of poverty. The conservative proposals are bereft of goals that deal in any way with poverty, and in their silence they acquiesce to the expansion of poverty, the increase in homelessness, and the increasing disadvantage and oppression of all individuals and families in the lower 60 per cent of the income distribution, in particular the marginalization and oppression of single mothers, children, the handicapped, visible minorities, and Aboriginal peoples.

2. *Equity and diversity.* There is a failure to recognize the processes of domination that have led to women, lesbians, gays, visible minorities, and Aboriginal peoples being marginalized and oppressed. At every turn the conservatives oppose measures to counteract historic oppression and achieve social justice. The need for a society in which pluralism is an important value is not understood.

3. *Community.* The central role of the community and of community-based visions of social welfare is not appreciated. The silence condemns communities to the vicissitudes of the global marketplace.

4. *Unpaid work.* Unpaid work, principally caring roles carried out in the home, is invisible to the economist, yet the contribution of such work to collective well-being is essential. The conservative failure to value what is not paid for depreciates the contribution of all women and distorts the economists' understanding of social welfare.

5. *International injustice.* The conservative vision and the associated global economy have led to an international order characterized by enormous differences of wealth and power. There is no attention to the unfairness of such an order; indeed, its inequalities are glorified. It is assumed that the values of global capitalism, and of the United States of America as world leader, have universal application and that

differences of wealth and power can be ascribed to the failure of other nations and peoples to follow the American path.

A more extreme expression of the conservative agenda comes from Walter Block, the senior economist of the Fraser Institute, who is quoted as answering the question, 'What services should the public sector provide?' by stating:

> Little or none. The classical liberal tradition, the tradition of Adam Smith, John Stuart Mill, and David Hume, was that government was mainly for defence, judiciary. And when it tries to act in the public good it actually worsens the situation of the people that it is acting in behalf of. The Fraser Institute would certainly advocate the government as a safety net of last resort but not one of first resort as is all too popular in this province and this country.[9]

The commitment of the more extreme conservatives to a continued reduction in all forms of social welfare alarms social welfare liberals, socialists, and the members of the various social movements. It suggests a 'race to the bottom' between provinces and between nations to do the least. It suggests that the interests of the transnational corporations in the highest possible profits and the greatest freedom of action can and should determine the future of social welfare.

The position of the social conservatives is also a cause for concern. Social conservatives challenge all the social policies that have been developed to increase respect for diversity. If social conservatives had their way, social deterrence and social control would have a larger role to play in social welfare policy. In time, key rights that protect private behaviour from state interference or from social discrimination would be reduced. Many conservatives reject the social policies of the social conservatives. However, politically the social conservatives are part of the overall conservative alliance, and through that alliance they are able to ensure a public platform for their views. Where there is a coincidence of social conservative views and economic conservatism, for example, in the view that welfare payments to single parents encourage the formation of more single-parent families, the resulting alliance can be a formidable force in shaping public policy.

All the forms of conservatism point to the continued moral blindness of capitalism and of its advocates. They also overlook the history of capitalism. On several occasions in the past, capitalist accumulation and speculation have exceeded the regulatory and offsetting capacity of government to stabilize market behaviour. The result in each case has been not only social disaster but also serious internal problems for capitalism itself. The most devastating example in the Western developed countries was the Great Depression of the 1930s, but there has been no lack of the disruptions caused by massive inflation in all other parts of the world, where capitalism has been less regulated than it was in the West and less balanced by the existence of a developed social welfare system. Furthermore, there are signs that the unbridled greed of capitalism can undermine major international companies.

The problems of capitalism and the conservative position are internal to it and have nothing to do with governments or social policies. The economist Robert Heilbronner reviews the capitalist protest about the growth of government and concludes:

> If the great scenarios teach us anything, it is that the problems that threaten capitalism arise from the private sector, not the public. . . . all successful capitalisms, I further believe, will find ways to assure labour security of employment and income, management of the right to restructure tasks for efficiency's sake, and government as the legitimate coordinator of national growth.[10]

Looking to the twenty-first century, he continues:

Two formidable self-generated problems are certain to disturb the capitalist world. One of these is the approach of ecological barriers. . . . These barriers imply a coming necessity to curtail industrial growth. . . . The second problem is the internationalizing tendency of capital that continues to outpace the defensive powers of individual governments. Thus capitalism itself encroaches on the political independence of nations in a manner that exposes the centre to the very forces that have sowed so much economic disarray on the periphery. . . . In so far as the malfunctions exist on a transnational scale, they require transnational political counter-force, and nothing of the kind exists.[11]

To these forces one should add that the inequalities generated by international capitalism are of an order that increasingly generates national oppositions requiring suppression by the establishment of non-democratic governments and the assertion of police and military power. In a world of instant communication, differences of living standards and wealth are glaringly apparent. In addition, parts of the international global economic system are vulnerable to disruption and to criminal activity. Thus the capitalist global economy faces problems of its own that can be addressed in one of two ways: increasing suppression of dissent and disruptive behaviour or increased redistribution of income and wealth to offset the capitalist concentration process. The conservative view favours the first approach but the history of social reform in Canada and other developed societies shows that in the end, and after some intensive struggles, a more balanced approach based on principles of equity and social justice is needed.

The Marxist/Socialist Vision

The Marxist/socialist writers of the political economy school of social policy analysis have little confidence in the social welfare institutions that have been established. They recognize the triumph of the conservatives and of corporate capitalism as representing the sum of all their fears but differ as to whether anything can be done. The starkest vision is provided by Gary Teeple. Social democracy and the liberal welfare state are dismissed as a product of economic conditions and national government authority that no longer exist.

> The social democratic left has become, in effect, part of the problem. It remained wedded to a notion of reformed capitalism until the 1980s and since then has produced little analysis of alternatives to neo-liberalism [a reference to what we have termed conservatism in this text]. Where it came to power, it has sooner or later introduced new right policies in the face of an electorate desirous of protecting the social security of the working class. . . . By accepting this agenda in theory and practice, social democracy has lost much of its credibility as a party representing the working population, and hypocrisy has become its hallmark.
>
> Social democracy as we know it has no future, because the conditions that gave rise to it are being transformed and because its policies and programs—the reforms of the nation-state era—were nothing more than what these conditions allowed or demanded.[12]

The work of the social movements is acknowledged as offering the seeds of an alternative, but:

> Both . . . resistance and . . . alternatives face enormous odds as long as the current system continues to provide a tolerable existence for the majority and second, control over the ideological and political systems remains a monopoly of the powers that be.[13]

Instead, the future promises only a continuing process of economic concentration and political repression. As Teeple sees it, this 'is a tyranny unfolding—an economic regime of unaccountable rulers, a totalitarianism not of the political sphere but of the economic.'[14]

Not all writers of this school are as pessimistic as Teeple. F.J. Tester emphasizes the emerging ecological limits to capitalism:

> The evidence that global environments are threatened by the economic growth mindlessly celebrated by World Bank and IMF officials . . . is overwhelming. . . . Ultimately, the failure to deal with the failure of the global environment must leave national governments with the responsibility of protecting their own environments by regulating the activities of transnational and other corporate interests. . . . It is the democratic will of people to act against vested interests which threaten their well-being that is the key to solving these problems.[15]

Diana Ralph, while not disagreeing with the direction of Teeple's argument, places more reliance on the social movements, strengthened by international connections between movements. Ralph makes three suggestions for the future:

> (1) Prioritize building the popular base of our movements and connections between them, as well as people's movements elsewhere in the world. We are not strong enough now to have much impact on policies or even electoral outcomes. So we need to retrench and rebuild our bases. Because our main strength is people, we need to focus first on building and re-building grassroots groups and training participatory leaders. Our emphasis needs to be on building the movement, not on initially expecting to influence the TNC [transnational corporation] giants. (2) Research the opposition better. At this point, little is known about the BCNI [Business Council for National Issues] members, the shadow government behind Federal and provincial decisions. If we want to take back the initiative, we need to anticipate their next

moves and their likely response to our tactics. We need to investigate their vulnerabilities. . . . We also can develop linkages with their employees and consumers elsewhere in the world. . . . (3) Plan strategically for the long haul, rather than reactively protesting each new injustice. . . . It will take a long time for us to turn around the twenty years of losses we've endured. . . . To win victories, we need to identify focused targets and aim our tactics at their vulnerable areas grounded in our areas of strength.[16]

Mullaly's structural social work tactics of working 'within (and against) the system' and 'outside (and against) the system' are also part of the future vision of the socialist/Marxist school. Mullaly sees these as strategies towards 'the ultimate goal . . . the transformation of liberal-capitalist society to one that is more congruent with socialist principles.'[17] In Mullaly's view this transformation will take place gradually through changes in the institutions of social welfare resulting from the work of structural social workers. There are few signs that this is about to happen. Indeed, all the structural forces that Mullaly analyzes point in the opposite direction, towards the transformation of social welfare to a more conservative form. A major problem for Mullaly and for structural social work generally is the credibility of the view that a new form of social work practice will be able to achieve the objective of beginning the transformation of society.

Leonard, in his interpretation of postmodern welfare, writes:

Can we any longer speak of the future, of the prospects for human welfare, in other than cataclysmic terms, because the 'party is over'? Especially when associated with emancipatory claims, all talk of plans for the future must now be greeted with profound skepticism, or more likely, cynicism. Within modernity, political talk of the future has always been articulated in terms of progress, of human betterment: the

postmodern condition makes such metanarratives appear hollow or dishonest.[18]

Leonard continues to struggle with this dilemma throughout his book, but ultimately finds hope in:

a confederation of diversities . . . a long-term commitment of participant organizations and individuals to a federation which is envisaged as representing their diversities as well as furthering the common interest. . . . The establishment of a party as a confederation of diversities would be a difficult task but one which would be, after all, a particular discursive and material expression of a growing realization that establishing solidarity between particular interests is the only way to mount resistance to the depredations of globalizing late capitalism and to establish the possibility of alternative forms of modernity. There are four major social movements whose interests in the effective meeting of common needs appear to be converging: the feminist movement, trade union movement, anti-racist movements and the ecology movement.[19]

The Marxist/socialist and postmodern visions gain their strength from their ability to connect with the experience of service consumers, social workers, community advocates, and the social movements. By directing attention to structural forces they make the movement towards a more conservative social order understandable. But as a guide to action there are problems. The analysis is too deterministic and the conclusion overstates the current problems of social welfare. Although the achievements of social welfare are much less than the objectives, the operation of social welfare and health programs by the state remains a principal form of public expenditure and a hallmark of Canadian and other developed societies. In an international context the programs that Canada has are regarded as a major achievement by most of the countries of the world.

The Feminist, Anti-Racist, and Aboriginal Communitarian Visions

Community has always been a major concept for social welfare. In the 1990s, several different applications of the concept of community moved towards establishing their own visions of the future. Of particular importance for the continued development of social welfare are the visions articulated by the feminist, Aboriginal, and anti-oppressive (anti-racist) social movements. Each of these social movements is broadly based and contains a wide range of internal differences. However, in the context of their relationship to social welfare they also have important common features.

1. *A defined constituency of 'marginalized' people.* Each of the social movements defines itself as having been excluded from power on the basis of the difference of its members from the establishment stereotype. The establishment stereotype is male, white, European, Protestant, and heterosexual. The world view of the social movement constituency and their experience of social welfare result from their life experience on the margins of the society, rather than as the powerful and defining establishment. The development of social welfare by liberals is seen as being primarily the work of liberal men, deeply influenced by patriarchy, British origins, Protestant values, and traditional forms of family life. The resulting institution entrenched those values and reproduced the marginalization of those who were not members of this well-intentioned mainstream liberal establishment.

2. *A goal of inclusion.* The experience of each of the groups has been of oppression and exclusion from some forms of social welfare on the basis of their position in society. Consequently, an important objective of each of the groups has been equity of treatment for its members. Equity of treatment is defined to include both equality of treatment and the recognition in policy of distinctive needs. Thus, women have wanted both equality of treatment to men and recognition of

the responsibility for caring roles that most women have contributed to society. Aboriginal people have sought equality of access to mainstream benefits and recognition of claims based on their history and colonization.

3. *Resistance.* In the context of conservative social reforms and cutbacks each of the groups is committed to resistance. Often the members of each group form the majority of welfare program beneficiaries and so the results of cutbacks, and conservative ideology, fall most noticeably on them. Establishment liberals may be tempted to compromise with the conservatives to maintain their participation in social policy processes, hoping to find some middle way, hoping to ameliorate conservative objectives. In contrast, the social movements are not prepared to compromise and define a path of continued resistance to conservative policies (see Box 8.1).

4. *Political organization.* Each of the groups has organizations of its own that can articulate the collective views and, where necessary, take political action. In this regard each of the groups has some similarity to labour unions and can often form alliances with labour unions in organizing rallies and street protests.

5. *A literature and discourse of their own.* Each of the groups has its own literature and discourse and some policy analytic capacity. Within this discourse differences of opinion are common, often mirroring some of the differences between liberal and socialist visions referred to earlier.

6. *A role in the development of social welfare services.* Each of the groups also has community experience in the development and operation of social welfare services.

In addition to these common characteristics, each of the social movements has a distinct vision of the social welfare policies needed for the twenty-first century.

The Feminist Vision

Women have been active in the building of social welfare from its earliest days, providing

Box 8.1 A 12-Step Plan to Take Back the Nation

The corporate takeover of Canada's economic and political agenda is forcing people to stand up for their rights. Dr Jane Kelsey, an economist at the University of Auckland in New Zealand, has developed the following list of proposed tactics and strategies to resist the corporate agenda:

1. Be skeptical about fiscal and other 'crises'.
Examine the real nature of the problem, who defines it as a crisis, and who stands to gain. Demand to know the range of possible solutions, and the costs and benefits of each to whom. If the answers are not forthcoming, burn the midnight oil to produce the answers yourself.

2. Don't cling to a political party that has converted to neo-conservatism.
Fighting to prevent a social democratic party's capture by right-wing zealots is important. But once the party has been taken over, maintaining solidarity on the outside while seeking change from within merely gives them more time. When the spirit of the party is dead, shed the old skin and create something new.

3. Take economics seriously.
Neo-liberal economic fundamentalism pervades everything. There is no boundary between economic, social, environmental or other policies. Those who focus on narrow sectoral concerns will lose their battles and weaken the collective ability of the rest. Leaving economics to economists is fatal.

4. Expose the weakness of their theory.
Neo-liberal theories are riddled with dubious assumptions and internal inconsistencies. Expose them as self-serving rationalizations which operate in the interests of the elites.

5. Expose the masterminds.
Name the key corporate players behind the scenes, document their interlocking roles and allegiances, and expose the personal and corporate benefits they receive.

6. Maximize every obstacle.
Federal systems of government, written constitu-
tions, legal requirements and regulations, supranational institutions like the International Labour Organization and the United Nations, and strong local governments can provide barriers that slow down the pace of corporate takeover.

7. Maintain the concept of an efficient public service.
Build support among client groups and the public which stress the need for public services and the risks of cutting or privatizing them.

8. Encourage community leaders to speak out.
Public criticism from civic and church leaders, folk heroes and other prominent 'names' make corporate and political leaders uncomfortable. It also makes people think.

9. Avoid anti-intellectualism.
A pool of academics and other intellectuals who can expose the fallacies and failures of the corporate agenda, and develop viable alternatives in partnerships with community and sectoral groups, is absolutely vital. They need to be supported when they come under attack, and challenged when they fail to speak out or are co-opted or seduced.

10. Develop alternative media outlets.
Once the mainstream media are captured by the right, it is difficult for critics to enter the debate, and impossible to lead it. Alternative media and innovative strategies must be put in place.

11. Raise the levels of popular economic literacy.
Convince people that economic policy affects everyone and that alternatives to the corporate agenda do exist.

12. Hold the line.
The corporate takeover is not yet complete. Social programs have not yet been entirely dismantled. Unions have not yet been destroyed. Not all environmental protections have been eliminated. There is still time, through sustained and co-ordinated action, to hold the line.

Source: Excerpted from Jane Kelsey's *Economic Fundamentalism: The New Zealand Experiment*, published by the Auckland University Press. It is reprinted from the June 1999 issue of *The Long Haul*, the newspaper published by End Legislated Poverty in Vancouver.

most of the leadership when the initial institutions of social welfare were developed around the beginning of the twentieth century. Women have also been predominant as consumers of social welfare, receiving through social welfare limited but important support for family and caring roles. In the 1990s, when social welfare was cut back, the burden of the cutbacks fell disproportionately on women and became known as 'the feminization of poverty'. When the child welfare system shifted in emphasis from support to families to investigating child neglect, women were implicitly 'blamed' for not looking after children. Most social workers are women and much of the research on poverty, child welfare, and social welfare programs is done by women. Thus women, and feminists, are strong supporters of a well-developed and just social welfare system.

There is no single feminist vision for the future of social welfare, but recurring ideas in the feminist literature deserve restating because collectively they offer a view of a better and more socially just social welfare system. These ideas include the following.

1. *Safety and security of the person.* On the international and global level a world free of violent conflict is sought in which daily life can be conducted in safety and security. In local communities a world free of sexual violence, sexual mutilation, child prostitution, and pornography is sought.[20] Both of these concerns look for a world in which violence is eliminated as a basis on which human relations are conducted. Too often women and children are the victims of men's violence. Too often violence is used to suppress women's autonomy and lives. Too often violence is used to create situations of terror. Violence, once started, feeds on itself. On the other hand, social welfare programs, by increasing equality and promoting equity, can reduce the social conditions in which desperation turns to violence.

2. *Women's independence.* Social policies are sought that support the independence of women.[21] This begins with fair employment practices and with an adoption of pay equity principles for all remuneration. It includes policies to provide for effective child care for working mothers, income support policies that attend to women's needs, and an expanded role for social housing. It also includes policies to encourage a less gendered division of caring responsibilities.

3. *Collaborative working relationships.* The feminist vision emphasizes the need to democratize social welfare systems, to establish strong relationships of trust between women on both sides of the social welfare counter, and to promote co-operation and collaboration rather than hierarchy and competition.

4. *Community focus.* Although individual rights for women are important there has been a recurring interest, too, in finding collective, community-based solutions to social problems. This focus on community 'challenges [the] trickle-down theory of social progress. Instead it argues that all social institutions, be they public businesses or private families, should embrace notions of collective well-being, rather than simply serve as sites for individual opportunity.'[22]

The Aboriginal Vision

The Aboriginal vision begins in a position of respect for the land and for the many different Aboriginal peoples that lived in Canada prior to settlement. A cornerstone of the vision is found in the inherent right of Aboriginal people to govern themselves.

There is now general support for the principle that Aboriginal people should have the right to manage their own social services. However, to this point, most services have been transferred to Aboriginal peoples from mainstream organizations under funding and organizational conditions that require Aboriginal people to follow mainstream policies, constituting a form of neo-colonial rule of Aboriginal people by Aboriginal people. This is clearly an inadequate form of self-government, and consequently a strong case is made for Aboriginal people to assert an independent policy agenda informed from the start by Aboriginal culture, historical experience, and values. The agenda includes:

- the assertion of Aboriginal philosophy, values, and customs as the basis for social policy and social welfare;[23]
- the eradication of colonialism;
- respect for treaties and for Aboriginal rights;
- respect for Elders;
- strong, bold leadership;[24]
- an emphasis on health and healing policies and programs;
- independent thinking, including Aboriginal research, literature, and education.[25]

The Aboriginal vision cannot be made compatible with the structures through which Aboriginal people have been ruled since settlement. The Indian Act, the imposition of provincial policies on Indian people, and the administrative and delegated relationships through which neo-colonial welfare operates are all considered to be unacceptable.[26]

The Anti-Racist and Anti-Oppressive Visions

The anti-racist and anti-oppressive visions look towards social policy in which the white, European, able, and heterosexual biases and assumptions are exposed and set aside. The fundamental claim of anti-racist and anti-oppressive policy is for inclusion in the policy-making process and for the development of services that serve rather than 'manage' consumers. To approach these goals all measures of exclusion have to be exposed and dealt with. One example of what this vision means is provided by Lena Dominelli's anti-racist agenda for social work:

- Change the current definition of the social work task to one that does not make oppression invisible.
- Negate the 'objectivity' currently imbedded

in a professionalism underpinning a status quo that has been found seriously wanting.
- Alter the existing power relationships between the users of services and workers. The voice of the 'expert' should not substitute for that of the oppressed.
- Stop denying consumers the right to determine the types of welfare provisions on offer.
- Stop treating people's welfare at both individual and collective levels as a commodity that can be rationed for the purposes of controlling people and their aspirations. Instead, it should enhance personal fulfillment and well-being.
- Change the basis of training that assumes a false neutrality on the major social and ethical issues of the day to make explicit its value base and to take moral and political stances against oppression in any of its forms.
- Terminate an allocation of power and resources perpetuating injustice and misery and replace it with one committed to implementing justice and equality for all.
- End the theoretical separation between social work and (a) other elements of the state, especially welfare sectors, e.g., housing, education, health, and social security; and (b) the 'law and order' apparatus, including the police and the courts.
- End the separation between policy and practice, exposing the connections between them.
- Replace the lack of political commitment to end racial inequality with a commitment to end racial inequality.[27]

A second example is provided by the need to change the philosophy of disability services away from managing the 'problem' of disability towards supporting disabled persons and their families in living in a common society.[28] Table 8.1 illustrates the changes that are needed.

The communalist visions also have important linkages with international social movements of Aboriginal peoples and of social development under conditions of deprivation and oppression, especially as these have developed in Latin America.[29] The communalist visions are an important and inescapable part of the future of social welfare. Each indicates a commitment to resistance to the changes that conservatives seek. In addition, they call for fundamental change in the social welfare policies that operated for the last half of the twentieth century.

Conclusion

The original liberal vision that guided a half-century of Canadian social welfare policy has been weakened in its power to find a middle ground between the excesses of capitalism and the seeming impossibility of a world order based on any other set of political, economic, and social processes. In its place there is a dominant conservative vision that accepts a link between economic and social policy, and hence between US policy and Canadian policy. It is a vision of reduced reliance on collective welfare and equalizing measures, to be replaced by individual risk, responsibility, and inequality. Needless to say, this vision has little appeal to those who are committed to the original objectives of social justice. The socialist/Marxist vision provides a strong critique of conservative changes and a chilling understanding of where they may lead. Communalist visions, each representing the understanding of the constituency from which it is drawn, seek to remake social welfare in forms that respond more fully to the ideals of social justice that were central when the current social welfare policies were conceived in the mid-twentieth century.

The commitment of the United States to a 'war on terrorism' after the destruction of the World Trade Center on 11 September 2001 is also now an inescapable part of our world. What effect will these events have on social welfare in Canada? The first effect is on international relationships and priorities. Canada is linked too closely to the United States to have independent policies for security or trade and thus, perforce, is governed indirectly from Washington. Spending on security, policing, and the military is already increasing, and the priority of social policy on the federal government agenda has fallen. Once again, needed action on child poverty, child care, and other critical social issues is being delayed. Once again, the conservatives have been given an opportunity to achieve long-term objectives to

Table 8.1 Warehouse, Greenhouse, and Open House Social Services for the Disabled

	EVOLUTION OF SYSTEMS	
Warehouse	*Greenhouse*	*Open House*
• Segregated services	• Specialized services	• Mainstream services
• Centre-based delivery	• Community-based delivery	• Self-managed
• Large residential institutions	• Group homes	• Individual living arrangements
• Treatment only	• Rehabilitation	• Disability-related supports
• No labour force capability	• Specialized training and placement	• Range of employment opportunities
• Primary prevention	• Secondary prevention	• Promotion/advocacy/education
• Categorical funding	• Special needs/social assistance	• Level playing field/incentives
• Institutional funding		• Individualized funding

Box 8.2 Reflections on a War

The Americans say 'you are either on "our" side or the "other" side.' But what does that really mean?

There is a recurring image in the Qur'an. It is the image of a fountain. When talking about Paradise, the Qur'an says: 'In a garden sublime, wherein thou wilt hear no empty talk, countless fountains will flow therein, and there will be thrones (of happiness) raised high.'

I am drawn to this image of fountains; it reminds me of the fountains that you find everywhere in Islamic architecture; in the courtyards of beautiful mosques, palaces, and libraries. Fountains are symbols of reflection, they make one meditative, the rhythmic fall and rise of the waters, the gurgling sounds and a sense of perspective that they lend to a landscape all work to induce a sense of self-reflection. It is no wonder that fountains in Arabic share the same root word ('ayn') as the word for eye in Arabic.

When I reflect on the images that remain with me from the last few weeks, since the tragedy of Sept. 11, one of the first is that of a man, having jumped from the top floor of the tower, falling head-first into the abyss of his death. He is perfectly straight except for his left knee, which is slightly crooked. It is this image that haunts me. What was he thinking? Was he conscious as he fell? Amazingly, my mind keeps going back to the knee. Why the crooked knee when his body is perfectly straight? 'Out of the crooked timber from which humanity has sprung, no straight thing can ever be fashioned', reflected Kant. Nobody, but nobody, I tell myself should have to die like this.

The next image that remains with me is of the planes crashing into the twin towers of the World Trade Center and the Pentagon. Again and again the same images are played on television; the economic and military symbols of American Might being hit by three angry planes. I remember my heart filling with terror as I watch. Much like the Palestinian-New Yorker, Suheir Hammad, I pray: 'first, please god, let it be a mistake, the pilot's heart failed, the plane's engine died, then please god, let it be a nightmare, wake me now. Please god, after the second plane, please don't let it be anyone who looks like my brothers'.

When the pictures of the terrorists start appearing, with dismay, I see that the faces of these people could look like my brothers, cousins, friends. I stare at these men's eyes, searching for clues, for answers as to why they would do such a thing. Congealed in their photographs, they look back, almost serene. 'Why this shame at our door?' I demand of them. 'Did you wish to enter and partake of the fountains of Paradise by creating fountains of Blood?' 'How did Hell become a way to Paradise?' Silence, no answers.

One of the most beautiful fountains found in Islamic architecture is in the courtyard of the Alhambra Palace in Grenada, Spain. The interior of the palace is very beautiful, consisting of ornamental columns that fill the space by repeating themselves innumerably. You could stand anywhere and the same vista of pillar after pillar opens up in front of you. The experience of being in that space, I imagine, must be like none other, reflecting a profound truth—that the centre only exists from the perspective of where you stand.

From the perspective of the US (at least its official voice) there are only two sides: the side of the terrorists and the side of democracy; the side of the barbaric, against the side of the civilized world. You are either on 'our' or on the 'other' side. But what side is 'our' side? Is it the side which is allied with Pakistan, Uzbekistan and Russia, all of which were charged until last month with being involved in terrorist activities?

If a thing of beauty, such as a fountain, has any place at all in all this hideousness, it is only because it serves as a reminder of the importance of self-reflection. Yet when the American leadership looks at the events of Sept.11th, what they see reflected back are the faces of Brown, Turbaned, Muslim, Men who inexplicably hate 'America'. This emperor has no clothes, no colour, works on a misdirected sense of certainty; it does not see itself at all and therefore is engaged in very little self-reflection.

Mehmoona Moosa-Mitha is an Assistant Professor at the School of Social Work. Her research interests include children's rights and child welfare practice and policy.

Source: Mehmoona Moosa-Mitha, 'Reflections on a war', *The Ring* (University of Victoria), 18 Oct. 2001.

contain or reduce social welfare expenditures, this time linked to the need to prioritize security questions. Internationally, the world is becoming more divided between rich and poor, and US President George W. Bush talks in terms of 'good' and 'evil' and wars against distant peoples of indefinite duration, rather than about how to achieve social justice for all. This lack of reflection imperils what is left of the vision of a world in which social justice is a founding principle (see Box 8.2). The future of social welfare in Canada is uncertain in such a world.

Additional Readings

J. James Rice and Michael J. Prince, *Changing Politics of Canadian Social Policy*. Toronto: University of Toronto Press, 2000, 232–55. Chapter 10, 'Creating a New Policy Agenda', is a contemporary statement of the liberal vision for Canadian social welfare policy.

John Richards, *Now That the Coat Fits the Cloth: Spending Wisely in a Trimmed-Down Age*, C.D. Howe Institute Commentary 143. Toronto: C.D. Howe Institute, June 2000. Richards delineates the conservative agenda now being followed by federal and provincial governments.

Gary Teeple, *Globalization and the Decline of Social Reform: Into the Twenty-First Century*. Toronto: Garamond Press, 2000, 133–54. In a chapter titled 'The Era of the "Triumph of Capitalism"' Teeple forecasts the dark path that Marxist analysis suggests will be the fate of society and social welfare in the twenty-first century.

Study Questions

1. Review Appendix B: Chronology of Social Welfare in Canada. What early measures continue to exist? Does this mean that they are now so much a part of our society that they will probably be maintained in the future?

2. Take one social policy that you consider to be outdated and indicate where change is needed and how it fits, or does not fit, in the context of one or more of the future visions contained in this chapter.

3. This book has been written from a 'liberal' perspective but concludes with doubts that the liberal perspective is now in a position to provide leadership and a clear future vision. Articulate your own vision for social welfare policy, saying where you agree and disagree with the conclusions in this chapter.

Notes

1. Karen Swift, *Manufacturing 'Bad Mothers': A Critical Perspective on Child Neglect* (Toronto: University of Toronto Press, 1995).

2. Allan Cochrane and John Clarke, eds, *Comparing Welfare States: Britain in International Context*, 2nd edn (London: Sage Publications, 2001).

3. John Crane, *Directions for Social Welfare in Canada* (Vancouver: University of British Columbia Press, 1994), 129.

4. J. James Rice and Michael J. Prince, *Changing Politics of Canadian Social Policy* (Toronto: University of Toronto Press, 2000), 232–55.

5. Thomas Courchene, *Social Canada in the Millennium* (Toronto: C.D. Howe Institute, 1994), 322.

6. David Bull and Paul Wilding, eds, *Thatcherism and the Poor*, Poverty Pamphlet 59 (London: Child Poverty Action Group, Apr. 1983), 10–11.

7. John Richards, *Now That the Coat Fits the Cloth: Spending Wisely in a Trimmed-Down Age*, C.D. Howe Institute Commentary 143 (Toronto: C.D. Howe Institute, June 2000), summary.

8. Ibid.

9. Crane, *Directions for Social Welfare*, 129.
10. Robert Heilbronner, *Capitalism in the Twenty-First Century* (Concord, Ont.: Anansi, 1992), 113.
11. Ibid., 114.
12. Gary Teeple, *Globalization and the Decline of Social Reform* (Toronto: Garamond Press, 1995), 148.
13. Ibid., 194.
14. Ibid., 151.
15. Frank James Tester, 'The Disenchanted Democracy: Canada in the Global Economy of the 1990s', *Canadian Review of Social Policy* 29/30 (1992): 132–57.
16. Diana Ralph, 'Tripping the Iron Heel', in Jane Pulkingham and Gordon Ternowetsky, eds, *Remaking Canadian Social Policy: Staking Claims and Forging Change* (Halifax: Fernwood, 1995).
17. Bob Mullaly, *Structural Social Work*, 2nd edn (Toronto: Oxford University Press, 1997), 134.
18. Peter Leonard, *Postmodern Welfare: Reconstructing an Emancipatory Project* (London: Sage Publications, 1997), 27.
19. Ibid., 177.
20. Marilyn Callahan, 'Feminist Community Organizing in Canada', in Brian Wharf and Michael Clague, eds, *Community Organizing: Canadian Experiences* (Toronto: Oxford University Press, 1997), 190.
21. Patricia Evans, 'Women and Social Welfare: Exploring the Connections', in F. Turner and J. Turner, eds, *Social Welfare in Canada*, 3rd edn (Scarborough, Ont.: Allyn and Bacon, 1995), 150–64; Marjorie Griffin Cohen, 'Social Policy and Social Services', in Ruth Roach, ed., *Canadian Women's Issues* (Toronto: Lorimer, 1993), 265–84.
22. Callahan, 'Feminist Community Organizing', 201.
23. Leroy Little Bear, 'Jagged Worldviews Colliding', in M. Battisits, ed., *Reclaiming Indigenous Voice and Vision* (Vancouver: University of British Columbia Press, 2000), 77–85.
24. Strater Crowfoot, 'Leadership in First Nation Communities: A Chief's Perspective on the Colonial Millstone', in R. Ponting, ed., *First Nations in Canada: Perspectives on Opportunity, Empowerment and Self-Determination* (Toronto: McGraw-Hill Ryerson, 1997), 299–325.
25. Anne Marie Mawhiney, 'First Nations in Canada', in J.C. Turner and F.J. Turner, eds, *Canadian Social Welfare*, 3rd edn (Scarborough, Ont.: Allyn and Bacon, 1995), 213–29.
26. Taiaiake Alfred, *Peace, Power, and Righteousness: An Indigenous Manifesto* (Toronto: Oxford University Press, 1999).
27. Lena Dominelli, *Anti-Racist Social Work* (London: Macmillan, 1988), 162.
28. Anne Chricton and Lyn Jongbloed, *Disability and Social Policy in Canada* (North York, Ont.: Captus Press, 1998), 279–86.
29. Herbert Campfens, 'Forces Shaping the New Social Work in Latin America', *Canadian Social Work Review* 5 (1988): 19.

Glossary

Ableism Ableism means an attitude that defines being human as having a 'normal' set of physical and mental attributes and presumes that public policy should be based on the needs of 'normal' people. Ableism results in considering people with differing capacities to be 'abnormal', 'handicapped', or 'disabled' and therefore subject to lesser rights.

Aboriginal peoples Aboriginal peoples are the original inhabitants of a country or territory. The term is plural as there are many Aboriginal peoples in Canada, each of which is properly referred to by their Aboriginal name. The Canadian government recognizes three main groups of Aboriginal peoples: the Indian peoples, also known as First Nations, the Inuit, and the Métis.

Assimilation Assimilation as a social policy is the deliberate attempt to incorporate a minority population into the majority. Assimilation also occurs through social contact when the identity and origin of individuals and families are replaced by the identity of the majority population in which they are residing.

Child welfare Child welfare is a specific field of practice inclusive of a series of community-based and case-oriented measures designed to protect children. The primary services included are family support, homemakers, child and youth care, protection, foster care of children, and adoption. The term is used in modified form as in the title Children's Aid Society. It is also used in some provinces as part of the title of a senior administrator in the provincial department of social welfare, as in Superintendent of Child Welfare.

Colonialism The process through which the European peoples took control of overseas territories, expropriated land, exploited resources, and displaced and/or controlled indigenous populations.

Communalism A theory or system of government in which communes or local communities, sometimes based on ethnicity or religion, have virtual autonomy within a federal state. When applied to social welfare the focus is on the government of a community's social welfare functions, which may or may not be part of a larger process of self-government.

Community development Community development refers primarily to a community self-help methodology.[1] The term is also used to refer to a program designed to apply the methodology in specified communities, as in the 'community development program' of _____. In some literature, the term is used to indicate the product rather than the methodology, that is to say, the development of the community. Such uses can only be found through inspection of the context.

Community economic development (CED) CED is the application of the community development process to the development and ownership of self-sustaining economic enterprises.

Corrections Corrections is a field of practice inclusive of a series of measures designed to protect society from criminal behaviour and to rehabilitate those judged criminal. Corrections includes probation and parole programs.

Demogrant A demogrant is a cash payment to an individual or family based solely on demographic characteristics (usually age). No recognition is given of differential needs. Old Age Security is a demogrant.

Feminism Feminism is a social movement of women who seek political, economic, and social rights equal to those held by men and who seek social policies that recognize the distinct problems faced by women and the distinct contribution made by women.

Field of practice Field of practice refers to a subdivision of the totality of social work practice. Thus child welfare, corrections, mental health, etc. are fields of practice.

First Nations The First Nations are the separate peoples who lived in Canada, south of the treeline, prior to European settlement. In the nineteenth century the government of Canada registered families and individuals, giving them 'status' under the Indian Act. 'Status' was accompanied by whatever treaty rights had been agreed when settlement occurred. 'Status' also meant that the individual status Indian was governed under the Indian Act. Until the middle of the twentieth century 'status Indians' could not vote, retain legal counsel, or live off reserve. The schooling of children was principally through residential schools operated by the churches, under contract to the government of Canada.

Guaranteed income Guaranteed income is a term that has had wide use and several different meanings. The primary use is to indicate a social objective—the provision of a guarantee of minimum income for individuals and families. The term is also used to indicate the means for obtaining this objective. Since there are several different means available and each of these may be referred to as a guaranteed income program, there is confusion in meanings. The different means include social insurance, social assistance, negative income taxes, and demogrants. Which method of income guarantee is intended by a particular author can usually be discerned from the context.

Heterosexism Heterosexism is the assumption that heterosexuality is the 'normal' and superior form of sexual attraction and that any other sexual orientation is 'abnormal'. Heterosexism can take the form of personal prejudice and can be incorporated into public policies, taking such institutional forms as discriminatory laws or practices of exclusion.

Human service organization A human service organization is one having a mandate to protect, maintain, or enhance personal well-being. Human service organizations take many forms. This book differentiates between government service organizations and the social movement service organizations. Examples of government organizations include schools, welfare agencies, mental health services, correctional facilities. Examples of social movement service organizations include transition houses, rape and sexual assault centres, First Nations band offices and tribal councils, and HIV/AIDS services.

Income security Income security refers to all programs in which a cash payment is made to beneficiaries. In some uses, as in this book, the term has an expanded meaning, including all those programs where tax expenditures, goods, or services are provided by government in order to distribute economic benefits more equitably than is achieved by the market economy.

Internal colonialism This occurs when an Aboriginal population is subject to colonialism by a settler population who live in the same country.

Inuit The Inuit are the Aboriginal people who lived north of the treeline prior to European settlement. They were not registered under the Indian Act or confined to reserves, but in the mid-twentieth century many of their settlements and their nomadic lifestyle were disrupted and they were required to live in communities formed in the Arctic primarily for administrative convenience.

Métis The Métis are the Aboriginal people who, following intermarriage of First Nations peoples with traders and settlers in the eighteenth and nineteenth centuries, founded a distinct society on the Prairies. This society was disrupted in the latter half of the nineteenth century by increasing settlement of what was then the North-West Territories, which was instrumental to the Riel Rebellion of 1869, which in turn led to the establishment of the province of Manitoba.

Negative income tax Negative income tax refers to a proposed program of payments to individuals and families in which the amount of payment would be determined on the basis of an income declaration. The paying agency might be the relevant income tax department rather than a traditional welfare agency. The precise form of program envisaged by a particular author can usually be discerned from the context.

Neo-colonialism This refers to a situation in which the European people (or settler population) retain control of an indigenous people through Aboriginal leaders who agree to govern the Aboriginal people in accord with required financial conditions, laws, and administrative measures.

Poverty line Canada has no 'official' definition of poverty. However, the Statistics Canada low-income cut-offs (LICOs) are the best-known and most widely used measure of poverty and are used by the National Council of Welfare in its annual reports on poverty in Canada. LICOs are based on Statistics Canada's annual survey of incomes and expenditures and use a 'relative' approach to define poverty that compares expenditure patterns at different income levels and in different regions. The Montreal Diet Dispensary and the Fraser Institute have developed more restrictive definitions of poverty that are based on a 'market basket' approach, which defines poverty in terms of subsistence necessities.

Racism Racism refers to an assumption of superiority by one people that, for them, justifies their dominating of other peoples. Racism is usually based on colour or ethnic origin. *Personal racism* refers to prejudice and harassment in daily life; *institutional racism* refers to laws, administrative measures, and attitudes used by the state to make distinctions based on race in the practice of governing; *cultural racism* refers to the assumption that the institutions and culture of one people are superior to those of another.

Social administration Social administration refers to the planning and management of all aspects of social welfare. It is an activity engaged in by 'social administrators', who are usually identified as being the senior officials of social welfare organizations. In the British literature, 'social administration' is used to indicate a field of studies. In turn, university departments are sometimes entitled Schools of Social Administration.

Social assistance Social assistance, sometimes referred to colloquially as 'welfare' or, in the past, 'the dole', refers to income security programs that use a 'means' or 'needs' test to determine eligibility for benefits. These programs are also referred to as *social allowance* programs. In the American literature, they may be referred to as *public assistance* programs. The term is also used as the title of specific income security programs. Thus, some provinces have a Social Assistance Act.

Social development Social development is used to indicate the entire field of social welfare, with particular emphasis on change and on the future. The term, with various meanings, has been employed in a number of recent books. What a particular writer means, beyond an orientation to the future, has to be discovered from the context. In addition, the term has been used by a number of government departments, as in the Department of Health and Social Development; it also forms part of the title of the former Canadian Welfare Council, now the Canadian Council on Social Development. These uses may or may not indicate change in the functions of the organizations concerned. That, too, can only be discovered by studying what they did and what they do. Changes in name are easier to accomplish than changes in substance.

Social indicators Social indicators are a set of time series statistics that provide a representation of the social affairs of the society. Examples include the unemployment rate, the poverty rate, the CCSD Personal Social Security Index, UN indexes on welfare, etc.

Social insurance Social insurance refers to income security programs in which eligibility for benefits is determined on the basis of a record of contribution and on the occurrence of a foreseen social contingency, such as unemployment, retirement, injury, or widowhood.

Social planning Social planning refers to a professional activity carried out as part of social administration. The activity centres on the design and evaluation of social programs. In the American literature, particularly the writing of Alfred Kahn, the term 'social planning' is used very broadly. In such use, it encompasses all parts of the process whereby social programs are introduced. The term is also used in the title of a number of local bodies, such as the social planning councils. These are typically voluntary social welfare organizations that engage in studies of social needs and programs.

Social policy Social policy encompasses not only social welfare but other activities of government affecting social life. Marriage and divorce legislation and support to culture and the arts are examples of social policy that lie beyond the field of social welfare. The term is also linked with 'economic policy'. In this sense, it usually contrasts a concern for people with a concern for economic issues and growth. Shankar Yelaja identifies four key assumptions implicit in social policy. (1) The government has responsibility to meet the needs of the less fortunate members of society. (2) The state has a right to intervene in areas of individual freedom and economic liberty. (3) Governmental and/or public intervention is necessary when existing social institutions fail to fulfill their obligations. (4) Public policies create social impacts, the consequences of which become the moral obligation of some group to act upon.[2]

Social security Social security refers to particular programs. It has had a number of uses and some inspection of the context is usually necessary to understand the writer's meaning. In United Nations and most Canadian writings, the term refers to income programs plus social services. Thus, the total of both is referred to as 'social security'. The existence in the United States of a major government department and a number of programs using 'social security' as parts of their title further affects the term's meaning. These programs are all income programs and most use a social insurance technique. Thus the Social Security Act established a program of retirement benefits. As a consequence, 'social security' in American writing frequently has the reduced meaning of income security and may have the even narrower meaning of 'social insurance'.

Social service Social service is a broad term used to indicate the provision of services other than income support. Thus adoption, daycare, protection, and probation are all social services.

Social service worker This term has received increased usage as the social work profession has sought to restrict 'social worker' to its own members. 'Social service worker' has been used to cover not only professional social workers but all those who perform similar functions, for example, case aides and probation officers. The term indicates an occupational class.

Social utilities Social utilities, a term introduced into wide usage through the writings of Alfred Kahn, refers to 'a social invention, a resource, or facility, designed to meet a generally experienced need in social living'.[3]

Social welfare Social welfare is the term used in this book, and elsewhere, to describe the totality of the enterprise under study. There is a tendency to use it to describe the present rather than the future, hence the connection in meaning to the more future-oriented term 'social development'. There is also a tendency to use the term to indicate both intended and unintended consequences. Social welfare is what has been produced, warts and all. In earlier writing, social welfare has rather more of a future orientation than it has in contemporary use. The term is also used as part of the title of government departments, as in the Department of Social Welfare.

Social work Social work refers to a professional skill used principally in social welfare. The skill can be applied to individual and small-group activities, to communities, and to social administration. Social work is also the name of a profession. In some provinces the title 'Social Worker' is restricted to registered members of the profession. In others the term is used more loosely and employer job descriptions define employees as 'social workers' even though they do not have professional credentials.

Voluntary agency A voluntary agency is one in which the sponsorship is not government. The term is used to refer to at least three types of non-governmental organizations. The *quasi-non-governmental agency* is privately incorporated but depends on government for most if not all of its support. Children's Aid Societies and children's treatment institutions are typical examples. The *private service agency* may be answerable not to a membership but to itself, that is, to a paid professional staff and a self-perpetuating board of trustees. It is legitimized by the utility of its program rather than by its status as the representative organ of defined bodies of citizenry. A family service agency and the YMCA are typical examples. The truly *voluntary association* is created by private citizens of their own volition, is not for profit, and is outside the initiative and authority of government. Social movement service organizations are examples of this type of voluntary agency.

Welfare state The welfare state is a state (government, bureaucracy, and institutions) in which there is a commitment to use resources primarily for the collective welfare. Originally, the 'welfare state' was contrasted with the fascist 'warfare state'. In the immediate post-war period the term was used to indicate that totality of legislation whereby social security (in its broad sense) was obtained, plus the commitment to maintain a focus on welfare into the future. In recent writing there has been less of a tendency to use 'welfare state'—perhaps because the commitment is now lacking.

Workfare Workfare is a system in which the performance of work is a required condition for receiving social assistance. Workfare is a form of forced labour: the type of work and the conditions under which it is performed are set by the social assistance agency.

Notes

1. See W. and L. Biddle, *The Community Development Process* (New York: Holt, Rinehart and Winston, 1965).

2. Shankar Yelaja, ed., *Canadian Social Policy*, 2nd edn (Waterloo, Ont.: Wilfrid Laurier University Press, 1987), 1.

3. Alfred Kahn, *Theory and Practice of Social Planning* (New York: Russell Sage Foundation, 1969), 178.

Chronology

This annotated chronology is intended to provide the student with an overview of the sequence of development of legislation and institutions. It is not intended to provide a history of the development of Canadian social welfare institutions. Major sources used in the development of the chronology are the articles by Bellamy and Willard in the *Encyclopedia of Social Work*,[1] Guest's text, *The Emergence of Social Security in Canada*,[2] and the chronology of events between 1985 and 1993 provided by Courchene.[3] Guest's work provides the best liberal treatment of the history of Canadian social welfare. For a good summary account of changes in Indian policy, read Mawhiney, *First Nations in Canada*.[4]

Pre-1900

The development of Canadian social welfare provision is principally a twentieth-century phenomenon. Pre-1900 programming[5] included the following major features:

- Limited municipal responsibility for the poor and indigent—responsibility assumed *only* for the sick, elderly, young, and women with dependent children, *only* after all the family financial resources have been exhausted, and *only* where local residence was clearly established.
- Custodial institutions for the mentally ill and mentally retarded.
- Custodial institutions for criminals, with some provision for the segregation of young offenders into reformatories.
- Beginnings of major voluntary welfare organizations, principally in Toronto: Toronto Children's Aid Society (1891); Red Cross (1896); Victorian Order of Nurses (1897).
- Early forms of workers' compensation legislation (1886).
- Separate authority for services to Native peoples based on treaty obligations incurred by the Crown and, subsequently, on the Indian Act (1876).

1900–1920

During this period there was a continuation of the pattern of programming noted for the pre-1900 period, with some expansion and modification. These changes include the following:

- Major voluntary welfare organizations grew. Children's Aid Societies were formed to serve other urban areas; the Toronto Family Service Agency was founded in 1914, the Canadian Mental Health Association in 1918, the Canadian National Institute for the Blind in 1918, the Canadian Council on Social Development in 1920, etc.
- Segregation of juveniles in criminal proceedings was increased. The Juvenile Delinquents Act (1908) provided for juveniles to be charged as delinquent rather than as offenders and provided for a broad range of court dispositions.
- A mothers' allowance program was introduced in Manitoba in 1916, providing for payments by the province to morally upright women with dependent children. Character references were required for eligibility. The program removed one category of destitute persons from dependence on municipal relief. Subsequently, many other categories were added (veterans, unemployed, elderly, etc.) and the whole relief function has been progressively transferred to provincial and federal governments.
- Services to Indian people were provided through a church-state alliance, under which the churches accepted responsibility for the residential school system.

1920–1930

The first substantial involvement by the federal government in the field of income security began during this decade. The federal involvement was a product not only of high regard for veterans but also of social unrest, including the Winnipeg General Strike of 1919. Returning veterans were not assured work and found a marked contrast between the society's rhetoric and their destitute circumstances. Principal events during this period included:

- Various pieces of legislation were enacted in the years following World War I to assist veterans. These included Returned Soldiers Insurance (1920), which provided for veterans to purchase private retirement annuities to a value of $5,000, the Soldiers Settlement Act (1927), and War Veterans Allowances (1930) payable to veterans, widows, or orphans who by age or incapacity were unable to earn an income and had insufficient means. These federal programs were introduced on the basis of the federal responsibility for the armed services.
- The Old Age Assistance Act (1927) was the first federal-provincial shared-cost program. An allowance was paid to the elderly on the basis of a means test. The provinces administered the program but were able to obtain 40 per cent of their costs from the federal government.
- The Canadian Association of Social Workers was founded in 1928.
- The emphasis of Indian policy shifted from measures to manage what had been seen as the inevitable decline and fading away of Aboriginal peoples, to measures to ensure their assimilation. Aboriginal customs like the potlatch of the Northwest Coast Indians, which had been banned in 1884 but still generally tolerated, were stopped. Indian leaders were imprisoned and the proportion of Indian children in residential schools increased.

1930–1940

This period was dominated by the Great Depression. Millions of Canadians were unemployed and, on the Prairies, a period of drought destroyed farms and farm income. Many people turned to their municipalities for relief. However, the municipalities' source of income was principally the local property tax and the same circumstances that caused the need for relief payments also caused much tax delinquency. The result was municipal bankruptcy or near bankruptcy. Provincial governments were the guarantors of municipal bond indebtedness. As a result, the provinces had to assume responsibilities, including the 'relief' responsibility from municipalities.

Some provinces, notably Saskatchewan, had the same problems in supporting relief payments as had been faced by municipalities: they lacked a sufficient income to cover their responsibilities as governments. In response, the federal government was increasingly involved in payments to the unemployed. As in the case of veterans' payments, the federal role was also a response to serious disorder. In Regina in 1935, workers on their way to Ottawa to protest inadequate programs were met with force by the RCMP. Principal actions by government during the dirty thirties included the following:

- Several unemployment relief measures were enacted by the federal government. Between 1930 and 1935 these took the form of ad hoc, short-term measures, allowing federal funds to be used to provide relief. The emphasis was on work projects for the unemployed, including the establishment of labour camps. In southern Saskatchewan, the federal government took over the entire relief function through the establishment of the Saskatchewan Relief Commission.
- In 1935, the federal government passed the Employment and Social Insurance Act, which was intended to institutionalize the federal unemployment role. The Act was challenged in the courts by Ontario and was eventually ruled ultra vires by the British Judicial Committee of the Privy Council in 1937.
- In 1937 the federal government appointed the Royal Commission on Dominion-Provincial Relations (the Rowell-Sirois Commission). The Commission was charged with responsibility for 'a re-examination of the financial and economic basis of Confederation and of the distribution of legislative powers in the light of the economic and social developments of the last 70 years' (since Confederation).

1940–1950

During this period the foundations of the modern Canadian social welfare institutions were created. This was done, in part, through the reports of a series of inquiries related to the structure of social welfare in Canada. Principal inquiries that reported during this period included the following:

- The Royal Commission on Dominion-Provincial Relations reported in 1940. A central conclusion was that 'Not only national duty and decency, if Canada is to be a nation at all, but equity and national self-interest demand that the residents of these [impoverished] regions be given average services and equal opportunities.'[6] The Commission proposed a federal unemployment program and a system of equalizing grants to the poorer provinces, but that the general responsibility for welfare should remain provincial.

- The Committee on Health Insurance (Heagerty Committee) was appointed in 1942. The Committee proposed a reorganization of health services, including a full range of medical benefits: physician, dental, pharmaceutical, hospital, nursing, etc. Coverage was to be provided on payment of an annual $12 registration fee with financing from provincial and federal governments.
- The House of Commons Advisory Committee on Post-War Reconstruction reported in 1943 (the Marsh Report). The Marsh Report suggested a twofold classification of income security risks: universal risks such as medical care and pensions; and employment risks, unemployment, disability, etc. Marsh's report shared ideas with the British Report on Social Insurance and Allied Services of 1942 (the Beveridge Report). A comprehensive set of income security proposals designed to protect national minimums was proposed.
- The Dominion-Provincial Conference on Reconstruction, Proposals of the Government of Canada, 1945 (the Green Book proposals) presented formal proposals of the federal government 'for establishing the general conditions of high employment and income policies, and for the support of national minimum standards of social services'.

The results of these inquiries were twofold. General objectives for Canadian social welfare policy were established. In addition, some specific legislation was passed.

- With the Unemployment Insurance Act, 1940, the provinces agreed to a constitutional amendment giving power to the federal government for Unemployment Insurance.
- The National Employment Service (the forerunner of the Department of Manpower) was established in 1941.
- The universal Family Allowances program was legislated in 1944 and introduced in 1945.
- The National Housing Act was legislated in 1944, and the Central Mortgage and Housing Corporation was established in 1946.
- Although there were no federal health insurance acts, some provinces began to provide specific

types of health insurance, for example, hospital insurance acts in Saskatchewan (1947) and British Columbia (1949).

1950–1960

The fifties were a time of incremental extension in Canadian social welfare legislation. Several important measures were enacted during this decade.

- Income security provisions for the elderly and incapacitated were substantially revised. These revisions included universal Old Age Security payments (1951) beginning at age 70 and a revised Old Age Assistance Act (1951) for persons aged 65 to 70. A Blind Persons Act (1951), similar in its provisions to the Old Age Assistance Act, was also legislated. In 1955, those federal shared-cost, means-tested programs were extended to the permanently disabled through the Disabled Persons Act.
- In 1951 the Indian Act was amended so that provincial laws of general application, such as child welfare legislation, applied to Indians living on reserves.
- In 1956 the Unemployment Assistance Act was passed, whereby the federal government agreed to furnish 50 per cent of the costs of provincial social assistance payments.
- Also in 1956 a federal Hospital Insurance Act was passed, whereby the federal government agreed to share in the costs of provincial hospital insurance programs.

The 1951 changes in the Indian Act were particularly significant as they marked a decision by the federal government to move towards integrated services for Aboriginal people that would complete the process of assimilating them into an undifferentiated Canadian citizenship.

1960–1970

The decade 1960–1970 saw more substantial progress than had the preceding decade. During this period, action was taken to develop the social welfare institutions that had been foreseen during the 1940s. By the end of the decade, the only major fields in which the objectives of the 1940s had not been legislated were housing, particularly housing for low-income persons, and maternity allowances. In addition, new action was begun, centring on the subject of poverty. Finally, the issue of responsibility for social welfare was reopened during the series of federal-provincial conferences that followed Quebec's Quiet Revolution.

- In 1961, the Royal Commission on Health Services (the Hall Commission) was appointed. In 1962, Saskatchewan enacted the first universal government medical care insurance program in North America. Despite a doctors' strike on its introduction, the program was generally regarded as successful. In 1964–5, the Hall Commission reported, advocating a universal medical insurance plan. In 1968, the federal Medical Services Act came into effect, whereby the federal government agreed to share in the cost of provincial programs of medical insurance. Despite initial provincial opposition, all provinces had enacted medical insurance legislation within three years.
- In 1962, the Royal Commission on Taxation (the Carter Commission) was appointed. The subject of government payment programs to individuals (income security) was outside the terms of reference of the Commission. When it reported in 1966, the Commission asserted a principle of equity in the treatment of income, regardless of source. The Commission's proposals were the subject of a government White Paper, 'Proposals for Tax Reform', in 1969 (the Benson proposals). Revised income tax legislation, incorporating some but not all of the Carter Commission's proposals, was introduced in 1971 and came into effect in 1972.
- There was substantial revision in provision for the elderly and incapacitated. The Canada Pension Plan, covering retirement, widowhood, disability, etc. through social insurance, was introduced in 1966. A companion plan, the Quebec Pension Plan, provided similar coverage in that province. In addition, the Old Age Security Guaranteed Income Supplement program (1966) was introduced. This program supplemented Old Age Security payments, ensuring that no elderly person's monthly income fell below a prescribed level.
- The Canada Assistance Plan (1966) extended federal cost-sharing in provincial social welfare programs. The plan provided for a consolidation of previous cost-sharing programs, unemployment assistance, old age assistance, blind and disabled persons assistance, the inclusion of child welfare measures, and the inclusion of administrative costs.
- The War on Poverty, begun in the United States in 1964, had an effect on Canadian social welfare programs. The objectives of the Company of Young Canadians (1965) showed similarities to those of the American Office of Economic Opportunity community action programs. The objectives

of the Canada Assistance Plan, 'the prevention and removal of the causes of poverty', are similar to the early War on Poverty declarations. In addition, careful study of poverty in Canada was begun. In 1968, the *Fifth Annual Review* of the Economic Council of Canada indicated that one in five Canadians lived in poverty. Also in 1968, the Special Senate Committee on Poverty (the Croll Committee) was appointed.

- In 1968, the federal-provincial constitutional conference agreed to undertake a complete review of the Constitution of Canada. Federal proposals on income security and social services were presented at a meeting in 1969. It was apparent, during the meeting, that the federal proposals (which basically affirmed the status quo) did not provide Quebec with the increased social policy responsibility that province sought.
- In 1969, the federal government issued a White Paper on Indian affairs that would have led to the repeal of the Indian Act, the ending of separate legal status for First Nations, and the conversion of reserve lands to private tenure. The White Paper was rejected by First Nations, which began a sustained campaign for separate constitutional and policy recognition as independent nations within Canada.

1970–1980

The 1970s, in particular the first five years of the decade, were a period of major change and development in welfare programs. The future foreseen was characterized by expanded social welfare measures and restructuring of existing programs.

- The process of constitutional review continued and proposals were presented to a federal-provincial conference on the Constitution in Victoria (1971) that increased provincial jurisdiction over welfare. However, the increased authority was not adequate to satisfy Quebec and the proposals were rejected.
- The Unemployment Insurance Act was amended in 1971, extending coverage to groups not previously covered, e.g., fishermen, and expanding coverage to include sickness and maternity leave. These changes, along with the previously enacted Canada Pension Plan, provided Canada a full range of social insurance coverage for the major insurable life contingencies foreseen by Marsh and Beveridge in the 1940s.
- The concern with poverty continued with the publication of the Report of the Special Senate

Committee on Poverty in 1971. This concern was institutionalized at the federal level with the establishment of the National Council of Welfare and the publication by Statistics Canada of regular data on poverty.

- The major federal initiative aimed at the design of a guaranteed income was initiated in 1971 with the federal proposal, *Income Security for Canadians*. A two-level system was foreseen, one level for unemployable people and a second level, integrated with working income through wage supplementation, for unemployed but employable people. These proposals were published in 1973 in the *Working Paper on Social Security in Canada*, but, for technical and financial reasons, no basic changes were enacted.
- The personal social services were substantially expanded at the provincial level and major initiatives were undertaken to improve their integration and co-ordination. These initiatives took the form of an expanded provincial jurisdiction in relation to services previously provided by local government and private societies. There were also changes in inter-ministry jurisdiction to integrate services more closely, and new structures for the accountability of services to the local community were introduced. In most jurisdictions child welfare legislation was revised to reflect rights and due process. These changes were influenced by the British Seebohm Report (1968). However, they were not always consolidated, and legislation, such as British Columbia's Community Resource Board Act (1974), was both introduced and withdrawn again by the end of the decade.
- The Canadian Council on the Status of Women was established in 1973, following a recommendation from the Royal Commission on the Status of Women.

1980–1990

The 1980s began with much uncertainty. The first referendum on the separation of Quebec was held; separation was defeated by a 60 to 40 margin. The federal income security review failed to produce a guaranteed income plan, and most provinces (Quebec is an exception) failed to reform personal social services in the manner foreseen. The welfare state was under conservative review in the United States and Britain on both ideological and financial grounds. Major events included:

- The Canadian Constitution (formerly called the British North America Act, now renamed, in part,

the Constitution Act, 1867) was repatriated from Britain in 1982. The newly crafted Constitution Act, 1982, included the Canadian Charter of Rights and Freedoms, incorporating fundamental civil rights into the Constitution. However, Quebec was not a signatory due to concerns about the amending formula and the federal spending power, as these impacted on provincial jurisdiction for language and social policy.
- The 1982 Penner Committee on Indian Self-Government recommended that First Nations should be recognized as 'a distinct order of government in Canada'.
- The Canada Health Act of 1984 was passed to arrest the deterioration of universal medical coverage through the growth of provincial fee-for-service practices.
- The Report of the Royal Commission on the Economic Union and Development Prospects for Canada (Macdonald Commission, 1985) refocused attention on the unfinished business of income security reform, arguing that a better system was needed to assist in the process of economic adjustment that would follow from a free trade agreement with the United States.
- Registered Retirement Savings Plan and Registered Pension Plan contribution limits were raised as the first step towards increased tax expenditures to support retirement incomes.
- The principles on which Quebec's full agreement to the Canadian Constitution could be obtained were mutually agreed upon by the Prime Minister and the provincial premiers in the Meech Lake Accord (1987), wherein the federal government agreed to permit provinces to exclude themselves from federal-provincial shared-cost social programs in areas of exclusive provincial jurisdiction and receive financial compensation if they undertake initiatives compatible with the national objective. The Accord was never ratified by all the provinces within the three-year limit for legislative ratification, as Manitoba and Newfoundland, for differing reasons, withheld assent.
- The Child Care Act (1988) was introduced to replace daycare provisions of the Canada Assistance Plan. It was never passed, and following the 1988 federal election it was not reintroduced.
- The Canada-US Free Trade Agreement was signed in 1988. Although the agreement made no mention of social policy, it established a trade and investment relationship that provided capital with increased freedom of choice as to which country to invest in, restricting the Canadian ability to

develop taxation policies on corporations dissimilar to those in effect in the United States.

- The House of Commons resolution to eliminate child poverty by the year 2000 was passed unanimously (1989).
- 'Clawback' was imposed in 1989 on Family Allowances and Old Age Security for incomes over $50,000/year.

1990–2000

In the early part of the decade Canada's fiscal problems became more significant as industrial recession in central Canada between 1990 and 1992 reduced government revenue while raising government expenditures for social security. In the latter part of the decade federal and provincial governments 'dealt' with the deficit problem by sharply reducing social expenditures and increasing poverty and inequality. Measures in the early 1990s included the following:

- In 1990 the full cost of Unemployment Insurance was shifted to employers and employees and government support from general revenue was ended. Expenditures under the Canada Assistance Plan were restricted to 5 per cent annual increases for Ontario, Alberta, and British Columbia. Canada Pension Plan contributions were raised.
- In 1993 Family Allowance payments, the child tax credit, and the child personal exemption were terminated and the Child Tax Benefit introduced.
- The contribution level of individuals to the CPP was raised each year from a maximum of $594.20 in 1990 to $806.00 in 1994; contributions to UI were raised each year from a maximum of $737.51 in 1990 to $1,245.24 in 1994.
- The social housing budget was frozen at $2 billion (no new commitments) in 1993.
- The Canada-US Free Trade Agreement was expanded to include Mexico in 1993, and leaders of the three countries signed the North American Free Trade Agreement (NAFTA), with provision for other countries in the Americas to join in the future.

The latter part of the decade saw further steps by governments to attack the welfare state.

- The Canada Assistance Plan (CAP) was repealed and the Canada Health and Social Transfer (CHST) was introduced.
- Through a succession of deficit reduction budgets by both federal and provincial governments, expenditures on social programs were sharply reduced and poverty and inequality increased.
- Unemployment Insurance became Employment Insurance and benefit rules were tightened.
- Canada Pension Plan contributions were increased progressively, reaching $1,496 in 2001, with further increases to come each year until 2004.
- Social service programming became increasingly coercive and oriented to 'risk' and social control measures as families and children became more desperate with the increase in poverty.
- In 1999 the federal and provincial governments adopted the Social Union Framework Agreement in which mutual consultation was promised before either party made major change in social programs.

Also, the Royal Commission on Aboriginal Peoples was appointed in 1992 and reported in 1996. The Royal Commission strongly advocated measures to increase the independence of Aboriginal people and strengthen self-government. A second referendum on Quebec independence was also held on 30 October 1995. It was defeated by a margin of barely 1 per cent—50.6 per cent to 49.4 per cent.

2000-present

The new century began with conservative principles in a dominant position. As a result new social expenditures had low priority and the results of having dealt with deficit problems by reducing social expenditures allowed governments to reduce debt and taxes. The attacks on the Pentagon and the World Trade Center on 11 September 2001 gave increased impetus towards the integration of Canadian and United States security and trade policies, making the development of independent social policies less likely.

Notes

1. D. Bellamy, 'Social Welfare in Canada', and J. Willard, 'Canadian Welfare Programs', in *Encyclopedia of Social Work* (New York: National Association of Social Workers, 1965).
2. Dennis Guest, *The Emergence of Social Security in Canada*, 2nd edn (Vancouver: University of British Columbia Press, 1985).
3. Thomas Courchene, *Social Canada in the Millennium* (Toronto: C.D. Howe Institute, 1994), 341–55.

4. Anne-Marie Mawhiney, 'First Nations in Canada', in J.C. Turner and F.J. Turner, eds, *Canadian Social Welfare*, 3rd edn (Scarborough, Ont.: Allyn and Bacon, 1995).

5. For an account of pre-1900 social welfare provision, see R. Splane, *Social Welfare in Ontario, 1791–1898* (Toronto: University of Toronto Press, 1965); T. Copp, *The Anatomy of Poverty: The Condition of the Working Class in Montreal, 1897–1929* (Toronto: McClelland & Stewart, 1974).

6. *Report of the Royal Commission on Dominion-Provincial Relations*, vol. 2 (Ottawa: King's Printer, 1940), 128.

Major Canadian Social Welfare Policy Web Sites

Most of the documents and reports that deal with Canadian social welfare policy are now available on the Internet. Although some information, for example, press releases and basic statistics, is available by simply connecting to the site, longer documents and reports usually require a computer with Acrobat Reader installed. The list that follows shows the main sites that were used in preparing this book. New sites continue to be added.

Federal Government
Canada Mortgage and Housing Corporation:
www.cmhc.ca/
2001 Census of Canada:
www.statcan.ca/english/census2001/
Department of Citizenship and Immigration:
www.cic.gc.ca/
Department of Finance: www.fin.gc.ca
Human Resources and Development: www.hrdc-drhc.gc.ca/
Department of Indian Affairs and Northern Development: www.ainc-inac.gc.ca/
National Parole Board: www.npb-cnlc.ca/
National Library of Canada: www.nlc-bnc.ca/
Statistics Canada: www.statcan.ca/

Provincial Governments
Alberta: www.gov.ab.ca/
British Columbia: www.gov.bc.ca/
Manitoba: www.gov.mb.ca/
New Brunswick: www.gov.nb.ca/
Newfoundland and Labrador: www.gov.nf.ca/
Nova Scotia: www.gov.ns.ca/
Ontario: www.gov.on.ca/
Prince Edward Island: www.gov.pe.ca/
Quebec: www.gov.bc.ca/
Saskatchewan: www.gov.sk.ca/

Territorial Governments
Northwest Territories: www.gov.nt.ca/
Nunavut: www.assembly.nu.ca/
www.stats.gov.nu.ca/
Yukon: www.yk.ca/

Quasi-Government
National Council of Welfare: www.ncwcnbes.net/

Organization for Economic Co-operation and Development: www.oecd.org/

Non-Profit Organizations
Caledon Institute: www.caledonist.org/
Canadian Centre for Policy Alternatives: www.policyalternatives.ca/
Canadian Council on Social Development: www.ccsd.ca/
C.D. Howe Institute: www.cdhowe.org/
Fraser Institute: www.fraserinstitute.ca/
Child Welfare League of Canada: www.cwlc1/cwlc.ca/
National Action Committee on the Status of Women: www.nac-cca.ca/
Roeher Institute: www.roeher.ca/

Aboriginal Organizations
Assembly of First Nations: www.afn.ca/
Congress of Aboriginal Peoples: www.abopeoples.org/
Inuit Tapirisat of Canada: www.tapirisat.ca/
Metis National Council: www.metisnation.ca/
National Association of Friendship Centres: www.nafc-aboriginal.com/
Native Action Committee on the Status of Women: www.nwac-hq.org/

Bookshops
Renouf Publishing: www.renoufbook.com/

National Newspapers and Media
Canadian Broadcasting Corporation: www.cbc.ca/
Canadian Television Network: www.ctv.ca/
Globe and Mail: www.globeandmail.com/
National Post: www.nationalpost.com

Social Research

University of Calgary, Centre for Social Work
Research: fsw.ucalgary.ca/rcentre/
University of Regina, Social Policy Research Unit:
www.uregina.ca/spru
University of Toronto, Bell Canada Child Welfare
Research Unit: www.canadachildwelfarere-
search.org/
University of Victoria, Research Initiatives for Social
Change: web.uvic.ca/socw/research.htm/

Wilfrid Laurier University, Partnerships for
Children and Families:
www.wlu.ca/-wwwfsw/

Additional Canadian social research Web sites,
including a guide to French-language sites, are
provided in the *Canadian Review of Social Policy*
45–6 (2000).

Bibliography

Abele, Frances, and Michael J. Prince. 2002. 'Alternative Futures: Aboriginal Peoples and Canadian Federalism', in Herman Bakvis and Grace Skogstad, eds, *Canadian Federalism: Performance, Effectiveness and Legitimacy*. Toronto: University of Toronto Press.

Alfred, Taiaiake. 1999. *Peace, Power, and Righteousness: An Indigenous Manifesto*. Toronto: Oxford University Press.

Armitage, Andrew. 1993. 'The Policy and Legislative Context', in Wharf (1993).

————. 1993. 'Family and Child Welfare in First Nations Communities', in Wharf (1993).

————. 1995. *Comparing the Policy of Aboriginal Assimilation: Australia, Canada, and New Zealand*. Vancouver: University of British Columbia Press.

————. 1998. 'Lost Vision: Children and the Ministry for Children and Families', *BC Studies* 118 (Summer).

————, Marilyn Callahan, Michael Prince, and Brian Wharf. 1990. 'Workfare in British Columbia: Social Development Alternatives', *Canadian Review of Social Policy* 26 (Nov.).

Assembly of First Nations. 1989. *National Inquiry into Child Care*. Ottawa: AFN.

Barlow, Maud, and B. Campbell. 1995. *Straight Through the Heart: How the Liberals Abandoned the Just Society*. Toronto: Harper Collins.

Baines, Carol, Patricia Evans, and Sheila Neysmith, eds. 1998. *Women's Caring: Feminist Perspectives on Social Welfare*, 2nd edn. Toronto: Oxford University Press.

Barter, Ken. 2000. 'Reclaiming Community: Shaping the Social Work Agenda', *Canadian Social Work* 2, 2 (Fall).

Battle, Ken, and Leon Muszynski. 1995. *One Way to Fight Child Poverty*. Ottawa: Caledon Institute.

Battle, Ken, and Sherri Torjman. 1993. *Opening the Books on Social Spending*. Ottawa: Caledon Institute.

Baxter, Sheila. 1986. *No Way to Live*. Vancouver: New Star Books.

Bauer, Raymond. 1966. *Social Indicators*. Cambridge, Mass.: MIT Press.

Bellamy, Donald. 1965. 'Social Welfare in Canada', *Encyclopedia of Social Work*. New York: National Association of Social Workers.

Beveridge, William. 1942. *Social Insurance and Allied Service*. New York: Macmillan.

Biddle, W. and L. 1965. *The Community Development Process*. New York: Holt, Rinehart and Winston.

Bottomore, T.B. 1969. *Critics of Society: Radical Thought in North America*. New York: Random House.

Boulding, Kenneth. 1967. 'The Boundaries of Social Policy', *Social Work* 5, 12.

Boygo, Terrence J. 1995. 'Workers' Compensation: Updating the Historic Compromise', in John Richards and William G. Watson, eds, *Chronic Stress: Workers' Compensation in the 1990s*. Toronto: C.D. Howe Institute.

Boyle, Michael. 1991. 'Children's Mental Health Issues', in Laura Johnston and Dick Barnhorst, eds, *Children, Families and Public Policy*. Toronto: Thompson Education Publishing.

British Columbia. 1991. *Closer to Home: The Report of the British Columbia Royal Commission on Health Care and Costs*. Victoria.

————. 1992. *Liberating Our Children*. Victoria: Ministry of Social Services.

Brown, David M. 1994. 'Economic Change and New Social Policies', in Watson et al. (1994).

Brown, Leslie, Lise Haddock, and Margaret Kovach. 2000. 'Watching Over Our Families: Lalum'utul' Smun'eem Child and Family Services', unpublished paper, School of Social Work, University of Victoria.

Bruyere, Gord. 1998. 'Living in Another Man's House: Supporting Aboriginal Learners in Social Work Education', *Social Work Review* 15, 2 (Summer).

Bull, David, and Paul Wilding, eds. 1983. *Thatcherism and the Poor*, Poverty Pamphlet 59. London: Child Poverty Action Group, Apr.

Burman, Patrick. 1996. *Poverty Bonds: Power and Agency in the Social Relations of Welfare*. Toronto: Thompson Educational Publishing.

Callahan, Marilyn. 1993. 'Feminist Approaches: Women Recreate Child Welfare', in Wharf (1993).

————. 1997. 'Feminist Community Organizing in Canada: Postcards from the Edge', in Wharf and Clague (1997).

———— and Karen Callahan. 1997. 'Victims and Villains: Scandals, the Press and Policy-Making in

Child Welfare', in Jane Pulkingham and Gordon Ternowetsky, eds, *Child and Family Policies: Struggles, Strategies and Options*. Halifax: Fernwood.

———, Colleen Lumb, and Brian Wharf. 1994. 'Strengthening Families by Empowering Women', unpublished research monograph, University of Victoria, School of Social Work.

——— and Brian Wharf. 1982. *Demystifying the Policy Process: A Case Study in the Development of Child Welfare Legislation in B.C.* Victoria: School of Social Work, University of Victoria.

Campfens, Herbert. 1988. 'Forces Shaping the New Social Work in Latin America', *Canadian Social Work Review* 5.

Canada. 1940. *Report of the Royal Commission on Dominion-Provincial Relations*. Ottawa: King's Printer.

———. 1966. *Canada Assistance Plan*. Ottawa: Queen's Printer.

———. 1969. *Statement of the Government of Canada on Indian Policy*. Ottawa: Queen's Printer.

———. 1969. *Income Security and Social Services*. Ottawa: Queen's Printer.

———. 1970. *Report of the Royal Commission on the Status of Women in Canada*. Ottawa: Queen's Printer.

———. 1971. *Income Security for Canadians*. Ottawa: Queen's Printer.

———, Special Senate Committee on Poverty (Croll Committee, Senator David Croll, Chairman). 1971. *Poverty in Canada*. Ottawa: Queen's Printer.

———. 1973. *Working Paper on Social Security in Canada*. Ottawa: Queen's Printer.

———. 1984. *Report of the Royal Commission on Equality in Employment*. Ottawa: Ministry of Supply and Services.

———. 1985. *Report of the Royal Commission on the Economic Union and Development Prospects for Canada*. Ottawa: Queen's Printer.

———. 1986. *Report of the Commission of Inquiry on Unemployment Insurance*. Ottawa: Queen's Printer.

———. 1994. *Agenda: Jobs and Growth–Creating a Healthy Fiscal Environment*. Ottawa: Department of Finance.

———. 1996. *Report of the Royal Commission on Aboriginal Peoples*. Ottawa: Supply and Services Canada.

———. 1998. *In Unison: A Canadian Approach to Disability Issues*. Ottawa: Human Resources Development Canada and Social Union.

———. 1999. *A Framework to Improve the Social Union for Canadians: An Agreement between the Government of Canada and the Governments of the Provinces and Territories*. Ottawa, 4 Feb.

———. 2001. *Annual Financial Report 2000–01*. Ottawa: Ministry of Finance.

———, Department of Indian and Northern Affairs. 1996, 2000. *Basic Departmental Data*. Ottawa: Supply and Services.

———, Human Resources Canada. 2001. *Income Security Programs Statistics Book*. Ottawa.

———, Human Resources Development Canada. 1995. *National Welfare Grants: Community Economic Development Products*. Ottawa: HRDC.

———, Status of Women Canada. 1986. *Report of the Task Force on Child Care*. Ottawa: Queen's Printer.

Canada Mortgage and Housing Corporation. 2001. *Children and Youth in Homeless Families: Shelter Spaces and Services*. Ottawa: CMHC.

Canadian Advisory Council on the Status of Women. 1986. Brief presented to the Commission of Inquiry on Unemployment Insurance. Ottawa.

———. 1987. *Integration and Participation: Women's Work in the Home and the Labour Force*. Ottawa.

———. 1988. *Planning Our Future: Do We Have To Be Poor?* Ottawa.

———. 1990. *Women and Labour Market Poverty*. Ottawa.

Canadian Centre for Policy Alternatives. 2000. *Healthy Families: First Things First. Alternative Federal Budget 2000*. Ottawa: CCPA.

——— and Choices: A Coalition for Social Justice. 1998. *Alternative Federal Budget Papers 1998*. Ottawa: CCPA.

Canadian Council on Social Development. 2000. *Report Card on Child Poverty in Canada 1989–1999*. Ottawa: CCSD.

———. 2001. *The Progress of Canada's Children*. Ottawa: CCSD.

———. 2001. *Gaining Ground: The Personal Security Index, 2001*. Ottawa: CCSD.

Canadian Labour Congress. 1973. *Labour's Social Objectives*. Ottawa: CLC.

Canadian Social Work Review. 1993. Special issue, 'Women and Social Work: Celebrating Our Progress', vol. 10, no. 2 (Summer).

Canadian Welfare Council. 1970. *Unemployment Insurance in the '70's*. Ottawa: Queen's Printer.

Carniol, Ben. 1990. 'Social Work and the Labour Movement', in Wharf (1990).

———. 2000. *Case Critical*, 4th edn. Toronto: Between the Lines (1st edn, 1987).

Chricton, Anne, and Lyn Jongbloed. 1998. *Disability and Social Policy in Canada*. North York, Ont.: Captus Press.

Clague, Michael. 1997. 'Thirty Turbulent Years: Community Development and the Organization of Health and Social Services in British Columbia', in Wharf and Clague (1997).

Cochrane, Allan, John Clarke, and Sharon Gewirtz, eds. 2001. *Comparing Welfare States: Britain in International Context*, 2nd edn. London: Sage.

Commission on Emotional and Learning Disorders in Children. 1970. *One Million Children*. Toronto: Leonard Crainford.

Copp, Terry. 1974. *The Anatomy of Poverty: The Condition of the Working Class in Montreal, 1897–1929*. Toronto: McClelland & Stewart.

Council of Canadians with Disabilities. 1994. 'Submission to the Standing Committee on Human Resource Development', Ottawa, 9 Mar., in *Canadian Review of Social Policy* 34.

Courchene, Thomas. 1994. *Social Canada in the Millennium: Reform Imperatives and Restructuring Principles*. Toronto: C.D. Howe Institute.

Crane, John. 1994. *The Public's View of Social Programs*. Vancouver: University of British Columbia Press.

Crowfoot, Strater. 1997. 'Leadership in First Nations Communities: A Chief's Perspective on the Colonial Millstone', in R. Ponting, ed., *First Nations in Canada: Perspectives on Opportunity, Empowerment and Self-Determination*. Toronto: McGraw-Hill.

Dahl, R.A. 1967. *Pluralist Democracy in the United States: Conflict and Consent*. New York: Rand McNally.

Demers, Andrée, and Deena White. 1997. 'The Community Approach to Prevention: Colonization of the Community?', *Canadian Review of Social Policy* 39.

Deschweinitz, Karl. 1943. *England's Road to Social Security*. London: Oxford University Press.

Dicken, Peter. 1992. *Global Shift: The Internationalization of Economic Activity*. London: Paul Chapman.

Dominelli, Lena. 1988. *Anti-Racist Social Work*. London: Macmillan.

Economic Council of Canada. 1968. *Fifth Annual Review, 1968*. Ottawa: Queen's Printer.

Esping-Andersen, Gosta, ed. 1996. *Welfare States in Transition: National Adaptations in Global Economics*. London: Sage.

Etzioni, Amitai. 1964. *Modern Organizations*. Englewood Cliffs, NJ: Prentice-Hall.

Evans, Patricia. 1995. 'The Claims of Women: Gender, Income Security, and the Welfare State', in *7th Conference on Canadian Social Welfare Policy: Remaking Canadian Social Policy: Selected Proceedings*. Vancouver: Social Planning and Research Council of BC, 25–8 June.

———. 2001. 'Women and Social Welfare: Exploring the Connections', in F. Turner and J. Turner, eds, *Social Welfare in Canada*. Scarborough, Ont.: Allyn and Bacon.

——— and Gerda R. Wekerle. 1997. *Women and the Canadian Welfare State: Challenges and Change*. Toronto: University of Toronto Press.

Fallis, George, et al. 1995. *Home Remedies: Rethinking Canadian Housing Policies*. Toronto: C.D. Howe Institute.

Ferguson, Evelyn B. 1988. 'Liberal and Socialist Feminist Perspectives on Child Care', *Canadian Social Work Review* 5.

Finnie, Ross. 1995. 'The Economics of Divorce', in Richards and Watson (1995).

Fleras, Augie, and Jean Leonard Elliott. 1992. *The Nations Within: Aboriginal-State Relations in Canada, the United States and New Zealand*. Toronto: Oxford University Press.

Friendly, Martha. 2001. 'Is This As Good As It Gets? Child Care as a Test Case for Assessing the Social Union Framework Agreement', *Canadian Review of Social Policy* 47.

Galbraith, Kenneth. 1958. *The Affluent Society*. London: Penguin.

Galloway, Burt, and Joe Hudson. 1994. *Community Economic Development*. Toronto: Thompson Educational Publishing.

Geller, Gloria, and Jan Joel. 1995. 'Struggle for Citizenship in the Global Economy: Bond Raters versus Women and Children', Seventh Conference on Canadian Social Welfare Policy, Vancouver, June.

Gilroy, Joan. 1990. 'Social Work and the Women's Movement', in Wharf (1990).

Gonick, Cy. 1987. *The Great Economic Debate: Failed Economics and a Future for Canada*. Toronto: James Lorimer.

Great Britain. 1834. *Report of the Royal Commission on the Administration and Practical Operation of the Poor Laws*. London: King's Printer.

Green, Christopher. 1967. *Negative Taxes and the Poverty Problem*. Washington: Brookings Institution.

———, Fred Lazar, Miles Corak, and Dominique Gross. 1994. *Unemployment Insurance: How To Make It Work*. Toronto: C.D. Howe Institute.

Gross, Bertram, ed. 1967. 'Social Goals and Indicators for American Society', *Annals of the American Academy of Political and Social Science* 371 (May).

Guest, Dennis. 1997. *The Emergence of Social Security*

in Canada, 3rd edn. Vancouver: University of British Columbia Press.

Hacker, Andrew. 1992. *Two Nations: Black and White, Separate, Hostile and Unequal*. New York: Charles Scribner's Sons.

Hackler, Jim. 2001. 'Brief on Proposed Criminal Justice Act', presented to Senate Legal and Constitutional Affairs Committee, 24 Oct.

Hasenfeld, Y. 1983. *Human Service Organizations*. Englewood Cliffs, NJ: Prentice-Hall.

Heilbronner, Robert. 1992. *Capitalism in the Twenty-First Century: The Massey Lecture Series*. Concord, Ont.: Anansi.

Helmes-Hayes, Rick, and James Curtis, eds. 1998. *The Vertical Mosaic Revisited*. Toronto: University of Toronto Press.

Higgins, Joan. 1981. *States of Welfare*. Oxford: Basil Blackwell.

Hogg, Peter W., and Mary Ellen Turpel. 1995. 'Implementing Aboriginal Self-government: Constitutional and Jurisdictional Issues', *Canadian Bar Review* 74 (June).

Hollander, Marcus. 1999. 'The Cost-effectiveness of Community-based Long-term Care Services for the Elderly Compared to Residential Care: A British Columbia Perspective', Ph.D. thesis, University of Victoria.

Ife, James. 2000. 'Localized Needs in a Globalized Economy: Bridging the Gap with Social Work Practice', in Rowe (2000).

Johnston, Patrick. 1983. *Native Children and the Child Welfare System*. Toronto: James Lorimer.

Kahn, Alfred. 1969. *Theory and Practice of Social Planning*. New York: Russell Sage Foundation.

———. 1987. *Social Policy and Social Services*. New York: Random House.

Katz, Arnold. 1973. 'Income Maintenance Experiments: Progress Towards a New American National Policy', *Social and Economic Administration* 7, 2 (May).

Keynes, John Maynard. 1933. *The Means to Prosperity*. New York: Harcourt Brace.

———. 1957 [1936]. *The General Theory of Employment, Interest and Money*. New York: Macmillan.

Kitchen, Bridget. 1997. 'The New Child Tax Benefit: Much Ado About Nothing', *Canadian Review of Social Policy* 39.

Kly, Y.N. 1991. 'On the Meaning and Significance of the United Nations Convention on the Rights of the Child', *Canadian Review of Social Policy* 27 (May).

Kymlicka, Will. 1995. *Multicultural Citizenship: A Liberal Theory of Minority Rights*. Oxford: Clarendon Press.

LaMarsh, Judy. 1968. *Memoirs of a Bird in a Gilded Cage*. Toronto: McClelland & Stewart.

Land, Kenneth. 1971. 'On the Definition of Social Indicators', *American Sociologist* 6, 4 (Nov.).

Land, Newman, Michael Prince, and James Cutt. 1993. *Reforming the Public Pension System in Canada*. Victoria: Centre for Public Sector Studies.

Lappin, Ben. 1970. *The Community Workers and the Social Work Tradition*. Toronto: School of Social Work, University of Toronto.

Lazar, Fred. 1994. 'UI as a Redistributive Scheme and Financial Stabilizer', in Richards and Watson (1994).

Leonard, Peter. 1994. 'Knowledge/Power and Postmodernism: Implications for the Practice of Critical Social Work Education', *Canadian Social Work Review* 11, 10.

———. 1997. *Postmodern Welfare: Reconstructing an Emancipatory Project*. London: Sage.

Levin, Michael D., ed. 1993. *Ethnicity and Aboriginality: Case Studies in Ethnonationalism*. Toronto: University of Toronto Press.

Lewis, Mike. 1994. 'The Scope and Characteristics of Community Economic Development in Canada', in Galloway and Hudson (1994).

Li, Peter, ed. 1990. *Race and Ethnic Relations in Canada*. Toronto: Oxford University Press.

Lithwick, N.H. 1970. *Urban Canada: Problems and Prospects*. Ottawa: Central Mortgage and Housing Corporation.

Little, Margaret Hillyard. 1998. 'No Car, No Radio, No Liquor Permit': *The Moral Regulation of Mothers in Ontario, 1920–1997*. Toronto: Oxford University Press.

Little Bear, Leroy. 2000. 'Jagged Worldviews Colliding', in M. Battisits, ed., *Reclaiming Indigenous Voice and Vision*. Vancouver: University of British Columbia Press.

McIntyre, Ewan. 1993. 'The Historical Context of Child Welfare in Canada', in Wharf (1993).

Macpherson, C.B. 1965. 'The Real World of Democracy', *Massey Lectures, 4th Series*. Toronto: Canadian Broadcasting Corporation.

———. 1985. *The Rise and Fall of Economic Justice and Other Papers*. New York: Oxford University Press.

MacPherson, Stewart. 1982. *Social Policy in the Third World: The Social Dilemmas of Underdevelopment*. Brighton: Wheatsheaf.

Marcuse, Herbert. 1966. *One Dimensional Man*. Boston: Beacon Press.

Marsh, Leonard. 1943. *Report on Social Security for Canada*. Ottawa: King's Printer.

Marshall, T.H. 1965. *Class, Citizenship and Social Development*. Garden City, NY: Anchor Books.

Martin, E.W., ed. 1972. *Comparative Development in Social Welfare*. London: George Allen and Unwin.

Mawhiney, Anne Marie. 1995. 'First Nations in Canada', in Turner and Turner (1995).

Maynes, W.G. 1993. 'Child Poverty in Canada: Challenges for Educational Policy Makers', *Canadian Review of Social Policy* 32.

McQuaig, Linda. 1993. *The Wealthy Banker's Wife: The Assault on Equality in Canada*. Toronto: Penguin.

———. 1995. *Shooting the Hippo:Death by Deficit*. Toronto: Viking.

Mendelson, Michael. 1999. 'The New Social Union', *Canadian Review of Social Policy* 43.

Mills, C. Wright. 1942. 'The Professional Ideology of Social Pathologists', *American Journal of Sociology* 69.

———. 1959. *The Sociological Imagination*. New York: Oxford University Press.

Mishra, Ramesh. 1981. *Society and Social Policy: Theoretical Perspectives on Welfare*, rev. edn. London: Macmillan.

———. 1984. *The Welfare State in Crisis*. Brighton: Wheatsheaf.

———. 1990. *The Welfare State in Capitalist Society: Policies of Retrenchment and Maintenance in Europe, North America and Australia*. Toronto: University of Toronto Press.

———. 1999. 'After Globalization: Social Policy in an Open Economy', *Canadian Review of Social Policy* 43 (Spring).

Moran, Bridget. 1988. *Stoney Creek Woman Sai'k'uz Ts'eke: The Story of Mary John*. Vancouver: Tillicum Library.

———. 1994. *Justa: A First Nations Leader*. Vancouver: Arsenal Pulp Press.

Mosca, Gaetano. 1939. *Ruling Class*. New York: McGraw.

Moscovitch, Alan. 1996. 'Canada Health and Social Transfer: What Was Lost?', *Canadian Review of Social Policy* 37 (Spring).

Mullaly, Bob. 1997. *Structural Social Work: Ideology, Theory, and Practice*, 2nd edn. Toronto: Oxford University Press.

———. 2002. *Challenging Oppression: A Critical Social Work Approach*. Toronto: Oxford University Press.

Myrdal, Gunnar. 1958. *Beyond the Welfare State*. London: Duckworth.

Naidoo, Josephine C., and R. Gary Edwards. 1991. 'Combatting Racism Involving Visible Minorities: A Review of Relevant Research and Policy Development', *Canadian Social Work Review* 8, 2 (Summer).

National Council of Welfare. 1973. *The Press and the Poor*. Ottawa.

———. 1988. *Child Care: A Better Alternative*. Ottawa.

———. 1995. *Poverty Profile 1993*. Ottawa.

———. 1998. *A New Poverty Line: Yes, No, or Maybe*. Ottawa.

———. 2000. *Welfare Incomes 1999*. Ottawa.

———. 2001. *Poverty Profile 1998*. Ottawa.

Naylor, Nancy. 1995. 'A National Child Benefit Program', in Richards and Watson (1995).

Ng, Roxana. 1996. *The Politics of Community Services: Immigrant Women, Class and the State*. Halifax: Fernwood.

Nozick, Marcia. 1993. 'Five Principles of Sustainable Community Development', in Shragge (1993).

O'Connor, Julia S. 1998. 'Social Justice, Social Citizenship and the Welfare State, 1965–1995: Canada in Comparative Context', in Helmes-Hayes and Curtis (1998).

Ontario. 1988. *Transitions: Report of the Social Assistance Review Committee*. Toronto: Ministry of Community and Social Services.

Organization for Economic Co-operation and Development (OECD). 1994. *OECD Economic Survey, 1993–4: Canada*. Paris: OECD.

———. 2001. *Society at a Glance: OECD Social Indicators, 2001*. Paris: OECD.

Pal, Leslie. 1992. *Public Policy Analysis: An Introduction*, 2nd edn. Toronto: Methuen.

Panitch, Leo V. 1990. 'Elites, Classes and Power in Canada', in Whittington and Williams (1990).

Pareto, Vilfredo. 1935. *Mind and Society*. New York: Dover.

Phipps, Shelley. 1995. 'Taking Care of Our Children', in Richards and Watson (1995).

Pinker, Robert. 1971. *Social Theory and Social Policy*. London: Heinemann.

Piven, Frances Fox, and Richard A. Cloward. 1972. *Regulating the Poor: The Public Functions of Welfare*. New York: Random House.

Poirier, Guy. 1994. 'Neo-conservatism and Social Policy Responses to the AIDS Crisis', in Andrew Johnson, Stephen McBride, and Patrick J. Smith, eds, *Continuities and Discontinuities: The Political Economy of Social Welfare and Labour Market Policy in Canada*. Toronto: University of Toronto Press.

Pomeroy, Steve. 2001. *Towards a Comprehensive Affordable Housing Strategy for Canada*. Toronto: Caledon Institute.

Popham, Rosemary, David Hay, and Colin Hughes. 1997. 'Campaign 2000 to End Child Poverty: Building and Sustaining a Movement', in Wharf and Clague (1997).

Porter, John. 1965. *The Vertical Mosaic*. Toronto: University of Toronto Press.

Prince, Michael J. 2002. 'Ready or Not? Hide and Seek Politics of Canadian Federalism, the Social Union Framework Agreement, and the Role of National Aboriginal Political Organization', in Tom McIntosh, ed., *Canada's Social Union: Perspectives and Directions*. Regina: Canadian Plains Research Centre.

———— and Frances Abele. 2000. 'Funding an Aboriginal Order of Government in Canada: Recent Developments in Self-Government and Fiscal Relations', in Harvey Lazar, ed., *Canada: The State of the Federation 1999/2000*. Montreal and Kingston: McGill-Queen's University Press.

Pulkingham, Jane. 1993. 'Community Development in Action: Reality of Rhetoric', *Canadian Review of Social Policy* 32.

Quebec. 1971. *Report of the Commission of Inquiry on Health and Social Welfare*. Quebec City: Quebec Official Publisher.

Ralph, Diana. 1993. 'Anti-Poverty Policy under NDP Governments', *Canadian Review of Social Policy* 31.

————. 1994. 'Fighting for Canada's Social Programs', *Canadian Review of Social Policy* 34.

————. 1995. 'Tripping the Iron Heel', in Jane Pulkingham and Gordon Ternowetsky, eds, *Remaking Canadian Social Policy: Staking Claims and Forging Change*. Halifax: Fernwood.

Rawls, John. 1973. *A Theory of Justice*. Oxford: Oxford University Press.

————. 1993. *Political Liberalism*. New York: Columbia University Press.

Reid, Darrell. 2002. 'You Better Get Used To Us', *Globe and Mail*, 23 Jan., A11.

Rekart, Josephine. 1995. *Social Services and the Marketplace*. Vancouver: Social Planning and Research Council of British Columbia.

Reynauld, André. 1973. 'Income Distribution: Facts and Policies', speech to The Empire Club, Toronto, 1 Feb.

Rice, J. James, and Michael J. Prince. 2000. *Changing Politics of Canadian Social Policy*. Toronto: University of Toronto Press.

Richards, John. 1994. *The Case for Change*. Ottawa: Renouf.

————. 1995. 'A comment', in Richards and William Watson, eds, *Market Solutions to Native Poverty:*

Social Policy for the Third Solitude. Toronto: C.D. Howe Institute.

————. 1997. *Retooling the Welfare State: What's Right, What's Wrong, What's To Be Done*. Toronto: C.D. Howe Institute.

————. 2000. *Now That the Coat Fits the Cloth: Spending Wisely in a Trimmed-Down Age*. C.D. Howe Institute Commentary 143. Toronto: C.D. Howe Institute, June.

————. 2001. 'The Social Union Framework Agreement: Disappointing and Irrelevant', *Canadian Review of Social Policy* 47.

———— and Aidan Vining. 1995. 'Welfare Reform: What Can We Learn from the Americans?', in Richards et al. (1995).

———— and William Watson, eds. 1994. *Unemployment Insurance: How To Make It Work*. Toronto: C.D. Howe Institute.

———— and ————, eds. 1995. *Helping the Poor: A Qualified Case for 'Workfare'*. Toronto: C.D. Howe Institute.

———— and ————, eds. 1995. *Family Matters*. Toronto: C.D. Howe Institute.

Riches, Graham. 1986. *Food Banks and the Welfare Crisis*. Ottawa: Canadian Council on Social Development.

————. 1987. 'Feeding Canada's Poor', in J. Ismael, ed., *The Canadian Welfare State*. Edmonton: University of Alberta Press.

Rioux, Marcel. 1971. *Quebec in Question*. Toronto: James Lewis and Samuel.

Rioux, Marcia H. 1994. *The Canadian Disability Resource Program: Offsetting Costs of Disability and Assuring Access to Disability-Related Supports*. Toronto: Roeher Institute.

Roeher Institute. 1993. *Social Well-Being: A Paradigm for Reform*. Toronto: Roeher Institute.

Romanyshyn, John. 1971. *Social Welfare: Charity to Justice*. New York: Random House.

Ross, David. 2000. *The Canadian Fact Book on Poverty*. Ottawa: Canadian Council on Social Development.

———— and Louise Hanvey. 2001. *Gaining Ground: The Personal Security Index 2001*. Ottawa: Canadian Council on Social Development.

————, E. Richard Shillington, and Clarence Lochhead. 1994. *The Canadian Fact Book on Poverty*. Ottawa: Canadian Council on Social Development.

Rowe, Bill, ed. 2000. *Social Work and Globalization*. Ottawa: Canadian Association of Social Workers.

Rubin, Sandra. 1994. 'If I have children, I'll raise them very differently', *Victoria Times Colonist*, 17 Apr.

Runciman, W.G. 1972. *Relative Deprivation and Social Justice*. London: Pelican.

Rutman, Deborah, and Andrew Armitage. 1993. 'Counting on Kids: An Overview of "State of the Child" Reports', *Canadian Review of Social Policy* 31.

Samuelson, Paul. 1966. *Economics*. Toronto: McGraw-Hill.

Sarlo, Christopher. 1992. *Poverty in Canada*. Vancouver: Fraser Institute.

Schellenberg, Grant. 1994. *The Road to Retirement*. Ottawa: Canadian Council on Social Development.

Shewell, Hugh. 1990. 'History and Social Policy: Understanding the Context of Canada's Native Indian Policies', *Canadian Review of Social Policy* 25 (May).

——— and Anabella Spagnut. 1995. 'The First Nations of Canada: Social Welfare and the Quest for Self-Government', in John Dixon and Robert P. Scheurell, eds, *Social Welfare with Indigenous Peoples*. London: Routledge.

Shragge, Eric. 1993. *Community Economic Development*. Montreal: Black Rose Books.

———. 1997. *Workfare: Ideology for a New Under-Class*. Toronto: Garamond.

——— and Sherri Torjman. 1998. 'Civil Society: Reclaiming our Humanity—a Debate', *Canadian Review of Social Policy* 41 (Spring).

Smiley, Donald, ed. 1963. *The Rowell-Sirois Report*. Toronto: McClelland & Stewart.

Smith, Dorothy. 1986. 'Institutional Ethnography: A Feminist Method', *Resources for Feminist Research* 15, 1.

Sniderman, Paul M., and Thomas Piazza. 1993. *The Scar of Race*. Cambridge, Mass.: The Belknap Press of Harvard University.

Splane, Richard. 1965. *Social Welfare in Ontario, 1791–1898*. Toronto: University of Toronto Press.

———. 1980. 'Whatever Happened to the G.A.I.?', *The Social Worker* 48, 2.

———. 1987. 'Social Policy-Making in the Government of Canada: Reflections of a Reformist Bureaucrat', in Yelaja (1987).

Statistics Canada. Various years. *Census of Canada*. Ottawa: Statistics Canada.

———. 1990. *Projections for Canada and the Provinces, 1989–2011*, Catalogue no. 91–520. Ottawa: Supply and Services.

———. 2002. *Census Definitions*. Ottawa: Statistics Canada.

Stone, Leroy O. 1967. *Urban Development in Canada*. Ottawa: Dominion Bureau of Statistics.

Swift, Karen J. 2001. 'The Case for Opposition: Challenging Contemporary Child Welfare Policy Directions', *Canadian Review of Social Policy* 47.

Teeple, Gary. 1995. *Globalization and the Decline of Social Reform*. Toronto: Garamond.

Tester, Frank James. 1992. 'The Disenchanted Democracy: Canada in the Global Economy of the 1990s', *Canadian Review of Social Policy* 29–30 (Summer-Winter).

——— and Peter Kulchyski. 1994. *Tammarniit (Mistakes): Inuit Relocation in the Eastern Arctic 1939–63*. Vancouver: University of British Columbia Press.

Timpson, Joyce. 1995. 'Four Decades of Literature on Native Canadian Child Welfare: Changing Themes', *Child Welfare* 74, 3.

Titmuss, Richard M. 1968. *Commitment to Welfare*. London: George Allen and Unwin.

———. 1968. *The Gift Relationship*. London: George Allen and Unwin.

Tobias, John. 1976. 'Protection, Civilization, Assimilation: An Outline of the History of Canada's Indian Policy', *Western Canadian Journal of Anthropology* 6, 2.

Trist, Eric. 1967. *The Relationship of Welfare and Development in the Transition to Post-Industrialism*. Ottawa: Canadian Centre for Community Studies.

Turner, Joanne C., and Francis J. Turner, eds. 1995. *Canadian Social Welfare*, 3rd edn. Scarborough, Ont.: Allyn and Bacon.

Ujimoto, K. Victor. 1990. 'Studies of Ethnic Identity and Race Relations', in Li (1990).

United Kingdom Home Office. 1968. *Report of the Committee on Local Authority and Allied Personal Social Services*. London: HMSO.

United Nations. 1948. *Universal Declaration of Human Rights*. New York.

Van Kessel, G.C.J. 1998. 'The Canadian Immigration System', address to International Conference on Migration, Baden, Austria, 26 Nov. Available at: <www.cic.gc.ca/english/refugee/kessel>.

Wachholz, Sandy, and Bob Mullaly. 1997. 'Towards a Research Model for Structural Social Work', *Canadian Social Work Review* 14, 1.

Walter, Dorothy. 1972. 'Social Intelligence and Social Policy', in *Social Indicators*. Ottawa: Canadian Council on Social Development.

Warren, Roland. 1963. *The Community in America*. Chicago: Rand McNally.

Watson, Ken. 1994. 'A Review of Four Evaluations of CED Programs: What Have We Learned in Two Decades', in Galloway and Hudson (1994).

Watson, William G., John Richards, and David M. Brown. 1995. *The Case for Change: Reinventing the Welfare State*. Toronto: C.D. Howe Institute.

Watts, H.W. 1964. 'Graduated Work Incentive: An Experiment in Negative Taxation', *American Economic Review* 59, 2 (May).

Weeks, Wendy. 1992. 'Gender in the Social and Community Services: Implications for Management', *Human Services Management Network Conference*. Brisbane: Queensland University of Technology, Apr.

Wharf, Brian, ed. 1990. *Social Work and Social Change in Canada*. Toronto: McClelland & Stewart.

————, ed. 1993. *Rethinking Child Welfare in Canada*. Toronto: McClelland & Stewart.

————. 1995. 'Organizing and Delivering Child Welfare Services: The Contributors of Research', in Joe Hudson and Burt Galloway, eds, *Child Welfare in Canada: Research and Policy Implications*. Toronto: Thompson Educational Publishing.

———— and Michael Clague, eds. 1997. *Community Organizing: Canadian Experiences*. Toronto: Oxford University Press.

Whittington, Michael, and Glen Williams. 1990. *Canadian Politics in the 1990s*. Scarborough, Ont.: Nelson.

Wiggins, Cindy. 1996. 'Dismantling Unemployment Insurance: The Changes, the Impacts, the Reasons', *Canadian Review of Social Policy* 37.

Wilensky, H.L., and C. Lebeaux. 1965. *Industrial Society and Social Welfare*. New York: Macmillan.

Willard, J.W. 1965. 'Canadian Welfare Programs', *Encyclopedia of Social Work*. New York: National Association of Social Workers.

Williams, Fiona. 1989. *Social Policy: A Critical Introduction*. Cambridge: Polity Press.

Woodsworth, David. 1971. *Social Policies for Tomorrow*. Ottawa: Canadian Council on Social Development.

Yelaja, Shankar, ed. 1987. *Canadian Social Policy*, 2nd edn. Waterloo, Ont.: Wilfrid Laurier University Press.

Index